Theatre

A WAY OF SEEING

Theatre

A WAY OF SEEING

SEVENTH EDITION

Milly S. Barranger

The University of North Carolina at Chapel Hill

Cengage

Australia • Brazil • Canada • Mexico • Singapore • United Kingdom • United States

Cengage

***Theatre: A Way of Seeing*, Seventh Edition**
Milly S. Barranger

Product Director: Monica Eckman

Product Manager: Kelli Strieby

Content Developer: Rebecca Donahue

Product Assistant: Marjorie Cross

Media Developer: Jessica Badiner

Executive Brand Manager: Ben Rivera

Senior Content Project Manager: Michael Lepera

Senior Art Director: Linda May

Manufacturing Planner: Doug Bertke

Rights Acquisition Specialist: Stacey Dong

Production Service and Compositor: QBS Learning

Text and Cover Designer: Chris Miller Design

Cover Image: Scene from the Performance poem, "Red Beads," a Mabou Mines production, September, 2005, directed by Lee Breuer with choreography by Clove Galilee. From an original story by Polina Klimovitskaya with music composed and arranged by Ushio Torikai. Photography by © BEATRIZ SCHILLER 2013.

Library of Congress Control Number:

ISBN-13: 978-1-133-30989-5
ISBN-10: 1-133-30989-5

Cengage
200 Pier 4 Boulevard
Boston, MA 02210
USA

Printed in the United States of America
Print Number: 07 Print Year: 2022

BRIEF CONTENTS

CONTENTS

PART FIVE: THEATRE'S CRITICS

FEATURES

FOCUS ON PEOPLE IN THEATRE

Founding Artistic Director

Performance Artists

Playwrights

Playwrights' Agent

Playwright-Director-Designer

Producers

Producer-Director

Puppeteers

FOCUS ON THEATRE

FOCUS ON PLAYS

PREFACE

Theatre as a way of seeing is the subject of this book. Theatre, a complex and living art, requires a number of people engaged in the creative process to craft and sustain this vibrant form of artistic expression. Many individuals—writers, actors, directors, designers, choreographers, technicians, craftspeople, managers, and producers—contribute to the creation of this performing art that has endured for 2,500 years.

In the creation of a theatrical event, writers and artists devise a form of theatrical art for others to watch, experience, feel, and understand. Chiefly through the actor's *presence*, theatre becomes humanness, aliveness, and experience. As such, theatre does not exist in any book, for books can only *describe* the passion, wisdom, and excitement that derive from experiencing theatre's stories, colors, sounds, and motion.

FEATURES OF THIS BOOK

This edition of *Theatre: A Way of Seeing* discusses theatre as a composite experience of art, life, and the human imagination. Arranged in fifteen chapters, the discussions include spaces, artists, audiences, plays, designs, staging, styles, productions, performances, and theatrical criticism. Chapters 1–3 address the complex answer to the question: What is theatre? And, who contributes to this collaborative form of artistic expression? These chapters include discussions of aesthetics, theatrical spaces, audience expectations, dramatic writing, the artistic process, and stage conventions. Chapters 4–8 discuss playwrights, writing styles, structures, conventions, and language, with examples taken from classical, Elizabethan, modern, and postmodern texts. Chapters 9–13 examine the contributions of artists and producers to the theatrical event. Chapter 14 introduces the musical, the most popular of American theatrical genres, and Chapter 15 examines the influence of theatre critics on the life of productions and audience attendance.

- **Cultural diversity.** Cultural diversity and intercultural expressions of world theatre are threads woven throughout the fifteen chapters. Western and Eastern cultural and theatrical traditions, stages, and architecture are presented in their historical and present-day contexts. Given the fact that so much has taken place in the theatre of the United States since the mid-twentieth century, discussions about the artistic expressions of emerging American playwrights, performers, and solo artists dedicated to cultural and ethnic diversity are also woven throughout the book.
- **Artists' insights.** All discussions are supported by the insights of writers and artists talking about their work, texts and scenes from plays, biographical sketches, diagrams and definitions, and colorful photographs of Eastern and Western stages and productions. Of course, none of these discussions takes the

place of sitting with others in a theatre and experiencing the actors, texts, sets, costumes, lights, music, and sound effects in a carefully crafted event demonstrating the human imagination in its theatrical form.

- **Model plays.** Written as an introduction to the theatrical experience, *Theatre: A Way of Seeing* introduces readers to theatre as a way of seeing women and men in action in the creation of onstage reality and theatrical worlds. After all, Shakespeare said that "All the world's a stage, / And all the men and women merely players . . ." (*As You Like It*). To assist readers discovering theatre for the first time and perhaps even attending their first performances, this edition features a number of "model" plays as examples of trends, styles, and forms of theatrical production. They range from ancient playwrights to postmodern writers and include such plays as *Oedipus the King, Macbeth, The Cherry Orchard, The Caucasian Chalk Circle, The Glass Menagerie, A Streetcar Named Desire, Death of a Salesman, The Life of Galileo, Fences, Juan Darién, the CIVIL warS*, and *Glengarry Glen Ross*. The musical stage is represented by such musicals as *Oklahoma!, West Side Story, Hair*, and *Miss Saigon*. Each of these plays has a special place in the ongoing history of theatrical writing and performance. From Sophocles's *Oedipus the King* to Tony Kushner's *Angels in America*, these model plays represent the extraordinary range and magnitude of human expression as theatrical achievement.
- **Texts of several plays.** In addition, abbreviated texts of several plays are included to illustrate styles and conventions of theatrical writing. Excerpts and scenes from Euripides's *The Trojan Women*, William Shakespeare's *As You Like It, Hamlet*, and *Macbeth*, Anton Chekhov's *The Cherry Orchard*, Luigi Pirandello's *Six Characters in Search of an Author*, Bertolt Brecht's *The Caucasian Chalk Circle*, Samuel Beckett's *Waiting for Godot*, Tennessee Williams's *The Glass Menagerie* and *A Streetcar Named Desire*, Arthur Miller's *Death of a Salesman*, August Wilson's *Fences*, Tony Kushner's *Angels in America*, and David Mamet's *Glengarry Glen Ross* are included.
- **Detailed discussions of artists and craftspeople.** This new edition also features expanded discussions of the artists and craftspeople who engage in making theatre come alive: stage directors and auteurs (Anne Bogart, Peter Brook, Martha Clarke, Jerzy Grotowski, Elia Kazan, Ariane Mnouchkine, John O'Neal, Robert Lepage, Andrei Serban, Peter Schumann, Julie Taymor, and Robert Wilson); playwrights, choreographers, and solo performers; composers and librettists; producers and artistic directors; dramaturgs and literary managers, actor-voice-and-movement trainers and coaches; and theatrical designers and production teams. Moreover, new color photographs illustrate ancient and modern stages, theatrical designs, international productions, and celebrated performances.
- **Tools to clarify theatre details.** There are also tools to clarify details of theatre history, biography, modern stage history, and terms that belong to the business of theatre. *Synopses* of the model plays along with *short biographies* of

playwrights, actors, directors, designers, composers, librettists, producers, and critics parallel the discussions. End-of-chapter features include a *list* of theatrical terms, *websites* for research and entertainment, and a list of *InfoTrac® College Edition search terms* students can use for further reading and to help them research supporting materials for written assignments. A *glossary* at the end of the book defines key terms to assist the reader.

Finally, *Theatre: A Way of Seeing* is by no means a definitive treatment of theatre practice, history, or literature. Its aim is to put readers in touch with theatre *as a performing art and humanistic event*. Most important, it introduces theatre as an *immediate* experience, engaging actors and audiences for a brief time in a special place. The Greeks called that special place—where audiences sat to watch performances—a *theatron*, or "seeing place." The idea of the "seeing place" has been our guide as readers and theatregoers to understanding and enjoying theatrical writing and performance.

IN THIS NEW EDITION

- **Chapters have been revised to incorporate new subjects, artists, productions, and photographs.** Key topics include discussions of the emergence of women artistic leaders in the nonprofit and regional theatres, new trends in stage adaptations, alternative voices to mainstream playwrights, and performance diversity. A discussion of "theatre as a way of seeing" introduces the book (Chapter 1). The section on Eastern theatre practices includes their influences on staging and design in Western theatre (Chapter 2). Discussion of environmental theatre traces the international movement in the use of alternative playing spaces from the Polish Laboratory Theatre to the Bread and Puppet Theatre in Vermont (Chapter 3). The overview of solo texts and performance art includes Spalding Gray, Anna Deavere Smith, and others (Chapter 6). Analyses of play structures, stage conventions, and language are found in chapters (Chapters 4, 5, 6, 7, 8), along with examples from plays by William Shakespeare, Henrik Ibsen, Anton Chekhov, Luigi Pirandello, Bertolt Brecht, Tennessee Williams, Arthur Miller, David Mamet, Paula Vogel, Robert Wilson. Also included are solo texts and postmodern visual and audio texts. The chapters on theatrical design have been expanded to include the emergence of women-designers in the commercial theatre, and the increasing use of puppetry in design and staging (Chapters 11, 12). The chapter on producers features the new producers and the choreographer-directors who are shaping American drama and musicals along with the new producing organizations whose purpose is to bring diversity onto America's stages (Chapters 13, 14). Finally, the chapter on theatre criticism ranges from pioneering critics (Brooks Atkinson, Claudia Cassidy, Edith Oliver) to an expanded list of national critics who influence the audience interest in shows from Chicago to Seattle to the Web (Chapter 15).

- **A chapter on musical theatre** discusses American musicals, composers, librettists, and the new choreographers-directors; British megamusicals on Broadway; and Broadway audiences (Chapter 14).
- **Issues of cultural and ethnic diversity in performance have been incorporated throughout** to illustrate this dynamic at work in world theatre. The section on writing and staging diversity in U.S. theatres has been incorporated in the discussions of alternative writing for the theatre and producing in nonprofit regional theatres (Chapters 4, 13).
- **Expanded discussions** of audiences, types of playwriting, visual and audio texts, and actor-training in America are included throughout.
- **Examples of artists, writing, and performance styles have been updated.** For instance, audition and casting issues are examined from the actor's and the director's perspective (Chapters 9 and 10); and discussions of the work of August Wilson, Edward Albee, Suzan-Lori Parks, Nilo Cruz, David Henry Hwang, David Ives, Lynn Nottage, and Tony Kushner are found in the chapter on playwriting (Chapter 4).
- **Feature and margin boxes have been added, rearranged, and updated** to complement ongoing discussions of playwrights, artists, creative teams, producers, staging conventions, hip hop expressions, and theatrical business, such as "open calls."
- Moreover, **a greater number of colorful photographs** of artists and productions are incorporated throughout to illustrate with visual images the artists and productions being discussed.
- Finally, **suggested readings and reference sources** have been moved to the book's companion website.

SUPPLEMENTARY MATERIALS

The seventh edition of *Theatre: A Way of Seeing* is accompanied by a suite of integrated resources for students and instructors.

Student Resources

- *Theatre CourseMate* Cengage Learning's Theatre CourseMate brings course concepts to life with interactive learning, study, and exam preparation tools that support the printed textbook. Watch student comprehension soar as your class works with the printed textbook and the textbook-specific website. Theatre CourseMate goes beyond the book to deliver what you need! Learn more at cengage.com/coursemate.
- *Theatregoer's Guide* This brief introduction to attending and critiquing drama enhances the novice theatregoer's experience and appreciation of theatre as a living art. This essential guide can be packaged for free with this text.

Instructor Resources

- ***Instructor's Resource Manual*** This guide is designed for beginning as well as seasoned instructors. It includes suggested course syllabi and schedules, teaching ideas, chapter objectives, lecture outlines, discussion questions and activities, and test questions for each chapter.
- ***Cognero Online Testing Program*** Theatre: A Way of Seeing 7e provides a flexible online testing system that allows you to author, edit, and manage the author created test bank content. You can create multiple test versions instantly and deliver them through your Learning Management System from your classroom, or wherever you may be with no special installs or downloads.
- ***Evans Shakespeare Editions*** Each volume of the Evans Shakespeare Editions is edited by a Shakespearean scholar. The pedagogy is designed to help students contextualize Renaissance drama, while providing explanatory notes to each play. The plays included in the series are *The Tempest, A Midsummer Night's Dream, As You Like It, Hamlet, Macbeth, Richard III, Measure for Measure, The Winter's Tale,* and *King Lear*. These critical editions can be packaged with a Cengage Learning theatre title. Consult your local sales representative for packaging options.
- ***A Pocketful of Plays: Vintage Drama*** This selection of some of the most commonly taught plays satisfies the need for a concise, quality collection that students will find inexpensive and that instructors will enjoy teaching. The plays include source materials to encourage further discussion and analysis, as well as comments, biographical and critical commentaries, and reviews of actual productions. The plays featured in the book are Susan Glaspell's *Trifles*, Sophocles's *Oedipus the King*, William Shakespeare's *Hamlet*, Henrik Ibsen's *A Doll's House*, Tennessee Williams's *The Glass Menagerie*, and Lorraine Hansberry's *A Raisin in the Sun*. Consult your local sales representative for packaging options.

ACKNOWLEDGMENTS

My thanks are due to friends and colleagues for their encouragement and assistance in the preparation of the previous and current revisions of this book. Those who assisted and advised on the seventh edition are designers, directors, scholars, teachers, critics, agents, managers, and editors. It is important to mention the contributions of Judy Adamson, Costume Director, PlayMakers Repertory Company, NC; McKay Coble, Designer, PlayMakers Repertory Company, NC; Bill Clarke, New York-based set and costume designer; F. Mitchell Dana, lighting designer and Professor at the Mason Gross School of Arts, Rutgers University, NJ; Mary Louise Geiger, Arts Professor and Associate Chairman of the Department of Design for Stage and Film, New York University; Alexis Greene, New York-based author, editor, and critic; Kimball King, Professor Emeritus of English, University of North Carolina, Chapel Hill; Mary Porter Hall, production stage manager for *Fosse*; Carrie F. Robbins, costume designer for *M. Butterfly* and *Irving Berlin's White Christmas*, Tazewell Thompson, director of *Porgy and*

Bess, City Center Opera Company, New York City; and Liz Woodman, Casting Director, C.S.A., New York City. Those who suggested useful revisions incorporated in this new edition were Carey Hansen, University of Mississippi, Oxford; Christopher J. Herr, Missouri State University; Tracy L. McAfee, Washington State Community College, Marietta, OH; Jay Malarcher, West Virginia University, Morgantown; Kevin Malloy, University of Mississippi, Oxford; Donald Stevens, Louisiana Tech University, Ruston; and Daniel Volonte, Citrus College, Glendora, CA.

Also, my special thanks to the Cengage Learning team for their efforts on behalf of the seventh edition of *Theatre: A Way of Seeing*: Michael A. Rosenberg, Publisher Humanities; Megan Garvey, Managing Development Editor; Rebecca Donahue, Content Coordinator; Jessica Badiner, media developer; Ben Rivera, executive brand manager; Michael Lepera, senior content production manager; Paul Blake and Scott Dunay for G&S Book Services; and Linda Sykes, photograph researcher.

Rhona Justice-Malloy has served as consultant on this seventh edition. She brings her background as editor of *Theatre History Studies*, former chairwoman of the Theatre Department, and Professor of Theatre at the University of Mississippi, Oxford. She has brought thoughtful suggestions, skillful editing, and useful revisions to this new edition. She is a colleague to be praised for her knowledge of theatre history, her commitment to excellence in research and writing, and for her friendship as a colleague and collaborator.

Again, my special appreciation to Linda Sykes for undertaking another edition of *Theatre: A Way of Seeing* and for her patience and persistence in the collection of remarkable images to illustrate the theatrical experience over several editions of this book.

Milly S. Barranger

© Joan Marcus

1

DISCOVERING THEATRE

I can take any empty space and call it a bare stage. A man walks across this empty space whilst someone else is watching him, and this is all that is needed for an act of theatre to be engaged.[1]

— PETER BROOK, *THE EMPTY SPACE*

THE IMMEDIATE ART

Theatre is a form of art and entertainment that places actors before a group of people—an audience—in an act of engagement and discovery about life. Theatrical performances have taken place for thousands of years and in almost all world cultures with few exceptions. The great societies of Europe, China, and India first nurtured theatre as a means of gathering citizens together to celebrate civic accomplishments, warn of personal errors, or ridicule society's fools. In doing so, ancient civilizations in the East and West created dramatic art and stage traditions lasting centuries.

DEFINITIONS

Since early times, *immediacy* and *presence* have set theatrical art apart from other forms of art. For theatre to happen, actors and audiences must come together at a certain time and in a certain place. On a stage, or in a prearranged space, actors present themselves to an audience in a story involving intensely personal aspects of human behavior. Audiences share in the story and the occasion. They actively listen, gather information, feel emotions, and respond to events taking place before them during the performance. Audiences are not passive observers. They engage as responders to the words, music, song, and spectacle created by the

PREVIEW

While we are watching, men and women make theatre happen before us. We see human beings in action—what they do and why they do it—and we discover things about ourselves and our world.

The musical *Wicked*, a revisionist look at *The Wizard of Oz* with music and book by Stephen Schwartz and Winnie Holzman, has enchanted audiences since its Broadway opening in 2003. By featuring Glinda, the "Good Witch," and her rival the "Wicked Witch of the West," audiences rediscover this tale of discrimination based on superficial features ("green skin") and the triumph of inner truth over appearances.

© Stratford Shakespeare Festival, Stratford, Ontario

The Matchmaker
Seana McKenna as Dolly Levi in *The Matchmaker*, Stratford Festival, Ontario, Canada.

theatre's artists for the audience's entertainment and understanding.

Theatre has been defined as a way of seeing men and women in action, of observing what they do, why they do it, and the results of their actions. It is an art form that engages human beings to tell stories about other human beings. Theatre's subjects and its means of expression through human form are one and the same. For this reason, it can be said that theatre is an immediate way of experiencing what it means to be human.

A recent production of Thornton Wilder's *The Matchmaker* is a good example of how theatre engages actors in a very human story about true love. In a production at the Stratford Festival (Ontario, Canada), actors playing Mrs. Irene Molloy, the milliner, and Mrs. Dolly Levi, the matchmaker, engage audiences in Wilder's enduring story about the course of true love failing to run smoothly. Audiences delight in the machinations of young lovers outwitting their elders to find true love—a story as old as Roman comedy. When actors breathe life into Wilder's characters, they give form to an enduring story about our humanity for audiences to delight in.

To begin our discussion of theatre, let us consider basic questions: What is theatre? How is theatre *a way of seeing*? How do we, as audiences, respond to, interact with, and experience theatre? What are theatre's special qualities that set it apart from other art forms and popular entertainments? Let us first search for answers in theatre's *living* quality—its immediacy, aliveness, spaces, and spectators.

Theatre's *living* quality, its immediacy, is our first concern.

THEATRE'S IMMEDIACY

Theatre happens when actors and audiences come together in the here and now. Audiences watch, listen, and react in the presence of the actor's work in a prearranged space—what is normally called a stage or platform. The two living, breathing groups are central to an act of theatre taking place. This immediacy of human beings sets theatre apart from such media and digital technologies as film, television, iPhones, and the Internet. Theatre's essential difference is the *physical presence* of actors and audiences together within a space arranged for seeing and being seen. Although plays are filmed and seen by millions of people (for example, the now-classic film of Tennessee Williams's play *A Streetcar Named Desire*) the theatre itself—its aliveness and distinctive artistic quality—is lost in the transfer to another medium.

A Streetcar Named Desire
Rachel Weiz as Blanche DuBois in *A Streetcar Named Desire*, London.

As a form of live entertainment, theatre is often defined by its differences from live concerts, dance performances, and sporting events. Certainly theatre, especially musical theatre such as *The Lion King* and *Wicked*, can be diversions. Its farces and thrillers, such as *The Addams Family* and *Perfect Crime*, can serve as amusing diversions from such serious events as civil unrest and unfolding wars. But, unlike concerts, dance, sports, and mass-media programs, theatrical entertainment presents us with the actor's body, voice, mind, and soul enacting stories that challenge us to enjoy human inventiveness, or to think about uncomfortable truths, or to come to higher understandings of human affairs. No one wants to ride that "streetcar named desire" in quite the way that Tennessee Williams's character Blanche DuBois does, but through her we come to know the sadness and despair of the human condition.

Mass Media and Spectators

Theatre does not involve the huge audiences that attend such popular entertainments as rock concerts and sporting events and watch films and television programs. Mass-media audiences number in the millions of viewers (24.88 million viewers watched one episode of television's *Dancing with the Stars*). In contrast, a theatrical event is restricted to a fixed number of seats in a single building. Most New York or London playhouses seat approximately 700 to 2,000 people nightly. Contrast this number to the tens of thousands who attend Super Bowl games in gigantic stadiums. Moreover, television has worldwide viewers. Nightly newscasts are beamed into various corners of the world, and recorded images of human events are sent in "real time" from Kabul to New York City, Beijing, and Cairo. These images find their way into our living rooms in Chicago, Los Angeles, and Austin, Texas. In comparison to the global outreach of the mass media, theatre is limited in almost all respects: in number of spectators, size of markets, and resistance to reproducibility. Its *immediacy* is its defining character and its limitation.

Nevertheless, theatre's immediacy has had a profound effect on media arts. The imitative "reality" television programs (*Extreme Makeover, Survivor,* and *Project Runway*) aim to inject a sense of happening-on-the-spot immediacy as a new television genre. Unlike theatre's "reality," which is limited to a direct exchange between actor and spectator in the present time of the performance, reality television is pretaped, edited, and broadcast and rebroadcast to millions.

Whereas we respond to the theatre event from moment to moment over a period of an hour or more, films and radio and television shows require no immediate feedback from viewers, except as tweets, blogs, and Facebook postings. In an effort to create feedback, the broadcast media has recently engaged viewers directly through on-camera interviews, call-in talk shows, email responses, and blogs to questions and issues. Following singer Janet Jackson's infamous "wardrobe malfunction" during a prime-time television broadcast, the networks instituted time lapses of seven seconds to screen the language and behavior of performers, thereby avoiding the broadcast of socially inappropriate behavior and fines levied by the Federal Communications Commission.

It is undeniable that media arts and popular entertainments have a large and significant place in our daily lives. Music on iPhones is often background to such activities as driving a car or studying for an exam. Television sets and home-theatre centers are part of our household furniture, and iPads and e-readers let us select and show films of our own choosing. Moreover, the Internet has transformed entertainment, messaging, and communication. The computer has made possible "interactivity" between sender and receiver. There are interactive games, home shopping, Internet searches, Facebook postings, electronic voting, online courses, blogging, and so on. Communication theorists argue that the Internet extends the power of the individual as audience member to intervene, to talk back to senders, to gain access to information through Google and Yahoo! Nevertheless, the viewer seated before the computer terminal communicates electronically; this interaction is very different from the interactive experience of theatre audiences in communion with others around them and onstage before them.

In contrast to the interactivity of digital media, theatre engages us in an *active* and kinetic physical construction of behavior and meaning. Shakespeare's *Hamlet* engages us in untimely revenge and deadly consequences; John Patrick Shanley's *Doubt* shows the clash of wills and generations in a school setting; María Irene Fornés' *The Conduct of Life* confronts us with the family as mirror of totalitarian societies; and so on.

Unlike products of digital media, theatre cannot be replicated in another medium. Once the theatrical performance ends, it is gone forever. What is unique (and even disheartening) about the theatre is that, even as it is taking place, it is being lost to future generations. We can read firsthand accounts about the early performances of Shakespeare's plays and even try to reconstruct them and the Globe Theatre, but we can never fully know what it was to experience *Hamlet* onstage as Elizabethan audiences did. We can have our own first experience of a Shakespeare play, but we cannot make permanent our experience except in memory, in photographs, or on film. What is it, then, that makes this ancient art so elusive? The answer is, once again, the centrality of human beings—actors and spectators—to the art.

FOCUS ON THEATRE

Audience Viewpoints: Audience as Motley Crew

Since the time of ancient Greece, audiences of all ages have assembled in amphitheatres and playhouses to be entertained and challenged with the deepest truths about the human condition.

Greek audiences assembled at dawn to witness multiple plays performed through daylong festivals. Today, audiences buy tickets for matinees or evening performances of a single play. In earlier centuries, evening dress was required for men and women seated in the "dress circle," but there are no dress codes enforced today. Modern audiences are a motley crew of dress, age, and ethnicity who freely laugh, applaud, weep, but otherwise give respectful attention to the actor's work as the world of the play unfolds.

As we pass through the theatre's foyer and enter the auditorium, ushers take our tickets, hand us playbills, and help us find our seats. We settle down to watch a revival of *Hamlet* in an open-air playhouse, such as the reconstructed Elizabethan theatre of the Oregon Shakespeare Festival in Ashland, and actors as castle guards walk onto the platform stage and introduce us to Hamlet's murderous world of ghosts, graveyards, and avengers. The two sentinels, Bernardo and Francisco, engage us at the outset in their discomfort and fear:

Bernardo: *Who's there?*

Francisco: *Nay, answer me. Stand and unfold yourself.*

© Photo by Jennifer Donahoe/Courtesy Oregon Shakespeare Theatre

The Oregon Shakespeare Festival Theatre in Ashland (founded in 1935) is an open-air theatre. The audience sits in front (and to the sides) of a platform stage. A multilevel building serves as a permanent background for plays by Shakespeare and other playwrights.

As director Peter Brook says, "A man walks across the empty space whilst someone else is watching him, and this is all that is needed for an act of theater to be engaged." In other words, theatre presents human beings playing characters who move, speak, and "live" in the here and now. As we watch, they become recognizable people, events, and places. For a short time we share an experience with actors that is imitative, provocative, entertaining, and magical. Theatre's *living quality* on both sides of the "footlights" sets it apart from its popular mass-media competitors.

THEATRE'S ALIVENESS

In many ways, theatre parallels life. Onstage, actors represent our humanness in an imitation of human truths and realities. In *Tartuffe*, for example, Molière presents the perils to a family of a phony religious person's greed; in *The Caucasian Chalk Circle*, Bertolt Brecht demonstrates the selfless act of a young woman saving a child in time of war. As we sit in the audience, we also constitute a human community—a collective presence—as we laugh, cry, enjoy, and applaud.

Theatre is thus "alive" as actors tell a story in immediate communion with its audience. Film is a means of recording and preserving that "aliveness" for all time. The television series *Live from Lincoln Center* is one highly successful effort to provide HD broadcast transmissions of a stage performance with its audience. From our homes we can hear the audience's enthusiastic response, but we are removed from the original event. We know that both theatre and film are equally convincing in their storytelling powers, but their modes of presentation are vastly different.

For example, the great performances of Marlon Brando as Stanley Kowalski and Vivien Leigh as Blanche DuBois in *A Streetcar Named Desire* are captured in the 1951 film. But the wonderful theatrical performances of Laurette Taylor, Jessica Tandy, Cate Blanchett, and others in plays by Tennessee Williams are lost to us as the performance ends.

Theatre is an evanescent art, lasting only those two or three hours it takes to see the play-in-performance. The experience can be repeated night after night as long as the show is running, but once the play closes and the cast disperses, that performance is lost.

Although admittedly frustrating, this intriguing quality of theatre, which the critic Brooks Atkinson calls the "bright enigma," is the source of its vitality and our pleasure.

Theatre, then, is a *living* art form, continuing in present time until that final moment when Shakespeare's Hamlet is lifted from the stage to Fortinbras's command, "Take up the bodies," or when Samuel Beckett's tramps "do not move" from the appointed place for their meeting with Godot, who never comes. Theatre also bears a unique relationship to the humanity it mirrors. What are these parallels between theatre and life? There are six essential parallels:

actors	↔	humanity
simulation	↔	reality
rehearsal	↔	discovery
improvisation	↔	spontaneity
stage	↔	world
audiences	↔	society

Theatre's Doubleness

At all times in the theatre there is a doubleness. The actors are human beings representing the playwright's imaginative expression of our humanity and the human condition; the stage is a platform that convinces us it is another world. Shakespeare said it best in *As You Like It*: "All the world's a stage/And all the men and women merely players." Theatre's doubleness—art mirroring life, and life mirroring art—is another special quality of this complex art.

FOCUS ON PLAYS

Theatre and Life

Michael Cumpsty (center) as Jaques in the Williamstown Theatre Festival, MA, production of *As You Like It*.

© Courtesy of Williamstown Theatre Festival/Richard Feldman

Jaques's speech from Shakespeare's *As You Like It* provides us with one of the most famous discussions on the similarities between theatre and life:

All the world's a stage,
And all the men and women merely players:
They have their exits and their entrances;
And one man in his time plays many parts,
His acts being seven ages. At first the infant,
Mewling and puking in the nurse's arms.
And then the whining school-boy, with his satchel
And shining morning face, creeping like snail
Unwillingly to school. And then the lover,
Sighing like furnace, with a woeful ballad
Made to his mistress' eyebrow. Then a soldier,
Full of strange oaths, and bearded like the pard,
Jealous in honour, sudden and quick in quarrel,
Seeking the bubble reputation
Even in the cannon's mouth. And then the justice,
In fair round belly with good capon lined,
With eyes severe and beard of formal cut,
Full of wise saws and modern instances;
And so he plays his part. The sixth age shifts
Into the lean and slipper'd Pantaloon,
With spectacles on nose and pouch on side,
His youthful hose, well saved, a world too wide
For his shrunk shank; and his big manly voice,
Turning again toward childish treble, pipes
And whistles in his sound. Last scene of all,
That ends this strange eventful history,
Is second childishness and mere oblivion,
Sans teeth, sans eyes, sans taste, sans everything.
(2, vii)

REFLECTIONS IN THE MIRROR

The doubleness about the theatrical experience reflects a sense of life lived onstage. For instance, the audience experiences the actor both as actor—the living presence of another human being—and as fictional character. Audiences experience Ralph Fiennes as Hamlet and Al Pacino as Shylock. Likewise, the performing space is a stage and at the same time an imaginary world created by playwrights, designers, directors, and actors. Sometimes this world is as familiar to us as a St. Louis tenement in *The Glass Menagerie* or a midwestern farmhouse in *Buried Child*. The stage might resemble a modern living room or a hotel room or a front yard. Sometimes it is unfamiliar, for example, Macbeth's blighted castle at Dunsinane, Oedipus's plague-ridden city of Thebes, or Othello's storm-tossed island of Cyprus.

Elizabethans thought the theatre mirrored life. Shakespeare's Hamlet describes the purpose of acting, or "playing," in this way:

> ... *the purpose of playing, whose end, both at the first and now, was and is to hold as 'twere the mirror up to Nature, to show Virtue her own feature, scorn her own image, and the very age and body of the time his form and pressure.* (3, ii)

Hamlet speaks here of the Elizabethan idea that the stage, like a mirror, shows audiences both their good and bad qualities along with an accurate reflection of the times.

The Elizabethan idea of the stage as a mirror, related as it is to the act of seeing, can help us understand the dynamics of theatre and its aesthetics. Looking into a mirror is, in a sense, like going to the theatre. When we stare into a mirror, we see our double—an image of ourselves and possibly a background and anyone standing

© Sara Krulwich/The New York Times/Redux

The Merchant of Venice
Al Pacino as Shylock in Shakespeare's *Merchant of Venice*, Broadway.

nearby in the reflection. The image can be made to move; we make certain judgments about it; it communicates to us certain attitudes and concerns about our humanness. As reflected in the mirror, our humanity has shape, color, texture, form, attitude, and emotion; it is even capable of movement within the limits of the mirror's frame. Onstage, the actor as fictional character—as Oedipus, Othello, Hamlet, or Blanche DuBois—creates the doubleness that is theatre's special quality. It is both a stage world and an illusion of a real world.

Theatre is life's double, but it is also something more than a reflection of life. As a form of art it is *a selected reflection* organized into stories and fictions about events and people to tell us something about our humanity.

THEATRE'S FICTIONS

Theatre presents itself as a fiction—the performance of stories about events and people. We are emotionally and intellectually pulled into the lives and feelings of the characters before us. We would like Blanche DuBois to find that handsome, mythical gentleman who will make life kind and tolerable for her, but we are made aware of her destructive tendencies with alcohol and sex, and cringe before the inevitable ending to her life.

In the case of such films as *Henry V* and *Much Ado About Nothing,* Kenneth Branagh, as film director and leading actor, rearranged Shakespeare's text while retaining the language pertinent to telling the story on film. The play's dimension is concentrated in certain scenes of *Henry V*, for example, when the comic rogue Falstaff exhorts his friend in the tavern, or when King Henry proposes marriage to Katharine of France. These scenes are lifted from the play. But in the film as a whole, the rapid editing from place to place, the contrasts of faces and images, the realistic scenes of horses falling in battle and men dying, and the rearranging of the old text into useful fragments create a cinematic version of the play.

In film, images transport us into new worlds of discovery. Theatre has other means to persuade us that we are sharing in new experiences. As the curtain goes up and the performance begins, we enter into an artistic illusion, guided by language and physical presence that is now 2,500 years old.

Theatre creates the *illusion*, as we watch, that we are sharing an experience with others *for the first time.* As members of the audience, we tacitly agree with the actors that, for the time of the performance, the play is a living reality. We know that theatre is not life, but we suspend this knowledge for the few hours that we watch the play. Moreover, actors contribute to the illusion, for they are both actors *and* characters. We are simultaneously aware that Oedipus, the central figure in *Oedipus the King*, is Sophocles's central character and that he is being played by an actor. Theatre's grand fiction is twofold: that the actors are other than who they are in the present moment, and that life is taking shape before us for the first time.

In the theatre we both believe in what is happening before us ("suspend our disbelief," as the poet Coleridge said) and disbelieve in the stage-world before us. We give way to theatre's magic and fiction as our minds and emotions are involved, yet we exist apart.

THEATRE'S SPACES

At the heart of the theatre experience, as Peter Brook suggests, is the act of seeing and being seen. That requires a special place. The word *theatre* comes from the Greek word *theatron*, meaning "seeing place." At one time or another during the history of Western culture, this place for seeing has been a primitive dancing circle, an amphitheatre, a church nave, an Elizabethan platform stage, a marketplace, a garage, a street, or a proscenium theatre. Today, it may be a Broadway theatre, a university playhouse, or a renovated warehouse. But neither the stage's shape nor the building's architecture makes a theatre. Rather, the use of space to imitate human experience for audiences to see makes *a seeing place*. This seeing place, or theatre, is where we are entertained and learn about ourselves and others. It is the place where we perceive the how, the what, and the why of our humanness in the company of others.

The three basic components of theatre are the actor, the space, and the audience. The history of theatre has been, in one sense, the changing physical relationship of actor and audience. This changing relationship mirrors the changing status of audiences and the changing social, economic, and political importance of theatre to society. The audience has moved from the hillside of the Greek open-air theatre to a place before the Christian altar, to standing room around the Elizabethan theatre's platform stage, to seats in a darkened hall before a curtained proscenium stage, to the floor or scaffolds of a modern environmental production.

In the same historical sequence, the actor has moved from the dancing circle of the Greek amphitheatre to the open stage of the Elizabethan theatre, to the picture-frame stage of the proscenium theatre, to contemporary environmental spaces. The effects of historical trends and social institutions on theatre are important. What is crucial is an

The Guthrie Theatre
The Wurtele Thrust Stage in the new Mississippi riverfront home of the Guthrie Theater, Minneapolis, opened in 2006 with three theatres, including the 1,100 seat Wurtele stage. The audience's relationship to the thrust stage (and the actors) is apparent in this photo of the performance space.

understanding of the common denominators, unchanged, as unsubstantiated legend has it, since the sixth-century BC poet Thespis introduced the first actor (himself) to converse with the chorus and created dialogue. It is no accident that the Greek word for actor is *hypokrites*, meaning "answerer." That first actor literally stepped apart and answered questions asked by the chorus.

Whether the physical space becomes more elaborate or less so, whether the performance occurs indoors or out, the actor–audience relationship is theatre's vital ingredient. In one sense, the formula for theatre is simple: *A man or woman stands in front of an audience in a special (or prepared) place and performs actions that lead to interactions with other performers and audiences.* For many theorists, theatrical communication begins and ends with the audience.

American Airlines Theatre

The Roundabout Theatre Company's new 740-seat flagship theatre on Forty-second Street, New York City. Formerly the Selwyn Theatre, then a neglected B-movie house, it was transformed in 2000 to its gilded 1918 neo-Renaissance origins and renamed. The proscenium stage is seventy-five feet wide and fifty feet deep.

THEATRE'S AUDIENCES

A modern audience enters a theatre lobby with an air of excitement and a sense of anticipation. There is usually a last-minute crush at the box office to pick up tickets, then to get programs and find seats. An audience is not an unruly crowd but a special group assembling for a special occasion; it is the final, essential participant in the creation of the theatre event. The audience is the assembled group for which all has been written, designed, rehearsed, and staged.

What, then, are the audience's expectations as they wait for the house lights to dim and the curtain to rise? We find that expectations are essentially the same whether theatregoers are in the American Airlines Theatre on Broadway or the Guthrie Theater in Minneapolis.

1. *Audiences expect plays to be related to life experiences.* (It goes without saying that audiences expect plays and performances to hold their attention and to be entertaining.) Audiences do not actually expect to have experienced the events taking place onstage. None of us would willingly exchange places with Oedipus or Blanche DuBois. Instead, we expect the play's events (and also the actor's performances) to be *authentic*, to "ring true," in feelings and experiences. We are moved by *A Streetcar Named Desire* because it rings true in terms of what we know about ourselves and others. It confirms what we have studied, read, and heard about human behavior. Williams's characters and situation may not be literally a part of our lives; yet, we all recognize the need for fantasies, self-delusion, and refuge from life's harsh realities. In short, we go to the theatre expecting the performance to be an authentic representation of some aspect of life as we know it or can imagine it.

© Photo by Richard Termine

A Streetcar Named Desire
Cate Blanchett as Blanche DuBois arriving at the New Orleans apartment of Stanley and Stella Kowalski in the Sydney Theatre Company production of *A Streetcar Named Desire*, directed by Liv Ullmann, Brooklyn Academy of Music, New York.

2. *Most audiences go to the theatre expecting the familiar*. These expectations are based largely on plays we have already seen or on our experiences with films and television. Audiences enjoy the familiar in plots, characters, and situations. For this reason, daily television soap operas, such as *The Young and the Restless* and *The Bold and the Beautiful*, are popular with all ages. Also, audiences frequently have difficulty understanding and enjoying plays from the older classical repertory or from the contemporary avant-garde. We are not as comfortable with the concerns of Oedipus or

Estragon (in *Waiting for Godot*) as we are with the domestic affairs of Ashton Kutcher or Melissa McCarthy.

All audiences come to the theatre with certain expectations that have been shaped by their previous theatregoing experiences. If those experiences have been limited to musicals, summer stock, or local community theatre, then they may find the first experience of a play by Anton Chekhov or Samuel Beckett a jarring, puzzling, or even boring experience. But masterpieces somehow ring true! In them we find authentic life experiences, even if the language is difficult, the situations strange, the characters weird, the writing styles unusual, or the production techniques unfamiliar.

The response to the first American production of *Waiting for Godot* is a good example of audiences being confronted with the unfamiliar and having their expectations disappointed on their first experience with the play. Audiences in Miami and New York were baffled by it. But in 1957, Jules Irving and Herbert Blau's San Francisco Actor's Workshop presented *Waiting for Godot* to the inmates of San Quentin Prison. No play had been performed at San Quentin since the French actress Sarah Bernhardt had appeared there in 1913, and the director and actors were apprehensive.

Of the 1,400 convicts assembled to see the play, possibly not one had ever been to the theatre. Moreover, they were gathered in the prison dining room to see a highly

FOCUS ON THEATRE

Samuel Beckett's *Waiting for Godot*

Waiting for Godot, by the Irish playwright Samuel Beckett, was first produced at the Théâtre de Babylone, Paris, in 1953. On a country road in a deserted landscape marked by a single leafless tree, Estragon and Vladimir are waiting for someone named Godot. To pass the time, they play games, quarrel, make up, fall asleep. In comes Pozzo, the master, leading his slave, Lucky, by a rope tied around his neck. Pozzo demonstrates that Lucky is his obedient servant, and Lucky entertains them with a monologue that is a jumble of politics and theology. They disappear into the darkness, and Godot's messenger (a boy) announces that Mr. Godot will not come today.

In Act II, a leaf has sprouted on the tree, suggesting that time has passed, but the two tramps are occupied in the same way. They play master-and-slave games, trade hats, argue about everything. Pozzo and Lucky return, but they are not the same: the master is blind, and the slave is mute. Godot again sends word that he will not come today, but perhaps tomorrow. As the play ends, Vladimir and Estragon continue waiting, alone but together. In this play Beckett demonstrates how each of us waits for a Godot—for whatever it is that we hope for—and how, so occupied, we wait out a lifetime.

© Sara Krulwich/The New York Times/Redux

Waiting for Godot
A Broadway revival of Samuel Beckett's *Waiting for Godot* with Nathan Lane, John Goodman, and Bill Irwin.

experimental play that had bewildered sophisticated audiences in Paris, Miami, and New York. What would be the response? It was simply overwhelming. The prisoners understood the hopelessness and frustration of waiting for something or for someone that never arrives. They recognized the repetitions and meaninglessness of waiting; they understood that if Godot finally came, he would probably be a disappointment.

By now, *Waiting for Godot* is no longer considered experimental, and audiences are no longer baffled by it. It has become a modern classic, exemplifying how initial audience expectations can change over a period of years in response to an unusual, but profound, play. Even though audiences desire to see the familiar—this is probably the reason there are so many revivals of *Arsenic and Old Lace* and *Charley's Aunt*—they also appreciate and look forward to novel experiences in the theatre. Imagine the surprise of audiences when director Peter Brook reinterpreted Shakespeare's *A Midsummer Night's Dream*, exploring the complications of young love in a white, boxlike setting with actors in circuslike clothing on trapezes. Most audiences around the world were delighted with the new concept for staging a very old play, although a few were dissatisfied by not having their expectations fulfilled.

Like all great art forms, the theatre gives us a heightened sense of life and greater self-awareness. Great theatre also provides a sense of *new possibilities*. We go to plays (often consciously aware of our reasons) to realize a fuller, deeper understanding of our lives, our society, and our universe. When we are satisfied, we no longer cling to our need for the familiar.

3. *Another facet of the audience experience is the collective response*. We experience a performance as a group—as a collective thinking and feeling *presence*. Psychologists tell us that being in an audience satisfies a deeply felt human need: the need to participate in a collective response, whether with laughter, tears, appreciative silence, or thundering applause. As part of an audience, we become very much aware of group dynamics at the conclusion of a powerful and moving play. Sometimes when audiences are deeply moved, there are moments of silence before the beginning of applause. At other times applause is instantaneous, with audiences leaping to their feet clapping and shouting "Bravo!" The response to a great performance is immediate and unrestrained.

Even though applause is a theatregoing convention, it is also a genuine expression of the audience's appreciation and approval. One major element of the experience of live theatre is this sharing of feelings with others around us. Sometimes this even happens in cinemas, especially during horror films, as when audience

A Midsummer Night's Dream

A radical adaptation of Shakespeare's *A Midsummer Night's Dream*, directed by Peter Brook for Great Britain's Royal Shakespeare Company. Oberon (Alan Howard) and Puck (John Kane) speak Shakespeare's lines while perched like acrobats on trapezes.

Death of a Salesman
Broadway revival of Arthur Miller's *Death of a Salesman*, directed by Mike Nichols.

members scream in mock terror at threats to Kristen Stewart in the vampire film *Twilight: Breaking Dawn*.

An audience by definition is a sharing with others—of laughter and tears, expectations and delight.

4. *Audiences must make preparations for attending a play and observe certain unwritten rules of decorum.* Once we decide to see a play, preparations must be made. Because theatres are often not conveniently located and have limited seating, it is important to reserve tickets online or by telephone with Telecharge or Ticketmaster or purchase tickets at the box office. Theatres have seating charts that can be studied when purchasing tickets at the box office. The play, date, seat number, and time of performance are indicated on the ticket. Ticket buyers are warned to make certain all the information is correct because tickets often cannot be exchanged.

For the most part, our behavior in the theatre is expected to be respectful of the performers and considerate of those people seated around us. A quiet demeanor is, of course, not expected of audiences attending sporting events or rock concerts.

As mentioned earlier in this chapter, there are no special dress codes for attending the theatre. Usually, opening nights are dressier affairs than weekday or weekend performances; open-air theatres encourage even less formality in dress because they are subject to the weather and usually located in public parks.

Nevertheless, the theatre has certain rituals that pertain to audience etiquette. As we move from the foyer into the auditorium (called *the house* in theatre jargon), ushers check our tickets and help us find our seats; they hand us programs (called *playbills*) listing the producers, playwright, designers, director, cast of actors, and production and front-of-house staff and indicating the number of acts and intermissions. Sometimes notes about the play and production are included in the program.

Love's Labour's Lost
A production of Shakespeare's *Love's Labour's Lost* presented by New York's Shakespeare Festival Public Theater in the outdoor Delacorte Theatre, located in Central Park, New York City.

As front-of-the-house staff, ushers are responsible for the comfort and safety of the audience. They guard against those bringing food and drink into the theatre (refreshments are available at intermission), ask that book bags and briefcases be stored under seats so others will not stumble over them, and even issue warnings if someone inadvertently places his or her feet or coat on the back of a nearby seat.

Before the performance begins, audiences mingle and talk with friends until the houselights dim, signaling that the performance is about to begin, and preshow announcements invite us to turn off our cell phones and all personal electronic devices and unwrap candies before the performance begins. We are also warned that taking photographs is illegal. The actors' concentration is paramount, and audiences are asked to give their full attention to what is happening onstage from moment to moment. An unexpected noise emanating from the audience has been known to distract actors. They will usually talk through the disturbance without stopping the scene. However, if there is a serious disruption of some length, such as an ill patron, actors will stop and wait until the ushers deal with the situation and then continue the scene. In the rare instance that an audience member becomes ill, ushers will call for medical assistance and help that individual exit the auditorium.

Sometimes audience participation is designed into a performance. Audiences are asked to participate in answering direct questions posed to them by actors and collaborate in the fun of the moment.

At the end of performances, spontaneous and heartfelt responses take the form of unrestrained applause, shouts of bravo, or even the silence of a deeply moved audience. These responses usually come at the end of the performance during the curtain call; the exception is comedy, in which a zinger, or one-liner, can result in spontaneous laughter and enthusiastic applause. (In opera, the singers of the great arias are applauded at the end of each aria.) Curtain calls are carefully choreographed during rehearsals (from minor to major actors reappearing onstage to take a bow). This is our opportunity to applaud the actors and loudly applaud, even stand for, our favorites, usually the leading actor and actress.

In general, there are no rules for experiencing a theatrical performance. Courtesy is possibly the only rule for audience members. It is important to be courteous to people nearby and to the actors onstage. We must remember that they are creating a living work of art and require the audience's collaboration to concentrate as they become characters and contribute to the unfolding story.

5. *The audience, or spectator, is central to the theatrical event*. In recent investigations, the role of the audience as a "co-creator" has received attention. In this view, the audience comes into the performance area as an active participant sharing in the cultural, social, and political issues set forth by the production. These groups are usually not mainstream audiences. They are likely to be found today in public parks, union halls, warehouses, and community centers. In these nontraditional areas, audiences compare and contrast social and cultural experiences during and after the theatrical occasion and broaden their understanding of different cultures. As an active participant in the theatrical occasion, audiences share in defining the "global village."

©Ed Bailey/AP Images

The Phantom of the Opera
Curtain Call for the long-running *The Phantom of the Opera*, Broadway.

TRANSITION

Theatre takes place as we watch actors present themselves before audiences in stories usually about human experience. The heart of the theatrical experience is the act of seeing and being seen; hence, we have called this introduction to theatre "a way of seeing."

Theatre, like life, happens within the present moment and has an immediacy that most other art forms do not have, or require. For theatre to happen, two groups of people—actors and audience—must come together in a prearranged space. The space, the actor, and the audience are three essential ingredients of the theatre event.

Theatre is also an act of discovery. When the curtain goes up, we discover new worlds and share in unlooked-for experiences. We also learn about ourselves, our society, and our world. Great plays raise questions about what it means to be a human being, and great performances communicate this knowledge to us in fresh, entertaining, and challenging ways.

As audiences, we enter a theatre and find, first, the theatrical space that influences the way we see and experience the theatrical event. That space is the focus of our next discussion.

Theatre: A Way of Seeing Online

Visit the CourseMate for Theatre: A Way of Seeing 7th Edition for quick access to the digital study resources that accompany this chapter, including links to the websites listed below, Theatre Workshop, digital glossary, a chapter quiz and more.

Websites

The *Theatre: A Way of Seeing* CourseMate includes links for all the websites described below. Simply select "Web links" from the Chapter Resources for Chapter 1, and click on the link that interests you. You'll be taken directly to the site described.

Artslynx International Theatre Resources
Comprehensive, well-maintained, and easy-to-use library of online theatre resources. Includes links to such topics as special effects, world and ethnic theatre, and employment in the theatre.

McCoy's Guide
A brief guide to a multitude of Internet resources in theatre and performance studies, maintained by Professor Ken McCoy of Stetson University. Scroll down to get to the links and information.

Playbill.com
A first stop for theatre links, theatre news, and theatre information, plus listings of plays in New York, London, and regional theatres. Scroll down, and click on "Theatre Central: Sites" for a number of links to theatre professionals and organizations throughout the world.

World Wide Web Virtual Library of Theatre and Drama
Links to resources in more than fifty countries around the world for professionals, amateurs, academics, and students of all ages—check out the links to theatre image collections, plays in print, theatre on film, and more.

Yahoo!'s Directory of Theatre Sites
Hundreds of links to all things theatre, such as In-Yer-Face Theatre, dedicated to cutting-edge British drama, and links to websites that highlight specific theatre genres and forms.

ODYSSEUS, the WWW Server of the Hellenic Ministry of Culture
A history of Greek theatre, plus links to modern-day theatre in Greece. From the home page, click on the link "Modern and Contemporary Cultural Creation" in the left-hand menu, then on "Theatre." (Click "Cancel" if you're asked to install a language pack.)

Royal National Theatre, London
Links to what's going on at one of London's most prestigious theatres.

© John Tramper/Globe Theatre

2

THE SEEING PLACE

There are, for example, privileged places, qualitatively different from all others—a man's birthplace, or the scenes of his first love . . . as if it were in such spots that he had received the revelation of a reality other than that in which he participates through his ordinary daily life.[1]

— MIRCEA ELIADE, *THE SACRED AND THE PROFANE: THE NATURE OF RELIGION*

Let us begin the discovery of theatre with another kind of privileged place—the stages, arenas, amphitheatres, and auditoriums where theatrical performance happens. With the exceptions of Mayan, Aztec, Sumerian, and some Islamic cultures, all cultures, from early to modern times, have encouraged theatrical performances and places for seeing these events. The earliest theatrical spaces were areas for performance of rituals dealing with life and death.

RITUAL AND THEATRE

When we examine the origins of ritual and theatre, we find that both are concerned with "the things done," with emphasis on the concrete and actual doing rather than the metaphysical or spiritual. They both deal with social relationships through enactment by living people. The difference between them is also distinctive. Theatre confines itself to showing and saying things about social needs; ritual reinforces or brings about change. For example, the marriage ritual, in which a young woman's status is forever changed in the community, and the rite of passage, or puberty rite, in which a young man is initiated into adulthood, are familiar rituals. Irrevocable change occurs as the young people are initiated by the community into a new life.

PREVIEW

Since its beginnings, theatre has been a place for seeing—for viewing, presenting, enacting, understanding. Places for theatre to happen are found in almost all societies, ancient and modern.

Throughout history the theatre space has been arranged so that audiences can see and performers can be seen.

The new Globe Theatre, London, is a modern reconstruction of Shakespeare's Globe, as a partially-open air theatre with surrounding covered balconies and an open area for standing around the thrust stage that features two columns supporting the roof above the stage.

© Charles & Josette Lenars/CORBIS

A Shaman Performs a Ceremonial Dance
A Dayak shaman performs a ceremonial dance ritual for villagers in Borneo, Indonesia.

But the young woman who dresses in ceremonial wedding clothes to play Rosalind in *As You Like It* is clearly an actress representing a bride, and she will do so repeatedly during the play's run. The marriage ritual has accomplished social change; the theatre has shown why and how Rosalind "got her man."

Early Performance Spaces

Ritual and theatre also share special places of enactment. The earliest agent, or "actor," performs in a special or privileged place. The priest, the guru, the dancer, or the actor performs in a threshing circle or in a hut, a building, or an enclosure that is shared with the onlooker or audience. In some ritual spaces, a circular area is surrounded by spectators in much the same way that the semicircular Greek theatre is configured or even the modern-day Guthrie Theater in Minneapolis. In other ritual spaces, special buildings are constructed for the occasion and often destroyed at the end of the rite in the same sense that a modern production is "struck," meaning scenery is removed from the stage at the end of the play's run. Some groups moved from place to place in early societies, as today's touring companies do.

For many years, theatre historians have connected the origins of theatre with agrarian and fertility rites and with *special places* for enactment of these rites. Early societies staged mock battles between death and life in which the king of the old year, representing death, perished in a duel with the champion of the new year. In such rituals we can see the beginnings of modern theatre—*enactment, imitation*, and *seasonal performances*—all held in special or privileged spaces designated by the community.

Dramatic overtones were added to early ceremonies designed to win favor from supernatural powers. Imitation, costumes, makeup, masks, gestures, and pantomime were elements in these rituals. The rain dance ceremonies of the Native Americans of the Southwest were meant to ensure that the tribal gods would send rain to make crops grow. Early societies acted out seasonal changes—patterns of life, death, and rebirth—until their ceremonies became formalized occasions. Harvest rituals, for example, celebrated abundant food supplies. Today's state fairs held in the fall celebrate the products grown by farming communities (animals, vegetables, fruits, etc.).

Whereas rituals of early societies were concerned with the protection of the community against hunger and illness, for example, theatre's most common objective is to please and entertain rather than to pacify, protect, or heal the community. And theatre's audiences are not secondary to what is happening onstage, as they may very well be in the practice of ritual ceremonies. As we have seen, theatre's actors and audiences are indispensable to the theatrical experience.

THEATRICAL PERFORMANCE

Theatre deals with the mystery, history, and ambiguity of human behavior and events. Plays speak to us of individuals, as well as of groups. They hold the mirror up to our joys and our sorrows, to our triumphs and atrocities, to our questions and our tentative answers about life. Theatre can motivate us to social, cultural, and political action. Theatre aims to provoke thought while entertaining us, rather than provide concrete answers or solutions. Since the beginning of the Greek festivals, playwrights have expressed concern for the human condition. Shakespeare demonstrates the sensitivity of a supreme dramatic artist in this speech by Hamlet:

> *What a piece of work is a man, how noble in reason, how infinite in faculties; in form and moving how express and admirable, in action how like an angel, in apprehension how like a god: the beauty of the world, the paragon of animals! And yet to me what is this quintessence of dust?* (2, ii)

Hamlet speaks about himself, but he also speaks in universal terms about all of us. He raises questions about human nature; insights are there for those who want them. But even so, the play's essential function is to entertain. For without diversion, all else in the theatre must inevitably fail, and audiences become bored, restless, "turned off." Although ritual performances are often entertaining, their objective is largely practical: crops will grow, the hunt will succeed, illness will be cured, warring tribes will be placated or defeated. In ritual, entertainment is a bonus for the onlooker; in theatre, we share in a complex experience that is simultaneously entertaining, imitative, provocative, subversive, and even magical.

Although theatre's origins share kinship with early rituals in seasonal themes of birth and death and enactment in special places reserved for communal interests, theatre differs in essential ways. Using the playwright's words to create a sense of place and life, actors present themselves on a stage, or in a special place.

What is certain in these early beginnings is that theatre, as we know it now, is a kind of ritual act performed not in a hut or other temporary structures that will be dismantled after the ceremony, but in a permanent building that will be used again and again. Theatrical space in modern terms has two components: *stage* and *auditorium*. And the first such permanent theatre building we know of in Western culture stands in the curve of a hillside in Greece.

WESTERN THEATRE

Greek Theatre

Orchestra and Skene

The most celebrated theatre of fifth-century BC Athens, called the Theatre of Dionysus in honor of the fertility god, was an open-air structure located on the slope of the hill below the Acropolis.

In time, there were two performance areas cradled within the curve of the hillside: the dancing circle (or *orchestra*) and later an open area backed by a scene building

The Theatre at Delphi
The Theatre at Delphi, an ancient Greek theatre, is built on a hillside with seating on three sides surrounding the dancing circle, or *orchestra*. The photo shows the stone benches placed on the hillside for the audience, the flat dancing circle for the chorus (and possibly actors) at the foot of the hill, and the entrance-way and remains of the stone foundation for the scene building and entrance-way (upper right).

(or *skene*). The chorus, usually portraying ordinary human society, performed in the dancing area. One speaking actor (later, three) portrayed mythical and historical characters. Actors first performed in an "empty space" and later in front of a rectangular, wooden scene building, which formed a neutral background easily representing many places—a palace, temple, house, cave, or whatever was needed in the story line. A late addition to the space was the wooden scene building erected on a stone foundation. Actors may also have performed in the *orchestra*, or on a raised stage, although no one knows for sure. The chorus, actors, and audience all entered the theatre through passageways called *parodoi*; on the hillside "auditorium" the audience stood, or sat on the ground, and later on wooden or stone benches.

In the ancient Greek theatre there were no barriers between the performing area and the auditorium. The audience on the hillside had an unbroken view of chorus and actor in the Theatre at Delphi. The spectators in the lower tiers near the dancing circle or orchestra, in fact, were so near the chorus that they were practically an extension of it.

Chorus as Spectator The Greek chorus, which was eventually reduced from fifty people to fifteen or twelve by the time Aeschylus, Sophocles, and Euripides were writing for the festivals, shared the audience's reactions to events and characters and sometimes interacted with the actors. Functioning as the spokesman for the play's community or society, the chorus gave advice, expressed opinions, asked questions, and generally set the ethical framework by which events were judged. They frequently served as the "ideal spectator," reacting to characters and events as the playwrights hoped audiences would. With their costumes, masks, and musical instruments, the chorus added spectacle, movement, music, song, dance, and visual interest to the occasion. Moreover, their moods heightened the story's dramatic effectiveness.

Unlike the chorus, the actor, representing a heroic figure such as Oedipus or Agamemnon, stood apart in the performance space, just as he stood apart from ordinary mortals in life. Thus, the dancing circle and the chorus formed a kind of bridge between actor and audience, serving as both commentator on and spectator to the deeds it witnessed.

The arrangement of spaces in the Greek theatre indicates how the Greeks saw their world: Classes separated by convention and social status found themselves on common ground when faced with spectacles of terror and misfortune. Individuals could measure their own experiences against the great human misfortunes enacted before them.

FOCUS ON PEOPLE IN THEATRE

PLAYWRIGHT

Aeschylus and the Athenian Festivals

© Araldo de Luca/CORBIS

Aeschylus (525/4–456 BC), Sophocles, Euripides, and Aristophanes are four Greek playwrights whose work has survived. Aeschylus began at an early age to write tragedies for the annual festivals in the Theatre of Dionysus, in Athens, winning thirteen first prizes during his lifetime.

Sometime before or during Aeschylus's career, the features of Greek tragedy became fixed: At an Athenian festival, three groups of male players, each consisting of a chorus and two (later, three) actors, competed in acting four sets of plays. Each set contained three tragedies and a satyr play—a burlesque of Greek myth, for comic relief. The plays were based on Greek legend, epic poems, or history. Costumes were formal, masks modest, physical action restrained; violent scenes occurred offstage. The playwright expanded and interpreted the characters and stories of legend or history.

Although Aeschylus wrote more than seventy plays, we have inherited scripts for only seven: *The Suppliants, The Persians, The Seven Against Thebes, Prometheus Bound, Agamemnon, The Libation Bearers*, and *The Eumenides*. These last three make up the *Oresteia* (458 BC), the only surviving Greek trilogy, or sequence of three tragedies. Its satyr play is missing.

We know little about Aeschylus as a person except that he fought at Marathon (490 BC) and probably at Salamis (480 BC) during the Persian Wars. His epitaph, which he wrote himself, shows that he was most proud of his military record:

> *Under this monument lies Aeschylus the Athenian, Euphorion's son, who died in the wheatlands of Gela. The grove of Marathon with its glories can speak of his valor in battle. The long-haired Persian remembers and can speak of it too.*

© Sandro Vannini/CORBIS

The Epidaurus Festival Theatre, Greece
The modern audience looks down upon the ancient *orchestra*, or dancing circle.

Sophocles's *Oedipus the King* speaks to master and slave when the chorus concludes: "Count no man happy until he has passed the final limit of his life secure from pain."

From the classical to the Hellenistic period (c. 990–30 BC), the Greek theatre underwent changes: wooden seats were replaced by stone; the addition of the scene building made the actors' area more complex, providing a neutral scenic background and dressing area; a low raised stage was probably added sometime after the fifth century BC for the actors to perform on. But the theatres, such as the Epidaurus Festival Theatre, remained in the open air, with well-defined places for the audience to sit and for the actors and chorus to perform. As we discover in later chapters, the division of space and other conventions, such as formal entrances, choral odes, and two to three speaking actors, dictated the structure of the plays performed there. The plays of Aeschylus, Sophocles, Euripides, and Aristophanes were shaped as much by the theatre's conventions as by the worldview of the playwrights.

Medieval Theatre

The medieval theatre (c. 950–1500) began in churches with Latin playlets performed by priests to teach Christian doctrine and encourage moral behavior. (An early example is the *Quem Quaeritis* trope.) Gradually, as performances became more concerned with entertainment and spectacle, they were moved out of the churches into the marketplaces. Lay performers replaced priests, and scripts grew longer and more complex, mixing the serious with the boisterous and farcical.

As in Greek and Roman practice, the medieval European theatre was an open-air festival theatre. There were few permanent structures. The plays, grouped in cycles, dealt with biblical events and ranged from the creation to the destruction of the world. One cycle contained as many as forty-two plays. They were performed in spring and summer months on religious holidays such as Corpus Christi, Easter, and Whitsuntide. Productions were sponsored by town councils, often with the help of local priests.

FOCUS ON THEATRE

Tropes

The trope, made up of chanted dialogue, was the beginning of medieval church drama and the first step toward creating plays after the Dark Ages. The tenth-century *Quem Quaeritis*, from a Benedictine abbey in Switzerland, consisted of questions and answers sung by the two halves of the choir during an Easter Mass. The Angels and the Marys were not actually impersonated, but the seeds of character and dialogue were there. Ultimately, the trope expanded into a little play or opera. It is significant that a question and answer, so familiar to us in theatrical dialogue today, was used so long ago to introduce the Easter Mass.

Question (by the Angels): *Whom do ye seek in the sepulcher, O followers of Christ?*

Answer (by the Marys): *Jesus of Nazareth, who was crucified, just as he foretold.*

Angels: *He is not here: He is risen, just as he foretold. Go, announce that he is risen from the sepulcher.*

Religious confraternities or secular trade guilds usually produced the cycles and hired a director or stage manager. Actors were recruited from the local population, who turned out en masse to be part of the event.

Types of Medieval Staging

The variety of theatrical activity in the Middle Ages is reflected in staging practices. Every place was potentially a site for theatre: streets, churches, guild halls, private manor houses, open fields, marketplaces, and innyards. In general, there were two approaches to staging: fixed (or linear) platforms and movable (or single-focus) rolling platforms or wagons.

Fixed Stages Precursors of medieval fixed stages are to be found in the permanent Greek and Roman theatres and in the Christian churches with their aisles, naves, and raised altars. The movable stage had its beginnings in the medieval processions that celebrated religious and state occasions. We can see the influence of medieval staging on our own fixed and movable stages, including open-air theatre buildings, amphitheatres, street and festival stages, and holiday parades with floats.

Valenciennes, France One of the best-known fixed stages was constructed in 1547 for the Valenciennes Passion Play, in northern France. Other important medieval fixed stages include the Roman amphitheatres; the "rounds" in Cornwall, England; and the stages, such as the Valenciennes stage, set up in public squares in France.

The Fixed Stage Used for the Valenciennes Passion Play, France, in 1547
The mansions or huts represent specific locations (from left to right): Paradise, Nazareth, the temple, Jerusalem, the palace, the golden door, the sea, and Hell's Mouth.

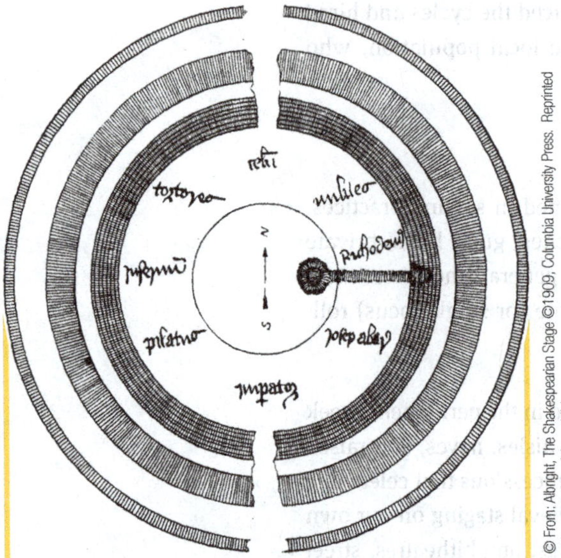

A Cornish Circular Amphitheatre (Fixed Stage)

A typical permanent open-air theatre in Cornwall (also called a *round*) was made out of earth with circular turf benches surrounding a level area 130 feet in diameter. Openings on two sides of the earthen mound provided entrances and exits. This diagram (of the fourteenth-century theatre at Perranzabulo) shows the staging for a biblical cycle called *The Resurrection of Our Lord Jesus Christ*. There are eight scaffolds located in the round's center. Action requiring a specific locale took place on the scaffolds; actors progressed from one scaffold to another around the circle. The audience, seated on the earthen tiers of seats, could follow the scenes with ease.

The fixed stage at Valenciennes was a rectangular platform with two chief areas. One contained the "mansions," or huts, which depicted specific locales; the other was the *platea*, an open playing space. There were no scene changes as we know them today. The actor merely went from hut to hut to indicate change in locale. Heaven and hell were usually represented on each end of the stage, with earthly scenes of humor, travail, and so on occurring between them. The fixed stage made it possible to present numerous scenes and actors, along with the required costumes, properties, and special effects.

In Cornish amphitheatres, such as the theatre at Perranzabulo, the audience probably viewed the action from two or more sides. When the stage was the platform type, viewers might be grouped around three sides of the playing areas, or they might gather at the front only. Whatever the arrangement, the stage was always in the open air; there was a definite performing space for the actors and areas for audiences. Actors were close to the audience, and performances sometimes continued from dawn to dusk.

Processional or Movable Stages Although fixed stages were common in many parts of Europe, theatrical space sometimes took on entirely different forms. In England and Spain, for example, the pageant wagon or processional, or portable, staging was used. The pageant wagon (in Spain called a *carro*) was a platform on wheels, something like our modern parade float.

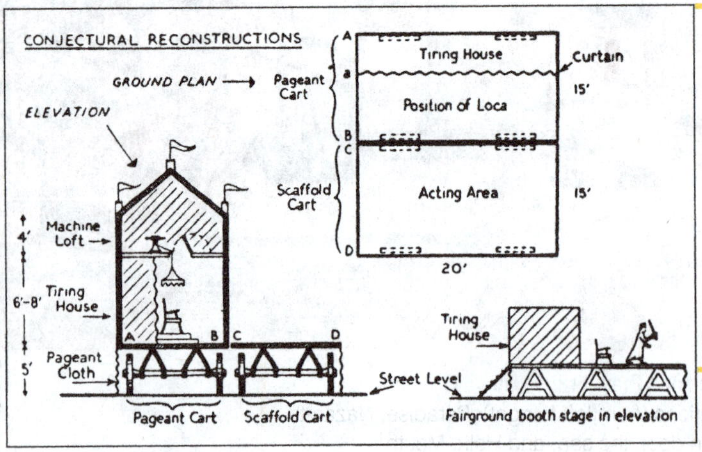

An English Pageant Wagon

Glynne Wickham's drawing is a conjectural reconstruction of an English pageant wagon and ground plan of the overall playing arrangement. The drawing shows the essential features of an Elizabethan playhouse: a platform acting area, a tiring-house with a recessed area (the *loca*) for interior scenes, a space for costume changes, and an area above the cart for machinery.

It was a portable playing area with a hut on top for the actors, which could also serve as a scenic background or acting area. No one is certain of the wagons' dimensions, but they had to fit through the narrow streets of medieval towns. The wagons stopped for performances at a number of places and may have been used individually or in groups.

The audience stood around the wagons to watch, so the actors were very close to the audience, just as they were on the fixed stages. The flexible playing space encouraged vigorous action (especially by the Devil, who was energetically booed and hissed); episodic, loose-knit plot structure; and some sort of scenic element to fix locale. *The Crucifixion Play*, one of thirty-two surviving plays of the English Wakefield cycle (c. 1375), is based on biblical scenes of Christ's torture at the hands of soldiers and his death on the cross. The cycle requires continuous action from the scourging of Christ to raising him on the cross in preparation for his death.

Elizabethan Theatre

By the late sixteenth century, permanent structures were being built in England and Europe to house a new kind of theatrical entertainment, one that was losing its ceremonial and festive qualities and focusing more on plays with commercial appeal performed by acting companies. In 1576, James Burbage built London's first theatre, naming it simply "The Theatre." It was an open-air structure that adopted features from various places of entertainment: inn-yards, pageant wagons, banquet halls, fixed platforms, and portable booth-stages.

Shakespeare's Globe

In 1599, Richard Burbage, James's son and leading actor for The Lord Chamberlain's Men (Shakespeare's company), and associates built the Globe Theatre, which became a showcase for Shakespeare's talents as actor and playwright. The most famous of all Elizabethan theatres, the Globe was an open-air building with a platform stage in the middle surrounded on three sides by open standing room. This space was surrounded in turn by a large enclosed balcony topped by one or two smaller roofed galleries. The stage was backed by a multilevel facade as part of the superstructure, called the *tiring-house.* On the stage level were places for hiding and discovering people and objects, highly influenced by the variety of medieval stages with their many huts or mansions. A roof jutting out above the stage platform was supported by two columns; the underside of the roof, called *the heavens*, was painted with moons, stars, and planets. After paying an admission fee, the audience stood around the stage or, for an additional charge, sat in the galleries or private boxes. Like the medieval audience, they were never far removed from the performers.

Swan Theatre
The De Witt drawing of the Swan Theatre in London dates from about 1596; it is the first sketch we have of the interior of an Elizabethan theatre.

FOCUS ON PEOPLE IN THEATRE

PLAYWRIGHT

William Shakespeare

William Shakespeare (1564–1616) was an Elizabethan playwright of unsurpassed achievement. Born in Stratford-upon-Avon, he received a grammar-school education and married a twenty-six-year-old woman when he was eighteen. He became the father of three children, Susanna and twins Judith and Hamnet.

Few other facts about Shakespeare's life have been established. By 1587–1588, he had moved to London, where he remained until 1611, except for occasional visits to his Stratford home. He appears to have found work almost at once in the London theatre as an actor and a writer. By 1592, he was regarded as a promising playwright; by 1594, he had won the patronage of the Earl of Southampton for two poems, *Venus and Adonis* and *The Rape of Lucrece*.

In 1594–1595, he joined James Burbage's theatrical company, The Lord Chamberlain's Men, as an actor and a playwright; later he became a company shareholder and part owner of the Globe and Blackfriars theatres. He wrote some thirty-seven plays for this company, suiting them to the talents of the great tragic actor Richard Burbage and other members of the troupe. Near the end of his life he retired to Stratford as a well-to-do country gentleman.

Shakespeare wrote sonnets, tragedies, comedies, history plays, and tragicomedies, including some of the greatest plays written in English: *Hamlet*, *King Lear*, *The Tempest*, *Macbeth*, and *Othello*.

The Globe Theatre
An enlargement of a theatre labeled "The Globe" from the engraving by J. C. Visscher, c. 1616.

Theatrical Influences

The Elizabethan theatre, like that of Greece and medieval Europe, was a festive theatre depicting cosmic drama that touched all people: peasant, artist, merchant, and noble. Its architecture, as we shall see, affected the structure of the plays written for it. Yet it all happened so long ago. What is our interest in these ancient modes of theatre, whose traditions are often so hard to trace? Do they really tell us anything about our own theatre buildings and stages? Are they related to the buildings and performance spaces that we think of as being so modern?

The answer is yes, and you will agree the next time you see a Mardi Gras parade float or an open-air theatre designed for summer productions of Shakespeare. In large parks, plays with historical themes are performed outdoors for audiences looking for family entertainment; touring groups travel widely to college campuses with portable stages, costumes, and properties to present plays about current themes. And street performers aided by puppets, mimes, musicians, loudspeakers, and colorful displays trumpet political and social messages with the spectacle and passion of medieval pageants.

FOCUS ON THEATRE

The Globe Restored

In *The Globe Restored* (1968), C. Walter Hodges describes the Elizabethan theatre as self-contained, adjustable, and independent of any surroundings other than its audience.

Hodges's detailed reconstruction (right) of the Globe Playhouse (1599–1613) shows the building's superstructure with galleries, yard, and railed stage. Notice the trapdoor in the stage, stage doors, curtained inner and upper stages, tiring-house (as backstage area with workrooms and storage areas), hut with machines, "the heavens," and playhouse flag.

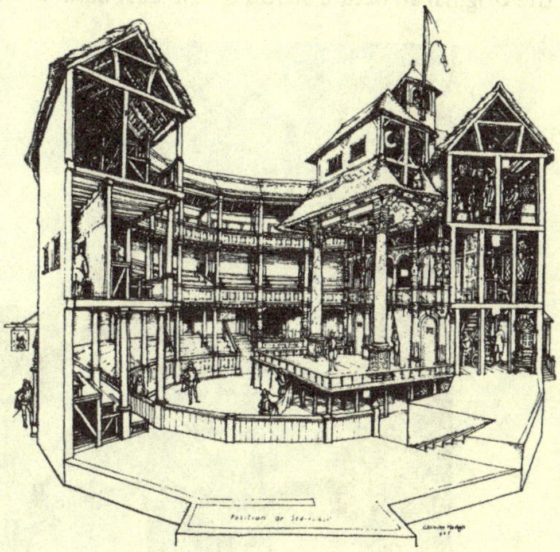

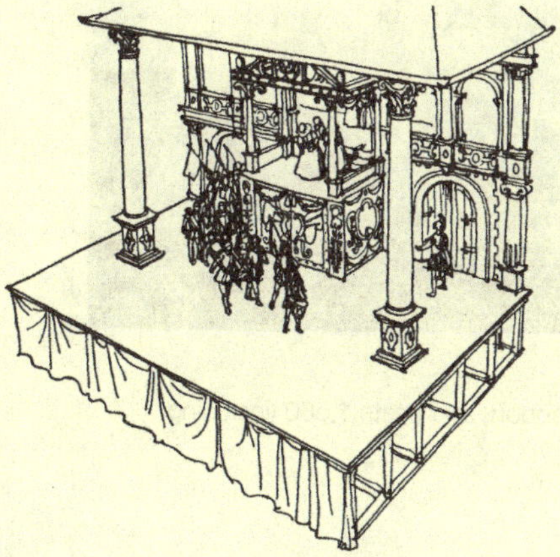

The inner stage or discovery space (left) is thought to be a small, recessed area with curtains in the tiring-house wall. Hodges shows a discovery area surrounded by curtains. The permanent upper level or upper stage is a characteristic feature of the Elizabethan stage; it was used for scenes such as the balcony scene in *Romeo and Juliet*. Hodges's reconstruction of the inner and upper stages brings them forward into the main acting area.

It is generally agreed that the tiring-house (right), the area around and within the wall at the back of the stage as shown in Hodges's drawing, was divided from the stage by hangings of some sort, usually curtains opening in the middle.

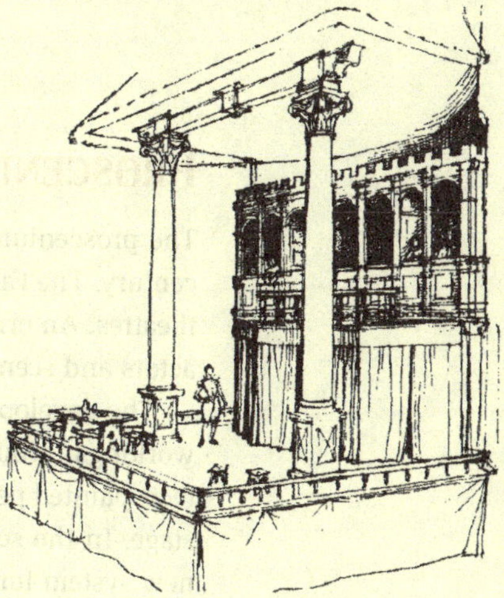

FOCUS ON THEATRE

Audience Viewpoints: London's New Globe

A reconstructed Globe Theatre opened in London in 1997. It is situated a few hundred yards from the site where the original structure stood on the East bank of the Thames River across from the City of London. Audiences enter the twenty-sided polygonal building, which has whitewashed, half-timbered walls and a thatched roof,

© Churchill & Klehr

Shakespeare's "New" Globe
The theatre is a modern reconstruction on Bankside, Southwark, London, and seats 1,500 (including standing room for 500 in an uncovered yard).

Proscenium Theatres and Modern Stages

The proscenium theatre dates from the Italian Renaissance of the early seventeenth century. The Farnese Theatre, built in 1618 at Parma, was one of the early proscenium theatres. An ornamental facade framed the stage and separated the audience from the actors and scene.

The development of the proscenium arch, framing the stage and masking its inner workings, brought innovative scenery and painting techniques. Renaissance architects painted perspective scenery on large canvas pieces placed on a raked, or slanted, stage. In the seventeenth century, an architect named Giambattista Aleotti created a new system for changing scenery, using movable, two-dimensional wings painted in perspective. This method, now called a wing-in-groove system (because grooves were placed in the stage floor to hold the scenery), replaced the raked stage.

FOCUS ON THEATRE

A performance of *Twelfth Night* at London's new Globe Theatre. The building, stage, and audience spaces duplicate as much as possible the performance conditions of Shakespeare's day.

and move toward the center, where they find an open theatre with a stage raised five feet above ground level; on the stage are two large pillars, painted to look like marble, supporting the "heavens," which are decorated with figures of the zodiac.

In imitation of Shakespeare's groundlings, the audience stands in the open space on three sides of the platform and looks toward the facade, or stage wall, which has a large opening at the center with doors on either side. The facade has a second level with a large open space that can be used by actors, musicians, and even spectators. Some 500 spectators can stand in sunshine or in rain around the stage, and another 1,000 can sit on benches in the three levels of covered balconies that surround the roofless yard.

Like its Elizabethan ancestor, the new Globe is a noisy theatre packed with spectators who become vocally and physically involved with the stage action, booing and hissing villains and shouting encouragement to lovers.

London's New Globe is a theatre without spotlights, microphones, or scenery where plays by Shakespeare and his contemporaries are performed. Moreover, the lively interaction of the tightly packed audience in the small, familiar space is reminiscent of Shakespeare's day.

Most of the theatres built in the Western world over the last 350 years are proscenium theatres. The concern of scenic designers working within this *picture-frame stage* was to create *illusion*, that is, to use perspective scenery and movable scenic pieces to achieve the effect of real streets and houses. The result literally framed the actors so that an audience could observe them in their setting. Playgoers were confined to the tiered galleries and to the orchestra or pit, as the ground-level seats were called.

Picture-Frame Stages

As audiences grew larger and playhouses became more profitable in the eighteenth century, the auditoriums of public theatres increased steadily in size. As auditoriums expanded, theatre architects added boxes for the affluent and cheap seats in the galleries for the less well-off. In the nineteenth century the proscenium opening was enlarged to exploit pictorial possibilities, and the auditorium was made shallower so that the audience was drawn closer to the stage, where spectators could better see the actors' expressions and the details of their environment.

An Early Proscenium Theatre

The Farnese Theatre in Parma, Italy, was one of the earliest to have a permanent proscenium arch. Our modern proscenium theatre with perspective scenery had its origins in Italy. Between 1500 and 1650, a typical theatre eventually developed with an auditorium, painted scenery, proscenium, curtain, and musicians' pit. Spectacle, illusion, and entertainment were its primary purpose.

Painted Scenery

The principles of perspective painting were introduced to theatrical scene design in the sixteenth century. Perspective scenery was painted to create the illusion of large streets or town squares, with houses, churches, roofs, doorways, arches, and balconies, all designed to appear exactly as they would seem to a person at a single point. This kind of painted background was intended to give a sense of depth to the scene. In his book *Architettura*, Sebastiano Serlio (1475–1554) explained the construction and painting of scenery for comedy, including the houses, tavern, and church shown in the drawing.

The Eisenhower Theatre
A proscenium theatre with seating and closed curtain at the John F. Kennedy Center for the Performing Arts in Washington, D.C.

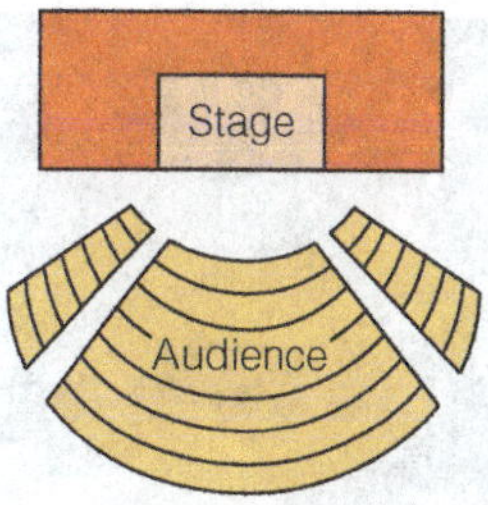

Proscenium Stage

Today, our proscenium theatres (many built in the early 1900s) contain a framed stage with movable scenery, machines, lighting, and sound equipment; an auditorium (possibly with balconies and orchestra pit) seating 500 to 1,500 or more; and auxiliary rooms, including foyers, box offices, workrooms, dressing rooms, and storage space.

The Box Set for *The Cherry Orchard*
The setting for the 1904 Moscow Art Theatre production of *The Cherry Orchard*, includes box set (three walls with ceiling), details of a recognizable room (doors, windows, curtains, furniture, dog), morning light coming through the windows, and the cherry trees in the distance.

© Auditorium and stage of the Stratford Festival of Canada. Photo by Terry Manzo/Courtesy of Stratford Festival of Canada

The Thrust Stage at the Stratford (Ontario) Festival Theatre
The stage has a permanent facade or background resembling the Elizabethan tiring-house.

The function of the proscenium theatre is to create pictorial illusion and recognizable worlds. For instance, the original box set of Anton Chekhov's *The Cherry Orchard* (1904) contains the world of the play—Madame Ranevskaya's drawing room on her bankrupt estate in rural Russia at the turn of the century.

In the proscenium theatre, the stage is usually hidden by a curtain until it is time for the play's world to be "discovered" by the audience. Staging, scenery, lighting, sound, and production style all work together to suggest that inside the proscenium arch is a self-contained world. The room may look like a typical living room. The street, kitchen, garden, or railway station may resemble places audiences know. But in the proscenium theatre, audiences are intentionally kept at a distance.

Thrust Stages

Variations of the proscenium theatre often display features from Elizabethan inn-theatres and open stages. Today's thrust or open stage is an example. Thrust stages were largely designed to minimize the separation of actor and audience created by the proscenium arch and the recessed stage. The actor literally performs on a platform that thrusts into the audience, and audiences have a keen sense of the actor in direct communication with them.

EASTERN THEATRE

The theatrical traditions of Eastern cultures throughout dozens of countries have been curiously removed from the West for centuries by geography, politics, language, and culture. The drama of India was first known to Westerners in the form of Sanskrit drama-theatre. Popular for more than a thousand years, Sanskrit drama was succeeded by regional dance-drama, named kathakali ("story play"), based on the many stories found in the two great Indian epics, *Ramayana* and *Mahabharata*. The music-drama (*xiqu*) of China flourished in the thirteenth century during the Yuan dynasty, with the Chinese opera becoming the dominant theatrical form by the mid-nineteenth century. The Japanese Noh theatre, developed in the late fourteenth century, has remained unchanged since the seventeenth century. Only recently have Noh staging practices influenced Western directors and designers. The same is true of Kabuki performances, despite their popularity in Japan since 1600. However, the traditional theatrical forms of the Middle East have been removed from cultures both in the East and the West.

Chinese Theatre

The Classical Theatre

China enjoyed one of the theatre's golden ages during the Yuan dynasty (1279–1368), the period during which the Italian explorer Marco Polo visited China and returned to tell Europeans of the wonders of this civilization. Yuan dramatists created the classical drama (*zaju*) of China with stories drawn from history, legend, epics, and contemporary events that advocated the virtues of loyalty to family and friends, and devotion to work and duty. Staging traditions in this period required a bare stage, with one door on either side at the rear for exits and entrances and an embroidered, decorative tapestry hanging between the two doors. Performers (both men and women) wore makeup, colorful clothes of the period with long, wide sleeves, and beards for the men.

Each play consisted of four acts with ten to twenty songs or arias, all sung by the main character. If the dramatic action was too complicated to be represented in four acts, a wedge (*chieh jie*), one or two short arias, provided a prologue or interlude. Simple, unadorned musical accompaniment using a seven-tone scale was played onstage by an orchestra consisting of gong, drums, clapper, flute, and *p'ip'a* (a plucked instrument similar to a lute).

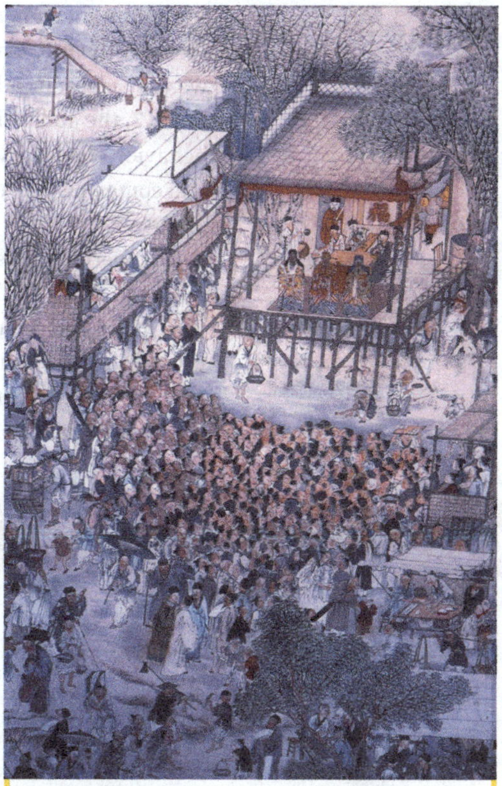

Early Chinese Stage
A performance of a drama during the Yuan dynasty. In the foreground are the actors with musicians. At the rear of the stage there is a decorative curtain. From a Quin dynasty stage painting (17th–18th century).

Beijing Opera (Jingxi)

By the mid-nineteenth century, the dominant theatrical form of the Chinese capital Beijing (formerly Peking) was *Jingxi*, or Beijing Opera. Primarily a theatrical rather than a literary form, its emphasis is upon rigidly controlled conventions of acting, dancing, and singing rather than upon texts, like those forms found in early Western operas by Wolfgang Amadeus Mozart (*The Marriage of Figaro*) or Giuseppe Verdi (*Aida*).
Many conventions of Beijing Opera, like theatrical conventions the world over, are related to the architectural features of the playhouse. The earliest stages were probably the porches of temples or other temporary outdoor stages. The traditional stage is an open platform, often square and raised a few feet above the ground, covered by a roof supported by lacquered columns. It is equipped with a carpet, and there are two doors in the rear wall (the one on stage right is used for all entrances and the one on stage left for all exits); a large embroidered curtain hangs between the doors. The only permanent properties are a wooden table and several chairs.

In the seventeenth century, actors began to perform in *teahouses*, where customers were seated at tables. When permanent theatres were built, traditions of the teahouses were retained and the ground floor was fitted out with tables and stools at which spectators were served tea while watching the play. The permanent theatres also included a raised platform around the sides and back of the auditorium, where poorer spectators sat on benches. A balcony, divided into sections much like the boxes of the Western theatre, was also added. In some periods the balcony was occupied by the wealthy class; in others, entirely by women. After the Chinese Republic was formed in 1912, the auditoriums were changed to include Western-style seating, but audience behavior changed very little. Spectators still carry on conversations, eat and drink, and come and go freely—usually remaining for their favorite passages while ignoring others.

The performance conditions for the music-drama, well-known to their audiences, are rigid. To circle the stage indicates a lengthy journey. An incense tripod on a table indicates a palace; a paper scroll and an official seal indicate an office; an embroidered divided curtain hung from a bamboo pole indicates an emperor's chamber, and so on. Throughout the performance, assistants dressed in ordinary street clothes help the actors with their costumes and bring on or remove the properties as needed.

FOCUS ON PEOPLE IN THEATRE

PLAYWRIGHT

Tang Xianzu

Tang Xianzu, also known as T'ang Hsien-tsu (1550–1616), was one of the finest Ming-dynasty dramatists whose four plays—called the "Four Dreams"—develop the theme that life is an illusion. The most admired of the four, *The Peony Pavilion*, tells the story with poetry and music (adapted from tunes of the time) of a girl who pines away for a lover that she has seen only in a dream. The lover appears at her grave, and she is resurrected. Romantic love, dreams, and the supernatural provide the emotional impact of the famous play.

The Peony Pavilion
This 400-year-old drama, written by Tang Xianzu (a contemporary of William Shakespeare), was directed by Chen Shi-Zheng and performed in its nineteen-hour form as part of the Lincoln Center Festival, New York City.

© Liu Liquin/ChinaStock

A Jingxi Stage

A Chinese opera stage (Temple of Jin, Taiyuan), probably in the grounds of a private mansion. The audience would have watched the performances from the courtyard, separate from the stage itself.

Music is an integral part of every opera performance. It provides atmospheric background, accompanies the many sung passages, controls the timing of movements, and fuses the performance into a rhythmical whole. Entrances and exits are signaled by brass gongs and cymbals and much of the onstage action is performed to a musical background of string, wind, and percussion instruments.

Beijing Opera Production The centerpiece of the Beijing Opera is the actor. On a bare stage furnished with only a few properties, the colorful and lavishly dressed actors speak, sing, and move according to prescribed conventions. The male roles (*sheng*) include scholars, statesmen, patriots, and similar types. Actors playing these roles wear simple makeup and, except for the young heroes, beards. The female roles (*dan*) are subdivided into six types: the good and virtuous wives and lovers, coquettish types, warrior maidens, young unmarried girls, evil women, and old women. Originally, all *dan* roles were played by women, but in the late eighteenth century, actresses were forbidden. After 1911, actresses returned to the stage and have now largely supplanted the male *dan* actors. The *jing* roles include warriors, courtiers, gods, and supernatural beings and are characterized by painted faces in brilliant patterns. The comic actor (*chou*), who combines the skills of a mime and an acrobat, speaks in an everyday dialect and is the most realistic of the characters.

The actor's delivery of lines is controlled by convention. Each role has a required vocal timbre and pitch; spoken passages are governed by strict rhythms and tempos; each work is accompanied by hand and arm gestures that have codified meanings.

FOCUS ON PEOPLE IN THEATRE

ACTOR

Mei Lanfang

Mei Lanfang in The Peony Pavilion (1959).

Mei Lanfang (1894–1961), one of the greatest of all Asian actors, was born in Beijing of an old theatrical family and trained at the Fuliancheng school there. He made his professional debut at the age of ten and became noted in *dan* (female) roles. He acted chiefly in Beijing until the Japanese occupied Manchuria in 1931; he moved to Shanghai and then to Hong Kong during the war years. He returned to Beijing in 1949 and remained there until his death in 1961.

Tours to the United States, Europe, and Russia in the 1930s established his fame and popularity as the foremost Chinese performer and brought the traditions of Beijing Opera to the West. He excelled in the female roles and in the aristocratic *kunqu* drama. His appearances in theatres in Moscow, Berlin, London, and Paris made lasting impressions on the leading theatre artists, including Bertolt Brecht, Vsevolod Meyerhold, and Sergei Eisenstein.

The actors' heavily patterned and colorful costumes likewise signify the wearers' ages, social status, and types. Color is always used symbolically: yellow for royalty, red for loyalty and high position, and dark crimson for barbarians or military advisors. Designs also have symbolic significance: the dragon is the emblem of the emperor; the tiger stands for power and masculine strength; the plum blossom, for long life and feminine charm. The actors' visual appearance is completed with makeup and beards for the *sheng* actors. The female roles, with the exception of old women, who wear very little makeup, require white-painted faces with the eyes surrounded by a deep red, shading into pink. The clown's distinguishing feature is the white patch around the eyes with distinctive black markings.

In its traditional form, Beijing Opera is now most fully preserved on Taiwan and to a lesser extent in Hong Kong and Singapore. Although Western influences have brought about changes in Chinese theatre and spoken drama, the Beijing Opera and its symbolic conventions continue to fascinate Westerners and influence modern productions.

Japanese Theatre

Theatre in Japan is a popular cultural activity for millions of modern Japanese. The major theatrical centers are located in Tokyo, Osaka, and Kyoto, but there are performances by a variety of companies throughout Japan. Since the late fourteenth century, the range of performance genres and styles has proliferated, from early performances (labeled *kagura*) at Shinto festivals to the serious Noh plays and comic Kyogen forms favored by the imperial courts and shogunates, to the latter-day Kabuki and Bunraku plays. Noh and Kabuki are the best-known Japanese performance styles in the West today.

Noh Theatre

The Japanese Noh (meaning "skill") theatre was established in the fourteenth century and has maintained its present form since the seventeenth century. Unlike Western drama, it is a highly stylized, restrained, and austere form of artistic expression and depends heavily on music and mime.

The Noh Stage The Noh stage is situated in a corner of a building at the audience's right hand. A temple roof rises above the stage floor, which is divided into two areas: the stage proper (*butai*) and the bridge (*hashigakari*). All elements on this stage, including the four columns supporting the roof, have names and significance during performances.

The stage proper is divided into three areas: The largest is about eighteen feet square and marked off by four pillars and a roof; at the rear of the stage are the musicians—a flute player and two or three drummers; and to the left of the main area sits the six- to ten-member chorus. The stage's two entrances are the bridge—a railed gangway that leads from the dressing room to the stage and is used for all important entrances—and the "hurry door." Only three-feet high, the hurry door is used by minor characters, musicians, chorus, and stage assistants for quick exits and entrances. Three small pine trees in front of the bridge symbolize heaven, earth, and humanity. Another pine tree, symbolizing the play's earthly setting, is painted on the center wall behind the musicians. This wall forms the scenic background for all Noh performances.

Noh Actors All features of a Noh performance are carefully controlled and fixed by tradition. The principal character (*shite*, or doer role) is usually a lavishly costumed aristocrat, lady, or supernatural being. The actor playing this character performs facing the column at the downstage (nearest the audience) right corner. The downstage left column is associated with the secondary character (*waki*, or sideman).

The conventions of performance are handed down from one generation of actors (all male) to the next. Every movement of the hands and feet and every vocal intonation follow a set rule. The orchestra supplies a musical setting and controls the timing of the action. The chorus sings the actor's lines while he is dancing and narrates many of the play's events.

Noh Performer
Noh performer with musicians in the background.

Principal actors wear painted wooden masks that designate basic types: men, women, elderly persons, deities, monsters, spirits. The women's masks are said to be neutral but express a range of emotions—grief, happiness, melancholy, innocence, and so on. The silk costumes and headdresses are rich in color and design. A few stage properties are used and tend to be symbolic—a fan becomes a drinking cup, for example.

Kabuki Theatre

By about 1600, the Noh theatre was replaced in popular taste, first by the Bunraku puppet theatre and then by Kabuki, described as the "rock" entertainment of the seventeenth

©AFP/Getty Images

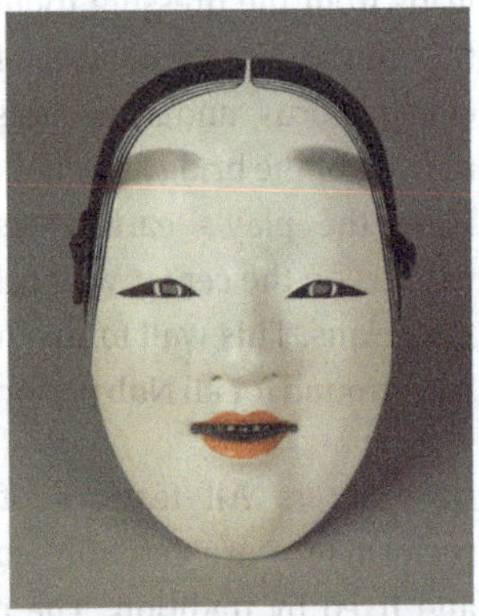

Japanese School/The Bridgeman Art Library

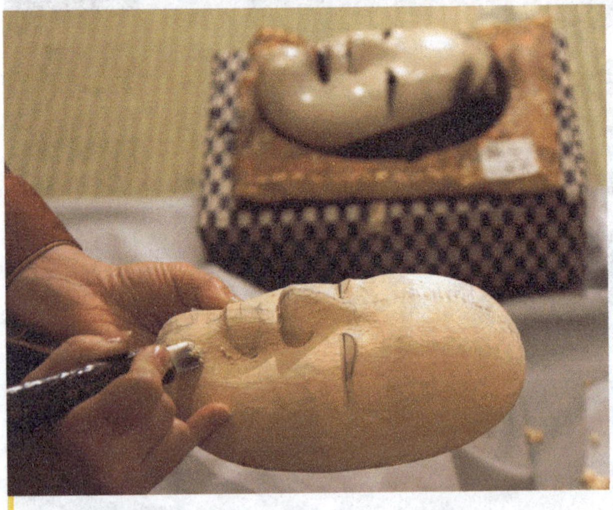

© Koichi Kamoshida/Getty Images

© Toshiyuki Aizawa/Reuters/Corbis

Mask Making
The ancient craft of *mask making* for the Noh theatre has been handed down from one generation of artists to the next. The masks are made of wood and painted. The purity and simplicity of the Noh mask reflect the highly formal theatre tradition of which it is a part.

FOCUS ON PEOPLE IN THEATRE

PLAYWRIGHT

Chikamatsu Monzaemon

© from Naniwa Miyage (souvenir from Naniwa, 1738.)

Born into a provincial samurai (warrior) family in the seventeenth century, **Chikamatsu Monzaemon** (1653–1724) became the most important Japanese playwright since the great period of Noh drama 300 years earlier. When he was thirty, Chikamatsu began writing for the Bunraku puppet theatre; he also wrote for the Kabuki theatre, and many of his puppet plays were later adapted for Kabuki.

Chikamatsu wrote both history and domestic plays—loosely constructed stories about the nobility, featuring military pageantry, supernatural beings, battles, suicides, beheadings, and many kinds of violent deeds, all rendered through choreographed movements. His domestic plays featured unhappy lovers driven to suicide. Every play was characterized by the beauty of Chikamatsu's poetry.

A prolific writer, Chikamatsu has been compared by Western critics to William Shakespeare and Christopher Marlowe for the power of his verse and the sweep of his social canvas. His best-known plays in the West are *The Battles of Coxinga* (his most popular work), *The Love Suicides at Sonezaki*, and *The Love Suicides at Amijima*.

century. Whereas Noh largely remained the theatre of the court and nobility, Kabuki—which originated in Edo, Kyoto, and Osaka, was less formal and restrained—had more popular appeal. The modern Kabuki stage is a rare combination of the old and the new, of thrust- and proscenium-type stages.

The Kabuki Stage The Kabuki stage covers the entire front of the theatre and is approached by a ramp, called a *hanamichi*, or "flower way," which is a raised narrow platform connecting the rear of the auditorium with the stage proper. The performers (all male) make dramatic entrances and exits on this runway. Occasionally, they perform short scenes on the *hanamichi* as well, literally in the middle of the audience.

The proscenium stage is long (some as long as ninety feet) but has a relatively low opening. Visible musicians (usually seated stage left) generally accompany the stage action. Kabuki plays originally required a full day in performance but today are about five hours long. They deal with vendettas, revenge, adventure, and romance. The plays feature elaborate, beautiful scenic effects, including a revolving stage that was developed in Japan before it was used in the West.

© Andrea Mohin/The New York Times/Redux

Kabuki Dance
Bando Kotoji in the celebratory dance "Sanbaso," in this presentation at Japan Society.

© Tristan Gregory/Camera Press/Redux

Kabuki Performance
A modern-day Kabuki performance in a presentation by the Japan Society.

Kabuki Actors Like Noh actors, Kabuki actors are trained from childhood in singing, dancing, acting, and feats of physical dexterity. Kabuki roles are divided into such basic types as brave and loyal men, villains, comics, children, and women. Male actors who play women's parts are called *onnagata*. They are particularly skillful in their ability to imitate feminine sensibilities through stylized gestures and attitudes.

The Kabuki actor does not use a mask but instead wears boldly patterned makeup—a white base with designs of red, black, brown, or blue. The makeup symbolizes the character and describes the role. *Onnagata* use only white makeup, along with false eyebrows and rouging to shape the mouth and the corners of the eyes. Each role has its conventional costume, based on historical dress and often weighing as much as fifty pounds.

The Kabuki actor's performance is always highly theatrical, colorful, and larger than life. Since he does not sing, he is often assisted by a narrator and chorus. The narrator may set the scene, speak dialogue, recite passages, and even comment on the action.

© Michael S. Yamashita/CORBIS

Bunraku doll-puppets
Bunraku doll-puppets with handlers.

Bunraku Puppet Theatre

The Japanese doll-puppet theatre, dating from the mid-seventeenth century, is a sophisticated, commercial entertainment. It is named Bunraku for a nineteenth-century theatre manager, Uemura Bunrakuen (or Bunrakuken), who moved from Awaji Island to Osaka, where he staged puppet plays at shrines and in professional theatres with an all-male company of professional performers.

The complex style of Bunraku consists of a domestic (three acts) or history play (five acts) written in alternating sections of spoken dialogue (prose) and sung narrative (verse) accompanied by music played on the *shamisen*. Chanters (one or several) "read" from the text (actually it is memorized) that

Drums on the Dike (Tambours sur la digue)
A production of Théâtre du Soleil, Paris, staged by Ariane Mnouchkine, uses actors as puppets in the style of Japanese Bunraku to tell a universal story of corporate greed and environmental catastrophe.

rests on a lacquered stand; the "star chanter" is reserved for the difficult scenes, usually at the end of each act. A *shamisen* player sits on a revolving dais to stage left of the proscenium in view of the audience.

Bunraku is performed on a small proscenium stage without a *hanamichi* or revolving stage. The stage is divided into three levels (front to rear) separated by low partitions, where the handlers sit to manipulate the puppets. The low front railing reaches to the handlers' knees and provides a ground level on which the puppet character can walk when moving outdoors. The innermost railing (*honte*, for "first" railing) is about hip level, allowing the puppet to sit on a mat of an inner room. Elaborate painted scenery surrounds the puppets with exterior and interior environments.

Some fifty puppet heads provide the variety of characters. In a long play, as many as five puppet heads, carved from paulownia wood and painted in realistic detail, may be used for a single puppet to show changes of emotion. Each puppet has three handlers to hold and move it and to work the mechanisms for moving eyes, eyebrows, mouth, hands, and fingers in stylized movements and gestures. Each puppeteer controls a part of the puppet's body:

— the chief puppeteer (*omo zukai*) controls a puppet's right arm (with his right hand) and head and body (with his left hand);

— the second puppeteer (*hidari zukai*) controls the left arm;

— the third puppeteer (*ashi zukai*) moves the feet of the male puppet or kimono hem of the female puppet that ordinarily does not have feet.

Berliner Ensemble/Bertoldt Brecht Archive/Akademie der Kunst, Berlin

The Caucasian Chalk Circle
Bertolt Brecht's production of *The Caucasian Chalk Circle* at the Theater am Schiffbauerdamm, in (formerly East) Berlin in 1954, shows the influence of Eastern theatre. On a bare stage, Grusha journeys with the child to the mountains. She mimes her journey before a simple white curtain with pine trees in the center.

In performance, puppets, puppeteers, chanter, and musician have a visual presence. The undisguised performing techniques found in Bunraku have influenced puppeteers and stage directors in the West. One recent innovation was French director Ariane Mnouchkine's variation on the Bunraku tradition in *Drums on the Dike.* She substituted actors for the doll-puppets in a Bunraku-style performance of an ancient marionette play.

Modern Western writers, directors, actors, and scholars have shown interest in the minimal staging; revolving stages; fixed conventions of movement, style, and dress; symbolic stage properties, costumes, and masks; and visible musicians and stage assistants found in Eastern theatrical practices. An admirer of the Asian actor Mei Lanfang, German playwright Bertolt Brecht described "alienation effects in Chinese acting" in a seminal essay and incorporated Asian-theatre techniques in his writing and staging, especially in *The Caucasian Chalk Circle.* Irish poet and playwright William Butler Yeats also incorporated elements of Japanese Noh theatre in his "four plays for dancers" that called for a bare stage with symbolic properties (a blue cloth for a well, for example) and the use of masks, dance, and music.

The influence of the main forms and styles of Eastern theatre have greatly influenced other Western playwrights and directors, including Peter Brook, Harold Prince, Peter Schumann, and Julie Taymor.

Theatre of India

India today is a country of over one billion people inhabiting a large subcontinent, practicing a variety of religions, and speaking a multitude of regional languages.

Similar to theatre in other cultures, theatre in India is a mix of ancient traditions and later practices introduced, in this case, by colonial powers.

Modern Indian theatre dates from the eighteenth century, when British governors introduced their brand of Western theatre to entertain their soldiers. The cities of Calcutta, Bombay, and Madras became centers of British education and culture. Modern Indian playhouses were constructed on the British model, with proscenium arch and raised stage separating the audience from the actors, a front curtain, lighting equipment, elaborate scenery, costumes, and makeup. Further cross-culturalization occurred, and Indian writers, such as Nobel prize-winning poet Rabindranath Tagore, began to write plays blending Indian and Western traditions in *The King of the Dark Chamber* and *The Cycle of Spring*.

With independence in 1947, the notion that traditional performance genres embodied the true national identity of Indian culture received official backing. Troupes began to rediscover older rituals and narrative dance-drama forms. Recent scholarship and the travels of Western artists to India have resulted in a resurgence of interest in traditional forms. Ariane Mnouchkine and Peter Brook have introduced Westerners to the performance modes of kathakali dance-drama and narrative drama found in the *Mahabharata* stories (discussed in Chapter 3, "Alternative Theatrical Spaces").

The King Stag
By Carlo Gozzi in the 1991 American Repertory Theatre (Cambridge, Mass.) production with Eastern costumes, masks, and puppetry influences. Directed by Andrei Serban. Designed by Julie Taymor and Michael Yeargan.

FOCUS ON THEATRE

Islamic Traditions of the Middle East

When the Byzantine Empire fell to the forces of Islam around 1453, the Muslim world expanded rapidly, carrying the teachings of Muhammad into North Africa and southern Europe, and eastward into Persia (Iran) and northern India. Early Muslims valued learning, mathematics, and philosophy, but religious leaders forbade artists from making images of living things because Allah was the sole creator of life. Consequently, Islamic art remained primarily decorative rather than representational.

The verbal arts of poetry, dramatic storytelling, and recitation of religious stories were widely practiced throughout the Islamic world. Only the nonrepresentational theatrical arts, such as shadow puppets—two-dimensional cutouts with perforated holes in the figures, manipulated with sticks and projected on a cloth by the light of lanterns or torches—overcame basic orthodox Islamic objections and survived as traditional performing arts.

The influence of European culture on the Middle East in the nineteenth century came about through travelers returning from European cities. A parallel Western-style drama developed in Cairo and Istanbul, and eventually theatres and opera houses were built. Egypt, Turkey, Syria, the Maghreb, and Iran have been central to theatrical development in the Middle East in the twentieth century. Nevertheless, the future of theatre and visual arts today is less certain in Muslim-controlled states.

Ancient Indian Forms of Drama and Theatre

Sanskrit Drama India's oldest writing and theatrical practice, Sanskrit drama and theatre, flourished as court entertainment. Primarily the language of India, Sanskrit emerged as literature between 1500 BC and 1000 BC. The rise of the great Hindu epic literature (the *Mahabharata*, *Ramayana*, and *Purana*) depicting ancient Indian beliefs and the life and exploits of Krishna, the incarnation of the god Vishnu, gave inspiration to dramatic compositions known as Sanskrit plays. The early fragments of Sanskrit drama, surviving in palm-leaf manuscripts, suggest a living theatrical tradition, although no physical evidence comparable to the remains of early amphitheatres found in Greece today exists to document its early history.

A treatise on the art of theatre, called *Natyasastra*, related the origins of Sanskrit writing and performance to the inspiration of Brahma, the god of creation who asked that India compose plays and that priests (*brahmana*) enact them.

Sanskrit plays, unlike Western forms, were concerned with presenting emotional states through words, action, costumes, and makeup. The eight *rasas*, or basic sentiments, were the erotic, the comic, pathos, rage, terror, heroism, odiousness, and the marvelous. These corresponded to basic human emotions or feelings (love, sorrow, fear, and so forth) represented by the actors and made harmonious at the play's end with good triumphant over evil.

The oldest surviving Sanskrit plays were by Bhasa, but the most revered playwright of the classical Sanskrit theatre, Kalidasa, was thought to have been a court poet. Writing in the mid-fifth century, he preserved the ideal example of classical Sanskrit drama in poems and plays, the most important of which is *Shakuntala and the Ring of Recognition*. His works adhere to the ancient rules and represent some of the finest examples of Sanskrit poetry.

FOCUS ON THEATRE

Natyasastra

A guidebook for ancient dramaturgy that includes acting, theatre architecture, costuming, stage properties, dance, music, and play construction, as well as the organization of theatre companies, audiences, dramatic competitions, and ritual practices. Requirements for dramatic composition are also spelled out in detail, including benediction, prologue, and ten types of drama for playwrights to choose from in order to depict ideals of human behavior.

The tenth century brings to an end the classical Sanskrit theatre as an influential force in Indian art. Once Islam became the state religion under the Mogul Empire of the fifteenth century, theatre no longer thrived in northern India. Islamic religion did not condone artistic imitations because of religious convictions, and followers of Islam discouraged, or forbade entirely, all representations, including theatrical performance.

Kutiyattam Only in Kerala, at the southern tip of the subcontinent, did traditions of Sanskrit theatre survive, in the form of *kutiyattam* performances. *Kutiyattam* preserves a tradition of performing plays in Sanskrit and regional dialects, written by well-known Sanskrit playwrights (Bhasa, Harsha, and Mahendra Vikrama Pallava). The plays were performed by actors maintained as a subgroup of temple servants in Kerala's temple compounds constructed for the early drama.

Nine theatres, representing the only permanent traditional theatre structures in India, have been built since the sixteenth century in various temples in Kerala. The largest is the Vatukumnathan Temple in Trichur. It is a rectangular building, seventy-two by fifty-five feet, located in the walled compound of the temple and situated in front and to the right of the main shrine. Pillars support a high roof, and the stage is a large, square, raised stone platform dividing the whole structure in half. Clusters of three pillars rise upward from each of the four corners of the stage to support an interior roof, very much like the pillars used in Noh stages in Japan. A back wall separates the dressing area from the stage.

FOCUS ON PEOPLE IN THEATRE

PLAYWRIGHT

Kalidasa

Kalidasa may have been a court poet of northern India in the mid-fifth century AD. He is the most revered playwright of classical Sanskrit drama and is known to have written plays and dramatic poems. His works, including the dramatic poem *The Cloud Messenger*, represent the finest examples of poetry and playwriting in the classical period.

As in Noh performance, convention mandates how the space is used in *kutiyattam* performances. The stage is equipped only with stools. A narrow door in the wall, upstage left, is used for entrances; and a door, upstage right, is reserved for exits. Large pot-shaped drums (*mizhavu*) for musicians are suspended in heavy wooden stands between the doors. Decorative carvings of deities and mythological characters are only faintly visible under the flickering light of a large bell-metal lamp placed downstage center.

Two female actors play small bell-metal cymbals that sustain the tempo in a *kutiyattam* performance. Both male and female actors wear elaborate costumes, headdresses, and fantastical makeup to represent various mythological characters representing gods and demons. Moreover, they use coded movements and gestures, exaggerated facial and eye expressions, and chanted speech. Drums and cymbals, oboe-like wind instruments, and a conch shell (*sanka*) accompany much of the action.

A typical *kutiyattam* performance lasts several days. During the first days, the play's characters and historical incidents are introduced and explored in detail. On the final day, the entire action of the play is performed in chronological order. In modern-day India, *kutiyattam* is performed once a year at Vatukumnathan Temple and in nearby Irinjalagauda Temple. In order to preserve the ancient art, state and national governments and private institutions support performances in various towns and cities of Kerala and elsewhere in India.

Les Atrides

The kathakali-inspired costumes and movements of the chorus in Mnouchkine's *Les Atrides*. Orestes seeks safety from the ensuing violence behind the walls of the arena.

© Jeremy Horner/CORBIS

Kathakali Dancers
Modern-day kathakali dancers, Kerala, India, with highly stylized costumes, makeup, and headdresses.

Kathakali The theatrical forms of rural India (puppet theatre, storytelling, and dance-dramas) evolved as expressions of religious rituals and later became secular in inspiration. One such form, kathakali, a vigorous dance-drama associated with early regional forms in the south of India, in particular Kerala, is performed today in commercial venues by professional troupes who tour internationally. Elaborate costumes with headdresses and energetic dances give insight into the early popular entertainments of village life.

Temple dancers preserved kathakali, which is now about 300 years old. Its subject matter is taken from Hindu epics. The stories center around the passions (loves and hates) of gods and demons that clash in desperate struggles, but good always triumphs in the end. To enact these wordless stories, dancers bring violence and death, forbidden in Sanskrit theatre, to the stage.

A kathakali performance can take place anywhere: in houses, village squares, proscenium stages, or temple compounds. A typical program for the dance-drama includes several favorite scenes from plays or a single play performed from beginning to end. Performances begin in the evening around nine o'clock with elaborate percussive overtures and conclude in the morning around six o'clock.

The theatre of India today is extremely diverse. Ancient Sanskrit plays share audience interest along with dance-dramas, folk plays, and modern realistic works in the Western style.

We have seen theatre's ritual origins in the East and the West in religious ceremonies, storytelling and dance, and enactments in spaces (with raised stages) configured for actors and audiences. We have looked briefly at the history of performance practices in Europe, China, Japan, and India. These early playing spaces and performance practices in world theatre are important because they serve as foundations for the writing and experimentation that shape our Western theatre in the twenty-first century.

TRANSITION

Both Western and Eastern theatres are divided into stage and auditorium. Beginning with ritual performances in early societies, the theatrical space has always been a "privileged" place where spectators share in the revelation of a reality separate from that of their daily lives, although related to it. Those creating theatre have traditionally sought out a variety of places—hillsides, streets, marketplaces, buildings—to engage audiences in the experience of seeing life imitated by performers to entertain and often to instruct. In all cases, conventions developed regarding the relation of spectator to performer, and vice versa.

A number of modern practitioners in Western theatre have played with these conventions, violated them, and even turned them upside down in their attempt to engage audiences by breaking established actor–audience relationships. The names *alternative* and *environmental* are given today to theatrical performances found in nontraditional spaces. In the modern theatre, most have been products of the theatrical avant-garde.

Theatre: A Way of Seeing Online

Visit the CourseMate for Theatre: A Way of Seeing 7th Edition for quick access to the digital study resources that accompany this chapter, including links to the websites listed below, Theatre Workshop, digital glossary, a chapter quiz and more.

Websites

The *Theatre: A Way of Seeing* CourseMate includes links for all the websites described below. Simply select "Web links" from the Chapter Resources for Chapter 2, and click on the link that interests you. You'll be taken directly to the site described.

Medieval Drama Links
Comprehensive collection of links to sites that highlight medieval theatre. Includes links to such topics as costumes, makeup, musical instruments, and medieval play manuscripts.

Shakespeare and the Globe Theatre
Many links to information about Shakespeare, the Globe Theatre, and the Elizabethan period.

Skenotheke: Images of the Ancient Stage
Hundreds of links to images of ancient Greek and Roman stages.

Theatre History Sites
Hundreds of links to sites about theatre history. Includes information about classical, medieval, Elizabethan, later English, illusionistic, and early American theatre.

Theatron Limited/Projects (Virtual Models of Historical Theatres)
Virtual reality tours of historical Greek, Roman, and European theatres. Click on "Gallery" and "Projects."

International Theatre Websites Théâtre du Soleil, Paris, France—"Tambours sur la digue"
Interesting article about Théâtre du Soleil's highly stylized performance of *The Flood Drummers*. Based on a fifteenth-century Chinese tale, this play was performed by actors elaborately dressed as Bunraku-style puppets who were lifted and manipulated by other actors dressed and masked in black.

National Theatre of Tokyo
Home page of the National Theatre of Tokyo. Check out "Facilities" for information about the layout of the theatre and "Stage Photos" for photos of past performances.

Theatre of India
Links to articles about the theatre of ancient India, including the text of the play *Chitra* by Rabindranath Tagore, based on a story from the *Mahabharata*.

New Amsterdam Theatre, New York City
History of the New Amsterdam Theatre in New York City, "The Crown Jewel of 42nd Street." If you're in New York City, check out the "Guided Tours" link for times when you can explore the theatre.

©Julio Donoso/Sygma/Corbis

3

ALTERNATIVE THEATRICAL SPACES

The elimination of the stage–auditorium dichotomy is not the important thing. The essential concern is finding the proper spectator–actor relationship for each type of performance and embodying the decision in physical arrangements.[1]

— JERZY GROTOWSKI, *TOWARDS A POOR THEATRE*

PREVIEW

Modern efforts to find new kinds of theatrical space have created different ways of experiencing theatre. In recent decades Jerzy Grotowski in Poland, Ariane Mnouchkine in Paris, Peter Schumann in Vermont, and Peter Brook in France have rearranged theatrical space to bring audiences and actors closer together.

All theatre people who have performed singly or in groups wherever an audience could be gathered around them are background to the modern avant-garde creation of alternative performance spaces. These alternative forms are associated in particular with the political protests of the Vietnam War era in the United States, although they are international in practice.

Much of the work of Julian Beck and Judith Malina (the Living Theatre), Jerzy Grotowski (the Polish Laboratory Theatre), Peter Brook (the International Centre for Theatre Research), Ariane Mnouchkine (Théâtre du Soleil), Peter Schumann (the Bread and Puppet Theatre), and John O'Neal and Gilbert Moses (Free Southern Theater) within the last five decades has been labeled alternative and/or environmental theatre. This type of theatrical performance rejects conventional seating and arranges the audience as part of the playing space.

ENVIRONMENTAL THEATRE

Writing about environmental production as a particular way of creating and experiencing theatre, American director and theorist Richard Schechner says, "The thing about environmental theatre space is not just a matter of how you end up using space. It is an attitude. *Start with all the space*

Peter Brook rehearsed *The Mahabharata* in a century-old abandoned theatre with peeling walls and stained floors in a working class section of Paris, France. Brook's choice of the derelict Théâtre des Bouffes du Nord as the permanent home for his company debunked the notion that performance needed a large house equipped with modern technology.

there is and then decide what to use, what not to use, and how to use what you use."[2] Polish director Jerzy Grotowski describes the essential concern as "finding the proper spectator–actor relationship for each type of performance and embodying the decision in physical arrangements."[3]

As noted, environmental theatre by definition rejects conventional seating and includes audiences as part of the performance space. Like the actors, the spectators become part of what is seen and done. They are both seeing and seen.

FORERUNNERS OF ALTERNATIVE APPROACHES

In modern Russia and Germany, such leaders as the inventive Vsevolod Meyerhold (1874–c. 1940) and Max Reinhardt (1873–1943) developed unorthodox production methods and uses of theatrical space. They are the chief forerunners of today's many experiments in nontraditional performance styles and alternative spaces. In the 1930s in Moscow, the Russian director Meyerhold, rejecting the proscenium arch as too confining for his actors, removed the front curtain, footlights, *and* proscenium. Stagehands changed properties and scenery in full view of audiences, and actors performed on trapezes, slides, and ramps to arouse exhilarating feelings in both performers and audiences.

Max Reinhardt explored vast acting areas such as Berlin's Circus Schumann arena, where he staged *Oedipus the King* in 1910. He thought of these spaces as a people's theatre—a "theatre of the five thousand." He dreamed of a theatre on the scale of classical Greek and Roman theatres to be used for spectacles and mass audiences. In 1920, he created his most famous spectacle (*Everyman*) in the square before the Salzburg Cathedral.

During the last sixty years, especially in the United States, many theatre directors and designers looked for new theatrical spaces in warehouses, garages, lofts, and abandoned churches. They reshaped *all* of the space available to audience and actor, bringing the actors into direct contact with the audiences, thereby making the audience a more essential part of the theatrical event.

This chapter discusses four alternative approaches to the use of theatrical space in modern times: the Polish Laboratory Theatre, the Théâtre du Soleil, the Bread and Puppet Theatre, and the Free Southern Theater.

THE POLISH LABORATORY THEATRE

JERZY GROTOWSKI'S "POOR" THEATRE

When Jerzy Grotowski founded the Polish Laboratory Theatre in Opole in 1959, he set out to answer this question: What is theatre? Grotowski first evolved a concept that he called "poor theatre." For him, theatre's essentials were the actor and the audience in a bare space. He found that theatre could happen without costumes, scenery, makeup, stage lighting, and sound effects; all a performance needed was the actor and audience in communion in a special place. Grotowski wrote:

> *I propose poverty in theatre. We have resigned from the stage-and-auditorium plant: for each production, a new space is designed for the actors and spectators .... The essential concern is finding the proper spectator–actor relationship.*[4]

"[Grotowski] was, with Stanislavsky, Meyerhold, and Brecht, one of the West's four great 20th century theatre theorist-practitioners."

—RICHARD SCHECHNER

Within the whole space, Grotowski created what he called "holy theatre": performance became a semireligious act in which the actor, prepared by years of training and discipline, undergoes a psychospiritual experience. Grotowski set about to engage the audience in this act, and thus to engage both actor and audience in a deeper understanding of personal and social truths.

FOCUS ON PEOPLE IN THEATRE

DIRECTOR

Jerzy Grotowski

©Max Waldman

Jerzy Grotowski (1933–1999) was founder and director of the Polish Laboratory Theatre, an experimental company located in Opole and then in Wroclaw (Breslau). Not a theatre in the usual sense, the company became an institute for research into theatre art in general and the actor's art in particular. In addition, the laboratory also undertook performances for audiences as well as instruction of actors, producers, students (many of them foreigners), and people from other fields. The plays performed were based on Polish and international classics. In the 1960s and 1970s, Grotowski's productions of Stanislaw Wyspianski's *Akropolis*, Shakespeare's *Hamlet*, Marlowe's *Dr. Faustus*, and Calderón's *The Constant Prince* attracted worldwide attention. His closest collaborators were actor Ryszard Cieslak and literary adviser Ludwik Flaszen. He wrote about his methods in *Towards a Poor Theatre* (1968)—a theatre that eliminates everything not truly required by the actor and the audience.

After 1970, Grotowski reorganized his company to explore human creativity outside the theatre and called this period *Holiday*. He intended to lead participants back to elemental connections between themselves and the natural world by exposing them to basic myths, and the elements of fire, earth, air, and water. In 1975, the event called *Holiday* took place in a forest, where participants were encouraged to rediscover the roots of theatre and their true being.

In 1982, at the University of California–Irvine, Grotowski began a third phase called "objective drama" to combine source materials with precise tools of actor training that he had developed in earlier years. In 1986, he established a Workcenter (*Centro di Lavoro*) in Pontedera, Italy, where he began the last phase of his work, called "art as vehicle," to explore how theatre differentiates performance "truths" in many cultures.

The 1999–2000 season was declared the "Year of Jerzy Grotowski" in Wroclaw, Poland, where his Theatre Laboratory began in 1965. Year-long festivities, exhibits, and symposia took place.

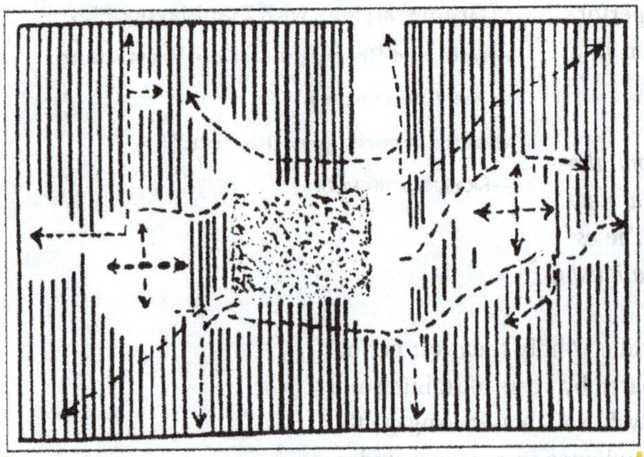

Grotowski's use of space for *Akropolis*
The lines with arrows indicate the actors' movements and areas of action; the straight lines show audience areas. The central playing space is a boxlike "mansion" where pipes are assembled and into which the actors disappear at the end of the performance.

Akropolis

In *Akropolis*, Grotowski adapted a text written by Polish playwright Stanislaw Wyspianski in 1904. In the original, statues and paintings in Cracow Cathedral come to life on the eve of Easter Sunday. The statues reenact scenes from the Old Testament and antiquity. But Grotowski shifted the action to a modern extermination camp, Auschwitz, in wartime Poland. In the new setting he contrasted the Western ideal of human dignity with the degradation of a death camp.

Akropolis takes place in a large room. Spectators are seated on platforms; passageways for the actors are created between the platforms. Wire struts are strung across the ceiling. In the middle of the room is a large, boxlike platform for the actors. Rusty pieces of metal are heaped on top of the box: stovepipes, a wheelbarrow, a bathtub, nails, hammers. With these objects the actors build a civilization of gas chambers. They wear a version of a camp uniform—ragged shirts and trousers, heavy wooden shoes, and anonymous berets.

The theatrical space at the beginning (top) and end of the performance of *Akropolis* (1962)
Note that at the beginning of the performance, the wire struts above the audience are empty. At the end, the actors have disappeared, leaving the stovepipes hanging from the wire struts as gruesome reminders of the events in the concentration camps.

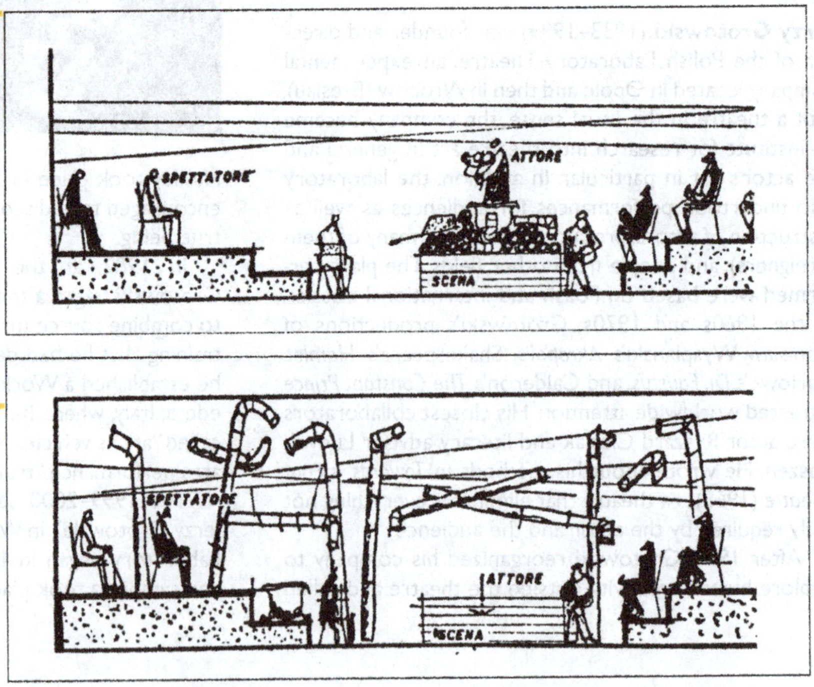

Grotowski juxtaposes Biblical and Homeric scenes and heroes against the grotesque reality of the modern death camp. The love of Paris and Helen, for instance, is played out between two men to the accompaniment of the laughter of the assembled prisoners; Jacob's bride is a stovepipe with a rag for a veil. *Akropolis* ends with a procession around the box in the center of the room led by a Singer carrying the headless corpse of the Savior. As Grotowski describes it:

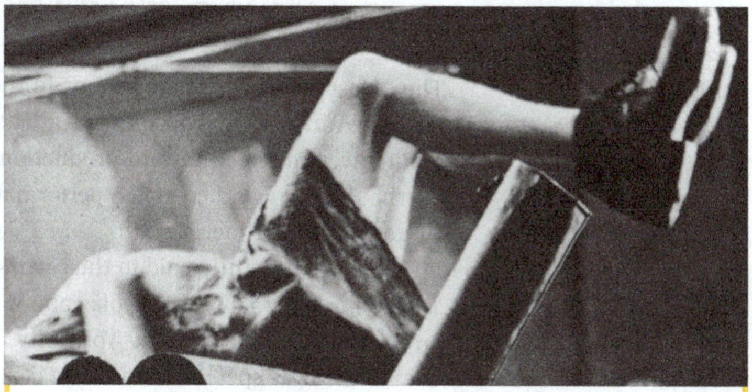

"Dialogue between two monuments."
The metal stovepipe and human legs with boots make a statement about the way human beings can be treated as objects. This is one of many statements in the performance about the effects of inhumanity throughout history. The actor is Zbigniew Cynkutis.

> *The procession evokes the religious crowds of the Middle Ages, the flagellants, the haunting beggars .... The procession reaches the end of its peregrination. The Singer lets out a pious yell, opens a hole in the box, and crawls into it, dragging after him the corpse of the Savior. The inmates follow him one by one, singing fanatically .... When the last of the condemned men has disappeared, the lid of the box slams shut. The silence is very sudden; then after a while a calm, matter-of-fact voice is heard. It says simply, "They are gone, and the smoke rises in spirals." The joyful delirium has found its fulfillment in the crematorium. The end.*[5]

Grotowski's poor theatre returns us to the essentials of theatre: actor, audience, space.

A view of the space converted into a monastery dining hall for Grotowski's production of *Dr. Faustus* (1963), based on the Elizabethan text by Christopher Marlowe
The spectators were guests at a banquet during which Faustus entertained them with episodes from his life. One hour before his death, Faustus offered a last supper to his friends (the audience) seated at the refectory tables.

THE LIVING THEATRE

The oldest of the collective groups in the United States began in 1948 in a basement on New York City's Wooster Street. The zeal and talents of Julian Beck and Judith Malina were directed toward productions that encouraged a nonviolent revolution to overhaul society and created a performance style to confront that society, namely, the United States of America.

Attention was fully paid to their work in 1958 with the production of Jack Gelber's *The Connection*, a disturbing play about heroin addicts, produced in a converted space on Fourteenth Street in New York City. The audience shared the addicts' naturalistic environment as spectators to the making of a documentary film about "real" addicts and their lifestyle. *The Brig* in 1963 re-created the senseless routine of a day in a Marine Corps prison.

Following an encounter in 1963 with the U.S. Internal Revenue Service over a failure to pay taxes, the company lost their space and went abroad, where they developed works in Rome, Berlin, and Paris. They performed in streets, prisons, even bars, provoking audience riots and confrontations with civil authorities. The Living Theatre returned to the United States in 1968 with significant works of their own creation advocating freedom from all restraints: *Mysteries and Smaller Pieces, Frankenstein*, and *Paradise Now*.

THE BRIG

A dazzling act of rebellion against the political and theatrical establishments, *The Brig*, written by Kenneth Brown, who had served in the Marine Corps, opened on May 15, 1963. As part of the Worldwide General Strike for Peace organized by the Becks a week earlier, *The Brig* addressed civil disobedience.

The Brig
The Living Theatre's 1963 production of Kenneth Brown's play re-created the routine of a day in a marine prison camp. The audience sat outside the fence as observers.

FOCUS ON THEATRE

Julian Beck and Judith Malina: The Living Theatre

©Fred W. McDarrah/Getty Images

©Fred W. McDarrah/Getty Images

Julian Beck (1925–1985) and **Judith Malina** (b. 1926) were the foremost gurus of the sixties' Off Off Broadway groups. Julian Beck grew up on New York City's Upper West Side and started out as a painter and writer. Judith Malina was born in Kiel, Germany; her father, a rabbi, brought the family to America in 1929. The two artists met in 1943 and married in 1948.

Finding that the Broadway theatre was closed to them, they made an unsuccessful attempt in 1948 to start a theatre in a basement on Wooster Street and eventually relocated to their own living room on West End Avenue. The first performance of the Living Theatre occurred in the Becks' apartment in 1951 with four short plays by Paul Goodman, Gertrude Stein, Bertolt Brecht, and García Lorca. These modest beginnings contained the abiding concerns of their future work: anarchism, poetry, Asian-inspired theatre, didacticism (via Bertolt Brecht), improvisation, and experimentation with language. The Living Theatre came of age with productions of *The Connection* (1958) and *The Brig* (1963).

Asked to give a quick assessment of the work of the Living Theatre, Julian Beck once said that "Our aim was to increase conscious awareness, to stress the sacredness of life, to break down walls."[6]

Directed by Judith Malina, who drew on interviews with marines, material from the *Guidebook for Marines* issued to recruits, and the desire to mold a genuine community among the company, *The Brig* was, first, an *environment* of intimidation and, second, a *plea* for nonviolence.

Kenneth Brown's script covers a single day (from reveille to bedtime) in a brig for U.S. military offenders on Okinawa. The eleven prisoners are drawn from a cross section of society. The atmosphere was one of isolation, intimidation, and brutality, by both victims and tormentors. In Beck and Malina's view, *The Brig* aimed at destroying violence by representing it. The actor became a "sacrificial" presence in the demonstration of mindless evil where no freedoms of the most basic kind exist.

©Max Waldman Archive

The Living Theatre
Actors in one of many theatrical rites that composed *Paradise Now: the Revolution of Cultures* (1968).

The production replicated the caged wire, the dormitory of bunk beds, and floor sectioned off by painted white lines. A blackboard listed offenses committed by the prisoners. Spectators sat before the barbed-wire cage as witnesses to the dehumanizing of the soldiers and as participants in society's responsibility for permitting such abuse of human beings.

THE LIVING THEATRE ON TOUR

The Living Theatre toured the United States in the late sixties, arousing bitter controversy and debate over the nature of theatre and the role of art in society. In 1970, the company returned to Europe and split into four groups, or "cells." The Becks' contingent went to Brazil for purposes of developing new methods for performance, methods that were less didactic and more responsive to the needs of specific communities. In 1984, the company returned to the United States and presented four works of "collective creation" in New York City, which critics found lacking in significant content. After Julian Beck's death in 1985, the future of the Living Theatre passed into the hands of Judith Malina, who continued to produce upon occasion until her retirement but without the same impact of the earlier company.

The significance of the Living Theatre rests on its naturalistic environmental productions and later techniques that included altering texts to argue for anarchy and social change, nudity and athleticism in performance, use of human voices and cacophonous sounds to assault the audiences' sensibilities, and confrontations with audiences with calls for revolution.

Julian Beck once said that "Art opens perception and changes our vision. I think without art we would all remain blind to reality. We go to the theatre to study ourselves. The theatre excites the imagination, and it also enters into the spirit."[7]

THÉÂTRE DU SOLEIL

ARIANE MNOUCHKINE'S ENVIRONMENTAL SPACE

Théâtre du Soleil ("Theatre of the Sun") is another group having impact on environmental production styles, especially in Europe. Founded in Paris in 1964 by Ariane Mnouchkine and a group of politically committed individuals, Théâtre du Soleil modeled itself on an egalitarian commune, dividing the theatre's profits equally among the company. The ensemble works on the notion of collaborative creation and democratic participation at all levels of decision making. Productions grow out of improvisations, discussions, and group study. All members share the various responsibilities of research, writing, interpretation, design, and construction in an effort to abolish the theatrical hierarchy that reaches upward from the ticket takers to the director of the production. Despite this egalitarian model, Théâtre du Soleil is primarily identified with its artistic director, Ariane Mnouchkine.

Théâtre du Soleil

Asian-inspired production of Shakespeare's *Richard II* staged in a former munitions factory in Vincennes, France, in 1981.

FOCUS ON PEOPLE IN THEATRE

DIRECTOR

Ariane Mnouchkine

©Martine Franck/Magnum Photos, Inc.

Of the French directors who have come to prominence since 1965, **Ariane Mnouchkine** (b. 1939) is one of the most important. She founded Théâtre du Soleil, a workers' co-operative composed of ten initial members, in 1964. Until 1970, they performed in Paris, creating a considerable stir with productions of Shakespeare's *A Midsummer Night's Dream* and Arnold Wesker's *The Kitchen*.

In 1970, the company moved to an abandoned munitions factory just outside Paris (the Cartoucherie de Vincennes), where they have since produced internationally celebrated environmental and intercultural productions of *1789* (in 1970) and *1793* (in 1972), treatments of the early years of the French Revolution that argued that the revolution was more concerned with property than with social injustice. *The Age of Gold* (*L'age d'or*, in 1975) dealt with various aspects of materialism. *The Terrible but Unfinished History of Norodom Sihanouk, King of Cambodia* (in 1985) and *The Indiade* (*L'indiade*, in 1987) centered on modern political history. The group traveled with their Asian-inspired productions of Shakespeare's *Richard II*; *Henry IV, Part I*; and *Twelfth Night* to the 1984 Olympic Arts Festival of Los Angeles. In 1992, the company returned to North America with the ten-hour, four-part cycle of Greek tragedy called *Les Atrides*. More recent works staged in Paris and on tour were *Le Dernier Caravansérail* (*Odyssées*) (also, *The Last Caravansary*) with actors-as-refugees performing on wheeled mini-stages resembling skateboards, and *Les Éphémères*, a seven-hour epic with twenty-nine scenes staged on multiple rotating table-size platforms to narrate stories about family and human fragility.

Théâtre du Soleil is one of France's finest theatre companies, inspired by its director Ariane Mnouchkine for fifty years. "Theatre is doubtless the most fragile of arts," she has said. "The theatre public is now really a very small group, but the theatre keeps reminding us of the possibility to collectively seek the histories of people and to tell them. . . . The contradictions, the battles of power, and the split in ourselves will always exist. I think the theatre best tells us of the enemy in ourselves. Yes, theatre is a grain of sand in the works."[8]

©Martine Franck/Magnum Photos, Inc.

Les Éphémères Part I

Actor propelling a wagon into the playing space in Théâtre du Soleil's *Les Éphémères, Part I*, Park Avenue Armory, New York City.

©Martine Franck/Magnum Photos, Inc.

Théâtre du Soleil's 1793

This view of the performance shows actors on raised platforms and scaffolds with the audience seated in a center pit.

©Stephanie Berger/Corbis

Drums on the Dike
A Théâtre du Soleil production that uses actors as puppets in the style of Bunraku theatre.

The company has challenged traditional modes of theatrical presentation in its attempts to create a populist theatre, using improvisation as well as techniques from mime, commedia, Chinese opera, Japanese Noh and Kabuki, and Indian kathakali dance-drama. Audiences move from platform to platform to keep up with the play's action or sit around the edge or even in the center of a large pit for many early productions.

Beginning with productions in the late sixties, the company attracted considerable international attention and was acclaimed for its radical environmental staging techniques and its explosive politicizing of dramatic materials. Its commitment to left-wing political beliefs and to the creation of vibrant "performance texts" out of the whole cloth of French history resulted in *1789*, then *1793*, and finally *The Age of Gold*. In the 1980s, the company's kathakali- and Kabuki-inspired productions of Shakespeare's plays blended Eastern and Western traditions. In the environmental space of a former munitions factory—which directly engaged audiences—these performances dealt with theatre as revolution, historical data, and contemporary social and political facts. The performances utilized improvised stage action and audience participation, and also emphasized spectacle and ritual.

Les Atrides

As political fervor waned worldwide in the late 1970s, along with the winding down of the Vietnam War, many groups either went out of existence or, like Théâtre du Soleil, turned to other artistic expressions, which overshadowed any "environmental" trendiness or political and social messages contained in their works. Théâtre du Soleil's Asian-inspired Shakespearean productions and *Les Atrides*, the four-part cycle of Greek tragedy based on Euripides's *Iphigenia in Aulis* and Aeschylus's three plays of *The Oresteia*, have further challenged contemporary notions of theatrical presentation.

More recently, Mnouchkine and her company have turned their attention to other Asian traditions. In 1998, the company created *Suddenly, Nights of Awakening* (*Et soudain, des nuits d'éveil*), which took the form of a touring Tibetan acting troupe putting on a play; in mid-performance the actors step out of the play to seek political asylum from the audience. As is now a familiar practice of Théâtre du Soleil, the production grew out of improvisations (shaped into a text by author-critic Hélène Cixous) and performed with a mix of Tibetan dance, Buddhist ritual, commedia dell'arte *lazzi* (clowning), political discourse, and actors wandering freely among audiences, speaking and passing out faxes as they argued their need for political asylum. *Drums on the Dike* (*Tambours sur la digue*) is an ancient marionette play adapted for the company in a Bunraku performance style to comment on corporate greed and environmental disaster.

THE BREAD AND PUPPET THEATRE

PETER SCHUMANN'S OPEN-AIR PERFORMANCES

Peter Schumann founded the Bread and Puppet Theatre in New York City in 1961. The group made its home on a farm in Glover, Vermont. Schumann's group did not attempt to create an environment but performed in almost any setting: streets, fields, gravel pits, gyms, churches, and sometimes theatres. Developed from biblical and legendary sources and using actors, stilt walkers, and larger-than-life-size puppets, Bread and Puppet plays advocated the virtues of love, charity, and humility.

The group took its name from two constant elements of their work: puppets and bread. Peter Schumann believed that "the theatre should be as basic as bread." At the start of a Bread and Puppet performance, loaves of bread were passed among the spectators. Each person broke off a piece and handed the rest to the next person, who did the same. When everyone had tasted bread, in an act of social and spiritual communion, the performance began. Through this act, the audience participated in an instantly recognizable ritual: sharing the staff of life, a symbol of humanity's most basic need.

DOMESTIC RESURRECTION CIRCUS

The Nineteenth Annual Domestic Resurrection Circus was performed each August on a Vermont farm in a grassed-over gravel pit with sloping sides that was as large as a football field. Free to the 6,000–8,000 people who attended this harvest weekend, the ten-hour extravaganza featured gods, demons, angels, peasants, dragons, and birds, along with a mélange of morris dancers, fire jugglers, rope walkers, and strolling jazz musicians. People enjoyed the corn and potato roast and the sourdough rye bread, which Schumann prepared each morning for six weeks.

The *Circus* began around four o'clock in the afternoon with a prayer for peace spoken in eight languages. The twenty-foot effigies and head-sized masks of the monstrous red figure of Yama, the King of Hell; the Nature God that resembled a Bigfoot dressed in cedar boughs; and a tall, careworn Madonna Godface with a cryptic smile

FOCUS ON PEOPLE IN THEATRE

PUPPETEER

Peter Schumann

©AP Images

Peter Schumann

With wife Elka Schumann surrounded by puppets and masks created for the 40th celebration of Bread and Puppets creativity and activism.

Peter Schumann (b. 1934 in Silesia) moved from Germany to the United States in 1961 and two years later founded the Bread and Puppet Theatre in New York City.

Until Schumann was ten years old, his family lived in a village near Breslau, renamed Wroclaw at the end of the Second World War when that part of Germany was incorporated into Poland. In late 1944, the family fled, barely ahead of the Soviet army, and survived on his mother's baked rye sourdough bread until they reached Schleswig-Holstein. The twin themes of family and survival in Schumann's work stem from this period. In 1956, he met American Elka Scott in Munich; they married and immigrated to the United States in 1961, where their artistic collaboration began with the creation and performances of street pageants, anti-Vietnam War parades, productions based on religious themes, and summer workshops with giant puppets.

In 1970, Schumann was invited to take up residency at Goddard College in Plainfield, Vermont, and "practice puppetry." Living in Glover, Vermont, Schumann assembled a small troupe of puppeteers, designers, musicians, and volunteers. Each August at harvest time, the troupe performed in a grassed-over gravel pit with actors walking on five- or six-foot stilts, musicians in strolling jazz bands, rope walkers, and fire jugglers. Sourdough rye bread that Schumann baked himself was passed among audiences.

Schumann's pageants have been about life and death, good and evil. His work with puppets reflected a traditionalism that harked back to Indian effigies, Japanese Bunraku and Noh theatre, and the masks of African and Alaskan shamans. Mistrusting the power of words, Schumann used puppets to simplify and caricature the horror of modern living in a time of potential global annihilation. His aim was to bring the spiritual into the lives of ordinary spectators.

In a Bread and Puppet performance the stories were simple, the giant puppets riveting, and the tempo majestically slow. Schumann's group was best known for his antiwar and nuclear disarmament pieces dating from 1965: *Fire, The Gray Lady Cantata, The Stations of the Cross,* and *A Man Says Goodbye to His Mother.*

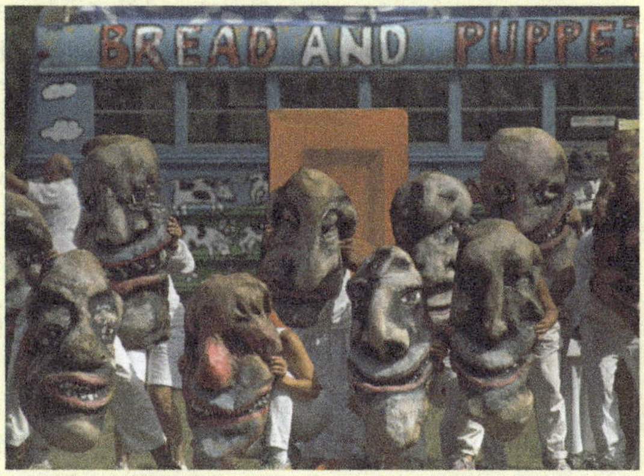

©AP Images/Craig Line

Puppeteers

Perform during the annual *Our Domestic Resurrection Circus*, Bread and Puppet Theatre, Glover, VT.

and hair woven of milkweed and goldenrod were central figures in the story that swept across centuries. Toward the end of each performance, white birds with wingspans of fifteen feet (flown by three puppeteers holding long poles) traveled fast, making sounds of seagulls crying and finally bringing peace to the kingdoms of animals and humans, as the Moon on an ox-drawn wagon appeared. On the horizon the real moon rose above a pinewoods, opposite the last rays of a real sunset. This pattern of

Domestic Resurrection Circus
The "Godface" from the *Domestic Resurrection Circus* in a field in northern Vermont.

events reinforced the "death-and-resurrection" theme that Schumann repeated in all of his Bread and Puppet events.

Of his unique work with puppets, Peter Schumann has said, "Puppet theatre, the employment of and dance of dolls, effigies, and puppets ... is an anarchic art, subversive and untamable by nature ... an art which does not aspire to represent governments or civilizations but prefers its own secret demeaning stature in society, representing, more or less, the demons of that society and definitely not its institutions."[9]

THE FREE SOUTHERN THEATER

The Free Southern Theater grew out of the civil rights movement in the United States to address issues of freedom, justice, equality, and voting rights in the South. In 1963, John O'Neal, Gilbert Moses, and Doris Derby—all staff members of the Student Nonviolent Coordinating Committee (SNCC)—discussed ideas for a "freedom theatre" in the rural South. That year in Mississippi, they founded the Free Southern Theater (FST), the American South's first legitimate black liberation theatre to tour poor rural areas, give free performances ("No tickets needed," a sign said), and train black artists in workshops. They received the energetic support of another coproducer, Richard Schechner, director and editor of *The Tulane Drama Review*, who was teaching at Tulane University in New Orleans at the time and later started the controversial environmental Performance Group, located in the Performing Garage in lower Manhattan.

FOCUS ON THEATRE

Cofounders of the Free Southern Theater : Gilbert Moses III, John O'Neal, and Doris Derby

Director and writer **Gilbert Moses**, born in Cleveland and educated at Oberlin College in Ohio, edited the *Mississippi Free Press* in Jackson before cofounding the Free Southern Theater in 1963. **John O'Neal** grew up in a small town in Illinois and graduated from Southern Illinois University in Carbondale. Bronx-born **Doris Derby** was a teacher and field secretary for SNCC's adult literacy program at Tougaloo College outside Jackson, Mississippi.

The theatre was organized with a home base at Tougaloo College but relocated to New Orleans. At the time, the founders' conversations were about the need for a theatre for black artists and black audiences. The idea developed into a touring company to take theatre into the rural South as part of a larger black theatre movement. Derby was more committed to sociopolitical ideals than to theatre and dropped out of the project in 1964.

After seventeen years of producing free theatre largely in rural areas and cities of the South, the Free Southern Theater failed for lack of funding, the absence of a creative home, and the collapse of an ideal based on "integrated" theatre that included black and white artists. Under pressure, the Free Southern Theater evolved into an all-black company.

The Free Southern Theater started as an experiment during the height of the civil rights movement and antiwar expression in the sixties. Its aim was to promote black theatre for the African American community. Gilbert Moses said, "We wanted freedom: for thought, and involvement, and the celebration of our own culture.… We wanted the theater to deal with black artists and the black audience. But its political aims reflected the political aims of the Movement at that time: integration."[10]

In White America

The Free Southern Theater toured its first production, Martin Duberman's *In White America*, from Tougaloo, Mississippi, to New Orleans in 1964. That summer, civil rights workers James Chaney, Andrew Goodman, and Michael Schwerner were brutally murdered in Mississippi. Against this backdrop of violence, FST toured a play to black communities about a legacy of pain and intolerance. Duberman's play was less a play and more a dramatic reading of black history based on historical documents dating back to the slave trade and forward to the Freedom Rides and bus boycotts of 1957. The material was readily adaptable to performances on porches of rural farmhouses and in cotton fields, local churches, and community centers.

Audiences of mostly black youths, many seeing a live play for the first time, sat in the afternoon sun on folding chairs, benches, cots, and on the ground in the backyard behind a small frame house in rural Mississippi to see *In White America*. The back porch became a stage; actors made entrances through the porch's screen door and around corners of the house. John O'Neal recalled that a pickup truck with a policeman at the wheel and a large police dog standing ominously in the back drove by several times, trolling for trouble.

©Herbert Randall

In White America

Free Southern Theater actors Stu House and Denise Nicholas performing Martin Duberman's play at the True Light Baptist Church in Hattiesburg, Mississippi, as part of the 1964 Freedom Summer.

The play, directed by Gilbert Moses, began with a musician and six actors (four men and two women) in the company—with members doubling as producers, directors, technicians, and wardrobe persons. The first tour took in thirteen Mississippi towns during three weeks. Audiences applauded the speeches of black Americans (Booker T. Washington and W. E. B. DuBois), laughed in unexpected places, and joined spontaneously in singing with the cast. As actor-characters made their pleas for justice, elderly women and young men shouted "That's right!" "Amen!" "You tell it!"[11]

With an orientation toward a populist theatre and "participatory democracy," FST's leaders looked for material in established plays written for black and white actors and worked toward incorporating the audience's open desire to participate in the play's events. Traveling by car and van in the second season, FST toured with productions of the wildly popular *Purlie Victorious* by Ossie Davis and the befuddling *Waiting for Godot* by Samuel Beckett.

As an extension of the civil rights movement, the company waxed and waned over the years as political ideology came into conflict with aesthetic standards. Finally, after seventeen years, with its leadership and monetary resources exhausted, the Free Southern Theater disbanded in 1980.

TRANSITION

Many theatrical groups in recent decades set about to rethink, reshape, and re-create the theatrical experience for actors *and* audiences. Jerzy Grotowski worked in large rooms and forests, Ariane Mnouchkine in a former munitions factory, Peter Brook in an abandoned theatre and rock quarries, Peter Schumann in streets and fields, and the Free Southern Theater in the rural American South.

Environmental or alternative theatre, as this type of nontraditional performance has been called since the 1960s, rejects conventional seating and arranges the audience as part of the playing space. Like the actors, spectators become part of what is seen and performed; they are both seeing and seen. In contrast, traditional theatre arranges the audience *before* a stage, where they see and hear at a distance.

Throughout the ages, the theatre's *space* has influenced those who work within it: playwrights, actors, directors, and designers. These artists are the theatre's "image makers," for they create the world of the production as theatrical metaphor for audiences to experience. The playwright, who creates the text, most often provides the blueprint for the production.

Theatre: A Way of Seeing Online

Visit the CourseMate for Theatre: A Way of Seeing 7th Edition for quick access to the digital study resources that accompany this chapter, including links to the websites listed below, Theatre Workshop, digital glossary, a chapter quiz and more.

Websites

The *Theatre: A Way of Seeing* CourseMate includes links for all the websites described below. Simply select "Web links" from the Chapter Resources for Chapter 3, and click on the link that interests you. You'll be taken directly to the site described.

The Centre for Study of Jerzy Grotowski's Work and for Cultural and Theatrical Research
Access to information about all things Grotowski, plus links to other interesting theatre sites (click on the English version).

Peter Schumann's Bread and Puppet Theatre
Information about past and present Bread and Puppet Theatre events, as well as a calendar of future events.

Polish Laboratory Theatre
Stories about Jerzy Grotowski's work told by his contemporaries after his death.

Théâtre du Soleil, Paris, France
Home page for Théâtre du Soleil, in French. To translate to English, search on Google with the term "theatre du soleil." On the results page, find the link to the home page, and click on the accompanying link "Translate this page."

The Legacy of the Free Southern Theater in New Orleans
Interesting history of the Free Southern Theater via interviews with Karen-Kaia Livers and Chakula Cha Jua, members of the New Orleans theatre community.

4

IMAGE MAKER: THE PLAYWRIGHT

The printed script of a play is hardly more than an architect's blueprint of a house not yet built or built and destroyed. The color, the grace and levitation, the structural pattern in motion, the quick interplay of live beings, these things are the play, not words on paper, not thoughts and ideas of an author.[1]

—TENNESSEE WILLIAMS, AFTERWORD TO *CAMINO REAL*

Who fills the theatrical space? Who is seen in the space? What methods and materials are used to create the stage environment, what a famous designer called "the machine for acting"? In theatre we continually encounter the idea of building. Actors speak of building a character. Technicians build the set, and costumers build costumes. The director often "blocks" the play. The word *playwright* is formed in the same way as *wheelwright* and *shipwright*: It means "play builder." Theatre is the creative collaborative effort of many builders. Creative artists using various methods and materials build an imaginary world, but the initial builder is most often the playwright.

The working methods of playwrights—their tools, perspectives, conventions, and writing styles—are discussed in the next several chapters.

THE PLAY AND THE AUDIENCE

When we take our places in a theatre, we tacitly agree to enter into the playwright's world. If we are in a proscenium theatre, we are usually seated before a curtain that conceals the scene and characters—the world

Tennessee Williams, Afterword to Camino Real (New York: New Directions, 1953): xii. Copyright ©1948, 1953 by Tennessee Williams. Reprinted by permission of New Directions Publishing Corporation.

Stage and film actors Denzel Washington and Viola Davis (as husband and wife Troy and Rose Maxson) in the Broadway revival of *Fences* by award-winning playwright August Wilson.

PREVIEW

The playwright envisions the play's world, its people, words, environment, objects, relationships, emotions, attitudes, and events. Playwriting is a creative act that enlarges our understanding of human experience and enriches our appreciation of life.

Othello
In the film *Othello*, Kenneth Branagh (Iago) observes Laurence Fishburne (Othello) and Irene Jacob (Desdemona) and plots against the Moor.

of the play. Many theatres with thrust stages have no front curtain but rely upon effects of lighting, sound, and actors to signal the play's beginning.

As we wait for the play to begin, we are aware of the conditions around us. Often the seats are cramped, strangers sit next to us, latecomers rush down the aisles, and the noises of an expectant crowd swirl around us. When the lights dim and the curtain rises, we are transported into another world removed from the sensory experiences surrounding us.

The playwright's onstage world, with its color, movement, human voices and speech, music, sound effects, and changing lights, persuades us emotionally and mentally that life is being lived before us. Aesthetic distance, or a psychological divide, keeps us grounded in the present, and we intuitively know that what we are watching is not real but a created situation at once removed from us. We respond with fear and disbelief as Othello and Desdemona are endangered by Iago's perfidy. Even as our minds grasp that Kenneth Branagh is an actor playing Iago, our hearts want us to warn Desdemona to be wary of her husband's jealousy. On the one hand, our empathy involves us in the emotional upheavals of Shakespeare's world; on the other, our aesthetic distance allows us to view events onstage objectively, but not dispassionately.

The Greek word for our emotional release is *catharsis*, a cleansing or purging of strong emotions. As we grapple with our emotions concerning Othello's self-inflicted punishment that begins with "Soft you! A word or two before you go . . . ," we are somehow better able to confront life's realities beyond the theatre.

Most playwrights encourage the audience's empathy, or emotional involvement, with characters and situations. In the mid-twentieth century Bertolt Brecht set about in epic theatre to "distance" audiences so that they would make judgments about the social and economic issues of his plays. His theory of distancing was called the alienation effect (*Verfremdung*, translated as "alienation"). Toward this end, he jarred audiences with cacophonous musical effects, disconnected songs, loudspeakers announcing events, and placards and signs carrying political messages. Brecht wanted a thinking audience to understand the injustices of the world and possibly do something about changing society.

Playwrights come to their craft with different aesthetic sensibilities. They create recognizable worlds with troubling relevance to human behavior and social themes. Others dismiss the "illusion of the real" to engage us in political arguments or absurdist metaphors. Thornton Wilder and Tennessee Williams, on the one hand, and Bertolt Brecht and Samuel Beckett, on the other, are playwrights with very different approaches to empathy and aesthetic distance. However, these writers have in common their means of artistic expression—the play.

The Play: A "Blueprint of a House Not Yet Built"

The playwright writes a play—crafts words on paper—to express some aspect of reality, some emotions and feelings connected with our humanity, some measure of experience, some vision or conviction about the world. Like any artist, the playwright shapes a personal vision into an organized, meaningful whole.

A playwright's script is more than words on a page—it is the playwright's *blueprint* of a special kind of experience, created to appeal as much to the eye as to the ear.

Cat on a Tin Roof
A Revival of Tennessee Williams's play with Phylicia Rashad and James Earl Jones, Broadway.

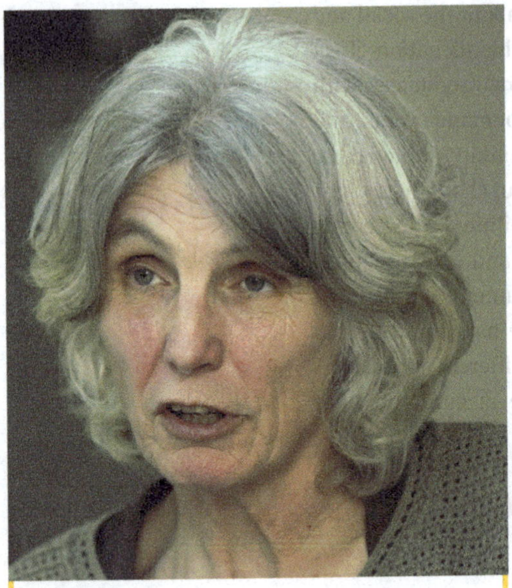

© Camera Press/Redux

Caryl Churchill
Caryl Churchill is a British writer associated with the Joint Stock Theatre Company, the Royal Court Theatre, and the Royal Shakespeare Company. She is best known for *Cloud 9*, *Top Girls*, *Fen*, *Serious Money*, *Mad Forest*, *Far Away*, and *A Number*. Churchill says, "I believe in the magic of theater, but I think it's important to realize that there is nothing magical about the work process behind it. I spend ages researching my plays and sitting alone writing them."[2]

As Tennessee Williams said, "The printed script of a play is hardly more than an architect's blueprint of a house not yet built." All in all, playwriting is the search for the truth of human experience as the playwright perceives it. Playwrights such as Henrik Ibsen write plays to expose truths about the realities of social injustice. Others, such as Bertolt Brecht and Caryl Churchill, make political statements about people, economies, and political systems. These writers use the theatre as a vehicle for a message or ideology. Most writers turn their personal experiences, wishes, and dreams into drama. For Adrienne Kennedy, writing is an outlet for psychological confusion and questions stemming from childhood. Other writers, such as Eugène Ionesco, ridicule the conventions of the theatre and certain kinds of human behavior to persuade us to see the world differently.

THE PLAYWRIGHT'S BEGINNINGS

Playwrights start with an idea, theme, dream, image, or notes and work out an action; or they begin with an unusual character or a real person and develop an action around that character; or they start with a situation based on a personal experience, their reading, or an anecdote. Working within groups, some playwrights evolve scenarios with actors and arrange a final script from the group's improvisations, suggestions, dialogue, and movement. Some write from scenarios or plot summaries; others write from outline, crisis scene, images, dreams, myths, or imagined or real environments.

> **"When I write a play, I write one draft of it because as I'm writing it, I see it and I hear it as a performed piece on stage. I know exactly what it looks like, I know exactly what it sounds like, and I have some accuracy about what the play does to me as an audience."[3]**
>
> —Edward Albee, Playwright

Bertolt Brecht usually worked from a story outline, which he called the draft plan. Next, he summarized the story's social and political ideas before developing scenes based on the outline. Sam Shepard first writes by hand in a notebook. He wrote literally a dozen different versions of *Fool for Love*, but the first five pages remained the same in each version. After spending a long evening in the theatre making script revisions with the director, Marsha Norman, author of *'Night, Mother*, returns to her residence and types the changes into her computer in the early morning hours. Some playwrights claim their characters talk to them and develop themselves; others claim they hear the play's voices and dialogue in their heads. Some playwrights speak lines out loud before writing them down or work from mental images of their characters moving and talking.

FOCUS ON PEOPLE IN THEATRE

PLAYWRIGHT
Edward Albee

© Martha Swope/The New York Public Library

With the passing of Eugene O'Neill, Tennessee Williams, and Arthur Miller, **Edward Albee** is today's reigning American playwright. Albee's (b. 1928) career has interestingly mirrored his private life. Adopted by Frances and Reed Albee, he was beloved as an infant, rejected as a youth, and finally left home when he was twenty. When he first exploded on the New York theatre scene in the early 1960s with *The Zoo Story* and *Who's Afraid of Virginia Woolf?*, he was celebrated by the critics, but they turned against his increasingly cryptic and abstract plays that followed: *Tiny Alice*, *A Delicate Balance*, *All Over*, *Seascape*, *The Lady from Dubuque*, and *Marriage Play*. His war with the critics ended on a happier note with *Three Tall Women* in 1991, which reinstated him as the country's top playwright with three Pulitzer Prizes, and forced a new appraisal of his earlier work. *The Goat, or Who Is Sylvia?* and *Peter and Jerry* followed with enthusiastic critical receptions.

© Sara Krulwich/The New York Times/Redux

Edward Albee's *The American Dream*
With (left to right) Myra Carter as Grandma, Judith Ivey as Mommy, and George Bartenieff as Daddy, directed by Edward Albee, Cherry Lane Theatre, Off Off Broadway.

THE PLAYWRIGHT'S ROLE

In the theatre the playwright is an anomaly. Although playwrights receive Pulitzer Prizes and Nobel awards, they are both central and peripheral to the production. In the privacy of the home, studio, or hotel room, the playwright turns on the computer or iPad and constructs an imaginary world. As the creative imagination takes over, people, events, conflicts, words, and whole speeches resound in the writer's inner eye and ear. The script belongs to the playwright, but once this original creative act—this blueprint for performance—is completed and handed over to director, designers, actors, and producers, the playwright in one sense becomes peripheral to the process. In the harrowing process of transforming the manuscript into a living performance, the writer takes a backseat in the rehearsal hall only to emerge a success or a failure on opening night. One exception is the playwright who also directs his or her own work, such as Bertolt Brecht, Samuel Beckett, Edward Albee, María Irene Fornés, or David Mamet. As directors, they remain central to the production process. Others, such as Shakespeare and Molière, were not only part owners of their companies but also actors in their plays. To prolong the New York run of *Small Craft Warnings* in 1972, Tennessee Williams, by no means a professional actor, took the role of narrator in his play and received critical acclaim.

In rehearsals, nevertheless, playwrights usually take a backseat to their collaborators. Huddled in a back row, often with iPad in hand, they note awkward lines and words that don't ring true, and rewrite speeches and even whole scenes when directors or actors find difficulties in making sense of the action or need a few more seconds to make a costume change or an entrance.

National Archives

Lillian Hellman

Lillian Hellman (1905–1984) was produced successfully on Broadway for almost thirty years. Best known for *The Children's Hour*, *The Little Foxes*, and *Toys in the Attic*, Hellman pioneered as a woman in the tough commercialism of the Broadway theatre. She said of the theatre: "The manuscript, the words on the page, was what you started with and what you have left. The production is of great importance, has given the play the only life it will know, but is gone, in the end, and the pages are the only wall against which to throw the future or measure the past."[4]

FOCUS ON PEOPLE IN THEATRE

PLAYWRIGHT

Sam Shepard

©AP Images

©Joan Marcus

Kicking a Dead Horse

With actor Stephen Rea attempting to bury the America West's galloping symbol of freedom, possibility, and redemption in Sam Shepard's lament for the nation's lost ideals and despoiled frontiers. New York Shakespeare Festival/The Public Theater.

Question: So, why are you writing plays?

Answer: I have to. I have a mission (*Shepard laughs*). No, I don't know why I do it. Why not?[5]

Sam Shepard (b. 1943) began his theatrical career as an actor. Since 1964, he has explored contemporary American myths among the refuse of our junk culture. His characters are Americans we all know, but his situations are often unfamiliar and jarring. Eight-time recipient of the Off Broadway Obie Award for distinguished playwriting, Shepard received the Pulitzer Prize for Drama in 1979 for *Buried Child*. Among his other well-known plays are *Cowboys, Chicago, Red Cross, La Turista, Operation Sidewinder, The Tooth of Crime, Angel City, Curse of the Starving Class, True West, Fool for Love, A Lie of the Mind, States of Shock, Simpatico, The Late Henry Moss, Kicking a Dead Horse*, and *Heartless*.

Shepard also acted in such films as *Days of Heaven, The Right Stuff, Country, Crimes of the Heart, Steel Magnolias, Thunderheart, The Pelican Brief*, and *Hamlet* with Ethan Hawke. Shepard wrote the screenplays for the films *Far North* and *Paris, Texas*.

The playwright's independence also makes him or her an anomaly in the theatre. Like novelists, playwrights usually create alone though there are exceptions. Their material, even for a political writer such as Bertolt Brecht, is highly personal. For example, Grusha in *The Caucasian Chalk Circle* is both a personal creation and a political statement on the human instinct for survival. We look to playwrights to give us insights into the world around us—to provide fresh perspectives and new visions. To do this, they reach inside themselves, in a private act, and pull forth intensely personal feelings, perceptions, and situations to construct the public world of the play.

© Boneau/Bryan-Brown/AP Images

Wit

Winner of the 1999 Pulitzer Prize for Drama, is Margaret Edson's first play. Between earning degrees in history and literature, she worked on the cancer inpatient unit of a research hospital. The material for the play grew out of her experiences with literature and cancer research. The Manhattan Theatre Club's 2012 revival featured Cynthia Nixon, New York City.

Where do playwrights come from? What are their origins? Their backgrounds? Playwrights have come from every conceivable background: acting, literary, gag writing, teaching, housewifery, politics, medicine, and so on. Lillian Hellman worked as a reader for a literary agent before writing her first play, *The Children's Hour*. Tennessee Williams worked in a shoe factory and wandered the United States writing poems, short stories, one-acts, and his first full-length play, *Battle of Angels*. Aeschylus was a soldier, Terence a slave, Shakespeare an actor, Luigi Pirandello a teacher, Anton Chekhov a doctor, Caryl Churchill a housewife, and Margaret Edson an elementary school and ESL teacher. Among playwrights, there is no common denominator other than the exercise of the creative imagination in plot, action, and dialogue—the conversion of dreams, fears, thoughts, and inner voices into a concrete, visible world that expands our understanding of ourselves, others, society, and the universe.

THE PLAYWRIGHT'S TOOLS

The essential tools of the playwright's craft are plot, character, and language. These are also the novelist's tools, and like novels, plays are studied as literature and read for pleasure. Although plays are an arrangement of words on a page (as dialogue), the play-as-text is incomplete, even though it has been published. It attains its finished form only in performance on a stage. That is why we call the text of the play a blueprint for performance. To look at several lines of dialogue without actors, scenery, lights, sound, and costumes is to be convinced of the "incompleteness" of a script. The following lines of *Waiting for Godot* strike us as wholly unfinished without the actors and production elements:

ESTRAGON:	*He should be here.*
VLADIMIR:	*He didn't say for sure he'd come.*
ESTRAGON:	*And if he doesn't come?*
VLADIMIR:	*We'll come back to-morrow.*
ESTRAGON:	*And then the day after to-morrow.*
VLADIMIR:	*Possibly.*
ESTRAGON:	*And so on. (Act I)*

Despite the bare-bones quality of a play's dialogue, the script is most often the foundation for the production.

"I feel like there are territories within us that are totally unknown. Huge, mysterious, and dangerous territories. We think we know ourselves, when we really know only this little bitty part. We have this social person that we present to each other. We have all these galaxies inside of us. And if we don't enter those in art ... whether it's playwriting, or painting, or music, or whatever, then I don't understand the point in doing anything."[6]

—SAM SHEPARD, PLAYWRIGHT

The playwright "builds" that foundation with plot, character, and language. A story is told with characters, physical action, and dialogue. But the building does not begin until the playwright conceives a whole event with *conflict* (the clashing of personal, moral, and social forces) and then develops a series of related events to resolve that conflict in new and unusual ways. The conflict and events must be compelling. Some are bold and unusual—such as Sophocles's Oedipus unwittingly chasing his own identity through a plague-ridden city, or Shakespeare's Hamlet avenging his father's murder at the invitation of a ghost. Some are seemingly ordinary, such as many domestic situations depicted in modern realistic plays. But, Blanche DuBois's encounter with her brother-in-law in a New Orleans tenement becomes life-threatening in Tennessee Williams's *A Streetcar Named Desire*, and Troy Maxson destroys his domestic tranquility through his need to control his son and assert his own manhood in August Wilson's *Fences*.

Playwrights conceptualize events—hear and see them in the mind's eye—for they are to be enacted and must hold the audience's attention. *Performability* is the key to the success of the playwright's story and dialogue. Whether the story is told in a straightforward manner (linear, point-to-point storytelling) or arranged as a series of nonlinear or discontinuous scenes, audiences respond to powerful and sustained dramatic impact. But that impact must be based on the dramatization of events with believable persons brought together in some sort of meaningful and satisfying fashion before audiences.

Tennessee Williams's *A Streetcar Named Desire*
A revival with Cate Blanchett as Blanche DuBois, Brooklyn Academy of Music, New York.

FOCUS ON PEOPLE IN THEATRE

PLAYWRIGHT

David Mamet

© Capital Pictures/Retna Ltd.

David Mamet (b. 1947), born in Chicago, worked as a bit player with Hull House Theatre, attended the Neighborhood Playhouse School of the Theatre (New York City) in 1960s, and graduated from Goddard College in 1969. He returned to Chicago and became a founding member of the Nicholas Theatre Company, where he began writing and directing plays. His early plays, *Sexual Perversity in Chicago*, *American Buffalo*, and *A Life in the Theatre*, established his style, language, and subjects.

Mamet is known as a playwright of the panic and poetry of the working class in America. He writes of the spiritual failure of entrepreneurial capitalism in the junkyards, real estate offices, and Hollywood agencies of America. Noted for his distinctive language, Mamet has his beleaguered characters demonstrate their frustration, rage, sense of humor, and incomprehension in undeleted expletives—what one critic called the "sludge in American language."

In 1984, Mamet wrote *Glengarry Glen Ross*, which received the Pulitzer Prize for Drama, *Speed the Plow*, *Oleanna*, *The Cryptogram*, *The Old Neighborhood*, *Boston Marriage*, and *Race*; and film scripts for *The Postman Always Rings Twice*, *The Verdict*, *House of Games*, *Glengarry Glen Ross*, *The Edge*, *Wag the Dog*, *The Spanish Prisoner*, and *State and Main*.

© T. Charles Erickson

David Mamet's *Glengarry Glen Ross*
The 2000 revival with Charles Durning (right) at the McCarter Theatre Center for the Performing Arts, Princeton, NJ.

In the playwright's so-called bag of tools, plot—what Aristotle called the "soul" of drama—requires compression, economy, and intensity. Romeo and Juliet meet, marry, and die within a "two hour's traffic" upon the stage. Although plots may encompass many years, the events are compressed so that the story is introduced, told, and resolved within a reasonable amount of time. The intensity of emotions, changed fortunes, and unexpected happenings account for our interest in the story and its outcome.

To sustain our interest, the playwright's characters must be believable, multifaceted, and psychologically complex. We may never meet a Hamlet, but his dilemma and responses are credible and far more complex and intriguing than people and events we encounter in our daily lives. Characters, according to Tennessee Williams, add the mystery and confusion of living to plays:

> *My chief aim in playwriting is the creation of character. I have always had a deep feeling for the mystery in life, and essentially my plays have been an effort to explore the beauty and meaning in the confusion of living.*[8]

"I think that people are generally more happy with a mystery than with an explanation. So the less that you say about a character the more interesting he becomes."[7]

—DAVID MAMET, PLAYWRIGHT

Plot and character are only two of the playwright's means of conveying the confusion and mystery of life. Language is the playwright's third essential tool. As dialogue, it must be speakable as words filled with potential for gesture and revelation of meanings—both obvious and hidden. As justification for the pain he causes his family, August Wilson's character, Troy Maxson, talks of his plight as an African American in a predominantly white society:

> *You born with two strikes on you before you come to the plate. You got to guard it closely ... always looking for the curve-ball on the inside corner. You can't afford to let none get past you. You can't afford a call strike. If you going down ... you going down swinging.* (2, i)[9]

Wilson's language is graphic, active, filled with gesture, emotion, and metaphor that convey the essence of Troy's plight and personal understanding of his situation in life. He has been born "with two strikes" against him before he steps up to the "plate" in the game of life.

In *Fences*, Troy Maxson speaks in language highly charged with feelings, gestures, and baseball images. Wilson's character swings his favorite baseball bat against a rag ball and delivers pronouncements on life in a manner that is at once believable and actable. No baseball diamond is required to convey Troy's philosophy of life as he stands in his front yard in reduced circumstances and swings the bat against defensive thoughts and lost dreams.

William B. Carter

August Wilson's *Fences*
The Yale Repertory Theatre's production, New Haven, CT with James Earl Jones as Troy Maxson.

FOCUS ON PEOPLE IN THEATRE

PLAYWRIGHT

Tennessee Williams

©Martha Swope/New York Public Library for the Performing Arts

Born Thomas Lanier Williams in Columbus, Mississippi, **Tennessee Williams** (1911–1983) was the son of a traveling salesman, and his mother was an Episcopalian minister's daughter. The family moved to St. Louis in 1918. He was educated at Missouri University, Washington University in St. Louis, and later the University of Iowa, where he received his bachelor's degree.

In 1939, *Story* magazine published his short story "A Field of Blue Children," the first work to appear under his nickname "Tennessee," which was given to him because of his Southern accent. That same year he compiled four one-act plays under the title *American Blues* and won a prize in the Group Theatre's American Play Contest. This aroused the interest of New York literary agent Audrey Wood, who asked to represent him.

The Glass Menagerie in 1944–1945 marked Williams's first major success and established him as an important American playwright. It was followed by his major plays: *A Streetcar Named Desire*, *The Rose Tattoo*, *Cat on a Hot Tin Roof*, *Sweet Bird of Youth*, and *The Night of the Iguana*. Although his later plays failed to please critics, he continued to write until his death.

© AP Images/Courtesy of the Goodman Theatre, Liz Lauren

Tennessee Williams's *Sweet Bird of Youth*
Diane Lane and Finn Wittrock star as Alexandra Del Lago and Chance Wayne in the Goodman Theatre (Chicago) revival, directed by David Cromer.

FOCUS ON PEOPLE IN THEATRE

PLAYWRIGHT

August Wilson

William B Carter

August Wilson (1945–2005), born in Pittsburgh, had seven plays produced on Broadway: *Ma Rainey's Black Bottom*, *Fences*, *Joe Turner's Come and Gone*, *The Piano Lesson*, *Two Trains Running*, *King Hedley II*, and *Gem of the Ocean*. He won two Pulitzer Prizes for Drama (for *Fences* and *The Piano Lesson*). At nineteen, Wilson left home to become a writer—he supported himself as a cook and stock clerk and in his spare time he read voraciously in the public library. Writing became his means of responding to changing race relations in America and to the violence erupting within African American families and communities. In 1968, he cofounded Pittsburgh's Black Horizons Theatre and secured a production of his first play, *Black Bart and the Sacred Hills*, in St. Paul, Minnesota, where he lived.

In St. Paul, Wilson was hired as a scriptwriter for the Science Museum of Minnesota, which had a theatre company attached to the museum. In 1981, a draft of *Ma Rainey's Black Bottom* was accepted by the Eugene O'Neill Theater Center's National Playwrights Conference in Waterford, Connecticut, and Wilson's career was launched.

Wilson's cycle of plays chronicles ten decades of the black experience set in different decades of twentieth-century America. The series includes his last plays *Jitney*, *King Hedley II*, *Gem of the Ocean,* and *Radio Golf*. Writing a history of black America, he probed what he perceived to be crucial oppositions in African American culture between those who celebrate black Americans' African roots and those who deny that historical reality.

© Jim Caldwell/The Alley Theatre

August Wilson's *Ma Rainey's Black Bottom*

Ma Rainey (Theresa Merritt) in the onstage recording studio. Produced at the Alley Theatre, Houston.

© Suellen Fitzsimmons/Courtesy of the Pittsburgh Public Theatre

August Wilson's *King Hedley II*

Directed by Marion Isaac McClinton, with Tony Todd as Hedley and Russell Andrews as Mister.

Speed of the Plow
As one of David Mamet's Hollywood types, William H. Macy, in *Speed the Plow*, Broadway.

THE PLAYWRIGHT'S INDUSTRY

Since the Greek festivals in ancient Athens, producers have clamored for new and better plays from playwrights. Today, hundreds of producers and literary agents are anxious to discover new authors and viable scripts. To do so, they employ a cadre of "readers" to find the exceptional manuscript: a play by a "new" David Mamet or an "undiscovered" Wendy Wasserstein. International Creative Management (ICM) and the William Morris Agency are the largest literary agencies in New York City, representing Edward Albee, Paula Vogel, and others. For years Tennessee Williams was represented by Audrey Wood, who guided him through the most successful part of his career. The agent and the producer are two essential connections for the playwright's success. Moreover, some writers develop working relationships with directors; for example, Arthur Miller and Tennessee Williams with Elia Kazan in the early part of their careers; August Wilson with Lloyd Richards, Marion McClinton, and Kenny Leon; Neil Simon with Mike Nichols and Jerry Zaks; and Sarah Ruhl with Les Waters. Others, such as David Mamet, Edward Albee, and Sam Shepard frequently direct their own plays.

For the successful Broadway playwright, the rewards are staggering, including television, film, recordings, and publishing contracts and interviews in glamorous magazines and on television. Prestigious awards are also forthcoming as indicators of success: the Pulitzer Prize, the Drama Critics' Circle Award, the Antoinette Perry "Tony" Award, and for some, even Nobel Prizes for Literature. Luigi Pirandello, Eugene O'Neill, and Samuel Beckett received Nobel awards.

In many respects, playwrights are the most respected of the theatre's artists, because audiences are aware that they sit in the presence of the writer's world. We listen to and experience a personal vision that makes us laugh and cry. The public may revere the actor—a Nathan Lane or an Audra McDonald—but the actor's creativity usually begins with the playwright's creation: the characters, environment, and situation of conflicts, feelings, and choices.

In one sense, playwriting is only one facet of the theatre profession and the theatrical machine—the industry. In another sense, it transcends both because when the curtain comes down on a production, the playwright's words remain. As Lillian Hellman, creator of *The Little Foxes*, said, "The manuscript, the words on the page, was what you started with and what you have left" after the production is over. Although we might not have an opportunity to see a production of *A Streetcar Named Desire* or *Fences*, we can read the playwright's published script and absorb the writer's world, incomplete though it may be.

FOCUS ON PEOPLE IN THEATRE

PLAYWRIGHT

Arthur Miller

© The Inge Morath Foundation/ Magnum Photos, Inc.

Arthur Miller and Tennessee Williams were the most influential American playwrights following the Second World War. **Arthur Miller** (1916–2005) had his first success with *All My Sons*, a realistic play about a wartime manufacturer of airplane engines who put profit above the safety of fighter pilots. He wrote the now-classic *Death of a Salesman*, followed by *The Crucible*, *A View from the Bridge*, and *The Price*. His reputation rests largely on these five plays. His later works received mixed critical reviews: *The Creation of the World and Other Business*, *The American Clock*, *The Archbishop's Ceiling*, *The Ride Down Mt. Morgan*, *Broken Glass*, *Mr. Peters' Connections*, *Resurrection Blues*, and *Finishing the Picture*.

Arthur Miller is often thought of as a moralist and social dramatist. His plays deal with the individual's responsibility in the face of society's emphasis on such false values as material success and personal happiness at any price.

© Jim Caldwell/Alley Theatre

Arthur Miller's *A View from the Bridge*
A revival at the Alley Theatre, Houston, with James Black and Annalee Jefferies (right) and Kevin Waldron (left).

NEW AMERICAN WRITING: ALTERNATIVE VOICES

Beginning in the late 1980s and continuing into the new millennium, an underrepresented, and often invisible, America emerged on stages throughout the country. The new writers were gay and lesbian, African American, Asian American, Mexican American, Latino/a, and Hispanic. The central issues of their lives became the material of their plays: oppression, racism, sexism, classism, homophobia. America's stages came to mirror ethnic, social, and political diversity among the many cultures that make up our society. Gender, ethnicity, and sexual orientation have become the defining subjects of the new writing.

Gay and Lesbian Writing

In the late 1960s, gay and lesbian issues came to be treated as serious dramatic subjects in the American theatre. In his groundbreaking play *Boys in the Band*, written in the 1960s, Mart Crowley introduced sexual orientation as a permissible romantic topic. What followed were mainstream Broadway musicals (*La Cage aux Folles*, *Falsettos*, *Kiss of the Spider Woman*) and serious dramas (*Bent*; *M. Butterfly*; *The Normal Heart*; *Angels in America*; *Baltimore Waltz*; *Love! Valour! Compassion!*; *Gross Indecency: The Three Trials of Oscar Wilde*; *Stop Kiss*; *The Laramie Project*). The onslaught of AIDS in the early 1980s, whose early victims in the United States and Europe were predominantly gay, produced writing that addressed political, medical, and personal issues in this new and terrible age. Larry Kramer, Terrence McNally, Tony Kushner, Paula Vogel, Paul Rudnick, and Diana Son have examined the political, cultural, and aesthetic implications of gay and lesbian issues in their plays.

© Dan McNeil/Courtesy of Denver Center Theatre Company

The Laramie Project
Written by Moisés Kaufmann in collaboration with the members of Tectonic Theater Project from interviews with the townspeople of Laramie, Wyoming, about the murder of Matthew Shepard. First presented in 2000 by the Denver Center Theatre Company.

African American Writing

African Americans writing for the theatre made inroads in the early years of the twentieth century with Langston Hughes' *Mulatto* in the 1930s and Lorraine Hansberry's *A Raisin the Sun* in the late 1950s, recently revived with Sean "P. Diddy" Combs and Phylicia Rashad. Paralleling the civil rights movement in the 1960s, Amiri Baraka's (then LeRoi Jones) writing became a revolutionary force. Baraka's plays *Dutchman* and *Slave Ship* confronted American racism head on.

Beginning in the 1960s, a growing number of African American playwrights emerged on the national scene, among them Charles Gordone (*No Place to Be Somebody*), Lonne Elder III (*Ceremonies in Dark Old Men*), Adrienne Kennedy (*Funnyhouse of a Negro*), Ntozake Shange (*for*

FOCUS ON PEOPLE IN THEATRE

PLAYWRIGHT

Paula Vogel

© Getty Images

Paula Vogel (b. 1951) grew up in suburban Maryland and arrived on the national scene by writing plays on such highly charged issues as pornography, domestic violence, gay parenthood, AIDS, feminism, pedophilia, and incest. Unlike most writers on political issues, she is not interested in persuading audiences to adopt political or moral positions but rather to understand that there are no easy answers. *The Baltimore Waltz*, her first success, grew out of her brother's dying of AIDS. It was followed by *Hot 'n' Throbbing, The Mineola Twins, The Mammary Plays, The Long Christmas Ride Home, Desdemona: A Play About A Handkerchief, And Baby Makes Seven, The Oldest Profession*, and *A Civil War Christmas. How I Learned to Drive* won the 1998 Pulitzer Prize for Drama.

Paula Vogel insists that her writing is not guided by political issues. "When I write," she says, "there's a pain that I have to reach, and a release I have to work toward for myself. So it's really a question of the particular emotional circumstance that I want to express, a character that appears, a moment in time, and then I write the play backwards."[10]

© Carol Rosegg

Paula Vogel's *How I Learned to Drive*
First-produced Off Broadway at the Vineyard Theatre with Mary-Louise Parker as Li'l Bit and David Morse as Peck.

colored girls who have considered suicide/when the rainbow is enuf), Suzan-Lori Parks (*The America Play*), John Henry Redwood (*The Old Settler*), Pearl Cleage (*Blues for an Alabama Sky*), Cheryl L. West (*Jar the Floor*), and George C. Wolfe (*The Colored Museum*). Lavishly produced musicals about the black experience with predominantly black casts found their way to Broadway: *Purlie*; *Bubbling Brown Sugar*; *The Wiz*; *Ain't Misbehavin'*; *Sophisticated Ladies*; *Dreamgirls*; *Five Guys Named Moe*; *Jelly's Last Jam*; *Bring in 'da Noise, Bring in 'da Funk*; *Ain't Nothing but the Blues;* and *The Gershwins' Porgy and Bess*. August Wilson, in his explorations of the twentieth-century history of black America in powerful and provocative plays from *Ma Rainey's Black Bottom* to *Gem of the Ocean*, became the leading African American playwright of his time.

FOCUS ON PEOPLE IN THEATRE

PLAYWRIGHT

Lorraine Hansberry

© AP Images

Lorraine Hansberry (1930–1965) is best known for *A Raisin in the Sun* (1959), which ran on Broadway for 530 performances and then was made into a film. She was the youngest playwright, the first African American writer, and only the fifth woman to win the New York Drama Critics' Award for the Best Play of the Year. Of playwriting, Hansberry said, "Plays are better written because one must, even if people think that you are being either artsy-craftsy or a plain liar if you say so. One result of this is that I usually don't say it any more, I just write—at my own dismally slow (and, yes, heartbreaking and maddening) commercially disinterested pace and choice of subject matter."[11]

© Joan Marcus

A Raisin in the Sun
Audra McDonald and Sean Combs in a Broadway revival of Lorraine Hansberry's *A Raisin in the Sun*.

Suzan-Lori Parks is the most experimental of recent African American playwrights. Using surreal landscapes ("the Great hole of History") in *The America Play*, she sets out boldly to rewrite, using theatrical conventions and musical "riffs," unrecorded segments of U.S. history, including the invisible servitude of black Americans. Her postmodern style is apparent in fantastical landscapes, nonlinear narrative, iconic characters (Abraham Lincoln is a recurring figure in her plays), and the reimagining of history in "the great hole" of theatrical space—the stage.

FOCUS ON PEOPLE IN THEATRE

PLAYWRIGHT

Suzan-Lori Parks

© Sara Krulwich/The New York Times/Redux

Suzan-Lori Parks (b. 1963), playwright and screenwriter, became interested in theatre during a writing course at Mount Holyoke College (MA) taught by novelist James Baldwin. Inspired by the works of Adrienne Kennedy and Ntozake Shange, Parks is one of the notable African American women writing for today's theatre. *Imperceptible Mutabilities in the Third Kingdom*, her first full-length play to be produced, was followed by *The Death of the Last Black Man in the Whole Entire World*, *The America Play*, *Venus*, *In the Blood*, *The Book of Grace*, and *Top Dog/Under Dog* that won the 2002 Pulitzer Prize for Drama. (She is the first African American woman to receive the prestigious award.) Parks exploded onto Broadway with revisions to the musical-book for the retitled *The Gershwins' Porgy and Bess* with Norm Lewis and Audra McDonald in the title roles.

Of her writing Suzan-Lori Parks, a MacArthur "Genius" Award recipient, says, "As a playwright I try to do many things: explore the form, ask questions, make a good show, tell a story, ask more questions, take nothing for granted ... I don't explode the form because I find traditional plays 'boring.' ... It's just those structures never could accommodate the figures which take up residence inside me."[12]

© Sara Krulwich/The New York Times/Redux

The Gershwins' *Porgy and Bess*

The Gershwins' musical masterpiece and timeless score set in Charleston, SC, with archetypal characters in a black community called "Catfish Row," is sung in this shorter version by Norm Lewis as Porgy, Audra McDonald as Bess (in red dress), and David Alan Grier as Sporting Life, Broadway, 2012.

"I'm interested in the dust that settles when worlds collide. Sometimes these worlds are cultural, as in my explorations of a Chinese past meeting an American present ... I am fascinated by America as a land of dreams—people pursue them and hope some day to own one."[13]

—David Henry Hwang, Playwright

David Henry Hwang, Contemporary American Dramatists, ed. K. A. Berney. St. James Press (1994): 285. Reprinted by permission of the Gale Group.

Asian American Writing

Asian theatre and opera traditions were imported by laborers from China as early as the 1850s and by Japanese and Filipinos settling in the United States at the turn of the twentieth century. As interest in traditional Eastern performance styles diminished, Asian stereotypes and stock characters dominated plays and films with Asian themes until the civil rights era. Beginning in the 1960s, new Asian American writers found it necessary to establish their own theatres to showcase their writing, which exploded narrow stereotypes and misperceptions about Asian culture, people, and traditions. Such playwrights as Philip Kan Gotanda (*Sisters Matsumoto*), Han Ong (*L.A. Stories*), and Diana Son (*Stop Kiss*) introduced complex issues of race, prejudice, family, compromise, and struggles for self-fulfillment into writing for the theatre. David Henry Hwang's *M. Butterfly* in 1988 was the play that effectively introduced the Asian American voice into mainstream American theatre.

© Getty Images

Diana Son
Her best-known work, *Stop Kiss*, was first produced at The Joseph Papp Public Theater/ New York Shakespeare Festival and received the 1999 Media Award from GLAAD (Gay and Lesbian Alliance Against Defamation) for Outstanding New York Theatre Production.

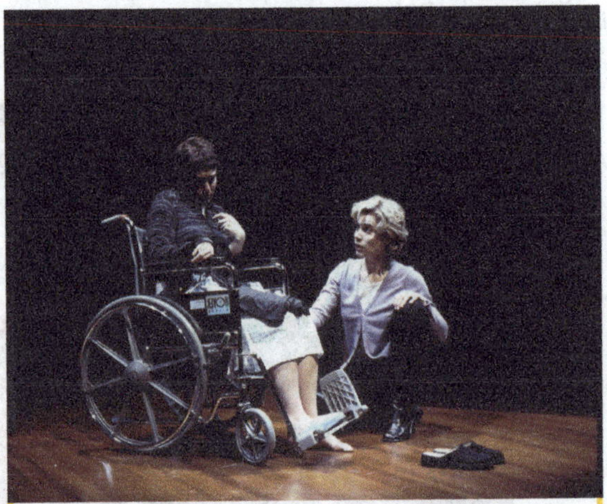

© Chris Bennion/Courtesy of Seattle Repertory Theatre

Diana Son's *Stop Kiss*
Directed by Sharon Off at the Seattle Repertory Theatre, WA, with Jodi Somers (left) and Amy Croise.

FOCUS ON PEOPLE IN THEATRE

PLAYWRIGHT

David Henry Hwang

© WireImage/Getty Images

David Henry Hwang (b. 1957), a second-generation Chinese American, grew up in Los Angeles and studied at Stanford University. His playwriting career began in 1979 following a writing workshop with Sam Shepard at the Padua Hills Playwrights Festival. *FOB*, *Family Devotions*, and *The Dance and the Railroad* were written as a Chinese American trilogy. He became the first Asian American to win Broadway's "Tony" Award for Best Play (*M. Butterfly* in 1988). *Face Value* and *Golden Child* ("Tony" Award nomination for Best Play in 1998), librettos for *1,000 Airplanes on the Roof* and *The Voyage* (with Philip Glass), and *The Silver River* (with music by Bright Sheng) followed. He cowrote the musical book for Elton John and Tim Rice's *Aida* and received the PEN/Laura Pels Award for a Master American Dramatist. His recent comedy, *Chinglish*, takes on absurdities of language-usage to depict culture clashes between a clueless American businessman in China and a top-level Chinese bureaucrat.

U.S. Latino/a Writing

A Spanish-speaking theatre whose purpose is to preserve Hispanic traditions and language for the minority culture has existed in North America since the late sixteenth century. In 1965, a Latino theatre under the wing of the United Farm Workers burst on the political scene to address the plight of migrant farm workers in California. Led by Mexican American theatre artist Luis Valdez and his bilingual Chicano company El Teatro Campesino (The Farm Workers' Theatre), Hispanic American writing found an aggressive contemporary voice. By 1967, El Teatro Campesino moved away from union involvement, expanding its subjects to address working-class and urban issues. A growing number of writers followed: Cuban-born María Irene Fornés (*The Conduct of Life*) and Eduardo Machado (*The Floating Island Plays*); Puerto Rican–born José Rivera (*Marisol*); Latina dramatist Milcha Sanchez-Scott (*Roosters*); and Chicano authors Josefina Lopez (*Real Women Have Curves*) and Carlos Morton (*The Miser of Mexico*).

Cuban-born Nilo Cruz, who took flight from Castro's Cuba at age nine, is the first Latin American dramatist to win the Pulitzer Prize for Drama. (He received the award in 2003 for *Anna and the Tropics*.) His plays—*Dancing on Her Knees*, *A Park in Our House*, *Two Sisters and a Piano*, *Hortensia and the Museum of Dreams*, *Anna and the Tropics*, *Hurricane*—give voice to the stories, hardships, and sensibilities of Cubans. His language of visceral imagery, lyrical emotions, and luxurious landscapes connects audiences with the richness of Cuban life and the paradoxes of identity in an adopted land.

FOCUS ON THEATRE

María Irene Fornés and Nilo Cruz

© Peter Bellamy

Cuban-born **María Irene Fornés** (b. 1930) immigrated to the United States in 1945. She emerged in the mid-1960s with New York City's Judson Poets' Theater and the Open Theater as a writer, director, and designer. She is legendary both as a playwright of ruthless self-exposure and disjunctive action and as a teacher with the INTAR Hispanic American Arts Center and the Padua Hills Playwrights Festival, where she has influenced Eduardo Machado, Tony Kushner, Paula Vogel, and Nilo Cruz, among many writers. Her more than thirty plays, produced largely Off Broadway, include *Promenade*, *Fefu and Her Friends*, *Evelyn Brown*, *Mud*, *The Conflict of Life*, *Abington Square*, *What of the Night?*, *Enter the Night*, *Drowning*, and *Letters from Cuba*. The Signature Theatre Company (New York City) produced a "*Fornés Retrospective*" in the 1999–2000 season.

Of playwriting she says: "We have to reconcile ourselves to the idea that the protagonist of a play can be a woman and that it is natural for a woman to write a play where the protagonist is a woman. Man is not the center of life. And it is natural when this fact reflects itself in the work of women."[14]

© Kathy Willens/AP Images

Nilo Cruz, born in Matanzas, Cuba, took a freedom flight in 1970 to Miami with his family. He credits the influence of María Irene Fornés on his development as a theatre artist. She gave a workshop in Miami in 1988, liked his writing, and invited him to join the now-defunct INTAR Hispanic Playwrights in Residency Laboratory in New York. He quit his job at a cargo airport, took a train to New York, and began the workshop. Thereafter he received commissions from regional theatres, where his early plays were produced, including *Anna and the Tropics*, before reaching Broadway. Of his writing style—he calls it "realism that is magic"—Cruz says, "I come from the Irene Fornés School. You don't write a play about an idea—you write a play about characters. I think it's the only way to write."

Also influenced by the writings of Federico García Lorca and Gabriel García Márquez, Cruz's "realism that is magic" veers into poetic chronicles of the harsh economic and political realities of Cuban life *sans* political agenda. "But what I'm interested in is the individual. I don't write with an agenda."[15]

Maria Irene Fornes, "The 'Woman' Playwright Issue," Performing Arts Journal, 7, No. 3 (1983): 91. Reprinted by permission.

©1999 Susan Johann

María Irene Fornés' *Drowning*
Two one-act plays *Mud* and *Drowning* opened the Signature Theatre's 1999–2000 retrospective of Fornés' work. In *Drowning*, Fornés explores the depths of the human soul as two men, with gestures of slow-moving underwater creatures, grapple with self-awareness and the limits of human compassion. Directed by David Esbjornson, Signature Theatre Company, Off Broadway.

TRANSITION

When the theatrical process starts with the playwright's script, the writer becomes the most essential artist in the collaboration. The playwright sets forth the play's world—its events, people, dialogue, and meaning—and places the playscript in the hands of director, designers, and actors. Endlessly fascinating are the playwright's tools, conventions, forms, and writing styles. The writer's creative strategies are the subjects of the next three chapters.

THEATRE: A WAY OF SEEING ONLINE

Visit the CourseMate for Theatre: A Way of Seeing 7th Edition for quick access to the digital study resources that accompany this chapter, including links to the websites listed below, Theatre Workshop, digital glossary, a chapter quiz and more.

Websites

The *Theatre: A Way of Seeing* CourseMate includes links for all the websites described below. Simply select "Web links" from the Chapter Resources for Chapter 4, and click on the link that interests you. You'll be taken directly to the site described.

Alex Catalogue of Electronic Texts
A collection of public domain documents from American and English literature and Western philosophy.

Google Directory of Gay and Lesbian Theatre
Dozens of links to information about gay and lesbian actors, playwrights, and theatre companies.

African American Theatre Companies
Links to professional and nonprofit theatre companies and organizations that present works from primarily an Afrocentric point of view.

Asian American Theatre Revue
Dozens of links to Asian American theatre companies, student theatre groups, performance artists, actors, and playwrights.

Association of Hispanic Arts
Your ticket to the Latino arts experience! Links to information, events, and job opportunities.

Dramatic Exchange
A web-based script exchange site where playwrights can post unpublished scripts and where readers and producers can look for plays.

The Dramatists Guild of America
Home page of the professional association of playwrights, composers, and lyricists.

National Endowment for the Arts (NEA)
Home page of the most well-known sources of public funding for the arts. Links to news, information about grants, and other resources.

The Eugene O'Neill Theater Center
A learning community dedicated to advancing the American theatre through programs that encourage creative excellence and develop diverse voices and new work.

The United States Copyright Office
The place to go to have your plays copyrighted.

5

THEATRICAL WRITING: PERSPECTIVES AND FORMS

If art reflects life it does so with special mirrors.[1]

—BERTOLT BRECHT, *A SHORT ORGANUM FOR THE THEATRE*

DRAMA'S PERSPECTIVES

Through the centuries, playwrights have developed ways of imitating behavior in a variety of dramatic forms and styles. Bertolt Brecht called them "special mirrors." Drama's forms have changed as societies and perceptions of the world have changed. This is what Peter Brook means when he says that every theatrical form, once born, is mortal.[2] Drama's forms fall into many categories: *tragedy, comedy, tragicomedy, melodrama, farce, epic,* and *absurd*.

Drama's essential forms are ways of viewing and understanding human experience. The words *tragedy, comedy,* and *tragicomedy* are not so much ways of classifying plays by their endings as ways of talking about the playwright's vision of experience—of the way he or she perceives life and its outcomes. The content and endings also furnish clues about how the play is to be taken or understood by audiences. Is the play a serious statement about, say, relationships between men and women or parents and children? Does it explore issues of gender and sexual orientation? Does it despair at the possibilities of mutual understanding? Or does it hold such attempts up to ridicule? Or does it explore humanity's unchanging existential situation?

PREVIEW

Playwrights use a variety of dramatic forms to express their understanding of human experience. Tragedy and comedy are the oldest and most familiar forms, but there are many other ways to classify plays and to label the playwright's vision—the way he or she perceives life in theatrical terms.

A reimagining of the blasted physical and moral landscape for Samuel Beckett's absurdist play *Happy Days* with Fiona Shaw as Winnie and directed by Deborah Warner, Brooklyn Academy of Music, New York.

TRAGEDY

It is not altogether simpleminded to say that a tragedy is a play with an unhappy ending. Tragedy, the first of the great dramatic forms in Western drama, makes a statement about human fallibility.

The Tragic Vision

The writer's tragic vision of experience conceives of people as both vulnerable and invincible, as capable of abject defeat and transcendent greatness. Tragedies such as *Oedipus the King*, *Medea*, *Hamlet*, *Ghosts*, *Death of a Salesman*, and *A Streetcar Named Desire* show the world's injustice, evil, and pain. Tragic heroes, in an exercise of free will, pit themselves against forces represented by other characters, by their own inner drives, or by their physical environment. We witness their suffering, their inevitable defeat, and sometimes, their personal triumph in the face of defeat. The trials of the hero give meaning to the pain and paradox of our humanity.

Some tragedies are concerned with seeking meaning and justice in an ordered world; others take up humanity's helpless protest against an irrational one. In both kinds, the hero, alone and willful, asserts his or her intellect and energy against the ultimate mysteries of an imperfect world.

In Sophocles's tragedy *Oedipus the King*, the hero is pitted against the workings of a supernatural order that is ruthless but not arbitrary or malevolent. Although the will of the gods is inscrutable, their predictions cannot be ignored or circumvented. In his search for the murderer of the old Theban king, Oedipus fulfills the gods' prophecy. In contrast, Euripides, arguably the most modern of the classical Greek writers, viewed humanity as victims of the irrationality of gods and humans alike.

The Tragic Realization

The realization (a *recognition* or *anagnorisis*) that follows the hero's failed efforts usually takes one of two directions for characters and audience: Despite suffering and calamity, a world order and eternal laws exist and people can learn from suffering; or human acts and suffering in an indifferent or capricious universe are futile, but at the same time the hero's protests against the nature of existence are to be admired. In *Oedipus the King* and *Medea*, we find examples of these two kinds of tragic realization in classical drama. In later plays, the consequences of human choice are less predictable and subject to arbitrary meaning.

Aristotle on Tragedy

In the first critical writing on drama in the West, called *The Poetics* (c. 335–323 BC), the Greek philosopher Aristotle spoke of tragedy as "an imitation of an action … concerning the fall of a man whose character is good (though not preeminently just or virtuous) … whose misfortune is brought about not by vice or depravity but by some error or frailty … with incidents arousing pity and fear, wherewith to accomplish the catharsis of these emotions."[3]

Aristotle emphasized the preeminence of plot over character and defined tragedy's action as an imitation of a well-meaning hero who makes a mistake and experiences a downfall, suffering, and even death. The heroes of ancient tragedies were usually aristocrats, to show that even the great among us are subject to the fate of the human condition. In modern plays, the hero's averageness speaks to us of kinship in adversity. Willie Loman, the father in *Death of a Salesman*, and Amanda Wingfield, the mother in *The Glass Menagerie*, are familiar parental figures whose lives go terribly wrong as they struggle to make a better life for their children.

FOCUS ON THEATRE

Sophocles's *Oedipus the King*

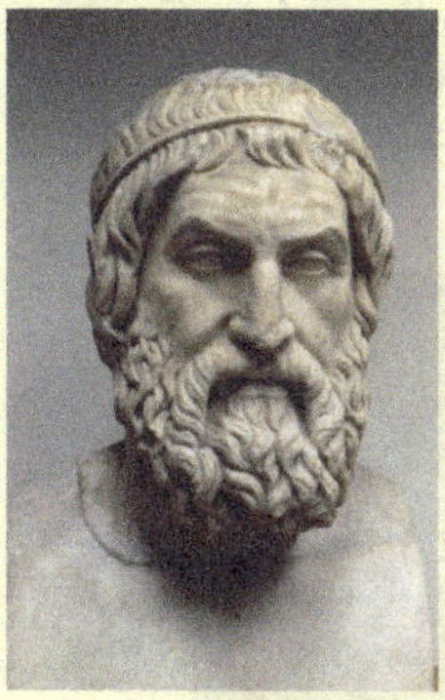

©The Bridgeman Art Library/Getty Images

One of several Greek playwrights whose work survives today, Sophocles wrote three plays about Oedipus and the House of Thebes. *Oedipus the King* (427 BC) is generally considered the greatest of Greek tragedies. (*Antigone* [441 BC] and *Oedipus at Colonus* [406 BC] are the other two.)

Oedipus the King tells the story of a man who flees from Corinth to avoid fulfilling a prophecy that he will kill his father and marry his mother. On his journey, at a place where three roads meet, he kills an old man (an apparent stranger but actually his real father, the king of Thebes). He then proceeds to Thebes and solves the riddle of the sphinx. As a reward, he is made king and married to the widowed queen, Jocasta, who is actually his mother. He rules well and has four children.

The play opens with Thebes stricken by a plague. Declaring that he will rid the city of this affliction, Oedipus sends his brother-in-law Creon to consult the Delphic oracle about the cause of the plague. As he pursues the plague's source, Oedipus comes face to face with himself as his father's killer, as his mother's son and husband, and as his children's father and brother. When the truth is learned, Jocasta kills herself and Oedipus puts out his eyes. By his own decree, Oedipus is exiled from Thebes and wanders blind, as a lowly beggar, into the countryside.

Oedipus the King explores human guilt and innocence, knowledge and ignorance, power and helplessness. Its fundamental idea is that wisdom comes to us only through suffering.

© Carol Rosegg

The Oedipus Plays

Avery Brooks as Oedipus in the production of *The Oedipus Plays* at the Shakespeare Theatre, Washington, D.C.

FOCUS ON PEOPLE IN THEATRE

PLAYWRIGHT

Euripides

©Gianni Dagli Orti/CORBIS

Euripides (c. 480–406 BC), one of three fifth-century BC writers of tragedy whose work survives today, won only five dramatic contests during his lifetime. Scholars attribute his relative unpopularity to his innovations with play structure and to the characters and subjects of his plays.

The son of aristocrats, Euripides held political office in Athens, where he became a member of the unpopular peace party during the Peloponnesian War and an opponent of Athenian imperialism. Toward the end of his life he sought exile at the court of Macedonia and died there, rumored to have been killed by the Macedonian king's hunting dogs.

Euripides is credited with writing eighty-eight plays (twenty-two sets of four), of which nineteen have survived. His best known are *Medea*, *Hippolytus*, *Electra*, *The Trojan Women*, and *The Bacchae*. His play *The Cyclops* is the only complete satyr play that now exists.

Aristotle, surveying Greek drama decades later, called Euripides the "most tragic of poets," presumably because of Euripides's dark materials: sexual repression, irrational violence, human madness, and savagery. Critics consider Euripides the most modern and innovative of the Greek tragic writers, for he speaks to audiences of the hero's demoralization and savagery and of the barbarity of armies at war.

© Joan Marcus

Euripides's Medea

Diana Rigg played Medea in the revival of Euripides's tragedy at the Almeida Theatre, London, and on Broadway.

Whether the hero is aristocratic or ordinary, his or her actions are shaped by the writer's tragic view of life, which focuses on the need to give meaning to our fate even though we are doomed to failure and defeat.

EURIPIDES'S *MEDEA* AS TRAGEDY

Produced in the City Dionysia festival (Athens) in 431 BC, Euripides's *Medea* tells the story of Jason's betrayal of his wife, Medea, to further his fortunes (and those of his two small sons) by marriage to the Princess of Corinth. The Athenian audience would have known the story of Medea, the barbarian princess and sorceress, related to the gods, who helped Jason and the Argonauts steal the Golden Fleece from her father. To help them escape, she murdered her brother and threw pieces of the body into the sea so that her father's pursuing fleet would be slowed in order to collect the fragments for burial.

With a background of violence, passion, and sorcery, Euripides's play begins in Corinth, where Jason and Medea have taken refuge. Whether because he wants to strengthen his economic and social position or because he has grown tired of his dangerous foreign wife, Jason decides to put her aside and marry the daughter of Creon, King of Corinth. At this point the action begins. Medea's jealous rage and desperate sense of betrayal by a husband for whom she sacrificed all spurs her revenge. She uses her magical powers to destroy both Creon and his daughter by means of a poisoned robe that clings to their flesh and melts them in a fiery death. Despairing of her children's safety and wishing to injure Jason totally, she kills her sons and escapes with their bodies in a supernatural chariot drawn by dragons to take refuge with the elderly Aegeus, King of Athens, who has promised asylum in exchange for her powers to restore his manhood.

Euripides uses the *Medea* story of unrequited love, unreasonable passion, and catastrophic revenge to depict a world where order is ever tenuous and where human beings are subject to the irrationality of gods and other humans. As the chorus says at the end in ironic explanation:

> ... *What we thought*
> *Is not confirmed and what we thought not God*
> *Contrives. And so it happens in this story.*

COMEDY

In the eighteenth century, Horace Walpole said, "The world is a comedy to those that think, a tragedy to those that feel." In comedy the playwright examines the social world, social values, and people as social beings. Frequently, comic action shows the social disorder created by an eccentric or foolish character who deviates from reasonable values such as sensibility, good nature, flexibility, moderation, tolerance, and social intelligence. Deviation is sharply ridiculed in comedy because it threatens to destroy revered social structures such as marriage and family.

Tragedy and comedy are two forms of dramatic writing that deal with the individual on the one hand and the social unit on the other. Comic action has consequences in the social world for the group; tragedy has consequences in the moral world for the individual. Central figures in comedy are usually a miser determined to hoard his money for all eternity or clever young lovers determined to marry despite the opposition of parents. Shakespeare, Molière, and Oscar Wilde wrote comedies of youthful determination and success in *As You Like It*, *The Miser*, and *The Importance of Being Earnest*.

The Importance of Being Earnest
Brian Bedford as Lady Bracknell in Oscar Wilde's *The Importance of Being Earnest*, Roundabout Theatre Company, NY.

The central figures in early comedy are usually ridiculous figures, such as the miser or the hypochondriac, who try for wholly selfish reasons to impede the happiness and well-being of others. Misers, hypocrites, fools, impostors, gluttons, and parasites are found in comedies dating from the days of the Greek and Roman writers Aristophanes and Menander. Later comedy centers on the high spirits and romance of young lovers who cleverly remove obstacles to their happiness by outwitting the rigid behavior and opposition of an older generation "set in their ways." Comedy, therefore, delights in entertaining with good-natured social criticism; for example, in Shakespeare's *A Midsummer Night's Dream*, Puck pronounces, "Lord, what fools these mortals be!"

Differences Between Tragedy and Comedy

Tragedy	Comedy	Tragedy	Comedy
Individual	Society	Terror	Euphoria
Metaphysical	Social	Unhappiness	Happiness
Death	Endurance	Irremediable	Remediable
Error	Folly	Decay	Growth
Suffering	Joy	Destruction	Continuation
Pain	Pleasure	Defeat	Survival
Life-denying	Procreative	Extreme	Moderation
Separation	Union/Reunion	Inflexible	Flexible

THE COMIC VISION

The writer of comedy calls for sanity, reason, and moderation in human behavior so that society can function for the well-being and happiness of its members. In comedy, society survives the threats posed by inflexible or antisocial behavior. In Molière's *Tartuffe* the title character's greed is revealed, and Orgon's family is returned to a normal, domestic existence at the play's end. For the seventeenth-century French playwright, as for some of his English contemporaries, the well-being of the family unit is a measure of the health of the society as a whole.

At the end of almost any comedy, the life force is ordinarily celebrated in a wedding, a dance, or a banquet symbolizing the harmony and reconciliation of opposing forces: young and old, flexible and inflexible, reasonable and unreasonable. These social ceremonies allow us to see that good sense wins the day in comedy and that humanity endures in the vital, the flexible, and the reasonable. Shakespeare said it another way: "All's well that ends well."

FOCUS ON PEOPLE IN THEATRE

PLAYWRIGHT

Molière

©Stock Montage/Getty Images

Molière (Jean-Baptiste Poquelin, 1622–1673), French playwright-actor-manager, was the son of Louis XIV's upholsterer. Poquelin spent his early years close to the court and received a gentleman's education. He joined a theatrical troupe in 1643 and became a professional actor with the stage name Molière. Molière helped found the Illustre Théâtre Company in Paris, which soon failed, and spent twelve years touring the French provinces as an itinerant actor and company playwright. He returned to Paris to become the foremost writer and comedian of his time. Within thirteen years (1659–1673), he wrote and acted in *Tartuffe*, *The Misanthrope*, *The Doctor in Spite of Himself*, *The Miser*, and *The Imaginary Invalid*. Written during France's golden age, Molière's comedies balance follies of eccentric and devious humanity against society's reasonable good sense.

Tartuffe (1664) is Molière's comedy about a hypocrite. Tartuffe disguises himself as a cleric, and his apparent piety ingratiates him with the gullible merchant Orgon and his mother, Madame Pernelle. As the play begins, Tartuffe has taken over Orgon's house. Both Orgon and his mother believe that Tartuffe's pious example will be good for the family. But everyone else in the family, including the outspoken servant Dorine, is perceptive enough to see through Tartuffe.

Despite the protests of his brother-in-law Cléante and his son Damis, Orgon determines that his daughter Marianne, who is in love with Valère, will marry Tartuffe. When Orgon's wife, Elmire, begs Tartuffe to refuse Marianne's hand in marriage, he tries to seduce her. Damis, who has overheard, denounces Tartuffe. Orgon banishes his son rather than his guest and signs over his property to Tartuffe.

Elmire then plots to expose the hypocrite. She persuades Orgon to conceal himself under a table while she encourages Tartuffe's advances. Orgon's eyes are opened, but it is too late. The impostor realizes he has been discovered and turns Orgon's family out of the house. He then reports to the authorities that Orgon has a strongbox containing seditious papers and contrives to have Orgon arrested. But, by the king's order, the arresting officer takes Tartuffe to prison instead.

The play ends with Damis reconciling to his father, Orgon reconciling with his family, and Valère and Marianne getting engaged.

©Jim Caldwell

Tartuffe

Tartuffe (James Black) attempts to seduce Elmire (Annalee Jefferies) in a revival of Molière's play at the Alley Theatre, Houston. Directed by Gregory Boyd in collaboration with the California-based Dell'Arte Players.

At the end of comedy, it is understood that a less rigid, freer society has been substituted for the old. Comedy's endings assure us that the newly married couple will live happily ever after or the reunited husband and wife will be more tolerant and forgiving of one another's foibles. The comic writer's vision attributes human error to folly, not to ill will or irremediable corruption, and celebrates human endurance and survival in unions and reunions.

TRAGICOMEDY

DEFINITIONS

Tragicomedy, as its name implies, is a mixed dramatic form. Up to the end of the seventeenth century in Europe, it was defined as a mixture of tragedy, which went from good fortune to bad, and comedy, which reversed the order from bad fortune to good. Tragicomedy combined serious and comic incidents as well as the styles, subject matter, and language proper to tragedy and to comedy, and it also mixed characters from all stations of life. The *ending* (up until the nineteenth century) was its principal feature: Tragicomedies were serious and potentially tragic plays with happy endings, or at least with averted catastrophes. Shakespeare's *All's Well That Ends Well* and *The Winter's Tale* are considered tragicomedies.

The term *modern tragicomedy* is used to designate plays with mixed moods in which the endings are neither exclusively tragic nor comic, happy nor unhappy. The great Russian playwright Anton Chekhov wrote plays of mixed moods in which he described the lives of "quiet desperation" of ordinary people in rural Russia around the turn of the twentieth century: provincial gentry, writers, professors, doctors, farmers, servants, teachers, government officials, and garrisoned military. What they had in common, finally, was their survival.

Chekhov's most frequently revived play, *The Three Sisters* (1901), tells of the provincial lives of the Prozorov family: three sisters (Olga, Masha, and Irina), their brother (Andrey), his wife (Natasha), their lovers, a brother-in-law, and military friends. The play's only action in the traditional sense is an offstage duel and the sounds of the departing military regiment from a small town after an interval of several years. For four acts the sisters dream of returning to Moscow to escape from the dull routine of their lives. But, unlike the regiment, they are unable to move on to new places and experiences.

As we scrutinize the seriocomic quality of Chekhov's play, a theme emerges: *the value of surviving in the face of social and economic change*. The three sisters are emotionally adrift in a society whose institutions supply avenues of change only for the soldier, the upstart, and the entrepreneur. The weak and ineffectual, such as the three sisters (and these women are products of their time), are locked into a way of life that is neither emotionally nor intellectually rewarding. The most that Chekhov's characters can do is endure the stultifying marriage, the routine job, and the tyrannical sister-in-law. But they survive. With no prescription for the future, Masha says only that "We've got to live."

FOCUS ON THEATRE

Anton Chekhov's *The Three Sisters*

©Time Life Pictures/Getty Images

Chekhov's most critically acclaimed work during his lifetime was first produced at the Moscow Art Theatre in 1901 with Olga Knipper as Masha, Konstantin Stanislavski as Lieutenant-Colonel Vershinin, and Vsevolod Meyerhold as Baron Tusenbach.

In a garrison town in rural Russia, the cultured Prozorov sisters think longingly of the excitement of Moscow, which they left eleven years earlier. Olga, the oldest, is constantly exhausted by her work as a schoolteacher; Masha, married at eighteen to a man she considered an intellectual giant, bitterly realizes that he is merely a pedant; Irina, the youngest, dreams of a romantic future and rejects the sincere love of Baron Tusenbach and the advances of Captain Solyony. Their brother, Andrey, an unambitious man, courts Natasha, the daughter of a local family. Into this circle comes Lieutenant-Colonel Vershinin. Like Masha, he is unhappily married. They are immediately attracted to one another.

The Prozorovs and their friends recognize the frustration of their lives, but hope in some vague future keeps their spirits high. For the sisters it is a dream of returning someday to Moscow. The situation changes when Andrey marries Natasha. The sisters' immediate prospects of returning to Moscow are dashed. Irina tries to find relief in her job in the telegraph office. Natasha takes control of the household, and as time goes on, the sisters are moved into smaller quarters to make room for her two children. Andrey takes refuge in gambling and mortgages the house that is owned jointly by him and his sisters.

News that the garrison is to be transferred brings depressing prospects for the future. Irina decides to marry Tusenbach, an unattractive but gentle man, who resigns his army commission in the hope of finding more meaningful work. As Masha and Vershinin, who have become open lovers, bid each other goodbye and the regiment prepares to leave, word comes that Tusenbach has been killed by Solyony in a duel over Irina. The sisters cling to one another for consolation. As the military band strikes up, the gaiety of the music inspires them to hope that there is a new life in store for them in another "millennium."

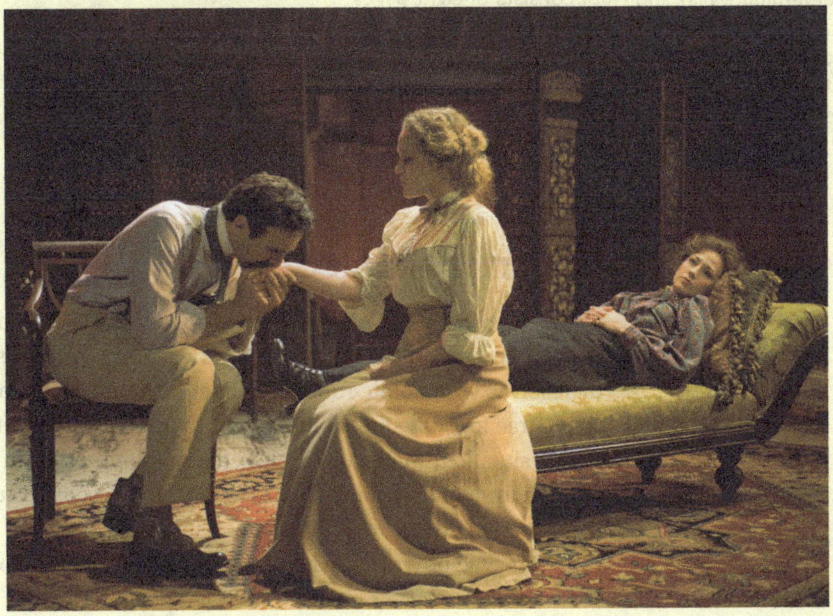

©Michael Brosilow

Anton Chekov's *The Three Sisters*
A revival of Chekov's *The Three Sisters* with Derek Gaspuh, Caroline Weff, and Carrie Coon, Steppenwolf Theatre Company, Chicago.

FOCUS ON PEOPLE IN THEATRE

PLAYWRIGHT

Samuel Beckett

©AFP/Getty Images

Samuel Beckett (1906–1989) was an expatriate Irishman who lived in France. Beckett grew up near Dublin and attended Trinity College, where he received two degrees in literature and began a teaching career. In the 1930s, Beckett left his teaching position, traveled in Europe, published his first book (*More Pricks Than Kicks*), and wrote poetry in French. During the Second World War, he worked with the French Resistance and barely escaped capture by the Nazis.

Beginning in 1953, Beckett wrote some thirty theatrical pieces, including radio plays, mime sketches, monologues, and four full-length plays (*Waiting for Godot*, *Endgame*, *Krapp's Last Tape*, *Happy Days*), which have become modern classics.

Beckett's last plays were minimal. *Come and Go* is a three-minute play, *Breath* is a thirty-second play, *Rockaby* is a fifteen-minute play, and *Not I* consists of eight pages of text. With these brief pieces Beckett constructed a theatrical image of how we come and go on this earth, briefly filling a void with our bodies and voices, and then disappear into darkness without a trace.

©Sara Krulwich/The New York Times/Redux

Samuel Beckett's *Waiting for Godot*
From left to right, Nathan Lane, John Goodman, and Bill Irwin in Samuel Beckett's *Waiting for Godot*, directed by Anthony Page, at Studio 54, New York City.

MODERN TRAGICOMEDY

Samuel Beckett subtitled *Waiting for Godot* a "tragicomedy," though it is also considered an enduring absurdist play of modern times. In this play, two tramps entertain themselves with comic routines while they wait in a sparse landscape adorned by a single tree for someone named Godot to arrive. But Godot never comes. As they react to this situation, their humor and energy are mixed with anguish and despair. In the modern form of tragicomedy, playwrights show people laughing at their anxieties and life's contradictions with little effect on their situations. Beckett's Vladimir summarizes this type of writing when he says, "The essential doesn't change."

FOCUS ON PEOPLE IN THEATRE

PLAYWRIGHT

Tony Kushner

©Brad Barket/Wireimage/Getty Images

Tony Kushner (b. 1956) grew up in Lake Charles, Louisiana, where his father, a professional musician, managed a lumber company that the family inherited. Kushner holds degrees (BA and MFA) from Columbia University in medieval studies and from New York University in directing. He wrote his first play, *A Bright Room Called Day*, in the 1980s and followed with *Angels in America: A Gay Fantasia on National Themes*. The first part (*Millennium Approaches*), staged by George C. Wolfe, reached Broadway in 1993 and won the Pulitzer Prize for Drama and four "Tony" Awards. The second part (*Perestroika*) opened later in that year and won another "Tony" Award for best play.

Kushner is a prolific writer and director. In addition to writing full-length plays, he has written essays, one-acts, screenplays, and libretti and has adapted plays by Corneille, Goethe, and Brecht. Recent works to receive favorable critical attention are *Homebody/Kabul; Caroline, or Change* (with book and lyrics by Kushner and music by Jeanine Tesori); and *The Intelligent Homosexual's Guide to Capitalism and Socialism with a Key to the Scriptures*. The film version of *Angels in America* premiered on HBO, and an opera version was staged in Paris in 2004.

© Joan Marcus

Tony Kushner's *Angels in America*
The Angel (Ellen McLaughlin) appears with spreading wings to Prior Walter (Stephen Spinella) at the end of *Millennium Approaches*, Part One of *Angels in America*.

Modern "American" Tragicomedy

The American tradition of writing tragicomedy, inherited from Henrik Ibsen and George Bernard Shaw, dramatizes contradictions in a realistic world of front yards, kitchens, living rooms, and bedrooms haunted by visions of apocalyptic angels. In the last decades of the twentieth century, playwrights expressed a tragicomic vision of the human condition with comic characters that were amusing and serious without being foolish and superficial. In Sam Shepard's *Buried Child* and August Wilson's *Fences*, central characters die, but the writers affirm humanity's endurance despite anguish, loss, and little potential for personal or social change. In Shepard's mid-western farmhouse, Hallie, the wife and mother, sees from the upstairs window magical crops growing in a barren field as a sign that the unearthing of a terrible crime (child murder) has lifted the family curse. Wilson's *Fences* shifts the emphasis to the younger generation. Troy Maxson's children—Lyons, Corey, and Raynell—experience at the play's end shifting winds of change blowing them into the turbulent new decade of the 1960s.

In the writing of *Angels in America*, Tony Kushner transcends the static endings characteristic of modern tragicomedy inherited from the plays of Chekhov, Ionesco, and Beckett. Kushner's darkly comic resolution transcends the devastations of disease, drug-induced utopias, dysfunctional families, and corrupt politicians. At the close of *Angels in America: Millennium Approaches*, a messenger appears, and Part One ends with what one critic called "luminous ambiguity."[4] Unlike Beckett's messenger in *Waiting for Godot*, who announces that Godot will not come today but "to-morrow," Kushner's messenger arrives to the sounds of beating wings and crashing ceiling to announce that "The Great Work begins." By using the arrival of the angelic messenger, Kushner cancels out the indeterminate endings of modern tragicomedy inherited from Samuel Beckett. His writing over the two parts of *Angels in America* thrusts the idea of social change into a transformative theatre of people, politics, history, dreams, fantasies, and angelic hosts.

In Part Two, called *Perestroika*, meaning "peaceful change," Kushner's dramatic world spins forward with the living, redeemed not by prophets but by the guarded optimism of ordinary human "angels" who champion tolerance, compliance, forgiveness, and hope for humankind.

MELODRAMA

Another mixed form, melodrama derives its name from the Greek word for music, *melos*. It is a combination of music and drama in which the spoken word is used against a musical background. Jean-Jacques Rousseau, who introduced the term's modern use in 1772, applied it to his *Pygmalion*, a *scène lyrique* in which words and music were linked in action.

The Mixed Form

Melodrama became widely used in the nineteenth century to describe a play without music but with a serious action usually caused by the villainy of an unsympathetic character. Melodrama's characters are clearly divided—either sympathetic or unsympathetic—and the villain's destruction brings about the happy resolution. Melodrama usually shows a main character in circumstances that threaten death or ruin from which he or she is rescued at the last possible moment. Like a film's musical score, incidental stage music can heighten the mood of impending disaster.

The term *melodrama* is most often applied to such nineteenth-century plays as *Uncle Tom's Cabin* (1852), based on Harriet Beecher Stowe's novel, and Dion Boucicault's *The Octoroon* (1859). Today, we apply the term to such diverse plays as Lillian Hellman's *The Little Foxes*, Lorraine Hansberry's *A Raisin in the Sun*, Sarah Ruhl's *In the Next Room or the Vibrator Play* and to such thrillers as *Sleuth* and *The Woman in Black*.

FOCUS ON THEATRE

Lillian Hellman's *The Little Foxes*

The Little Foxes, written by Lillian Hellman in 1938–1939, is a quintessential melodrama. The play takes place in the American South in 1900 and concerns the wealthy Hubbards, a prosperous family eager to parlay their success as merchants and bankers into vast industrial wealth. "To bring the machines to the cotton, and not the cotton to the machines," as Ben Hubbard says. Regina Hubbard Gibbons is the powerful villainess of a play that demonstrates the corrosive consequences of money and lust.

To compete with her brothers, Oscar and Ben, Regina must persuade her dying husband, Horace Gibbons, to invest one-third interest in their get-rich-quick scheme. Because of a heart condition, Horace has been in a Baltimore hospital. Regina sends their daughter Alexandra to bring him home so that Regina can invest his Union Pacific bonds in the scheme. Horace arrives but refuses to advance the money. Her brothers tell Regina they will go elsewhere for another business partner, although they would prefer not to bring in an outsider. When the brothers learn from Leo—Ben's son who works in the bank that holds Horace's bonds—that the bonds could be "borrowed" from the bank strongbox without fear of discovery, they take the bonds and tell Regina she's out of the deal. When Horace discovers the bonds are missing and learns of his wife's manipulations, he says he will claim that he loaned the bonds to his brothers-in-law. Regina's scathing verbal attack on Horace brings on his fatal heart attack. Because his death will eliminate her problems and make her rich, she stands immobile while he pleads with her for his medicine. She watches his desperate but futile struggle to climb the stairs to reach his medicine.

With her husband's death, Regina now owns the bonds, and she is once again victorious. Regina blackmails her brothers into giving her seventy-five percent interest in the venture for her unauthorized "investment." Their alternative is jail. Alexandra, who suspects Regina's complicity in her father's death, voices her disgust and leaves home, but this is only a dim shadow on the bright horizon of Regina's future.

Hellman's scenes turn on theft, blackmail, sudden and unexpected shifts of fortune, unrelenting greed, and major changes in the balance of power in the Hubbard money game. The play's characters range from the genteel Birdie Hubbard and naive Alexandra to the "little foxes that spoil the vines"—the vicious and manipulative Regina, Ben, and Oscar Hubbard.

Hellman does not attempt to deepen our understanding of society or of human values. Rather, she shows evil in conflict with evil and the good and decent as merely impotent onlookers. The fascination with Regina's manipulations and her victory over her pernicious brothers stimulate audiences into applauding her resourcefulness and withholding moral judgment before her wit, glamour, and cunning.

The Everett Collection

The Little Foxes

Lillian Hellman's *The Little Foxes*. with Tallulah Bankhead and Carl Benton Reid.

Melodrama's View of Life

The melodramatic view of life sees human beings as whole, not divided; enduring outer conflicts, not inner ones, in a generally hostile world; and sees these conflicts resulting in victory or defeat as they are pressed to extreme conclusions. Melodrama's characters win or lose in the conflict. The endings are clear-cut and extreme. There are no complex and ambiguous resolutions, as when Hamlet wins in the losing. Replying to critics complaining of her melodramatic plots, Lillian Hellman said, "If you believe, as the Greeks did, that man is at the mercy of the gods, then you write tragedy. The end is inevitable from the beginning. But if you believe that man can solve his own problems and is at nobody's mercy, then you will probably write melodrama."[5]

Melodrama oversimplifies, exaggerates, and contrives experience. In short, melodrama is the dramatic form that expresses the truth of the human condition as we perceive it most of the time. We have our victories, but we attribute our "accidents" or failures to external factors, or to the faults of others.

FARCE

Farce (from a Latin word meaning "stuffing" in its culinary sense) is best described as a punch-drunk comedy of situation in which plot depends upon a skillfully exploited situation rather than upon character development. We use the word to describe real-life encounters with the ridiculous or the unexpected and often say in mockery, "It's a farce!" In films and plays, farce is associated with such physical

The Frogs
A modern revival of *The Frogs* by Aristophanes with Nathan Lane as Dionysus observing the ensemble of frogs in costumes designed by William Ivey Long, Vivian Beaumont Theatre, Lincoln Center Theatre Company, New York.

humor as pies in the face, harmless beatings, mistaken identities, slips on banana peels—exaggerated physical activities growing out of situations.

Writers of farce present life as mechanical, aggressive, and coincidental; they entertain us with seemingly endless variations on a single situation. A bedroom crowded with concealed lovers as the cuckolded husband or deceived wife arrives on the scene is a typical farcical situation devised by the popular French playwright Georges Feydeau, with variations by Broadway's Neil Simon in *The Odd Couple* and London's Michael Frayn in *Noises Off*. In *Loot* and *Jumpers*, Joe Orton and Tom Stoppard entertain with devices of corpses "concealed in plain sight" as people come and go, blithely ignorant of the bodies present. Stoppard's *Jumpers* has been described as a "metaphysical" farce wherein a professor of moral philosophy repeatedly tries to compose a lecture on "Man—Good, Bad or Indifferent" while surrounded by acrobats (the Jumpers of the title) and his girlfriend, an ex-musical comedy star.

Farce has been part of theatre since the time of ancient Greece and Rome. In *The Frogs*, Aristophanes used the Greek chorus as rollicking frogs to debate the merits of plays by Aeschylus and Euripides (Aeschylus wins); Shakespeare introduced pranksters and tipplers in *A Midsummer Night's Dream* and *Much Ado About Nothing*; and commedia dell'arte players in the Italian Renaissance entertained with antics of pranksters, knaves, and self-satisfied fools with names such as Harlequin, Brighella, Dottore, and Pantalone. In general, farce's characters are broad outlines of the ludicrous in human behavior. They are monuments to human stupidity and mischievousness—reminders that fools and impostors are part of the human condition along with the sensible, virtuous, and noble.

THE "PSYCHOLOGY" OF FARCE

The "psychology" of farce, as Eric Bentley calls it, is that special opportunity for the vicarious fulfillment of our unmentionable wishes without having to take responsibility for our actions or suffer guilt for our transgressions.[6] As a popular dramatic form, farce gives us a fantasy world of violence (without harm), adultery (without consequences), brutality (without reprisal), and aggression (without risk). Unlike comedy's concerns for social values, the fast-paced, topsy-turvy world of farce trips over social proprieties. It entertains with escapades that appeal to our secret thoughts and innermost fantasies. In Michael Frayn's *Noises Off*, a character summarizes the improbable confusions of farce: "That's what it's all about. Doors and sardines. Getting on—getting off. Getting the sardines on—getting the sardines off. That's farce. That's the theatre. That's life."

Today, we enjoy farce in the films of Charlie Chaplin, W. C. Fields, the Marx Brothers, Woody Allen, Steve Martin, Eddie Murphy, Queen Latifah, and the Coen Brothers; in the plays of Georges Feydeau, Neil Simon, Elaine May, Alan Ayckbourn, Michael Frayn, David Ives, and Steve Martin; and in the performances of The Flying Karamazov Brothers, Blue Man Group, Penn & Teller, Bill Irwin, and Robin Williams.

FOCUS ON PLAYS

David Ives's *Venus In Fur*

Venus in Fur, described as a spooky sex farce, portrays an unknown actress giving the audition of a lifetime. Chicago native David Ives has not written a creaky old farce involving philandering bosses and naughty secretaries. Rather, Ives, known for his short plays presented under the titles *All in the Timing* and *Time Flies*, has written the full-length *Venus in Fur*, a suspenseful study of the "erotics of power" in which the two participants—the writer-director hosting an audition and the presumably struggling young actress, who arrives to audition accompanied by a thunderclap—prove adept competitors in their power games.

The actress arrives hours late for her scheduled audition and launches into a description of the humiliating life of a struggling actress who has already heard that she's too "young," too "old," too "big," too "small," and her resumé is "not long enough." The actress's name is likewise the name of the female lead (Vanda) in the director's own adaptation of the 1870s novel, *Venus in Fur* by Leopold von Sacher-Masoch (for whom masochism was named), which he has been trying to cast without success during the afternoon. The novel is also the source of Ives's title for his farce about power games at auditions—and other contexts.

Ninety minutes after her arrival, the elusive Vanda (or Venus) has destabilized the traditional sexual roles along with the time-honored power relationship between stage director and actress in this unrelenting farce whose central mystery involves the motives and identity of the elusive actress.

Venus in Fur
Nina Arianda as the "actress" auditioning for Hugh Dancy as the writer-director in the Manhattan Theatre Club's production of *Venus in Fur*, New York City.

Society's Safety Valve

Farcical moments have always been part of the world's great comedies and enlivened the plays of Shakespeare, Molière, and Chekhov. Moreover, absurdist writers Eugène Ionesco and Samuel Beckett exploited farce's practical jokes to comment on existence itself as the ultimate joke played by a Creator on human beings. Describing his work in *Notes and Counter Notes*, Ionesco called farce "the extreme exaggeration of parody," which in its broad and outrageous effects takes us back to the "unendurable."[7] In the broad context of the theatre of the absurd, farce—the extended practical joke—is a means of calling attention to the plight of human beings in a universe that has lost its meaning and purpose.

© Joan Marcus

***The Chairs* by Eugène Ionesco**
The Broadway production, with Geraldine McEwan and Richard Briers, directed by Simon McBurney.

In Ionesco's *The Chairs*, subtitled a "tragic farce," an elderly man and woman frantically fill an empty stage with chairs for imaginary guests to occupy and listen to a lecture by an Orator. Once the stage is filled with chairs and the Orator arrives, the couple fling themselves out of windows into a watery grave. Only then do we learn that the Orator is mute, unable to deliver an intelligible message on the meaning of life. Our bitter and puzzled laughter at the practical joke is Ionesco's way of using the tools of farce to demonstrate his view of a world without meaning. The hurly-burly of Ionesco's farce is also a way for audiences to contemplate grave issues without being asked for serious reflection at the time.

Beginning with early Greek and Roman plays, farce has been a way for audiences to indulge antisocial wishes for revenge (against the overbearing mother-in-law), aggression (against the school-yard bully), and offense (against all-too-proper rules of etiquette). It is one of drama's forms demonstrating how situations become hopelessly entangled until some amazing reversal frees the characters from harm—until their next escapade. In this context, farce is a safety valve in which we can vicariously indulge our antisocial thoughts in the hilarity of the situation. In effect, farce is a safety valve for audiences to partake of unmentionable desires without risk to themselves and harm to others.

FOCUS ON THEATRE

Stage Adaptations

The current explosion of interest in adapting nondramatic materials for the stage is not so much related to the availability of new plays as to the desire of theatrical artists and companies to create their own texts from nondramatic works familiar to audiences as readers. The novels of Charles Dickens, with their wealth of dramatic incident and social detail, have been prime properties for adaptation; for example, *A Christmas Carol*, *The Life and Adventures of Nicholas Nickleby*, *David Copperfield*, and *Great Expectations* have successfully been translated to the stage.

One method of adapting novels to the stage is to retain the novel's narrative voice (with actors serving as narrators or storytellers). The aim is to blend narrative techniques (descriptions, comments, interior monologues) with dramatic ones (characters talking to one another). In some cases, social documents relevant to the story are read aloud; for example, original trial transcripts and newspaper accounts are included in Moisés Kaufman's *Gross Indecency: The Three Trials of Oscar Wilde*. Descriptions are sometimes included and introduced with "he said" or "she said."

Playwright Moisés Kaufman said that he wanted to tell the story of Oscar Wilde's three trials and explore how the theatre can reconstruct history. To achieve both goals, he combined details from Wilde's life and historical documents to tell the story of the playwright's descent from the darling of London's theatre world in the 1890s, with two plays (*An Ideal Husband* and *The Importance of Being Earnest*) running simultaneously in West End theatres, to convicted felon imprisoned for two years at hard labor. In the third trial, Wilde was convicted of having sexual relations with young men (called "gross indecency" in the legal language of Victorian England), and the dramatic text made use of transcripts from the 1895 trials as centerpieces of the action. Moreover, nine actors played the narrators, journalists, friends, accusers, and historical characters (Oscar Wilde, Marquess of Queensberry, Sir Edward Clarke, Edward Carson, Lord Alfred Douglas). In all, the various accounts by the people involved told a complicated, often contradictory, story of an artist's defense of his art in a Victorian court of law.

The Elevator Repair Service, an Off Broadway company pushing theatrical boundaries since its founding in 1991 in Fort Green, Brooklyn, has translated from page to stage such American novels as William Faulkner's *The Sound and the Fury* and F. Scott Fitzgerald's *The Great Gatsby* under the title *Gatz*. Founding director John Collins aims to stage classic novels without altering the text with a consistent team of a dozen performers who take turns reading the novel aloud at rehearsals, speaking the dialogue, and acting out scenes to get a sense of how the text sounds onstage. Of the company's work it has been pointed out that contemporary theatre is not necessarily made the traditional way with a writer seated at a computer, working on a script. The Elevator Repair Service introduces a new collaborative process that, in terms of stage adaptations, is becoming more prevalent in the creative landscape.

© Joan Marcus

Gross Indecency: The Three Trials of Oscar Wilde
Michael Emerson was Oscar Wilde in the Off Broadway production of *Gross Indecency: The Three Trials of Oscar Wilde*.

©Sara Krulwich/The New York Times/Redux

Gatz
The Elevator Repair Service's seven-hour production of *Gatz* at the New York Shakespeare Festival/Public Theatre, helmed by Oscar Eustis. A dispute over the rights to the novel in 2008 prevented the company from performing the work for a second time in New York until 2012.

FOCUS ON PEOPLE IN THEATRE

PLAYWRIGHT

Bertolt Brecht

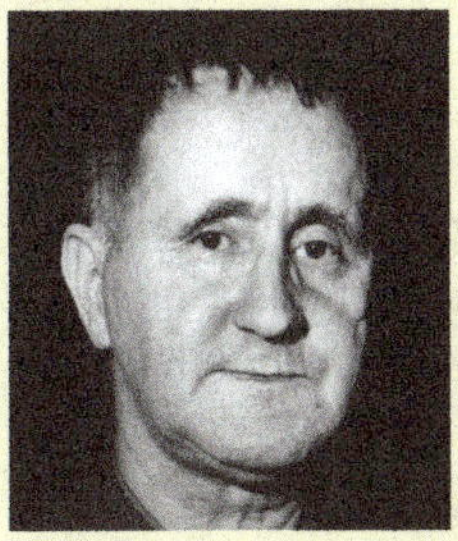

©Mondadon/Getty Images

Bertolt Brecht (1898–1956) was born in Augsburg, Germany, where he spent his early years. In 1918, while studying medicine at Munich University, he was called up for military service as a medical orderly. He began writing poems about the horrors of war. His first play, *Baal*, dates from this period.

After the First World War, Brecht drifted as a student into the bohemian world of theatre and literature, singing his poetry in Munich taverns and coffeehouses. By 1921, Brecht had seriously entered the German theatre as a reviewer and playwright. During the 1920s in Berlin, Brecht became a Marxist, wrote plays, and solidified his theories of epic theatre. *The Threepenny Opera* (1928)—produced in collaboration with the composer Kurt Weill—was an overnight success and made both Brecht and Weill famous.

With the rise of the Nazi movement, many German artists and intellectuals left Germany. Brecht and his family fled in 1933, first to Sweden and then to the United States, where he lived until 1947. In October 1947, Brecht was subpoenaed to appear in Washington, D.C., before the U.S. House Committee on Un-American Activities to testify on "Communist infiltration" of the motion-picture industry. He left the United States the day following his testimony, eventually settling in East Berlin, where he founded the Berliner Ensemble. This theatre company continues to perform his works today at the Theater am Schiffbauerdamm, where he first staged *The Threepenny Opera*. Brecht's greatest plays date from his years of exile (1933–1948): *The Good Person of Setzuan*, *Mother Courage and Her Children*, *Life of Galileo*, and *The Caucasian Chalk Circle*.

©Richard Feldman

Bertolt Brecht's *The Good Person of Setzuan*

Directed by Andrei Serban with music by Elizabeth Swados, at the American Repertory Theatre, Cambridge (MA). Like Brecht's *The Caucasian Chalk Circle*, this play combines a nonillusionistic performance style with the statement that it is hard for human beings to reconcile instincts for goodness with the need for economic survival.

EPIC THEATRE

Bertolt Brecht, the director and playwright who greatly influenced our postwar theatre, reacted against Western traditions of the well-made play and pictorial illusion. Over a lifetime, he adapted methods from Erwin Piscator (who pioneered the docudrama for German working-class audiences in the twenties), films, Chinese opera, Japanese Noh staging, English chronicle history plays, and music-hall routines to create "epic" theatre.

THE EPIC PLAY

When Brecht spoke of *epic* theatre, he was thinking of plays as *episodic* and *narrative*: as a sequence of incidents or events narrated without artificial restrictions as to time, place, or formal plot. Play structure was more like that of a narrative poem than of a well-made play having a beginning, middle, and end.

Because Brecht wanted to represent historical process in the theatre and have it judged critically by audiences, he departed from many time-honored theatrical traditions. First, he thought of the stage as a platform on which political and social issues could be debated. He rejected the idea that a play should be "well made," reminding us that history does not end but moves on from episode to episode. Why should plays do otherwise? Brecht's plays therefore were a series of loosely knit scenes, each complete in itself. The effect was achieved through the juxtaposition of contrasting *episodes*. The nonliterary elements of production—music, acting style, lighting, sound, and moving scenery—also retained their separate identities. His epic play is, therefore, *historical, narrative, episodic*, and highly *theatrical*. It treats humans as social beings in their economic, social, and political milieus.

Brecht's characters are both individuals and collective beings. This type of characterization dates to the morality plays of the late Middle Ages, in which "Everyman" is both a recognizable individual and a representative of all human beings.

In Brecht's plays, character emerges from the individual's social function and changes with that function. In keeping with the idea that the theatre is a platform to discuss political and social issues, theatrical language is discursive and polemical.

EPIC THEATRE AS EYEWITNESS ACCOUNT

Early in his career, Brecht admonished actors not to regard themselves as impersonating or becoming characters so much as narrating the actions of people in a particular time, place, and situation. The model he used to demonstrate this approach was the behavior of an eyewitness to a traffic accident.

In retelling the event, eyewitnesses clearly differentiate between themselves and the victim, although they may reconstruct the victim's reactions and gestures. So, too, Brecht argued, actors clearly differentiate between themselves as actors and the characters in the play. The eyewitness never *becomes* the victim. He further explained:

> It is comparatively easy to set up a basic model for epic theatre. For practical experiments I usually picked as my example of completely simple "natural"

> epic theatre an incident such as can be seen at any street corner: an eyewitness demonstrating to a collection of people how a traffic accident took place. The bystanders may not have observed what happened, or they may simply not agree with him, may "see things a different way"; the point is that the demonstrator acts the behavior of driver or victim or both in such a way that the bystanders are able to form an opinion about the accident.[8]

In Brecht's theatre, the actor did not "become" the character as in Konstantin Stanislavski's approach to acting; rather, actors "demonstrated" the characters' attitudes while retaining freedom to comment (with attitude and gesture) on the actions of the person whose behavior they were displaying. This device of the actor as eyewitness to the play's events was also part of Brecht's efforts to distance or "alienate" the audience emotionally from what was happening onstage.

©Erich Auerbach/Getty Images

The Threepenny Opera
From the original 1928 production of Bertolt Brecht's and Kurt Weill's *The Threepenny Opera* at the Theater am Schiffbauerdamm in Berlin, Germany.

©Sara Krulwich/The New York Times/Redux

The Threepenny Opera
From the 2011 New York production of *The Threepenny Opera* as reinterpreted by director Robert Wilson with Stefan Kurt (seated left) and Stefanie Stappenbeck (seated right).

---

[8] Brecht on Theatre, tranls. John Willett. Translation ©1964, renewed 1992 by John Willett. Reprinted by permission of Hill and Wang, a division of Farrar, Straus & Giroux, LLC.

FOCUS ON THEATRE

Bertolt Brecht's *Life of Galileo*

The seventeenth-century Italian astronomer and physicist Galileo Galilei (1564–1642) challenged prevailing notions of religion and science by suggesting that Earth was not the center of the universe but rather revolved around the sun. Subjected to a court of the Inquisition, he recanted his theory. Literally under house arrest for the remainder of his life, he secretly wrote his great scientific work, the *Discorsi*, which was smuggled out of Italy and ultimately changed the course of modern science.

Brecht wrote two versions of his play (*The Earth Moves* and *Galileo*) during the thirties and forties; the third version, titled *Life of Galileo*, was performed at the Berliner Ensemble in former East Berlin shortly after the playwright's death. Why did the Galileo story so intrigue the playwright? First, the scientist was a sensuous, intellectual man who outsmarted reactionary authority; and second, he presented Brecht with a way of looking at twentieth-century social, scientific, and political issues. In laying the foundations of modern science, Galileo had indulged his pleasures in food and drink and in scientific experimentation and discovery. Nothing else mattered. For Galileo's dismissal of ethical and social responsibility, Brecht, living in the nuclear age, condemned his hero.

Life of Galileo, written in the epic style with fourteen scenes, moves toward a turning point with the recantation scene (scene 12) in which, under threat of torture by religious authorities, Galileo recants his theories when he is merely shown the instruments of torture. Brecht struggled with his growing dislike of Galileo's choices 300 years earlier and his disgust with modern scientific-industrial-political systems of power that resulted in the creation and use of the atomic bomb in 1945. His flawed hero explains to his pupil Andrea Sarti that he failed his ethical responsibilities to humankind:

> As a scientist I had an almost unique opportunity.... I surrendered my knowledge to the powers that be, to use it, no, not use it, abuse it, as it suits their ends. I betrayed my profession. Any man who does what I have done must not be tolerated in the ranks of science. (scene 13)

In epic style, *Life of Galileo* draws historical material from seventeenth-century Italy to remind audiences of repressive governments and totalitarian regimes in modern times. Each scene in a loosely connected series begins with titles, or legends, written on placards and suspended above the stage or with other images projected on screens. Brecht's use of alienation (or distancing) devices has its clear purpose. Brecht argued that theatre should not treat contemporary social and political problems directly. By placing similar events from the historical past onstage, Brecht helps the audience see the parallels between past and present and understand what actions should have been taken in the past (and were not). By observing the failures of the past, audiences can see how to correct social and political problems in the present. Brecht's harsh view of the historical Galileo parallels his even harsher view of scientific progress based upon science's subservience to the state. Revising his play twice (between 1945 and 1956), Brecht was convinced that the development of the atomic bomb in Los Alamos, New Mexico—which was then used for military purposes over the Japanese cities of Hiroshima and Nagasaki—effectively placed science at the disposal of nonscientific people to serve their power politics.

Brecht's use of the stage as platform to confront ethical issues of modern science in the guise of Galileo's life and times effectively addressed present-day arguments on nuclear proliferation and global annihilation.

Life of Galileo
With F. Murray Abraham as Galileo, from the Classic Stage Company production of Brecht's play, directed by Brian Kulick, Off Broadway.

The Alienation Effect

Brecht called this jarring of the audience out of its sympathetic feelings for what is happening onstage his alienation effect (sometimes called *A-effect* or *Verfremdungseffekt*). He wanted to prevent the audience's empathetic "willing suspension of disbelief" and force them to look at everything in a fresh light and, above all, to think. Brecht wanted audiences to absorb his social criticism and to carry new insights out of the theatre into their own lives.

Brecht was certainly aware of the entertainment value of theatre. For Brecht, pleasure in the theatre came from observing accounts of past situations, discovering new truths, and enlarging upon an understanding of the present. What he opposed was a theatre solely of catharsis (what he called "culinary" theatre), where the audience lost its critical detachment by identifying emotionally with the characters. All of the epic devices—music, loudspeakers, scenery, harsh lighting, placards, projections, acting style—reminded audiences that they were in a theatre, that the stage was a stage and not someone's living room.

ABSURDIST THEATRE

In 1961, Martin Esslin wrote a seminal book called *The Theatre of the Absurd* about trends in theatre following the Second World War. He used the label to describe new theatrical ways of looking at existence devised by postwar European writers.

Absurdist writers, such as Eugène Ionesco and Samuel Beckett, made their breakthrough in dramatic writing by *presenting*, without comment or moral judgment, situations showing life's irrationality. The common factors in the absurdist plays of Ionesco, Beckett, and others are unrecognizable plots, mechanical characters, situations resembling dreams and nightmares, and incoherent dialogue. The absurdist writer does not tell a story or discuss social problems. Instead, the playwright presents in concrete stage images, such as two tramps waiting for a figure named Godot who never shows up, *a sense of being* in an absurd universe.

Samuel Beckett's *Krapp's Last Tape*
John Hurt as Krapp listening to his voice captured on tape in past years. Issuing from the tape recorder is a youthful Krapp's vibrant voice full of aspirations that increasingly contrast with the voice of his wasted present. As Krapp tries to record his thoughts on life on his last remaining tape, he gives up in despair: "Nothing to say—not a squeak."

The Absurd

Absurdist playwrights begin with the premise that our world is *absurd*, meaning irrational, incongruous, and senseless. Albert Camus—a French philosopher, novelist, and playwright—diagnosed the human condition as absurd in a book of essays called *The Myth of Sisyphus*:

> A world that can be explained even with bad reasons is a familiar world. But, on the other hand, in a universe suddenly divested of illusions and lights, man feels an alien, a stranger. His exile is without remedy since he is deprived of the memory of a lost home or the hope of a promised land. This divorce between man and his life, the actor and his setting, is properly the feeling of absurdity.[9]

Ionesco defined *absurd* as "anything without a goal … when man is cut off from his religious or metaphysical roots, he is lost; all his struggles become senseless, futile and oppressive."[10] The meaning of Ionesco's plays is simply what happens onstage. The old man and old woman in *The Chairs* gradually fill the stage with an increasing number of empty chairs and address absent people in the chairs. At the play's end, the Orator comes forward to address the empty chairs, but he can neither hear nor speak and cannot make a coherent statement. The subject of Ionesco's play—the emptiness and absurdity of the world—is conveyed by the presence of the empty chairs.

Ionesco subtitled his first play, *The Bald Soprano* (written in 1949), "the tragedy of language." In it, he became one of the first to confront the absurdity of the universe with new dramatic techniques. This farce, like many of his early plays, demonstrates the emptiness of middle-class life in a world devoid of significant problems.

FOCUS ON PEOPLE IN THEATRE

PLAYWRIGHT

Eugène Ionesco

©Paris Match Archive via Getty Images

Eugène Ionesco (1912–1994) was a Rumanian-born schoolteacher and refugee from Nazism who lived in France until his death. He puzzled and outraged audiences with plays about bald sopranos, octogenarian suicides, homicidal professors, and human rhinoceroses as metaphors for the world's absurdity. Today, *The Bald Soprano*, *The Chairs*, *The Lesson*, and *Rhinoceros* are modern classics.

After *The Bald Soprano* was first produced in Paris at the Théâtre des Noctambules in 1950, Ionesco wrote more than thirty plays in addition to journals, essays, and children's stories. Ionesco's theatre expressed the malaise of contemporary life, language's failure to bring people closer together, the strangeness of existence, and a parodic reflection of the world. Breaking with the theatre of psychological realism, Ionesco pioneered a form of theatre closer to our dreams and nightmares.

FOCUS ON THEATRE

Eugène Ionesco's *The Bald Soprano*

The Bald Soprano is Ionesco's "antiplay," which dramatizes the absurdity of human existence. In 1948, while taking a course in conversational English, Ionesco conceived the idea of using many of the practice sentences to create a theatre piece.

Mr. and Mrs. Smith talk in clichés about the trivia of everyday life. The meaninglessness of their existence is caricatured in dialogue in which each member of a large family, living and dead, regardless of age or sex, is called Bobby Watson. Mr. and Mrs. Martin enter. They converse as strangers but gradually discover they are both from Manchester, that they arrived in London at the same time, that they live in the same house, sleep in the same bed, and are parents of the same child. The Martins and the Smiths exchange banalities, a clock strikes erratically, and the doorbell rings by itself. A fire chief arrives. Although in a hurry to extinguish all fires in the city, he launches into long-winded, pointless anecdotes. After he leaves, the two couples exchange hurried clichés until language breaks down into basic sounds. The end of the play completes a circle: The Martins replace the Smiths and speak the same lines that opened the play.

Ionesco's *The Bald Soprano*
The maid dominates the scene with the Smiths, the Martins, and the fire chief. The photo is from the original Paris production of *The Bald Soprano* at Théâtre des Noctambules, 1950, directed by Nicholas Bataille.

In more recent plays, Ionesco's concerns about middle-class conformity have a more political cutting edge. In *Rhinoceros*, written in 1958, Ionesco's hero, Bérenger, is an individual in a world of conformists. Ionesco's political concern is with people who are brutalized by dogma (in this case, fascism) and changed by it into thick-skinned beasts. The rhinoceros, with its thick hide and small brain, is Ionesco's brilliant analogue for the herd mentality. Bérenger emerges as a lonely but authentic hero, for he resists the physical and moral conformity that overwhelms his world and his loved ones. Like other Ionesco heroes, he represents a genuine assertion of personal value in a world dominated by nationalism, bureaucracy, and "groupthink."

Ionesco's later plays, such as *Exit the King*, *Macbett*, *Man with Bags*, and *Scene*, are parables on human evil, the will to power, and the inevitability of death.

The "American" Absurd

The Zoo Story, written by Edward Albee in 1958, introduced the absurd into American playwriting. The p lay is a confrontation in New York City's Central Park between two men: Jerry, a carelessly dressed man in his late thirties, and Peter, a man in his early forties who wears tweeds and smokes a pipe. Peter is seated on a park bench reading

©Joan Marcus

Peter and Jerry

Edward Albee's *Peter and Jerry,* the back-story of the characters from *The Zoo Story,* with Bill Pullman and Dallas Roberts as Peter and Jerry, Second Stage Theatre, Off Broadway.

a book when he is accosted by Jerry, who at once teases, taunts, and threatens him. As Jerry challenges Peter for possession of the park bench and intentionally provokes his own death, Jerry not only sacrifices his life but passes on to Peter the suffering and truth of his experience.

With this short play about a bench, two men, and their inability to communicate, Edward Albee launched the American absurd in which two disaffected and disconnected strangers contend for a park bench and mutual understanding.

TRANSITION

Drama's forms are the organization of the playwright's vision of and statement about the world. Tragedy, comedy, tragicomedy, melodrama, farce, epic, and absurd are theatrical ways of labeling the playwright's view of the world's substance, shape, and meaning. However, there is a larger pattern of writing that has the potential for becoming living words and actions. We call this pattern for "doing" or "becoming" *drama.* It all begins with the *imitation* of human events, speech, and behavior shaped into a verbal and visual pattern of experience.

THEATRE: A WAY OF SEEING ONLINE

Visit the CourseMate for Theatre: A Way of Seeing 7th Edition for quick access to the digital study resources that accompany this chapter, including links to the websites listed below, Theatre Workshop, digital glossary, a chapter quiz and more.

Websites

The *Theatre: A Way of Seeing* CourseMate includes links for all the websites described below. Simply select "Web links" from the Chapter Resources for Chapter 5, and click on the link that interests you. You'll be taken directly to the site described.

The Ancient Greek World
Virtual gallery that explores such topics as daily life, religion, and economics in the ancient world.

Bertolt Brecht Biography
Site that features a detailed biography of Bertolt Brecht, as well as a list of selected works.

The Broadway Theatre Archive
Dozens of made-for-television productions of plays available on videocassette or DVD, including a version of *Tartuffe* (1978), Irene Worth in Samuel Beckett's *Happy Days* (1980), and James Earl Jones in *King Lear* (1974).

Lillian Hellman Biography
Excellent site that features a biography of Lillian Hellman, links to related topics (such as her FBI file), and a video clip titled "Hellman's Victory over the House on Un-American Activities Committee."

The Samuel Beckett Endpage
A multiple-resource site for all those interested in the life and works of Samuel Beckett, and the official page of The Samuel Beckett Society.

Tony Kushner Biography
Biography of Tony Kushner plus links to a list of plays and related playwrights.

6

STRUCTURES OF SEEING

The play is a quest for a solution.[1]

—DAVID MAMET, *WRITING IN RESTAURANTS*

THE PLAYWRIGHT'S ART

PREVIEW

To read the printed page of a script is to experience much of the playwright's art. Words on a page have the potential for becoming human speech, movement, and sound. Playwrights use many kinds of play structures and dramatic conventions to aid in the telling of their stories.

Drama, the playwright's art, takes its name from the Greek verb *dran*, meaning "to do" or "to act." Drama is most often defined as a pattern of words and actions having the potential for "doing" or "becoming" living words and events.

On the printed page, that pattern appears as *dialogue*—words arranged in sequence to be spoken by actors. Stage dialogue can be similar to the dialogue we speak in informal conversations with friends. In some cases, as with Shakespeare's blank verse or the complex verse forms of ancient Greek plays, dialogue is more formal. But in all cases, stage dialogue differs from ordinary conversation in one important way: the playwright creates it and the actor speaks it. *Performability* is the link between the playwright's words and the actor's speech.

Let us begin the discussion of drama as a way of seeing by considering childhood *play*, with which it shares similarities.

DRAMA AS IMITATION

Children at play are amateur playwrights as they imitate reality through playing at pretend "tea parties," action hero games, and electronic games such as "Super Mario" and "The Legend of Zelda: Twilight Princess." Children play to entertain themselves, to imitate adult behavior, and to help fit themselves into an unfamiliar world. In play, children try

The postmodern staging of Robert Wilson's *The Black Rider: The Casting of the Magic Bullets*, Hamburg, Germany, represents his "theatre of visions" that imparts the single vision of the stage director-designer and a sense of the importance of the visual, aural, and imaginative in theatre dominated by stage design.

© Sara Krulwich/The New York Times/Redux

***Ruined* by Lynn Nottage**
With Condola Rashad as Sophie, the 18-year-old bookkeeper and bar singer in war-torn Congo, Manhattan Theatre Club, New York City.

out and learn roles they will experience in their adult lives. In their imitations, they develop what American psychiatrist Eric Berne calls *life-scripts*.

What do we mean by imitation, especially imitation at the psychological level? In *Play, Dreams and Imitation in Childhood*, French psychologist Jean Piaget says that we tend to imitate through play those things that arouse ambivalent emotions within us. We do this to handle the fears evoked by the strangeness of things and situations. We imitate the unknown as a way of mastering and gaining dominance over it. Children, adults of early societies, and artists all use imitation and for many of the same reasons.

Imitation in life and art is a process through which we confront and transform our fears of the strange and unknown by becoming one with them, even managing them. Every drama is an imitation that confronts the mystery of human behavior. It does so concretely through *the living presence* of the actor, who is both a real person and a fictional character. The great British actor Laurence Olivier once remarked, "Acting is an almost childish wish. . . . Pretend to be somebody else. . . . Let's pretend—I suppose that's the original impulse of acting."[2]

Play and drama have much in common. The child pretending to be an astronaut or the actor playing *Hamlet* must start with a script or imagined situation, character, dialogue, and locale. Both play and drama entertain. They contribute to a sense of well-being and to an understanding of ourselves and others. They have their own fixed rules. Most important, they *imitate* human events.

In the fourth century BC, Aristotle described drama as *mimesis*—the imitation of human beings in action. In his *Poetics*, he showed that the playwright used certain devices to turn written material into human action: plot, character, language, thought or ideas, music, and spectacle. From our modern perspective, we add time and space to Aristotle's list of dramatic elements.

Drama's Elements

Plot, Character, Language, Meaning, Music, and Spectacle

Drama's chief elements are still often modeled on Aristotle's criteria, beginning with plot, character, and language. *Plot* is an arranged sequence of events or incidents usually having a beginning, middle, and end. These incidents spring from an action or motive. *Character* includes the physiological and psychological makeup of the persons in the play.

Language is the spoken word, including verbal symbols and nonverbal signs. The play's *Meaning* is its underlying idea—its general and particular truths about experience. Today, we frequently use the words "theme" or "message" when we talk about a play's meaning. A play may have more than one basic theme. *Macbeth*, for example, is a play about crime and punishment, but it is also about the destructive effects of power and ambition on the human psyche.

Aristotle used *spectacle* to include all visual and aural elements: music (musical instruments and choral odes), properties (swords and urns), machines (wagons and cranes), and lighting effects (torches and open flames). In the modern theatre, we add scenery, lighting, projected images, and sound effects to this list.

Time—Actual and Symbolic

The modern idea of a play's *time* refers not to *actual time*—the length of the performance—but to *symbolic time*, which is integral to the play's structure and may be spread out over hours, days, or years. *Hamlet* takes about four hours to perform, although the story covers many months. We are asked to believe that the incidents in Henrik Ibsen's *Ghosts* take place in little more than twenty-four hours.

Action

Action is a crucial element of drama. Aristotle did not use *action* to refer to those external deeds, incidents, situations, and events we tend to associate with a play's plot. He likened the relationship of action and drama to that of the soul and the body. He saw action as the source of the play's inner meaning, the spiritual and psychological forces that move through the play, holding its elements together in a meaningful way.

Critic Francis Fergusson defined action as "the focus or aim of psychic life from which the events, in that situation, result."[3] The source of the play's outward deeds, *action* embodies all the physical, psychological, and spiritual gestures and motivations that result in the visible behavior of the characters. The action of Oedipus in Sophocles's play occurs on several levels. On one level, Oedipus's action is to find the killer of Laius, the former Theban king, and to purify the city of plague by punishing the guilty person. During his investigation of the plague's cause, Oedipus discovers that he is the guilty man, that he unwittingly killed his father and married his mother. On another, deeper level, the action of *Oedipus the King* is really a man's efforts "to know himself." In short, action is the play's all-encompassing purpose.

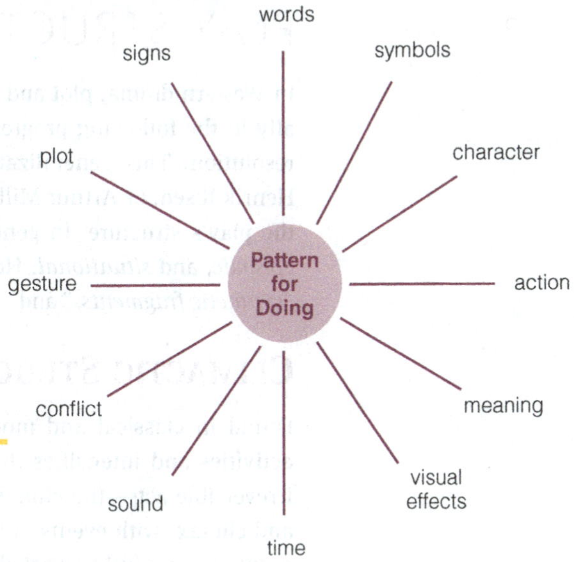

The Elements of Drama

Elements of Drama
The elements of drama make up a pattern for doing. Today, the list is more extensive than it was in Aristotle's time and includes words, symbols, character, action, meaning, visual effects, time, sound, conflict, gesture, plot, and signs.

FOCUS ON PEOPLE IN THEATRE

PLAYWRIGHT

Henrik Ibsen

© Hulton Archive/Getty Images

Henrik Ibsen (1828–1906), Norwegian playwright, is called the father of modern drama. Finding his early plays (celebrating his country's past glories) poorly received, Ibsen immigrated to Italy. There, he wrote *Brand* (1865), a symbolic tragedy in verse, which brought him immediate fame. For twenty-seven years he remained with his family in self-imposed exile in Rome, Dresden, and Munich, writing such plays as *A Doll's House, Ghosts, An Enemy of the People, The Wild Duck*, and *Hedda Gabler*. These plays changed the direction of the nineteenth-century theatre. In 1891, Ibsen returned to Norway; and in 1899, he completed *When We Dead Awaken*, the play that novelist James Joyce considered Ibsen's finest. He died there in 1906.

Ibsen wrote plays dealing with problems of contemporary life, particularly those of the individual caught in a repressive society. Although his social doctrines, radical and shocking in his own day, are no longer revolutionary, his portraits of humanity are timeless.

Through the centuries, playwrights have developed different ways of using dramatic forms, structures, and styles to mirror the changing intellectual and emotional life of their cultures. The play's structure is the playwright's way of *organizing* the dramatic material into a coherent whole.

PLAY STRUCTURES

In Western drama, plot and action are based on a central *conflict* and organized usually in the following progression: exposition > confrontation > crisis > climax > resolution. This generalization is true for plays written by William Shakespeare, Henrik Ibsen, or Arthur Miller. The way the playwright varies this pattern determines the play's structure. In general, plays are organized in three basic ways: *climactic, episodic*, and *situational*. However, entirely new structures, such as *"talking pieces," "synthetic fragments,"* and *"visual texts"* have been devised by contemporary writers.

CLIMACTIC STRUCTURE

Found in classical and modern plays, climactic structure confines the characters' activities and intensifies the pressures on the characters until they are forced into irreversible acts—the climax. The playwright begins late in the story, near the crisis and climax, with events of the past weighing heavily on the present situation. These events are not fully revealed until the play's final moments. Climactic structure, then, is a *cause-to-effect* arrangement of incidents ending in a climax and quick resolution. *Oedipus the King* and *Fences* are excellent examples of climactic structure.

In *Oedipus the King*, for example, Sophocles starts at the critical point in the ancient Theban story with the plague rampant throughout the countryside. The play's action consists of Oedipus's quest for the murdered king's slayer and ends with the revelation that he is both Thebes's savior and its defiler.

Henrik Ibsen's *A Doll's House*

A Doll's House, written two years before *Ghosts* in 1879, places climactic playwriting at the service of a social problem dealing with women's rights, both legal and personal. The background story of the Helmer marriage (Nora's forgery, her hidden efforts to repay the debt incurred during her husband's illness, those little signs of Nora's concealed nature as she eats the forbidden macaroons) points to a compressed past that surfaces with her girlhood friend's arrival. Mrs. Linde, like the Greek messenger, precipitates the revelations of Nora's past and ensures the catastrophe in the present. *A Doll's House* has a small cast (five principals), a short timespan (several days at Christmas), and a single setting (the Helmers' living room). Technical contrivances—a blackmail plot with reformed villain and fateful letter, the family crisis at Christmastime, the heroine's masquerade costume and frenzied dancing, the close friend's imminent death by inherited disease, the "debate" between husband and wife—are in the service of realistic writing that thrusts festering social and personal problems from the past into the present with unexpected and disastrous consequences.

One timely aspect of Ibsen's play is that the ending is not clear-cut. Nora's forgery of her father's signature despite her worthy reasons (to get money to save her husband during his grave illness) was legally wrong—no less than a criminal act. At the same time, she had no legal means of borrowing money in the society of the day. Her discovery that her secret pride in preserving her husband's health is looked upon as a felony in the eyes of her husband and the legal system shocks her into a larger understanding of herself and her situation.

The action of the play is the transformation of Nora Helmer from her father's, then husband's, doll and pet "squirrel" into a woman of unknown potential. At the end, as Nora sets out in quest of her "self" in an uncertain world, we see her as the product

A Doll's House
Ibsen's *A Doll's House* on Broadway, with Janet McTeer as Nora (right) and Jan Maxwell as Mrs. Linde, directed by Anthony Page.

of her social conditioning and a value system that stunted women's personal development, impoverished and trivialized their lives, and degraded them in their own eyes. Her story is the tragedy of wasted human potential and the unlikelihood that she can redeem that waste in the future. As Nora slams the door on family, husband, children, and friends, Ibsen makes a statement to his late nineteenth-century audiences: Both men and women are victims of a society that condones inequities in social conventions and legal systems.

Nora makes a ringing assertion of her new understanding:

Nora: *I have other duties equally sacred.*

Helmer: *You do not. What duties would they be?*

Nora: *My duties to myself.*

Helmer: *You are a wife and a mother before you are anything else.*

Nora: *I don't believe that any more. I believe I am first of all a human being, just as much as you—or at any rate that I must try to become one. (Act 3)*

A famous contemporary described the effect of the play on audiences of Ibsen's day: "The door Nora Helmer slammed shut on her marriage sent shock waves through thousands of homes."

Episodic Structure

Episodic play structure, found in medieval plays and the works of William Shakespeare, Bertolt Brecht, and Tony Kushner, traces the characters through a *journey* of sorts to a final action and to an understanding of what the journey meant. It can always take a new turn. In Shakespeare's plays, people are not forced immediately into unmaneuverable positions. Possibilities of action are usually open to them until the very end. Events do not accumulate to confine the characters because the play encompasses large amounts of time and distance. *Hamlet* takes place over several years and in several countries. And the expanding plot takes in a variety of events. In this loose structure, characters are not caught in circumstances but pass through them, as Grusha does in *The Caucasian Chalk Circle.*[4]

Bertolt Brecht's *The Caucasian Chalk Circle*

In *The Caucasian Chalk Circle*, Brecht tells two stories. The setting is a meeting of two Soviet collective farms in 1945 to decide which group should own a certain valley. Before they vote, they are told the stories of Grusha and the child Michael, which makes up the centerpiece of the play, and of the disreputable career of Azdak, a village rogue whom rebellious soldiers make a judge. The three stories come together as Azdak tries the case of the child's ownership and settles it by reversing the old test of the chalk circle. He awards the child to Grusha rather than to the biological mother (the governor's wife), who had abandoned him in wartime and now to win custody of the child, pulls him roughly from the circle. Brecht's moral is that both child and valley should belong to those who serve them best.

FOCUS ON THEATRE

Brecht's *The Caucasian Chalk Circle*

Storytelling in *The Caucasian Chalk Circle*, written by German playwright Bertolt Brecht in 1944–1945, begins in 1945 with two Soviet villages disputing the ownership of a fertile valley.

Before they decide the issue, a singer entertains them with a Chinese parable, the story of the chalk circle. The scene changes to a Georgian city being overthrown by a revolt against the ruling class. The governor is killed, and his wife abandons their son, Michael, in order to escape. Grusha, a peasant girl, rescues the child and flees to the mountains with him. In order to give the child a name and status, she marries a peasant whom she believes is near death. When the revolt ends, the governor's wife sends soldiers to get the child. The scene shifts again, to the story of Azdak, a rogue made village judge by the rebel soldiers. He is corrupt and prepares to judge the case of Grusha versus the governor's wife for possession of Michael. He uses the test of the chalk circle to identify the child's true mother, but reverses the outcome: The child is given to Grusha because she will not engage in the tug-of-war that is supposed to end in the child's being pulled out of the circle by maternal affection. He also decrees Grusha a divorce so that she can return to her soldier fiancé, Simon. Brecht's moral is that things—children, wagons, valleys—should go to those who serve them best.

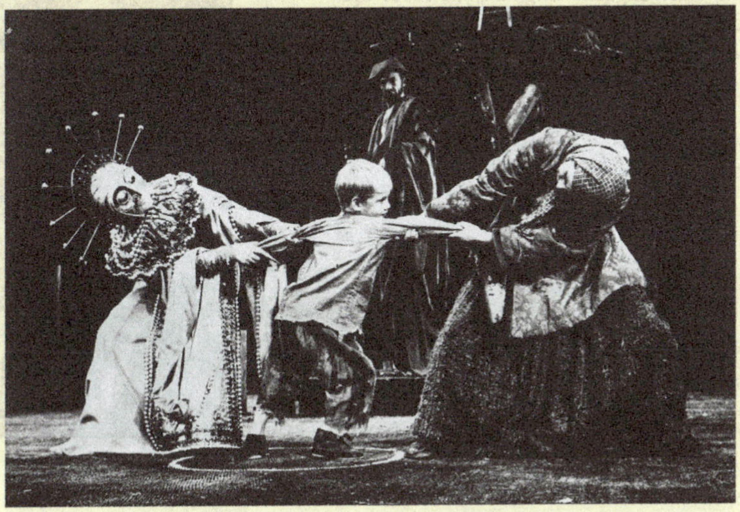

Marty Nordstrum/Courtesy Guthrie Theater

The Caucasian Chalk Circle
The circle drawn in white chalk on the stage signifies a test of true motherliness and rightful ownership based on mutual interest and well-being. The governor's wife (left) and Grusha (right) pull the child as Judge Azdak looks on. Grusha (Zoe Caldwell) releases the child before harming him. *The Caucasian Chalk Circle* staged at the Guthrie Theater, Minneapolis.

SITUATIONAL STRUCTURE

In modern absurdist plays, *situation*, not plot or arrangement of incidents, shapes the play. It takes the place of the journey or the pressurized events. The situation has its own inner rhythms, which are like the basic cycles of life: day, night, day; hunger, thirst, hunger; spring, summer, winter.

Eugène Ionesco's *The Bald Soprano*

In *The Bald Soprano* (1949), Ionesco introduces a fire chief and the Martins into Mr. and Mrs. Smith's typical middle-class English living room. After a series of absurd events, the dialogue crescendos into nonsensical babbling. The words stop abruptly, and the play begins again. This time, Mr. and Mrs. Martin are seated as the Smiths were at the play's beginning, and they repeat the Smiths' lines from the first scene. With this repetition, Ionesco demonstrates the interchangeability of middle-class lives.

FOCUS ON PLAYS

Eugène Ionesco's *The Bald Soprano*

The "Bobby Watson" exchange from Ionesco's *The Bald Soprano* presents the banality of middle-class suburban life in aural and visual images as Mr. and Mrs. Smith, seated in their middle-class English living room, discuss their middle-class English dinner and engage in conversation about Bobby Watson.

© Courtesy French Press and Information Office

The Bald Soprano
Ionesco's middle-class English couple, Mr. and Mrs. Smith, discuss dinner, the newspaper, and Bobby Watson in the original 1950 Paris production of *The Bald Soprano*.

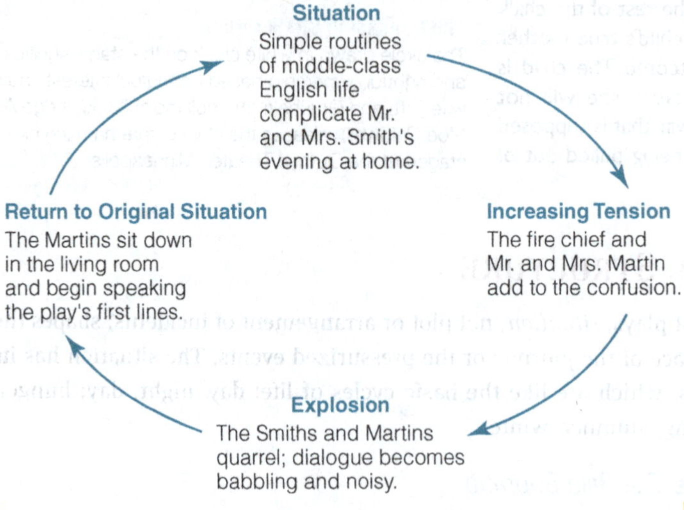
Situation
Simple routines of middle-class English life complicate Mr. and Mrs. Smith's evening at home.
Increasing Tension
The fire chief and Mr. and Mrs. Martin add to the confusion.
Explosion
The Smiths and Martins quarrel; dialogue becomes babbling and noisy.
Return to Original Situation
The Martins sit down in the living room and begin speaking the play's first lines.

Situational Play Structure in Ionesco's *The Bald Soprano*
The "theatre of the absurd" emerged in Europe following the Second World War. Absurdist plays convey a sense of alienation, of people having lost their bearings in an illogical or ridiculous world. Situational play structure mirrors this worldview.

©Sara Krulwich/The New York Times/Redux

Waiting for Godot
Samuel Beckett's groundbreaking absurdist play with five characters prepared the way for his later monodramas *Rockaby* and *Krapp's Last Tape*. In the Broadway revival of *Waiting for Godot,* Nathan Lane and Bill Irwin inhabit two of Beckett's characters, Vladimir and Estragon, as they "wait" for Godot.

Monodrama

Samuel Beckett's Monodramas

Since the original production of *Waiting for Godot* in 1953, Samuel Beckett has been a major influence on experimentalists looking for ways to introduce into the theatre intuitive events, talking pieces, interior monologues, and minimal staging. To do so required new dramatic forms. Cause-to-effect plots, soliloquies, and large theatrical moments were no longer adequate to express the mystery and pain of psychic distress and lives diminished by aging.

Beckett's monologues and narrative voices together with his minimalist staging (an old man, a table, and a tape recorder; a woman buried in a mound of dirt; two lips speaking) influenced the work of later absurdists. His stream-of-consciousness monologues (or monodramas) present the conscious and unconscious thought processes of the speaker. To take us into the character's consciousness, playwrights (following Beckett's lead) have added electronic amplification, sound tracks, holograms, and voice-overs.

FOCUS ON THEATRE

Samuel Beckett's *Rockaby*

Beckett's *Rockaby*, as interpreted by British actress Billie Whitelaw, is a fifteen-minute monodrama in which a woman, seated in a rocking chair, rocks herself into the grave. The actress speaks only one word ("more") four times. The single word is separated by a litany of words (prerecorded on tape) that represent the final thrashings of the woman's consciousness. As death comes, she ceases rocking. A single light picks out the actress' face; her eyes close. Then, darkness is total.

With a chair, one actor, few words, and scant movement, Beckett makes us feel the weight of the solitary, seemingly endless last night of a life. Death comes as a release—a "happy" ending.

© Irene Haupt

Rockaby
Billie Whitelaw as the Woman in the rocking chair in *Rockaby* at the Samuel Beckett Theatre, New York City.

RECENT STRUCTURES

SOLO TEXTS AND PERFORMANCE ART

Solo performances have a long stage history beginning with early shamans and medieval mimes, minstrels, and jugglers. In form and substance, the solo performer's antecedents stretch back to shamanistic practices in early cultures and forward to modern forms of art and entertainment found in vaudeville, cabaret, stand-up comedy, poetry readings, dance recitals, and European cubism, dadaism, and futurism. What these performers, ancient and modern, share is their singular presence and their aggressive interactions with audiences.

In the tradition of the artist entertaining as a single stage presence, solo performers are found in today's mainstream American commercial theatre and in the improvised spaces of the contemporary avant-garde. In the mainstream, solo performers are called upon to perform biographies of famous people. Julie Harris has been seen as Emily Dickinson, Hal Holbrook as Mark Twain, and Jefferson Mays as Charlotte von Mahlsdorf in *I Am My Own Wife*. The texts for these theatrical biographies performed by a single actor are usually written, directed, and performed by separate

© Jefferson Mays

I Am My Own Wife
With Jefferson Mays as Charlotte von Mahlsdorf.

artists (playwright, director, and actor). Hollywood celebrities and stand-up comics—Martin Short, Lily Tomlin, Louis Black, Whoopi Goldberg, Ellen DeGeneres, Chris Rock, Bill Maher, Wanda Sykes, and Billy Crystal—also bring their life stories, viewpoints, and sharp wit to Broadway's stages in what is most often called stand-up comedy.

"The question often comes up: Why is the solo show so endemic in the '90s? It would miss the heart of the artist's impulse to create solo work to simply echo the oft-cited bottom-line reasons—diminishing government funding for the arts, paucity of ensemble-size venues, the obvious showcase potential for an actor as a stepping stone to larger or more commercial work. Perhaps the primary reason for the proliferation of solo work in this decade lies in the great appeal for artists of having total aesthetic control of their material."[5]

—Jo Bonney, Director

In the experimental venues of Off Off Broadway, nonprofit theatres, and found spaces, the solo performer as the single creator (writer-actor) provides a low-budget means of exploring (often with nudity and explicit language) social, political, and cultural concerns. Positioned not so much on the aesthetic outskirts of the community as on its moral and social fringes, solo art has as its overriding concern such issues as class, identity, ethnicity, gender, environment, censorship, pornography, homophobia, and racism. Solo artists have become a vital part of the theatrical avant-garde, as evidenced in the work of Spalding Gray, Karen Finley, Holly Hughes, Eric Bogosian, Lisa Kron, Anna Deavere Smith, John Leguizamo, Guillermo Gómez-Peña, Eve Ensler, and Sarah Silverman.

Performance art is a term used to describe live art created in the moment by performers in the presence of spectators. It has been applied to such diverse events as the staged happenings of Alan Kaprow, the dance pieces of Anna Halprin, the dance/movements of Merce Cunningham, the collages of painter Claes Oldenburg, and the music experiments of John Cage. As *solo* performance art evolved in the late-twentieth century, the common factor among diverse artists was a self-created composition, called the *solo text*. Although widely varying approaches to written composition have been adopted, these texts share certain qualities: an improvisatory style, reduced emphasis on literary forms and language, rejection of traditional narrative or linear storytelling, lack of unity and coherence, and scatological language and presentational (In your face!) performance styles.

Solo performers usually take their materials from autobiography and from personal responses to the entire political, social, and cultural spectrum of American life. Deb Margolin, performer and author of the solo texts *Of Mice, Bugs and Women* and *Of All the Nerve*, calls solo performance art "a perfect Theater for One."[6]

Spalding Gray's "Talking Pieces"

As one of the recent progenitors of solo performance art, Spalding Gray (1941–2004) called his minimalist creations "talking pieces," meaning a series of simple actions using free associations as building blocks to turn a series of memories and everyday experiences into performance art. Gray's solo texts were composed of improvised memories, free associations, ideas of childhood, and private emotions shaped into such autobiographical sketches as *Sex and Death to the Age of 14*, *Monster in a Box*, *It's a Slippery Slope*, and *Swimming to Cambodia*. His texts were literally talked through with small audiences in what he called "an act of public memory." Once satisfied with the final product, Gray "set" the talking piece as a solo text.

Dressed casually in dark slacks and a plaid shirt, Gray performed seated at a small table with a glass of water, notebook (with outline), and pointer to identify images in slides projected on a screen behind him. Gray's minimalist use of set pieces, ordinary clothing, lighting, and sound are characteristic of most solo art, whose material is as individualistic and distinctive as the performers themselves.

© Paula Court

Monster in a Box
Spalding Gray performs *Monster in a Box* at Lincoln Center Theater, New York.

Anna Deavere Smith's *Fires in the Mirror*

The solo text is not only a highly personal response to current social and political issues but also a powerful means of speaking directly to America's collective conscience. Anna Deavere Smith began her "search for American character" as a solo artist in the early 1980s.

Fires in the Mirror brought her national attention for its deft biography of people involved in the 1991 Crown Heights riots in Brooklyn, New York. Her solo works (*Fires in the Mirror* and *Twilight: Los Angeles 1992*) are part of a series begun in 1983 as *On the Road: A Search for American Character*. She brings onstage "voices of the unheard"—the invisible in America. Taking on the roles of the many people she interviewed, she said of her process, "I try to represent multiple points of view and to capture the personality of a place by showing its individuals." In effect, her solo performances are a demonstration of the American character, what she calls "a parade of color," to assess race and class in America.[7]

Both *Fires in the Mirror* and *Twilight: Los Angeles 1992* are based on historical incidents. The racial conflict between the Lubavitcher and black communities in Brooklyn's Crown Heights, which resulted in the riots of 1991, became the subject of *Fires in the Mirror*. Racial divisions in Los Angeles between the Rodney King incident of March 3, 1991, and the federal trial that ended in April 1993 with the conviction of two Los Angeles policemen for violating King's civil rights provided the topic for *Twilight*. Of these communities, Anna Deavere Smith says, "They all have a very clear sense of their own difference. I'm interested in capturing the American character through documenting these differences."[9]

Fires in the Mirror: Crown Heights, Brooklyn, and Other Identities grew out of 100 interviews with a variety of participants and witnesses from the black and Lubavitcher communities in Crown Heights. Out of these many voices, Anna Deavere Smith crafted a performance by using the words of those she interviewed, thereby developing unique and often contradictory insights into a complex community and series of events. As the conflict unfolds, the voices of the Crown Heights community are heard: the Reverend Al Sharpton, civil rights activist; Robert Sherman, New York City's

FOCUS ON PEOPLE IN THEATRE

PERFORMANCE ARTIST

Anna Deavere Smith

© Janette Beckman/Retna Ltd.

Anna Deavere Smith (b. 1951), actress, playwright, and performance artist, grew up in Baltimore, Maryland, as the daughter of Deavere (pronounced "da-veer") Young, a coffee merchant, and Anna Young, an elementary school principal. She trained as an actress at the American Conservatory Theatre in San Francisco, graduating with a Master of Fine Arts degree in 1976. She taught at Carnegie-Mellon University, the University of Southern California, and Stanford University before joining the faculty of New York University's Tisch School of the Arts.

In 1983, she began a series of solo performances entitled *On The Road: A Search for American Character*. She gained national attention with the award-winning *Fires in the Mirror* in 1992 at the New York Shakespeare Festival/Public Theater and with *Twilight: Los Angeles 1992* at the Mark Taper Forum, Los Angeles, in 1993 and on Broadway. The next year, she appeared in the films *Dave* and Jonathan Demme's *Philadelphia*. She collaborated in 1994 on a ballet called *Hymn* for the thirty-fifth anniversary season of the Alvin Ailey American Dance Theater. *House Arrest*, begun during the 1996 presidential campaign with Smith as a member of the Clinton campaign's press corps, opened as a solo performance in March 2000 at the Joseph Papp Public Theater.

In *Let Me Down Easy*, Smith's many voices speak of the fragility and resilience of the human body in twenty vignettes—the cyclist, the dancer-choreographer, abandoned patients in a New Orleans hospital during Katrina, a supermodel, heavyweight boxer, bull rider, film critic—in stories about the nation's medical system and people fighting battles with cancer and death.

Of her work, Anna Deavere Smith has said that she tries to embody America by embodying its words. "In this case, they are words about the deepest human experiences: immortality and nobility of character, perseverance, hope and acceptance."[10]

© Sara Krulwich/The New York Times/Redux

Let Me Down Easy
Writer and performer Anna Deavere Smith explores issues of personal health and the healthcare system in her one-woman show *Let Me Down Easy*, Off Broadway.

commissioner on human rights; Norman Rosenbaum, Yankel Rosenbaum's brother; and Roz Malamud, a Crown Heights resident. It becomes apparent that there are no simple answers to the questions surrounding the controversy.

What Anna Deavere Smith clearly demonstrates, however, is that each person's perspective is a reflection of his or her background and experience of race, religion, and gender and is worthy of being heard and understood.

The historical moment occurred on August 9, 1991, in the Crown Heights section of Brooklyn when one of the cars in a three-car procession carrying the Lubavitcher Hasidic *rebbe* (spiritual leader) ran a red light, hit another car, and swerved onto the sidewalk, killing Gavin Cato, a seven-year-old child from Guyana, and seriously injuring his cousin.

Fires in the Mirror
Actress and solo performer Anna Deavere Smith in *Fires in the Mirror*, first performed in 1992 at the New York Shakespeare Festival/Public Theater.

Rumors spread throughout the community that a Hasidic-run ambulance service helped the driver and his passengers while the children lay bleeding and dying on the sidewalk. Members of the district's black community reacted violently against the police and the Lubavitchers. That evening, a group of young black men fatally stabbed Yankel Rosenbaum, a twenty-nine-year-old Hasidic scholar from Australia. For three days, blacks and Hasidic patrols fought one another and the police.

This conflict reflected long-standing tensions in the Crown Heights community as well as the pain, oppression, and discrimination these groups have historically experienced. Many of the Crown Heights black community were Caribbean immigrants from Jamaica, Guyana, Trinidad, and Haiti. They had experienced discrimination on the basis of their color and their national origin. The Lubavitchers—members of an Orthodox Jewish sect that fled the Nazi genocide of European Jews during the Second World War—were particularly vulnerable to anti-Jewish stereotyping because of their religion, style of dress, and insular community. Both communities felt victimized by the police, the press, and the legal system. Many viewed the jury acquittal of Yankel Rosenbaum's accused murderer as a stark example of injustice.

Anna Deavere Smith interviewed people engaged at all levels of this conflict. She distilled the interviews into a ninety-minute solo performance in which she speaks the words, thoughts, and emotions of eighteen people—male and female, black and Jewish, activist and resident, parent and teacher.

As a creator and performer, Smith sets out to use the words of the voiceless and the powerful in society, creating a sophisticated and poetic dialogue about race relations in contemporary America. Onstage among the clutter of chairs and tables, Smith, barefoot, with hair pulled back to make the changes of costume and gender easier, gives shape to the voices and words of others. She shows culturally diverse people

FOCUS ON THEATRE

Performance Diversity

Performance artists explore America's cultural diversity and social pluralism on traditional stages and in nontraditional spaces. At a time when theatre has been forced by the popularity and accessibility of film and television into the margins of cultural life, solo artists have stepped forward to give attention to the ostracized, the isolated, and the abandoned in American society.

© Timothy Greenfield-Sanders

Karen Finley became the center of controversy when the National Endowment for the Arts rescinded her grant to create performance art. Her work was considered offensive by local and national legislators for its explicit language, sexuality, nudity, and attacks on political and religious figures. In *We Keep Our Victims Ready*, about the degradation of women, Finley stripped nude and smeared her body with chocolate while comparing women to penned-up calves. She then toured the country with her *Return of the Chocolate-Smeared Woman* to continue her protest against government censorship of the arts. More recently, unable to find spaces for her work, she turned to embodying voices of other women in *The Dreams of Laura Bush* and *The Passion of Terri Schiavo*, merging national obsessions with right-to-life issues.

© Joseph Marzullo/Retna Ltd.

Eve Ensler—an award-winning playwright, activist, and screenwriter—compiled and performed *The Vagina Monologues* as an anthology on women and won a 1997 Obie Award for Best New Play. The world tour of *The Vagina Monologues* initiated V-Day, a movement to stop violence against women. This work has been performed as a solo piece and also with several actresses. Ensler's *Necessary Targets* has been performed on Broadway, in Sarajevo, and in London to benefit Bosnian women refugees. Her satirical comedy is angry, poignant, and deeply committed to women's issues. Ensler's recent work, *I Am an Emotional Creature . . . The Secret Life of Girls*, a series of monologues presented as a theatre piece and a book, aims to inspire young women to take charge of their minds, bodies, hearts, and curiosities.

© Kelly Campbell/Courtesy of Holly Hughes

Holly Hughes is another performance artist whose grant from the National Endowment for the Arts was rescinded for the allegedly indecent content of her work. She has since become a crusader against censorship of the arts.

FOCUS ON THEATRE

Credited with reinventing lesbian theatre, her solo performances explore her identity as a woman and lesbian. From her satires of detective fiction, *The Lady Dick* and *The Well of Horniness*, to her confrontational "queer theatre" pieces, *World Without End* and *Clit Notes*, Holly Hughes has been called "the poster child for indecent art." Her work has been recognized with an Obie and with a Lambda Book Award.

© Sara Krulwich/The New York Times/Redux

John Leguizamo is a Colombian-American stage and film/television actor and comedian. His best-known solo work, *Freaks*, is a comic, satirical, and poignant journey through his Latino neighborhood in Queens, New York, in which he plays a dozen different characters—male and female, young and old. Leguizamo's *Freaks* reached Broadway and was nominated for a 1998 Antoinette Perry "Tony" Award and later directed by Spike Lee as an HBO comedy special. Since then, along with his many film and television roles, he has performed *Klass Klown*, revised as *Ghetto Klown*, and garnered awards for outstanding solo performance.

© Jim Fogleman

Guillermo Gómez-Peña was born in Mexico City and came to the United States in 1978. A performance artist and writer, he also engages in video, audio, and installations, and writes poetry and critical essays on cultural theory. His performance pieces are politically charged critiques of xenophobia and U.S. imperialism often performed in marginally funded community centers and in museums and art galleries. By way of irony, humor, poetry, and wit, he uses performance to enter into dialogue on such complex issues as censorship, immigration, globalization, and Anglo-American attitudes toward Latinos and others. Overall, he projects a range of tensions, hopes, and fears that characterize U.S.–Mexican relations and envisions a utopian future where people live *without borders*. His performance work includes *The End of the Line*, *The Dangerous Border Game*, *The Mexterminator Project*, and the *Mapa/Corpo* series. In 1991, he became the first artist of Mexican birth and ancestry to receive a MacArthur ("genius" award) Foundation Fellowship.

> **"The model of cross-cultural interdisciplinary collaboration is still a very effective one. Sharing resources and skills, artists from different cultural backgrounds and métiers can effectively negotiate a common ground that supersedes temporarily our/their differences."**[8]
>
> —GUILLERMO GÓMEZ-PEÑA, PERFORMANCE ARTIST

struggling to make coherent their sense of rage, pain, and disbelief. She listens not for the facts but for the inner conflicts of the soul expressed in everyday speech. "I'm interested," she said, "in how language and character intersect."[11]

Fires in the Mirror, like *Twilight*, captures a multicultural America at the edge of consciousness about the death, pain, and guilt generated by racism and class. *House Arrest*, performed in 2000, refers to the captivity of the U.S. president, who inhabits the White House. Using historical documents and original interviews, she explores the presidencies of Thomas Jefferson, Abraham Lincoln, Franklin Delano Roosevelt, and William Jefferson Clinton to strip away the myths created by history, political systems, and newspaper headlines.

POSTMODERN TEXTS

In the 1970s, a movement in reaction against the "modern" emerged in architecture, painting, music, literature, and theatre. Called *postmodern*, the new movement most often called for *doubling*; that is, *placing contradictory experiences within the same frame of reference*—for example, the actor against the stenographic image in Philip Glass's opera *1,000 Airplanes on the Roof*, or, in the Wooster Group's *Hamlet*, in which the actor, playing Hamlet, is highlighted against a grainy, giant image of actor Richard

Hamlet
The Wooster's Group's postmodern staging of *Hamlet*, directed by founding artistic director Elizabeth LeCompte, places live performers before a gigantic black-and-white screen version of Richard Burton's filmic stage performance as Hamlet. Actor Scott Shepherd as Hamlet (right) seen in the foreground against the image of Richard Burton (left) in the Wooster Group's production, New York Shakespeare/Public Theater.

© Tom Caravaglia

1,000 Airplanes on the Roof
With music and direction by Philip Glass and libretto by David Henry Hwang. The actor is diminished by the 3-D stenographic projection of a modern high-rise building. Design by Jerome Sirlin.

Burton as Hamlet in the 1964 Broadway version with faintly heard voices from the film along with evaporating sounds and images. Giving flesh to the onstage *Hamlet*, Wooster actors juxtapose "this too, too, solid flesh" against gigantic screen images that literally "melt, thaw and resolve itself into a dew" (I. ii.). The Wooster Group's *Hamlet* is a gesture-by-gesture duplication of the action on screen with live actors as Hamlet, Gertrude, and Ophelia in the foreground in tribute to the ephemerality of greatness in the theatre.

Typical of postmodern art are artist Andy Warhol's repetitive screen prints of photographic images of Marilyn Monroe, Elizabeth Taylor, and Campbell's soup cans. The paintings are both a collection of images reproduced by technological means from an "original image"—the photograph—and not from the real person. This "reframing" of human experience with technology dispenses with realism and naturalism in art and celebrates the *fragmentation of experience*. When we talk today about "computer viruses," we are reframing experience to suggest that human biology is at work in computer networks. This kind of playful discourse (and even parody) is found in postmodern art.

In the theatre, postmodern works spring directly from the earlier antirealistic theatre of the symbolists and surrealists. Whereas symbolists and surrealists in the early part of the twentieth century set about to reveal inner truth, postmodernists celebrate the randomness of truth, in which experience is improvised, parodic, haphazard, self-referential, and arbitrary. Often called "assemblages" or "collages," brief texts (such as those of the German playwright Heiner Müller, for example) are composed of extended monologues, notations on stage images, notes on multiple sensory impressions, and paragraphs of word fragments that explore the world's cultural history. Unlike the Wooster's Group's *Hamlet*, Heiner Müller's theatre piece, called *Hamletmachine*, examines the collapse of Western civilization. Ophelia becomes a terrorist and Hamlet a

© Photo by Richard Termine

Máquina Hamlet
Adapted from Heiner Müller's play, *Hamletmachine* is the work of El Periférico de Objectos from Buenos Aires (Argentina) in a Spanish-language production called *Máquina Hamlet*, with Felictas Luna as Ophelia. Brooklyn Academy of Music, New York.

demolisher of "ideologues" Karl Marx, Lenin, and Mao Zedong to demonstrate modern Europe's political, intellectual, and social failures.

Theatre of Images

In 1976, critic Bonnie Marranca coined the term "Theatre of Images" to describe the postmodern work of American writer-director-designer-composers Robert Wilson, Philip Glass, and Lee Breuer of the Mabou Mines. (See Image from *Red Beads*, page 266.) Revolting against words and "old-fashioned" verbal texts, these innovators created theatrical events dominated by visual and aural images. Since the early 1970s, their avant-garde experiments evolved to resemble *the painter's collages*. Absent are climactic drama's cause-to-effect relationships of action, plot, and character and in their place we find actors juxtaposed with holographic shapes, atonal sounds, and sculpted images that develop as large-scale performances requiring more than a few hours to complete. This new mixture of creative sources (sound, music, light, technology, scenes) ultimately raises the same issues as more traditional theatre: questions of humanity's relationship to society, to the environment, to technology, and to itself.

FOCUS ON PEOPLE IN THEATRE

PLAYWRIGHT-DIRECTOR-DESIGNER

Robert Wilson

©Time & Life Pictures/Getty Images

Robert Wilson (b. 1941) created the Byrd Hoffman Foundation to work with autistic children, as well as performers of all ages, on developing a new kind of theatrical event. The results were unusually long performances—five to seven hours—intended to provoke contemplation rather than to tell a story.

Wilson's productions—many in collaboration with composer Philip Glass—"assemble" actors, sounds, music, sculptured scenery, light, and shadow to comment on American society and cultural myths. His epic productions stretch the audience's attention in an attempt to alter perceptual awareness of people, places, and things. They are known as much for their length and complexity as for their unique titles. Among the best-known are:

- *Einstein on the Beach*
- *A Letter for Queen Victoria*
- *the CIVIL warS: a tree is best measured when it is down*
- *The Forest*
- *The Black Rider: The Casting of the Magic Bullets*
- *The Voyage*
- *The Fables of de La Fontaine*

©Hermann and Clärchen Baus

The Black Rider
The Black Rider: The Casting of the Magic Bullets premiered in Hamburg, Germany, in 1990. Direction and design by Robert Wilson.

VISUAL AND AUDIO TEXTS

Robert Wilson says of his work: "Most theatre that we see today is thought about in terms of the word, the text. . . . And that's not the case with my work. In my theatre, what we see is as important as what we hear. What we see does not have to relate to what we hear. They can be independent."[12]

In his work, Wilson distinguishes between the "visual book" and the "audio book." He has described them as separate screens that can be adjusted to relate what

Robert Wilson's *Einstein on the Beach*

Originally produced in 1976 at the Metropolitan Opera House, New York City, *Einstein on the Beach* is a collaboration between Robert Wilson and composer Philip Glass. The five-hour production deals with the contradictions implicit in the genius of Albert Einstein and his legacy to our world. Dancers Sheryl Sutton and Lucinda Childs move as sculpted forms against a background image of the young Einstein.

the audience is *seeing* to what it is *hearing*, and vice versa. For the visual book of *the CIVIL warS: a tree is best measured when it is down*, a play about *civil* struggle throughout history, he collaborated with German playwright Heiner Müller and American composers Philip Glass and David Byrne (of the "Talking Heads"). Wilson thought of his projected seven-hour opera as an exploration of the American Civil War using Matthew Brady's photography. As he worked on the piece, his vision expanded to include all civilian struggles in families and countries from ancient Greece to modern times.

Robert Wilson's *The Knee Plays*

These short plays were originally intended as interludes between the fifteen scenes of *the CIVIL warS*. Nine dancers create a cascade of imagery—visual, aural, and choreographic—focusing on "a tree of life." Using square modules, puppets, and masks, *The Knee Plays* tell stories dealing with the life cycle through history. With words and music by David Byrne.

Robert Wilson's *the CIVIL warS*

Wilson's visual book for *the CIVIL warS* is structured with five acts and fifteen scenes. His audio book (words that audiences hear) is made up of texts—letters Frederick William I of Prussia sent to his son and a letter Franz Kafka wrote to his father; excerpts from plays by Shakespeare, Racine, and Goethe; verse from the *Song of Solomon*; and writings by Heiner Müller. The final text is generated by the juxtaposition of the visual and the audio books in performance with actors, music, and film images.

Robert Wilson explains that he is not a writer of words: "I usually find a form before I have content. Before I've gathered material, I have a form. Once I have a form, it's a question of how to fill the form."[13]

© Richard Feldman

the CIVIL warS
In Robert Wilson's *the CIVIL warS: a tree is best measured when it is down*, actors and puppets are juxtaposed in pinpoints of light. Abraham Lincoln, a sixteen-foot-tall figure (a singer suspended in a harness and wearing a long black coat)—is a startling image of "a tree" best measured when it has been cut down.

TRANSITION

Drama, the written text, is a special way of imitating human behavior and events. Depending upon the playwright's attitudes toward, and interpretations of experience, that imitation can take many forms. For 2,500 years, Western writers have used climactic, episodic, and situational play structures and a fairly consistent set of dramatic conventions.

In today's world of high technology and ambivalent meanings, writers and directors try different methods and tools to create texts that speak to audiences in tune with computer graphics, sophisticated sound systems, video equipment, and holographic effects. Almost in ironic juxtaposition with the elaborate technology is the minimalist art of Samuel Beckett, Spalding Gray, and recent performance artists.

Despite technology, drama's conventions and unique language continue to satisfy audiences as means of communicating the complexities of human experience.

Theatre: A Way of Seeing Online

Visit the CourseMate for Theatre: A Way of Seeing 7th Edition for quick access to the digital study resources that accompany this chapter, including links to the websites listed below, Theatre Workshop, digital glossary, a chapter quiz and more.

Websites

The *Theatre: A Way of Seeing* CourseMate includes links for all the websites described below. Simply select "Web links" from the Chapter Resources for Chapter 6, and click on the link that interests you. You'll be taken directly to the site described.

Interview with Spalding Gray
An interview with Spalding Gray about suicide and sadness, writing and regret.

The Playwriting Seminars
An opinionated Web companion on the art and craft of playwriting.

Robert Wilson Biography
Detailed biography of Robert Wilson, plus related links.

Einstein on the Beach
Article about Robert Wilson's opera *Einstein on the Beach*, plus a list of music, written by Philip Glass and featured in the production.

Anna Deavere Smith
Biography of Anna Deavere Smith and dozens of links to information about her plays, articles, and interviews.

John Leguizamo
Detailed site about John Leguizamo, including a biography, a list of his works, and a list of articles about this artist.

©Topfoto/The Image Works

7

DRAMA'S CONVENTIONS

All that lives by the fact of living, has a form, and by the same token must die—except the work of art which lives forever in so far as it *is* form.[1]

—Luigi Pirandello, Preface to *Six Characters in Search of an Author*

WRITING STRATEGIES

Through the years, playwrights have worked out various strategies, called *conventions*, to convey experience and activity to audiences. Drama's conventions are agreed-upon methods of getting something across quickly to audiences. Just as we have social conventions to help us meet strangers or answer our telephones and cellphones, so, too, playwrights have writing conventions to solve problems, pass along information, develop plot and action, and create interest and suspense. These shortcuts make it possible for playwrights to give information and present experiences that in life would require weeks or even years to occur, to tell two or three stories at once, and to complicate and resolve stage action.

What follows is a discussion of eleven widely used dramatic conventions: (1) stage directions, (2) exposition, (3) point of attack or inciting incident, (4) complication, (5) crisis, (6) climax, (7) resolution, (8) simultaneous or double plots, (9) time, (10) metaphor, and (11) the play-within-the-play.

PREVIEW

Playwrights have common strategies to develop plot, character, and action; to manipulate time; and to end plays. Taken all together, dramatic conventions are agreed-upon ways to communicate information and experience to audiences.

Stage Directions

Before the printing press made possible a general readership for plays, stage directions (if they existed at all) were used solely by theatre personnel. In modern editions of *Hamlet*, for example, we find such abbreviated directions as "A flourish," "Exeunt," "Aside," "Dies," and "Exit Ghost."

The chorus of gymnasts from Tom Stoppard's comedy *Jumpers* mirrors in physical terms the "athleticism" of the playwright's cascade of words and topsy-turvy world in interludes performed by the "jumpers," Broadway.

A Street Car Named Desire
Jo Mielziner designed the original set for *A Streetcar Named Desire* and incorporated the New Orleans French Quarter scene that Tennessee Williams described.

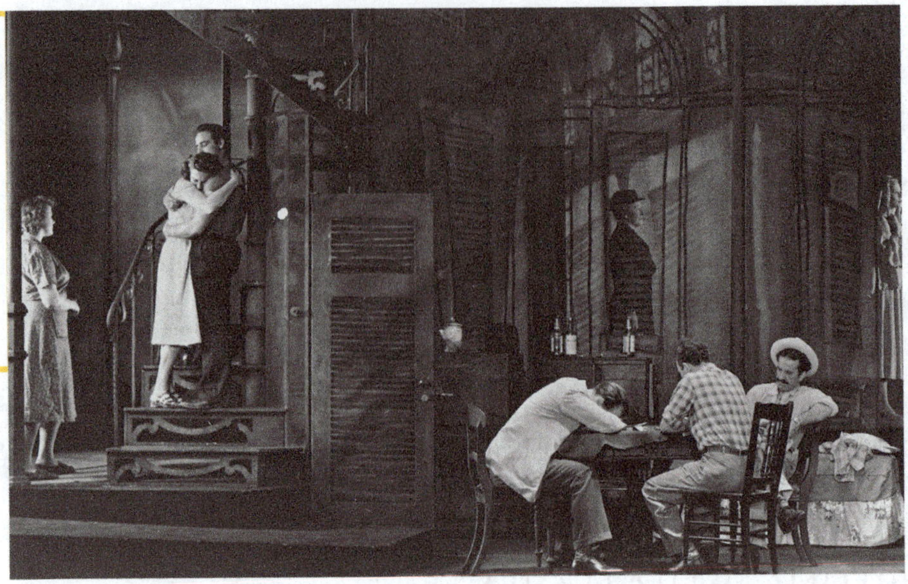

We assume that these directions were added to Shakespeare's original promptbook by players or printers. Nevertheless, by modern standards, these directions are sparse.

Modern stage directions are included at the beginning of each act to provide information about how the playwright imagines details of the stage or playing space, such as the Kowalski apartment in *A Streetcar Named Desire*. (Some stage directions are a result of the original director's and actors' contributions to the script during rehearsals and performance and often recorded by the stage manager.) The playwright's "directions" include facts about geography, season of the year, time of day or night, weather conditions, furnishings, dress, mood, stage properties, music cues, sound effects, and general impressions of place or environment. The opening stage direction in *A Streetcar Named Desire*, first staged in 1947, is a full page in length wherein Tennessee Williams provides atmosphere with graphic details of place, time, light, and sounds: New Orleans, Elysian Fields Avenue, a May twilight, blue sky, barroom piano music. The age, dress, and movements of Stanley Kowalski and his friend Mitch are also described.

Scene One

The exterior of a two-story corner building on a street in New Orleans which is named Elysian Fields and runs between the L & N tracks and the river. The section is poor but, unlike corresponding sections in other American cities, it has a raffish charm. The houses are mostly white frame, weathered grey, with rickety outside stairs and galleries and quaintly ornamented gables.

This building contains two flats, upstairs and down. Faded white stairs ascend to the entrances of both.

It is first dark of an evening early in May. The sky that shows around the dim white building is a peculiarly tender blue, almost a turquoise, which invests the scene with a kind of lyricism and gracefully attenuates the atmosphere of decay. You can

FOCUS ON THEATRE

Tennessee Williams's *A Streetcar Named Desire*

A Streetcar Named Desire was first produced at the Barrymore Theatre on Broadway. Her family's Mississippi estate sold, Blanche DuBois arrives at the New Orleans tenement home of Stella and Stanley Kowalski, her pregnant sister and her brother-in-law. Blanche's faded gentility clashes with Stanley's brutish masculinity. As she seeks protection from the world, she competes with Stanley for Stella's affections but finds herself no match for his sexual hold over her sister. She tries to charm Mitch, Stanley's poker-playing friend, into marrying her. However, Stanley destroys Blanche's hopes for marriage by telling Mitch about her drinking and promiscuity. As Stella reproaches Stanley for his cruelty, her labor pains begin and Stanley rushes her to the hospital.

Blanche is visited by a drunken Mitch, who accuses her of lying to him and tries to seduce her. Stanley returns to find Blanche dressed for a party, fantasizing about an invitation to go on a cruise with a wealthy male friend. Angered by her pretensions, Stanley starts a fight with her that ends in rape. In a final scene some weeks later, Blanche, her tenuous hold on reality shattered, is taken to a mental hospital.

The tragedy of *Streetcar* reveals human duplicity and desperation in Williams's modern South, where fragile people are overcome by violence and vulgarity.

Eileen Darby Images

A Street Car Named Desire

A tender moment between actors Jessica Tandy as Blanche DuBois and Karl Malden as Mitch in the original New York production of Tennessee Williams's *A Streetcar Named Desire* (1947), directed by Elia Kazan.

almost feel the warm breath of the brown river beyond the river warehouses with their faint redolences of bananas and coffee. A corresponding air is evoked by the music of Negro entertainers at a barroom around the corner. In this part of New Orleans you are practically always just around the corner, or a few doors down the street, from a tinny piano being played with the infatuated fluency of brown fingers. This "Blue Piano" expresses the spirit of the life which goes on here.

Two women, one white and one colored, are taking the air on the steps of the building. The white woman is Eunice, who occupies the upstairs flat; the colored woman a neighbor, for New Orleans is a cosmopolitan city where there is a relatively warm and easy intermingling of races in the old part of town.

Above the music of the "Blue Piano" the voices of people on the street can be heard overlapping.

[Two men come around the corner, Stanley Kowalski and Mitch. They are about twenty-eight or thirty years old, roughly dressed in blue denim work clothes. Stanley carries his bowling jacket and a red-stained package from a butcher's. They stop at the foot of the steps.][2]

Blanche, Stella's sister—dressed for a garden party in white suit, hat, gloves—comes unexpectedly into this setting. Williams describes her appearance:

She is about five years older than Stella. Her delicate beauty must avoid a strong light. There is something about her uncertain manner, as well as her white clothes, that suggest a moth.

In contrast, Shakespeare and his contemporaries did not have the advantage of modern print technology. Nor were they interested in the specifics of environment as a factor that shapes human events. Their writing tradition placed all indications of time, place, weather, and mood in the dialogue of minor characters in the play's beginning moments. They provided the background information and also captured the audience's attention preparatory to the entrance of the principals. In the jargon of the theatre, these are "weather lines." Within eleven lines at the beginning of *Hamlet*, the two guards give us a sense of place ("castle battlements"), time ("'Tis now struck twelve"), weather ("'Tis bitter cold"), mood ("I am sick at heart"), and what's happening ("Not a mouse stirring").

Stage directions are an important part of writing conventions, especially in the modern theatre. They provide crucial information for the reader, describing how the playwright has imagined the play's environment and the characters' ages and appearances. As a result of a recent legal ruling in the United States, only the playwright's stage directions, not the contributions of the original director, may be printed or otherwise used without permission in subsequent stagings.

FOCUS ON PLAYS

"Stage Directions" in Shakespeare's *Hamlet*

Bernardo: Who's there?

Francisco: Nay, answer me; stand, and unfold yourself.

Bernardo: Long live the King!

Francisco: Bernardo?

Bernardo: Here.

Francisco: You come most carefully upon your hour.

Bernardo: 'Tis now struck twelve; get thee to bed, Francisco.

Francisco: For this relief, much thanks; 'tis bitter cold. And I am sick at heart.

Bernardo: Have you had quiet guard?

Francisco: Not a mouse stirring.

Bernardo: Well, good-night. If you do meet Horatio and Marcellus, The rivals of my watch, bid them make haste.

Francisco: I think I hear them. Stand, ho! Who's there? (I, i)

FOCUS ON THEATRE

Euripides's Prologue in *The Trojan Women*

The Trojan Women, written by Euripides and produced in 415 BC at the Theatre of Dionysus, Athens, is the third (and only surviving) play in his trilogy about Troy—its destruction, the death of its defenders, and the enslavement of its women.

POSEIDON speaks:

....

I am Poseidon. Troy and its people were my city.
The ring of walls and towers I and Apollo built—
Squared every stone in it; and my affection has not faded
Now Troy lies dead under the conquering Argive spear,
Stripped, sacked and smouldering . . .

....

Farewell, then, city!
Superb masonry, farewell! You have had your day of Glory . . .

***The Greeks*, presented by the Royal Shakespeare Company, Stratford-upon-Avon Great Britain**
The Trojan Women, Part One: The War. Production directed by John Barton and designed by John Napier.

EXPOSITION

Classical Exposition

In a play's opening scene we are frequently given certain information (*exposition*) about what is going on, what has happened in the past, and who is to be seen. Exposition is usually conveyed through dialogue in short scenes or between several characters. In Euripides's *The Trojan Women*, a formal prologue is spoken by the gods Poseidon and Athene. The sea god Poseidon describes the treachery of the Greeks' use of the Trojan horse to gain entry into the city of Troy, the city's collapse, and the fate of its defenders. Athene, the goddess defender of Troy, describes how the Greeks defiled her altars. Then, Troy's Queen Hecuba tells of the physical and mental suffering of the Trojan people. Following this background information, the action begins. The fates of the Trojan women are decreed, and Hector's young son, Astyanax, is sentenced to die.

The expository prologue in Euripides's *Medea* is a lamentation by Medea's nurse describing her mistress' murderous assistance in the past to help Jason steal the Golden Fleece followed by his present desertion of his family to marry the Princess of Corinth. Medea's sufferings and the Nurse's fears that violence may come prepare for the play's beginning. The Nurse says of Medea, "I am afraid she may think of some dreadful thing,/For her heart is violent.... She's a strange woman."

Modern Exposition

In contrast to the formal exposition of Greek plays, some modern plays begin with a telephone ringing; the person answering—for instance, a maid or butler in drawing-room comedy—gives the play's background information by talking to an unseen party about the family, its plans, and conflicts.

In most cases, plays begin with informational exchanges of dialogue to establish who, what, when, and where. Contemporary drama presents less information of this kind. Instead of asking who these people are and what is going to happen next, we usually ask, "What's going on now?" Absurdist plays raise more questions about the who, what, and why of a situation than they answer.

Point of Attack

The moment early in the play when the story is taken up is the point of attack, or inciting incident. In *Macbeth*, the point of attack grows out of the victorious battle reports to King Duncan, who, learning of the death of the traitorous Thane of Cawdor, rewards Macbeth with that title. In the very next scene Macbeth encounters the witches, who greet him with many prophecies, including the title "Thane of Cawdor." Macbeth begins to believe the witches' prophecy that he will become the future king and writes to his wife, who plans the murder of King Duncan.

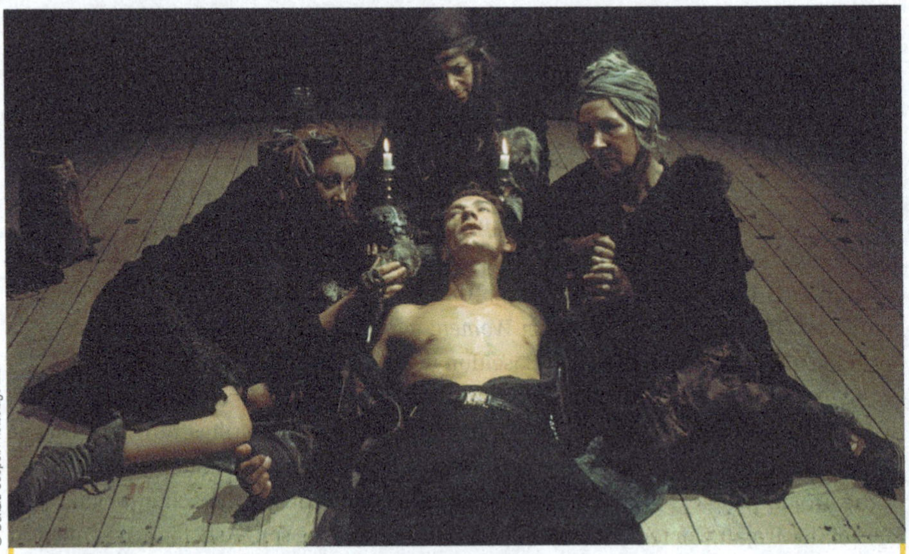

Macbeth

The witches entice Macbeth (Sir Ian McKellen) with voodoo dolls, as they paint symbols on his body in the Royal Shakespeare Company (Stratford-upon-Avon, Great Britain) production of *Macbeth*, directed by Trevor Nunn. The witches prophesy the titles and royal throne that will be bestowed upon Macbeth:

MACBETH: Speak, if you can. What are you?
1. WITCH: All hail, Macbeth! Hail to thee, Thane of Glamis!
2. WITCH: All hail, Macbeth! Hail to thee, Thane of Cawdor!
3. WITCH: All hail, Macbeth, that shalt be King hereafter! (I, iii)

FOCUS ON THEATRE

William Shakespeare's *Macbeth*

The last of Shakespeare's four great tragedies (the others are *Hamlet*, *Othello*, and *King Lear*), *Macbeth* (1606) was written when Shakespeare's creative powers were at their highest. Macbeth, King Duncan's noble warlord, hears witches prophesy that greatness will be his—that he will be king someday.

When his wife, Lady Macbeth, learns of the witches' prophecy, her imagination—overcharged with ambition—conceives the king's assassination. While he sleeps in their castle, the Macbeths murder Duncan, engendering a seemingly endless series of murders to conceal their original crime and to thwart other pretenders to the throne.

As the play progresses, the disintegrating effects of evil work on a once-noble man and his wife. Macbeth's crimes distort his judgment; he is terrified by hallucinations of the ghosts of his victims, symbolizing a warning of retribution to come. He becomes increasingly isolated from his followers and his wife, whose guilty conscience eventually leads her to suicide. Pessimism and despair take hold of Macbeth as he contemplates his inevitable punishment. Only in the end does he revive a part of his former self, as he duels with his rival (Macduff) to a certain death.

This story of crime and punishment illustrates the destructive effects of power and ambition on the human psyche. Macbeth's self-awareness endows the action with its tragic dimension: He feels responsibility for the moral chaos he has created and explores life's meaning in soliloquies that transcend his personal dilemma.

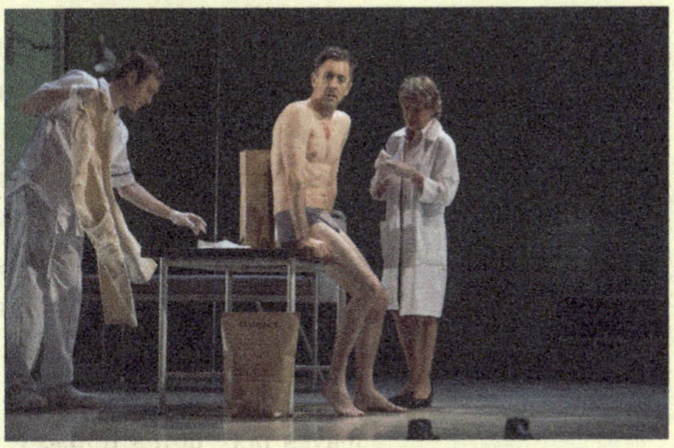

Macbeth
Alan Cumming as Macbeth in a reimagining of Shakespeare's "Scottish" play set in a psychiatric ward. As the lone patient with two attendants, Cumming inhabits some of Shakespeare's most complex and troubled characters in a production from the National Theatre of Scotland, at Lincoln Center Festival, New York City.

Complication, Crisis, Climax

The middle of a play is made up of *complications*—new information, unexpected events, or newly disclosed facts accompanied by increasing emotional intensity. Macbeth's unexpected encounter with the witches is the beginning of many violent complications. In Ibsen's *Ghosts*, Mrs. Alving overhears her son Oswald seducing Regina, the child of her husband and a servant, and, therefore, Oswald's half sister. Mrs. Alving must deal with this complication.

A play's complications usually develop into a *crisis*, or turning point of the action. The crisis is an event that makes the resolution of the play's conflict inevitable. In *Macbeth*, the crisis is the murder of King Duncan by the Macbeths. They have killed an anointed king, and a universal bloodbath will follow until the murderers are punished and the rightful heir restored to the throne.

A play usually ends when the conflict is resolved in the *climax*, or point of highest emotional intensity, and any loose strands of action are then tied off. In *The Trojan Women*, the moment of highest emotional intensity occurs when Hector's son, the heir to Troy, is sentenced to die and carried away to be executed. The consignment of the women to the Greek generals is almost anticlimactic because—without a male to procreate the tribe—Troy has no hope of future generations.

The climax of *Macbeth* is the appearance of the murdered Banquo's ghost at the banquet table—further evidence of Macbeth's ongoing bloody deeds and his unquiet conscience. After the ghost's appearance, forces turn against Macbeth, leading him finally to fight his rival Macduff; this secondary climax results in Macbeth's death and the restoration of the rightful heir to Duncan's throne.

Resolutions or Endings

The resolution usually restores balance and satisfies the audience's expectations. The captive Trojan women are marched away to board the Greek ships; Medea flies away on her magical chariot with her dead children to find refuge in another land. Macbeth pays for his crimes with his life, and Duncan's son is crowned king of Scotland. In *A Streetcar Named Desire*, Blanche is taken to an asylum and the Kowalski household settles back into its routines of poker, beer, and Saturday-night bowling.

An absurdist play, such as *The Bald Soprano*, usually completes a cycle in its resolution, suggesting that life's events repeat themselves over and over again. Some plays end with unanswered questions—for example, what is Nora Helmer's fate after she leaves her "doll's house"?—to stimulate audiences to think about the personal and social implications of the heroine's choice. Whatever the case, the resolution brings a sense of completed or suspended action, of conflicts resolved in probable ways, and of promises fulfilled.

Simultaneous Plots

Other dramatic conventions, such as simultaneous or double plots, relate past and present events and behavior. The Elizabethans used simultaneous or double plotting

Hamlet
As Hamlet, Jude Law portrays the Dane in modern dress, in a production imported from London's Donmar Warehouse to Broadway.

FOCUS ON THEATRE

William Shakespeare's *Hamlet*

Shakespeare's greatest tragedy, *Hamlet* (c. 1601), tells the story of a man who confronts a task that seems beyond his powers. The play begins as the Danish court celebrates King Claudius's wedding to Queen Gertrude; her son, Prince Hamlet, still mourns the death of his father. His father's ghost appears and tells Hamlet that he was murdered by Claudius. Hamlet swears to take vengeance, but he must first prove to himself that Claudius is guilty. He has a group of strolling players put on a play in which a similar murder is depicted. Claudius's reaction to the play betrays him, and Hamlet plots revenge.

By accident Hamlet kills Polonius, the Lord Chamberlain and father to Ophelia, a young woman who loves the prince. Hamlet is sent away from Denmark for killing Polonius, and Ophelia is driven mad by her loss. Time passes and Hamlet returns.

Laertes, Polonius' son, vows revenge and challenges Hamlet to a duel. To ensure that Hamlet is killed, Claudius poisons Laertes' sword and prepares a cup of poison for Hamlet to drink during the duel. In the closing scene, Gertrude accidentally drinks from the poisoned cup and dies, Hamlet kills Claudius, and Laertes—after mortally wounding Hamlet—is killed by Hamlet with the poisoned sword. Hamlet's cousin Fortinbras is made king of Denmark.

Hamlet is a tragedy about the power of evil to corrupt the innocent, bring chaos to a kingdom, and paralyze the human will. It contains some of the greatest poetry written by Shakespeare.

©Michal Daniel

Hamlet

Hamlet (Liev Schreiber, right) and Laertes (Hamish Linklater, left) in the dueling scene in Shakespeare's tragedy. Laertes' death concludes the story of his family and brings about Hamlet's death. New York Shakespeare Festival/Public Theater production, New York City.

to represent life's variety and complexity. Two stories are told concurrently; the lives of one group of characters affect the lives of the other group. *Hamlet*, for instance, is the story of two families: Hamlet-Claudius-Gertrude/Laertes-Polonius-Ophelia. The secondary plot or subplot is always resolved before the main plot to maintain a sense of priority. For example, Laertes dies before Hamlet in the duel, thereby ending that family's story.

CONVENTIONS OF TIME

DRAMATIC VS. ACTUAL TIME

During a performance, audiences experience time on several levels. First, there is the amount of actual time that it takes us to see a play. Dramatic time, however, is a phenomenon of the playwright's text.

Within the fictional world of the play, time can be expanded or compressed. Dramatic time can be accelerated by using gaps of days, months, and even years; or it can be slowed down by interrupting the forward action with soliloquies and flashbacks. Episodes may be shown out of their chronological sequence, or they may be foreshortened so that they occur more quickly than they would in actuality. Shakespeare's battle scenes, requiring only a few minutes of swordplay onstage, would require days or even months in real time. In Samuel Beckett's plays, characters experience the relentless passage of time as they wait out their uneventful lives. Often in Beckett's plays, the experience of dramatic time is cyclical—day becomes night, night becomes day, and so on.

Time in the fictional universe of drama is highly malleable. Consideration of dramatic time has always played a large part in the different theories and rules of drama. In his *Poetics*, Aristotle briefly suggested that the amount of time it takes the actors to enact the story should ideally be concurrent with the actual time it takes to perform the play. This attention to a *unity of time*, as it was later called, is still found in modern realistic plays in which a situation develops and is resolved within twenty-four hours or less.

CONVENTIONS OF METAPHOR

Figurative language has enriched stage speech since Aeschylus's Watchman at the beginning of *Agamemnon* described the chain of beacon fires on the hilltops between Argos and Troy set up to announce the capture of Troy. The Watchman says, "I wait; to read the meaning in the beacon light, a blaze of fire to carry out of Troy the rumor and outcry of its capture." The Watchman is speaking figuratively of the phenomenon of the beacon fires that will tell of Troy's destruction by fire and mayhem.

Metaphor and *simile* are both comparisons between things essentially unlike. The chief distinction is that "metaphor" equates two unlike objects to suggest similarities between them and "simile" compares two unlike things using *like, as, than,* or *similar to*. Both have survived in poetry and stage dialogue as principal components of figurative language.

Simile is a literal comparison. In William Congreve's *The Way of the World*, Mirabel, the suitor of Millamant, describes her as the nymph pursued by Apollo in Greek legend: "Like Daphne she, as Lovely and as Coy." On the other hand, metaphor allows us to make the connections between unlike objects and deeds. Othello struggles with the difference between snuffing out a candle, which can be rekindled, and the irremediable killing of Desdemona: "Put out the light, and then put out the light." Hamlet refers to his court world as an "unweeded garden that grows to seed." When he labels the inner play a "Mouse-trap" wherewith to catch the conscience of a king, he provokes us into thinking of Claudius as a "rat" approaching a trap that when sprung will reveal his guilt. Shakespeare's play-within-the-play has since become a chief convention of stage metaphor comparing the world to the theatre, and vice versa.

THE PLAY-WITHIN-THE-PLAY

Shakespeare used the play-within-the-play, and it is still found, most notably in the work of Bertolt Brecht, Luigi Pirandello, Peter Weiss, Tom Stoppard, and Michael Frayn. In *Hamlet*, the play-within-the-play (called *The Murder of Gonzago*, or "The Mouse-trap") is used in what is now thought of as a highly traditional way. The strolling players re-create a second play onstage for the entertainment of the court about the unusual murder of Hamlet's father. Claudius's violent reaction to it gives Hamlet proof of the king's guilt.

Brecht's *The Caucasian Chalk Circle*, like Pirandello's *Six Characters in Search of an Author* and Michael Frayn's *Noises Off*, is almost a play-within-the-play in its entirety. Brecht's singer-narrator links the outer play (the settling of the farmers' dispute over the ownership of the land) with the inner one (the stories of Grusha, Azdak, and the chalk-circle test). The long inner play manifests a kind of collective wisdom that has practical applications in the actual dispute over ownership of property (the outer play).

Shakespeare's *Hamlet*
Laurence Olivier, as Hamlet, devised "The Mouse-trap" to prove King Claudius's guilt. From the 1948 film of Shakespeare's play, also directed by Olivier.

FOCUS ON PEOPLE IN THEATRE

PLAYWRIGHT

Luigi Pirandello

©Bettmann/CORBIS

Luigi Pirandello (1867–1936), the son of a rich owner of sulfur mines in Agrigento on the southern coast of Sicily, studied philosophy at the University of Rome and earned a doctorate at the University of Bonn in Germany. In his early years, he wrote poems and short stories for his own enjoyment. He married the daughter of his father's partner in an arranged marriage. Both families lost their fortunes when the mines flooded in 1904. To earn a living for his new family, Pirandello became an instructor at a teacher's college for women in Rome. Shortly thereafter, his wife became mentally ill. Refusing to place her in a public institution and too poor to afford a private one, Pirandello lived with his wife's mental illness until her death in 1918. Writing to support the family, he attained international fame as a playwright by the 1920s. In 1925, he founded his own art theatre (*Teatro d'Arte*) in Rome and in 1934 was awarded the Nobel Prize for Literature.

Pirandello's plays demonstrate a brooding inquiry into the nature of reality. His belief that all experience is illusory and that life itself is a "sad piece of buffoonery" is best illustrated in *It Is So! (If You Think So)* (1917), *Henry IV* (1922), and *As You Desire Me* (1930) and in his "theatre trilogy"—*Six Characters in Search of an Author* (1921), *Each in His Own Way* (1924), and *Tonight We Improvise* (1930).

FOCUS ON PLAYS

Luigi Pirandello's *Six Characters in Search of an Author* (with text)

©Joan Marcus

Pirandello's "Six Characters" Make Their Mysterious Appearance in the Play-within-the-Play *Six Characters in Search of an Author* in the Arena Stage production, Washington, D.C., directed by Liviu Ciulei.

Six Characters in Search of an Author, written in 1921 by Italian playwright Luigi Pirandello, begins with a rehearsal of a "Pirandello comedy" (called *Mixing It Up*) by a second-rate acting company. A family of six fictional characters intrudes upon a rehearsal and demands that their story be performed. They have been deserted by their author and left in limbo, so to speak. The actors agree to give one rehearsal to the characters' story, and chaos ensues in their tale of domestic tragedy that becomes the play-within-the-play. During the rehearsal, the characters insist that the actors cannot portray them in any meaningful way. Characters and actors bicker in a radical questioning of theatrical art. The paradoxes of play and reality, characters and actors, illusion and truth are played out in the rehearsal and in the characters' inner play.

Pirandello's influential *Six Characters in Search of an Author* anticipated the theatricalism of the modern theatre, along with the mood and questioning of absurdist drama.

Act I

At this point, the ***Door-Keeper*** *has entered from the stage door and advances towards the manager's table, taking off his braided cap. During this manoeuvre, the* ***Six Characters*** *enter, and stop by the door at back of stage, so that when the* ***Door-Keeper*** *is about to announce their coming to the* ***Manager***, *they are already on the stage. A tenuous light surrounds them, almost as if irradiated by them—the faint breath of their fantastic reality.*

This light will disappear when they come forward towards the actors. They preserve, however, something of the dream lightness in which they seem almost suspended; but this does not detract from the essential reality of their forms and expressions.

He who is known as ***The Father*** *is a man of about 50: hair, reddish in colour, thin at the temples; he is not bald, however; thick moustaches, falling over his still fresh mouth, which often opens in an empty and uncertain smile. He is fattish, pale; with an especially wide forehead. He has blue, oval-shaped eyes, very clear and piercing. Wears light trousers and a dark jacket. He is alternatively mellifluous and violent in his manner.*

The Mother *seems crushed and terrified as if by an intolerable weight of shame and abasement. She is dressed in modest black and wears a thick widow's veil of crêpe. When she lifts this, she reveals a wax-like face. She always keeps her eyes downcast.*

The Step-Daughter, *is dashing, almost impudent, beautiful. She wears mourning too, but with great elegance. She shows contempt for the timid half-frightened manner of the wretched* ***Boy*** *(14 years old, and also dressed in black); on the other hand, she displays a lively tenderness for her little sister,* ***The Child*** *(about four), who is dressed in white, with a black silk sash at the waist.*

The Son *(22) tall, severe in his attitude of contempt for The Father, supercilious and indifferent to The Mother. He looks as if he had come on the stage against his will.*

DOOR-KEEPER [*cap in hand*]: Excuse me, sir . . .

THE MANAGER [*rudely*]: Eh? What is it?

DOOR-KEEPER [*timidly*]: These people are asking for you, sir.

THE MANAGER [*furious*]: I am rehearsing, and you know perfectly well no one's allowed to come in during rehearsals! [*Turning to the Characters.*] Who are you, please? What do you want?

THE FATHER [*coming forward a little, followed by the others who seem embarrassed*]: As a matter of fact . . . we have come here in search of an author . . .

THE MANAGER [*half angry, half amazed*]: An author? What author?

THE FATHER: Any author, sir.

THE MANAGER: But there's no author here. We are not rehearsing a new piece.

THE STEP-DAUGHTER [*vivaciously*]: So much the better, so much the better! We can be your new piece. . . .[3]

FOCUS ON PLAYS

Michael Frayn's *Noises Off*

Noises Off by British playwright Michael Frayn is a contemporary farce about playing farce. It ridicules the many clichés of the genre within the format of a play-within-the-play. Act I is the final dress rehearsal by a mediocre troupe of actors in *Nothing On*. The typical confusions of farce result from actors who can't remember their lines, their entrances, and their stage business. Plates of sardines, multiple doors, and telephones add to the actors' challenges. Frayn heaps onto his play-within-the-play a melee of stock characters: exasperated director, cheery housekeeper, incompetent burglar, unexpected lovers, outraged wife, and harried husband—who stampede in and out of the many doors.

The stage clichés of the farce *Nothing On* are repeated in Act I in the confusion of relationships among the actors during a dress rehearsal. Act 2 repeats Act I from backstage during a matinee performance. Act 3 returns onstage with an increasingly disastrous performance of *Nothing On*.

In Frayn's farcical contrivances of actors' mishaps and temper tantrums, the onstage versus the backstage views of the disorder of life-in-the-theatre mirror the many confusions and minor terrors of our daily existence.

©Topham/The Image Works

Noises Off
Noises Off by British playwright Michael Frayn at London's Old Vic Theatre brings to the stage another "play-within-the-play" with actors rehearsing a farce called *Nothing On*. Frayn contrives an onstage versus a backstage view of life.

Recent playwrights use the play-within-the-play in more complex ways than either Shakespeare or Brecht in order to demonstrate that life is like theatre, and vice versa. The stage itself becomes a metaphor for the world's fictions and self-imposed illusions. The outer play retains the realistic convention that the stage is a real-life living room (or situation), but that real-life living room is also viewed as a "stage."

In another modern use of the play-within-the-play, German playwright Peter Weiss, writing in the sixties, created a play about the French Revolution with two time frames (the inner play depicting the assassination of Jean-Paul Marat, and the outer play showing the Marquis de Sade producing a play in a madhouse fifteen years later). The two frames combine metaphors for the social themes, madness, and violence of modern political systems.

In his celebrated masterpiece *Marat/Sade (The Persecution and Assassination of Jean-Paul Marat as Performed by the Inmates of the Asylum of Charenton Under the Direction of the Marquis de Sade)*, set in 1808, Weiss depicts the production of a play by the inmates of an insane asylum in Charenton, France. Their text, about the events of 1793—the historical setting of de Sade's play about the French Revolution—that culminate in the assassination of Marat, has been composed by the Marquis de Sade, who is also director, fellow actor, and fellow inmate. The madhouse world of

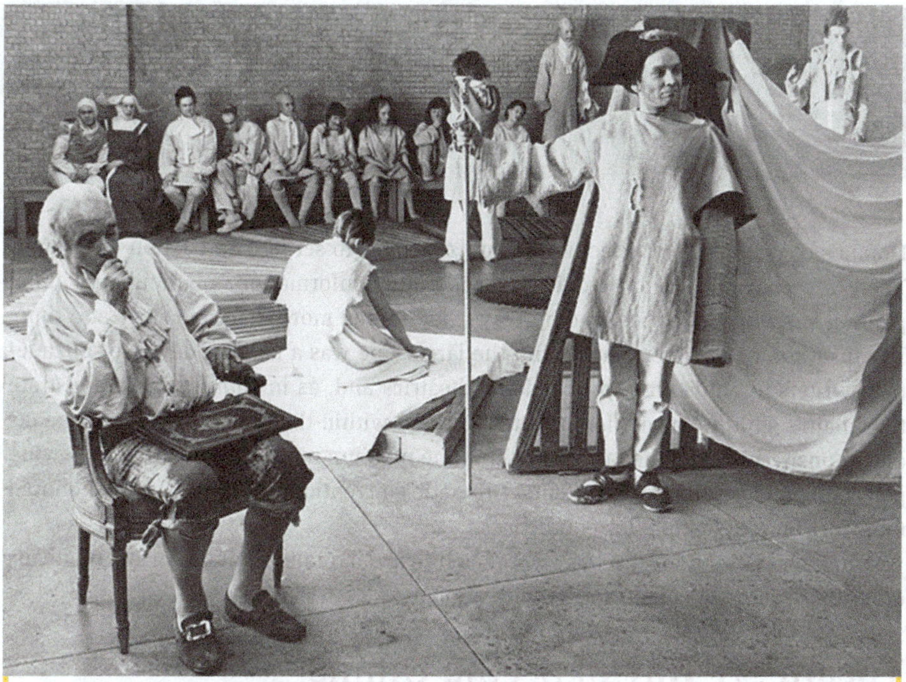

©Max Waldman Archive

Marat/Sade by Peter Weiss
The Marquis de Sade (Patrick McGee, left) rehearses the inner play with the inmates of Charenton asylum in the production, directed by Peter Brook, for the Royal Shakespeare Company (Stratford-upon-Avon, Great Britain).

Charenton and the play-within-the-play, the story of Marat's murder, force us to compare the manner in which conflicting political ideologies resolve their differences: then with the guillotine, and now with threats of nuclear annihilation.

In the modern theatre, the play-within-the-play, influenced by Luigi Pirandello's "theatre trilogy," has become a means for demonstrating life's theatricality. The stage is the most accessible medium to show life's artifice, playacting, and heightened moments of passion, anger, and even violence.

TRANSITION

Drama's conventions are effective writing strategies to set plot and action in motion. There are conventions for providing background information, manipulating time, plotting suspenseful stories, ending plays, and telling more than one story at a time. The insertion of an inner play within the larger one was a favorite device of Elizabethan writers to enliven the production's theatrics and, as in *Hamlet*, to demonstrate the villain's guilt. In the modern theatre, the play-within-the-play has become a means of demonstrating life's theatricality within the medium most appropriate for showing playacting and heightened moments. Dramatic conventions are a set of time-honored tools for communicating with audiences.

Language written for the stage also has its special qualities and a variety of means other than words to communicate with audiences.

Theatre: A Way of Seeing Online

Visit the CourseMate for Theatre: A Way of Seeing 7th Edition for quick access to the digital study resources that accompany this chapter, including links to the websites listed below, Theatre Workshop, digital glossary, a chapter quiz and more.

Websites

The *Theatre: A Way of Seeing* CourseMate includes links for all the websites described below. Simply select "Web links" from the Chapter Resources for Chapter 7, and click on the link that interests you. You'll be taken directly to the site described.

The Modern English Collection

Full texts of works of literature publicly available, dating from AD 1500 to the present.

The Theatre of Tennessee Williams

An online catalog of information for the seventy-plus full-length and one-act plays written by Tennessee Williams between 1930 and 1983. Includes such details as plot synopses and popular press reaction.

Structure of Plays

The Playwriting Seminars page about the structure of plays. Includes information and links about length, monologues, shape, style, and time. The Playwriting Seminars is "an opinionated Web companion on the art and craft of playwriting."

Joseph Cantwell
I'M JUST WILD ABOUT ARTIE

8

STAGE LANGUAGE

Theatre is more than words: drama is a story that is lived and relived with each performance, and we can watch it live. The theatre appeals as much to the eye as to the ear.[1]

—EUGÈNE IONESCO, *NOTES AND COUNTER NOTES: WRITINGS ON THE THEATRE*

Playwrights, directors, designers, and actors use a "language" that is both visual and aural to organize our perceptions in the theatre.

Spoken language in the theatre is both like and unlike the way people talk in real life. It is the playwright's means for expressing characters' thoughts and feelings and for developing plot and action. Actors speak highly selective words, unlike conversation in real life. Shakespeare's soliloquies express thoughts and feelings in blank verse and often advance the plot. This unusual and eloquent language is acceptable to us because it has its own reality, consonant with a world other than our own.

We are so used to equating language (and communication) with words that we must constantly remind ourselves that in the theatre, as in life, words are only a small part of our communications systems. Peter Brook called the words spoken onstage only "a small visible portion of a gigantic unseen formation."[2] The playwright's words in the theatre are supported, as in life, by a nonverbal language. Physical gestures, costumes, colors, masks, sounds, music, and lighting can speak eloquently to audiences of moods, attitudes, intentions, and meanings.

PREVIEW

Language for the theatre is special and complex. It organizes our perceptions of what is taking place before us, forcing us into self-discovery or radical changes of attitude. It communicates meaning and activity to us in ways that are verbal and nonverbal. Stage language is a way of seeing that engages our eyes, ears, and minds.

The finale of *Gore Vidal's The Best Man* was dominated by the American flag, a national symbol on display at political rallies whose meaning is understood by all. The revival was directed by Michael Wilson, with James Earl Jones as former President Arthur Hockstader, Broadway.

LANGUAGE FOR THE THEATRE

WORDS AND GESTURES

There is a direct connection in the theatre between words and gestures. To repeat George Steiner's comment about this connection: "Drama is language under such high pressure of feeling the words carry a necessary and immediate connotation of gesture."[3] Drama's language expresses not only the characters' thoughts, attitudes, and intentions but also the active presence of human beings in a living world.

It has been argued that the language we use for communication in real life is also multifaceted and theatrical: Our clothes are costumes, we speak words and make gestures, we carry props (book bags, sunglasses, cell phones), we wear makeup, and we are affected by the environment's sounds and silences. Although this is true, there is an important difference between language in the theatre and language in everyday life. In the theatre, language (both verbal and nonverbal) is selected and controlled. Much more must happen in conversation, or dialogue, in the theatre than in ordinary life. Our daily conversations with friends are often random and purposeless. But language in the theatre is carefully arranged by the playwright into a meaningful pattern, and actors, directors, and designers provide elements of support for this pattern of words to be meaningful night after night.

©Richard Feldman

Shakespeare's *The Tempest*
Caliban, wearing a mud mask from New Guinea, gestures to the frightened clowns in Shakespeare's *The Tempest*, directed and designed by Julie Taymor for the Theatre for a New Audience, New York City.

Suellen Fitzsimmons/Pittsburgh Public Theater

August Wilson's *King Hedley*

In *King Hedley II*, August Wilson's language is specific to urban black Americans and is rich in speechifying as characters explore their dreams, confusions, and disappointments in words and gestures.

Verbal and Nonverbal Language

On the page of a script, words are signs and symbols with the potential for making something happen in the theatre in an act of communication. In communication theory, a sign has a direct physical relationship to the thing it represents—to its referent. Thunder is a sign of rain. It has a physical connection with changes in the atmosphere. Symbols differ from signs in that they have an arbitrary connection to their referents. The American flag, for example, is a symbol of our country, and most people associate everything good in America with the flag that represents the United States. During wartime and political protests, U.S. opponents and antiwar activists burn the flag as a symbolic act of aggression against America. Today, flags have become

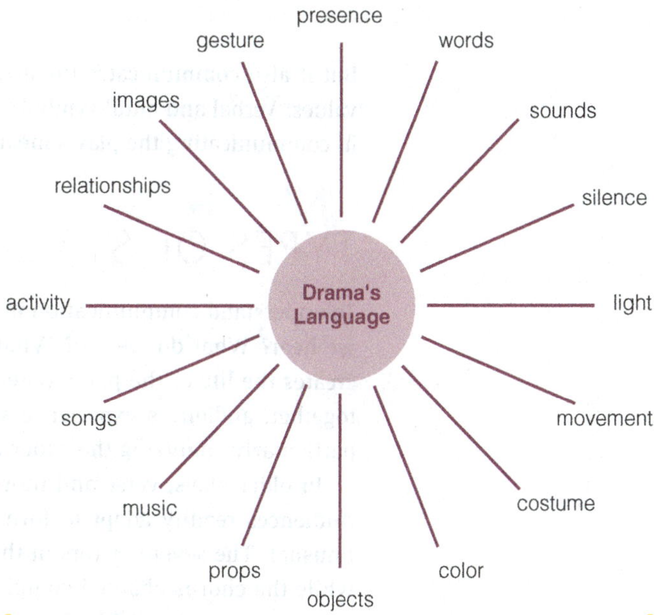

Drama's language

Drama's language has both verbal and nonverbal characteristics and can be divided into the many ways that meaning is communicated to audiences. The diagram lists sixteen ways that stage language communicates the stage's living reality.

©Martha Swope/New York Public Library for the Performing Arts

Hair
A politically active tribe of hippies in the rock musical *Hair*, first produced in 1968, whose lives are thrown into disarray when one of the tribe is drafted, Broadway.

domestic issues of legal and social debate, further emphasizing their symbolism.

In the theatre, both verbal and nonverbal symbols and signs are used to enhance audience perception of the actors' living presence. In Anton Chekhov's *The Cherry Orchard*, the orchard is a verbal symbol variously interpreted as the passing of the old way of life and/or of the coming of a new social order. Characters refer to the orchard as a family treasure, a local tradition, a beautiful object, and valuable property to be sold in order to save the estate from auction. The orchard is symbolic of the ways in which Chekhov's characters deal with or fail to deal with life's demands. The sound of the ax cutting down the trees at the play's end is a nonverbal sign, communicating the destruction of the family's treasure and their way of life. But it also communicates the arrival of a new social order with new strengths and values. Verbal and aural symbols and signs in Chekhov's plays reinforce one another in communicating the play's meaning.

TYPES OF STAGE LANGUAGE

To understand communication in the theatre, we must ask basic questions: What do we hear? What do we see? What is taking shape before us? What growing image creates the life of the play? When the many elements of the stage's language work together, audiences experience sensations, sounds, presence, and speech without particularly analyzing the experience in the moment.

In older plays, verse and prose alternate without seeming artificial and strange. Audiences readily adapt to forms and rhythms of speech that are unexpected or unusual. The several actors in the ancient Greek theatre spoke in heightened prose while the chorus chanted complex odes. Shakespeare's plays are written largely in iambic pentameter with fives stresses in each line. In order to vary the speech rhythms, advance the plot, and serve the emotional states of characters, Elizabethan playwrights introduced other forms of speaking, namely, the monologue, aside, and soliloquy.

The *monologue* is a character's extended, uninterrupted speech addressed to others. Marc Antony's uninterrupted, forty-two line speech to the citizens of Rome

©Todd Heisler/Redux

Samuel Beckett's *Eh Joe*
With Liam Neeson as the title character does not speak a single word in Samuel Beckett's portrait of a man on the edge of emotional collapse. A lover's voice (recorded words spoken by Penelope Wilton) emerges from the darkness of Joe's guilt-ravaged mind as the haunted image of his face grows larger in the background. The thirty-minute monologue, staged by Dublin's Gate Theater, was restaged for the Lincoln Center Festival, New York City.

in *Julius Caesar*, beginning "Friends, Romans, countrymen, lend me your ears," is a monologue. In modern plays by Samuel Beckett, the monologue becomes the entire play. The *aside* is a brief remark by a character spoken directly to the audience and is not overheard by other characters onstage. On the night that Iago maneuvers Othello into murdering Desdemona, he says in an aside to the audience: "This is the night/That either makes me or fordoes me quite." The *soliloquy*, best identified with Shakespeare, is a long speech delivered by a character, usually alone onstage, for the audience to overhear the character's inner thoughts. The soliloquies in *Hamlet*, *Macbeth*, *Othello*, and *King Lear* are some of the most beautiful in the English language.

Shakespeare's Verse

The soliloquy is a means of taking the audience into the character's mind to overhear unspoken thoughts and arguments with the self. Hamlet's "How all occasions do inform against me" begins with concern for his delayed revenge, then meditates on human nature and on the "thing" to be done. The precision of Hamlet's argument with himself reveals the brilliance of a mind that perceives the cause, proof, and means of revenge. The speech's length betrays Hamlet's habit of mind that delays his revenge against Claudius and fills time and space with words rather than actions. Measuring himself against his kinsman, the soldier Fortinbras, the man of action, Hamlet finds the example by which to act.

©Camerapresse/Redux

Shakespeare's *Hamlet*
As Hamlet, David Tennant delivers what is often thought of as a soliloquy to the skull of Yorick, but he is in the company of Horatio and the gravedigger. Royal Shakespeare Company, Stratford-upon-Avon, Great Britain.

FOCUS ON PLAYS

Soliloquy in Shakespeare's *Hamlet*

Hamlet: How all occasions do inform against me,
And spur my dull revenge! What is a man,
If his chief good and market of his time
Be but to sleep and feed? A beast, no more.
Sure, he that made us with such large discourse,
Looking before and after, gave us not
That capability and godlike reason
To fust in us unused. Now, whether it be
Bestial oblivion, or some craven scruple
Of thinking too precisely on the event,
A thought which, quartered, hath but one part wisdom
And ever three parts coward—I do not know
Why yet I live to say, "This thing's to do;"
Sith I have cause, and will, and strength, and means
To do't. Examples gross as earth exhort me.
Witness this army, of such mass and charge,
Led by a delicate and tender prince,
Whose spirit, with divine ambition puffed,
Makes mouths at the invisible event,
Exposing what is mortal and unsure
To all that fortune, death, and danger dare,
Even for an eggshell. Rightly to be great
Is not to stir without great argument,
But greatly to find a quarrel in a straw
When honor's at the stake. How stand I then,
That have a father killed, a mother stained,
Excitements of my reason and my blood,
And let all sleep, while to my shame I see
The imminent death of twenty thousand men
That for a fantasy and trick of fame
Go to their graves like beds, fight for a plot
Whereon the numbers cannot try the cause,
Which is not tomb enough and continent
To hide the slain? O, from this time forth,
My thoughts be bloody, or be nothing worth! (4, iv)

It is meaningful that Hamlet's speech is written as a soliloquy. He is, indeed, alone in the charge from his father's ghost and in the eventual killing of Claudius.

The speech moves in thirty-five lines from inactivity to activity, concluding with "O, from this time forth,/ My thoughts be bloody, or be nothing worth!" Hamlet, the hitherto invisible man of action, takes shape before our eyes, ears, and minds in sixty lines of blank verse.

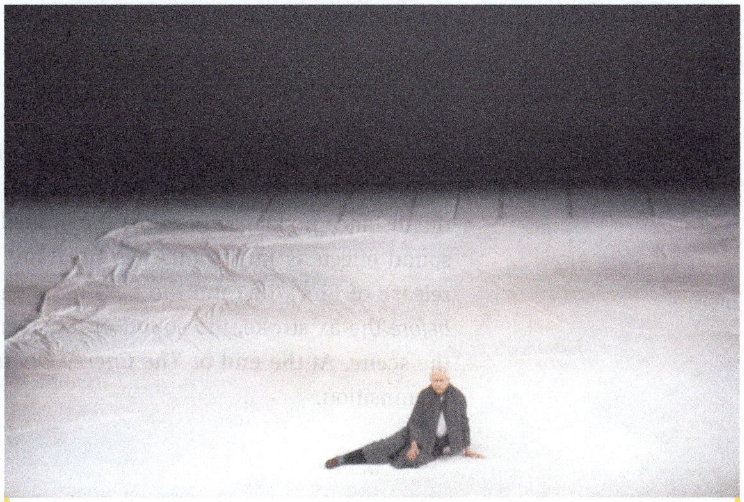

©George Joseph/New York Public Library for the Performing Arts

Chekov's *The Cherry Orchard*
Firs, the elderly valet, lies down alone—the final symbol of the passing of a way of life. The image of the dying man is reinforced by the sound effects that occur during the scene. *The Cherry Orchard*, directed by Andrei Serban, Lincoln Center Theater, New York City.

Sounds and Silences

Anton Chekhov ends *The Cherry Orchard* with verbal and nonverbal effects: sounds with silence, words with noise, physical activity with aural effects. Firs is the elderly valet left behind by the family in their hurried departure from the estate that has been sold at auction. His last speech is placed between stage directions suggesting offstage sounds

FOCUS ON PEOPLE IN THEATRE

PLAYWRIGHT

Anton Chekhov

Anton Pavlovich Chekhov (1860–1904) was born in southern Russia and studied medicine at Moscow University. During his student years, he wrote short stories to earn money. He began his playwriting career in the 1880s with one-act farces, *The Marriage Proposal* and *The Bear*. *Ivanov* (1887) was his first full-length play to be produced.

Chekhov redefined stage realism during the years of his association with the Moscow Art Theatre (1898–1904). The meaning of his plays is not in direct, purposive action but in the representation of a certain kind of rural Russian life, which he knew firsthand. Director Konstantin Stanislavski's style of interpreting the inner truth of Chekhov's characters and the mood of his plays resulted in one of the great theatrical collaborations.

©Time and Life Pictures/Getty Images

During his last years, Chekhov lived in Yalta, where he had gone for his health, and made occasional trips to Moscow to participate in the productions. He died of tuberculosis in a German spa in 1904, soon after the premiere of The Cherry Orchard.

During his short life, Chekhov wrote four masterpieces of modern stage realism: *The Sea Gull*, *Uncle Vanya*, *The Three Sisters*, and *The Cherry Orchard*.

of departure, of a breaking string, and of the stroke of an ax. The pauses in Firs's speech indicate the ending of a life, and also of a way of life. The fact that he is alone, locked in the house, forgotten and dying, tells us more vividly than his mutterings that "life has passed him by."

In Chekhov's plays, what people do is frequently more important than what they say. More important than Firs's words is the sound of the breaking string in the distance juxtaposed against the immediate sound of the ax. Even the order of the sound effects is important. The breaking string's mournful sound, symbolic of the release of Firs's life and the passing of the larger way of life, subsides into silence *before* the ax stroke, the sound of the aggressive new order taking over, intrudes on the scene. At the end of *The Cherry Orchard*, the audience hears and sees a world in transition.

FOCUS ON THEATRE

Anton Chekhov's *The Cherry Orchard*

After some years abroad, the widowed Madame Ranevskaya returns to her Russian estate to find that it has been heavily mortgaged to pay her debts and that it is to be auctioned. Generous and irresponsible, she seems incapable of recognizing her financial situation. A half-hearted attempt is made to collect money owed her by a neighboring landowner, but he is also in financial straits. Gaev, Madame Ranevskaya's brother, makes some suggestions, but his chief hope lies in an uncertain legacy from a relative or a rich marriage for Anya, Madame Ranevskaya's daughter. The only realistic proposal comes from Lopakhin, a merchant whose father was once a serf of the Ranevskaya family. He suggests cutting down the famous cherry orchard and dividing the land into plots for summer cottages. The family rejects the idea of destroying such beauty and tradition.

With no specific plan in mind for saving the estate, the family drifts aimlessly toward the day set for the auction. On the evening of the sale, Madame Ranevskaya gives a party she cannot afford. In the middle of the festivities, Lopakhin arrives; when questioned, he reveals that he has bought the estate and intends to carry out his plan for cutting down the orchard and subdividing the land.

With the estate and orchard now sold, the family prepares to leave. Forgotten in the confusion is the dying Firs, the devoted family servant. As the sound of the ax rings from the orchard, he lies down to rest and is soon motionless in the empty house.

©George Joseph/New York Public Library for the Performing Arts

© Richard Termine/The New York Times/Redux

The Cherry Orchard
(TOP) An early scene in *The Cherry Orchard*, directed by Andrei Serban, Lincoln Center Theater, New York City. (BOTTOM) Chekov's *The Cherry Orchard* with John Turturro as Lopakhin announcing his purchase of the estate with Dianne Wiest as Madame Ranevskaya in the background, directed by Andrei Belgrader, Classic Stage Company, Off Broadway.

FOCUS ON THEATRE

Chekhov's Sound Effects in *The Cherry Orchard*

In the modern theatre, stage directions are a means by which playwrights communicate imaginative worlds to directors, actors, designers, and readers. In the final scene of The Cherry Orchard, Chekhov describes the stage's appearance as he saw it in his mind's eye: Firs's costume, manner, and words; and the final powerful sounds.

LYUBOV: We are coming. (*They go out.*)

> *(The stage is empty. There is the sound of the doors being locked up, then of the carriages driving away. There is silence. In the stillness there is the dull stroke of an axe in a tree, clanging with a mournful lonely sound. Footsteps are heard. Firs appears in the doorway on the right. He is dressed as always—in a pea-jacket and white waist-coat with slippers on his feet. He is ill.)*

FIRS *(goes up to the doors, and tries the handles)*: Locked! They have gone ... *(sits down on sofa)*. They have forgotten me.... Never mind ... I'll sit here a bit.... I'll be bound Leonid Andreyevitch hasn't put his fur coat on and has gone off in his thin overcoat *(sighs anxiously)*. I didn't see after him.... These young people ... *(mutters something that can't be distinguished)*. Life has slipped by as though I hadn't lived. *(Lies down)* I'll lie down a bit.... There's no strength in you, nothing left you—all gone! Ech! I'm good for nothing *(lies motionless)*.

> *(A sound is heard that seems to come from the sky, like a breaking harp-string, dying away mournfully. All is still again, and there is heard nothing but the strokes of the axe far away in the orchard.)*
>
> *Curtain.*[4]

Brecht's Gestic Language

Bertolt Brecht's stage language includes music, song, placards, film projections, and *gest*. Brecht's concept of gest, or gestic language, is a matter of the actors' overall attitude toward what is going on around them and what they are asked to do within the circumstances of the text. In a reversal of emphasis, Brecht insisted that words follow the gest of the person speaking. He wrote:

> *"Gest" is not supposed to mean gesticulation: it is not a matter of explanatory or emphatic movements of the hands, but of overall attitudes. A language is gestic when it is grounded in a gest and conveys particular attitudes adopted by the speaker towards other men. The sentence "pluck the eye that offends thee out" is less effective from the gestic point of view than "if thine eye offend thee, pluck it out." The latter starts by presenting the eye, and the first clause has the definite gest of making an assumption; the main clause then comes as a surprise, a piece of advice, and a relief.*[5]

Bertolt Brecht's *The Caucasian Chalk Circle*

The characters' gestic language becomes visible in the test of the chalk circle. To decide who is worthy of rearing the child Michael, the judge orders that a circle be drawn on the floor and that the contestants pull the child from the circle. The materialistic

Courtesy Berliner Ensemble/Bertoldt Brecht Archive/Akademie der Kunste, Berlin

The Chalk-Circle Test from the 1954 Berliner Ensemble Production of Brecht's *The Caucasian Chalk Circle*

The circle drawn in white chalk signifies the test of true motherliness and rightful ownership. Judge Azdak gives the child to Grusha, who fails in the tug-of-war for fear of harming the boy.

attitudes of the lawyers and the governor's wife toward the child are contrasted with Grusha's humanity and love for the child. Grusha refuses to tug at the boy, whereas the governor's wife pulls the child from the circle two times. The wife's attitudes, words, and gestures betray the fact that her wealth and power depend upon her ownership of the child. We see that she is selfish and "grasping."

Brecht used music and song as well as dialogue to communicate his characters' thoughts and feelings. The narrator in *The Caucasian Chalk Circle* interrupts the play's action to sing songs that pinpoint social attitudes and injustices. He sings a song to reveal what Grusha thinks but does not say. As the Narrator sings, Brecht invites audiences to understand without becoming involved emotionally in the woman's selfless concern for the child.

THE SINGER: *Hear now what the angry woman thought and did not say:*
(Sings)
If he walked in golden shoes
Cold his heart would be and stony.

Courtesy Vikki Benner/Perseverance Theatre

The Caucasian Chalk Circle

Brecht's *The Caucasian Chalk Circle*, directed by Molly Smith, at the Perseverance Theatre, Alaska.

Humble folk he would abuse
He wouldn't know me.

Oh, it's hard to be hard-hearted
All day long from morn to night.
To be mean and high and mighty
Is a hard and cruel plight.

Let him be afraid of hunger
Not of the hungry man's spite
Let him be afraid of darkness
But not fear the light. (scene xi)[6]

CONTEMPORARY TRENDS IN AMERICAN THEATRE

INFLUENCES: ARTAUD'S "THEATRE OF CRUELTY"

French playwright and theatre theorist Antonin Artaud (1896–1948) adamantly opposed traditional dialogue that furthers plot, reveals character, and explores psychological and social problems. He opposed performing written plays and advocated staging themes, facts, or adapted works without regard for text. He also favored inducing in audiences, shock reactions and visceral responses. He called for a "theatre of cruelty" to purge the audience's feelings of hatred and violence against individuals and groups through use of nonverbal effects: shrill sounds, waves of light, and violent physicalizations in unusual theatre spaces, such as remodeled factories and airplane hangars, where audiences are seated in the middle of the space or in mobile chairs and follow the spectacle as it takes place around them. Above all, Artaud aimed to assault the audience's senses, thereby cleansing spectators morally and spiritually for the improvement of humankind.

Influenced by Artaud's theories, American playwrights of the sixties revolted against a stage language of ordinary conversation that defined character, furthered plot, and argued social themes. They set out to assault the spectator's senses with sounds, violent images, nudity, and physicalization in works that grew out of protests against the political, military, industrial, and cultural establishments in the United States.

By the end of the Vietnam War, American political consciousness was largely dissipated; the new performance techniques of experimental groups in the United States, such as the Open Theatre, the Living Theatre, and the Performance Group, had become predictable; and the games, transformations, and group improvisations of these companies had been appropriated by the commercial theatre as productions of *Hair* and *A Chorus Line* moved onto Broadway.

Powerful new voices emerged in the American theatre in the late sixties and throughout the seventies as a postwar wave of writers, including Edward Albee, Ed Bullins, Alice Childress, María Irene Fornés, John Guare, LeRoi Jones, Adrienne

"It has not been definitively proved that the language of words is the best possible language. And it seems that on the stage, which is above all a space to fill and a place where something happens, the language of words may have to give way before a language of signs whose objective aspect is the one that has the most immediate impact upon us."[7]

—Antonin Artaud, *The Theater and Its Double*

Kennedy, Arthur Kopit, Charles Ludlam, David Mamet, Terrence McNally, Marsha Norman, David Rabe, Sam Shepard, Megan Terry, Lanford Wilson, and many others. All tested the American character, family, and dreams and found them wanting.

David Mamet's Wordsmiths

In language at once fragmented and profane, David Mamet explores the myths of American capitalism—the loss of individual and national enterprise—in the salesmen, confidence men, and tricksters that inhabit *American Buffalo*, *Glengarry Glen Ross*, *Speed the Plow*, and *Race*.

Mamet's characters are *wordsmiths* who invent lies, sell reassurance, tell stories, and command experience through words alone. His world is composed of petty criminals (*American Buffalo*), dubious real estate salesmen (*Glengarry Glen Ross*), and second-rate Hollywood agents (*Speed the Plow*). His urban cowboys and gangsters speak a language that is self-serving, caustic, and exploitative as they hustle their "deals." These characters desperately wish to connect with one another, but they have forgotten how to do so except in their "business" relationships.

In *Glengarry Glen Ross*, Mamet contrives a neat paradigm (the real estate office) of a competitive capitalistic society. The play is set in and around a Chicago real estate office and takes its title from a subdivision ripe for the deal. The play concerns a group of none-too-successful real estate salesmen whose company has imposed a ruthless new regimen: The most successful salesman will receive a Cadillac; the runner-up, a set of steak knives; and the loser will be fired. The key to success lies in securing the addresses of likely buyers ("the leads"), and the pressure to succeed encourages unscrupulous methods with respect to clients and even the company. Increasingly desperate, one of the salesmen, Shelly Levene, breaks into the office and steals the premium address list of potential clients. Police are called to investigate the "crime." By contrast, the salesmen's day-to-day activities as they go about deceiving their customers are regarded as good business tactics, sanctioned by the ethics of a world in which success is the ultimate achievement.

Mamet's salesmen talk in code, deploying the jargon of the trade: leads, deals, sales, closings, percentages, marks, streaks, and so on. They talk in incomplete sentences sprinkled with profanity. The characters are consummate storytellers—wordsmiths. When the need arises, they improvise a drama or create stories of total plausibility to turn a situation into advantage, a sale, and cash.

It should not be assumed that the ethical failures of Mamet's confidence men lose them either the playwright's sympathy or the audience's. Mamet's concern for the individual's alienation from his or her moral nature forces us to look at the neediness and vulnerability among fellow tricksters and unwary customers.

In David Mamet's work, there is a yearning for that very sense of trust denied by every betrayal in the petty wheeling and dealing that he documents. Somewhere at the heart of his characters' being is a sense of *need* that is the beginning of their redemption (and our sympathy for them). Their words may snap under the pressure of fear

FOCUS ON PLAYS

David Mamet's *Glengarry Glen Ross*

David Mamet's wordsmiths, such as real estate salesman Shelly Levene in *Glengarry Glen Ross*, articulate in monosyllabic words the panic and sheer poetry of their beleaguered lives. Mamet's emphases (the italicized words) in the text underscore the hard-sell core of the salesmen's lives as they fend off failure in the guise of loss of influence, respect, leads, sales, closings, bonuses, new deals, and even the job. In Mamet's writing, words bring to the surface the characters' fear, greed, and desperation.

A booth at a Chinese restaurant, Williamson and Levene are seated at the booth.

Levene: John ... John ... John. Okay. John. John. Look: *(Pause.)* The Glengarry Highland's leads, you're sending Roma out. Fine. He's a good man. We know what he is. He's fine. All I'm saying, you look at the *board,* he's throwing ... wait, wait, wait, he's throwing them *away,* he's throwing the leads away. All that I'm saying, that you're wasting leads. I don't want to tell you your job. All that I'm saying, things get set, I know they do, you get a certain *mindset....* A guy gets a reputation. We know how this ... all I'm saying, put a *closer* on the job. There's more than one man for the ... Put a ... wait a second, put a *proven man out* ... and you watch, now *wait* a second—and you watch your *dollar* volumes.... You start closing them for *fifty* 'stead of *twenty-five* ... you put a *closer* on the ...

©Brigitte Lacombe

Mamet's *Glengarry Glen Ross*
Robert Prosky as Shelly Levene (left) argues for "leads" in the Goodman Theatre production, Chicago, of David Mamet's *Glengarry Glen Ross*, directed by Gregory Mosher.

Williamson: Shelly, you blew the last ...

Levene: No. John. No. Let's wait, let's back up here, I did ... will you please? Wait a second. Please. I didn't "blow" them. No. I didn't "blow" them. No. One kicked out, one I closed ...

Williamson: ... you didn't close ... *(Act I)*[8]

or greed; they may try to adjust themselves to the shape of myths and fantasies; or they may deny or exploit the desire for companionship. Deep down, however, below the broken rhythms of speech and the four-letter words, beyond the failed gestures at contact, is a need for connection.

Sam Shepard's Magical Realism

Sam Shepard's plays—*Buried Child, Curse of the Starving Class, True West, Fool for Love, A Lie of the Mind,* and *The God of Hell*—take audiences into the inner workings of the modern American family in carefully structured, seemingly realistic plays set in well-scrubbed kitchens and seedy living rooms. Shepard country is the American

Midwest, where farms are no longer worked and families are a dying species whose bucolic speech is laced with "deadpan surrealism."[9]

Sam Shepard's *Buried Child*

In Shepard's Pulitzer Prize-winning *Buried Child*, symbols of sexual impotence abound, fantastical crops grow in uncultivated fields, and a baby's corpse is mysteriously unearthed. Carrots are sliced up onstage with malicious energy, an amputee is robbed of his artificial leg, the elderly father's head is brutally shaved with an electric razor, and a baby's skeleton is brought onstage. Crops mysteriously grow in abundance—visible to the innocent and the redeemed.

Shepard's grown children have complicated relationships with dying or distant fathers, and events are transformed into theatrical poetry. The central action of *Buried Child* is the grandson Vincent's quest for his roots and identity. Shepard is writing here within the mainstream of Western drama, from Sophocles's *Oedipus the King* to Edward Albee's *Who's Afraid of Virginia Woolf?* The grandson returns to his family, who live in a midwestern farmhouse, to find out who he is. The past, once so promising, is filled with horror: one son killed in a gangland murder; a baby born of incest drowned; another son maimed in a chain-saw accident. Without the

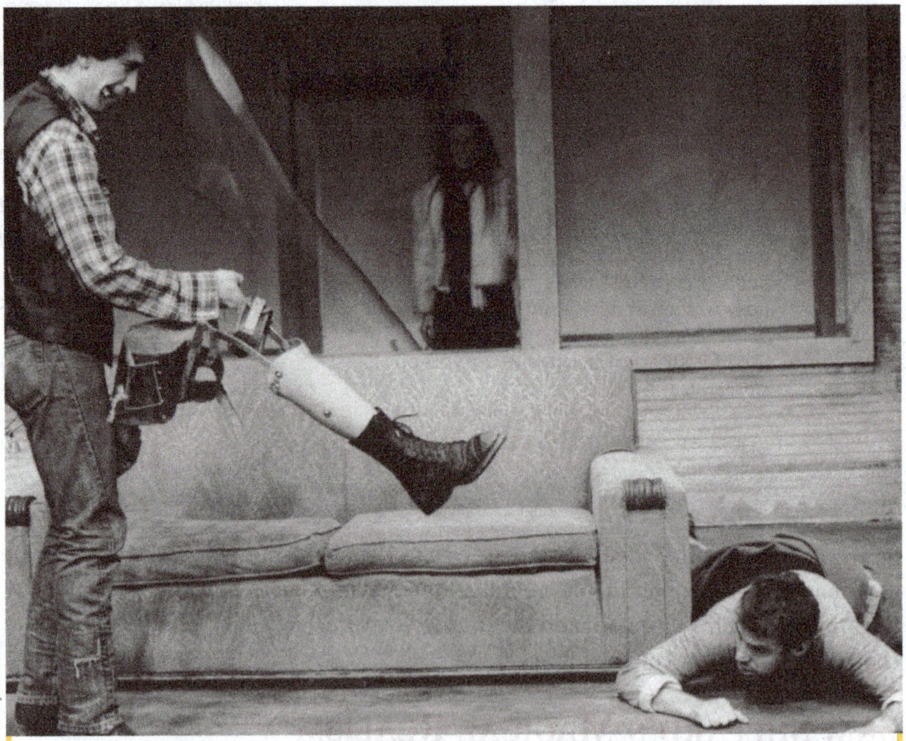

Sam Shepard's *Buried Child*
In *Buried Child*, Bradley (Jay Sanders, right) is threatened with his own artificial leg by Vincent (Christopher McCann). Shelly (Mary McDonnell), Vincent's girlfriend, looks on. Off Broadway production.

touchstones of normal family life and friendship, Shepard's characters live in a world that is indifferent to their betrayal, guilt, and violence. The family is locked together in mutual dependence, caring for the sick and looking after the physically and psychologically maimed. But these are conditioned responses. The characters do not really know one another. Hostile and ineffectual, they assert themselves with verbal and physical violence.

Almost thirty years after writing *Buried Child*, Shepard wrote *The God of Hell* (a coded reference to plutonium) and *Kicking a Dead Horse* (the supine horse is a now-dead symbol of freedom, possibility, and lost frontiers) to demonstrate, once again, that cherished American values of home, family, and country are chimeras, evaporating like morning fog in a new millennium of government oversight, corporate raiders, and radioactive doom. Shepard's more recent plays address loss and regret both personal and national in a postmillennial world.

TRANSITION

Playwrights are among the most important of the theatre's "image makers." The writing of plays is their medium for imitating human behavior and events. Other theatre artists interpret the playwright's text in the theatre's three-dimensional space, giving it shape, sound, color, rhythm, image, activity, and human presence.

Since the time of ancient Greek festivals, the actor's role in the theatre has been celebrated. Although acting styles and training have changed over centuries, the actor joins the playwright as one of the theatre's earliest "image makers."

Theatre: A Way of Seeing Online

Visit the CourseMate for Theatre: A Way of Seeing 7th Edition for quick access to the digital study resources that accompany this chapter, including links to the websites listed below, Theatre Workshop, digital glossary, a chapter quiz and more.

Websites

The *Theatre: A Way of Seeing* CourseMate includes links for all the websites described below. Simply select "Web links" from the Chapter Resources for Chapter 8, and click on the link that interests you. You'll be taken directly to the site described.

Anton Chekhov on Writing
A collection of quotations from Anton Chekhov on the subject of writing.

The Complete Works of William Shakespeare
Links to the complete texts of Shakespeare's plays and poetry, plus links to other information about Shakespeare.

The David Mamet Review
Website of the David Mamet Society. Click on the "Recent Issues" link to access articles about Mamet and reviews of his plays.

The Sam Shepard Website
A haven for all things Shepard: current productions, reviews, texts, and other resources of interest to both the casual playgoer and the scholar.

9

IMAGE MAKER: THE ACTOR

For it is not a game of charades, this acting world of ours; it is an everlasting search for truth.[1]

—Laurence Oliver, *On Acting*

Jerzy Grotowski's "poor theatre" expresses a desire to reduce the theatrical experience to *essentials*. In the American theatre, the trend has its roots in the 1938 Broadway production of Thornton Wilder's *Our Town*. Director Jed Harris took Wilder's straightforward play about recognizable townspeople in Grover's Corner, USA, and placed actors on a bare stage framed by the theatre's back wall. Virtually no scenery was used, costumes were muted, and properties were minimal. The actors told Wilder's story using only those properties, such as chairs and umbrellas, that they could move on and off the stage for themselves. The *actors* were the one indispensable element of the theatrical experience.

As Grotowski discovered, when everything else is stripped away, audiences *rediscover* the actor's presence and art.

PREVIEW

Acting combines belief and technique to create truthful behavior—of life taking place onstage, as if for the first time, and every time. Theatre is, after all, the art human beings make out of themselves.

ACTING—AS IMAGINATION AND TECHNIQUE

Acting Is Doing

As defined by acting teacher and director Sanford Meisner, acting is "living truthfully in imagined circumstances." That search for truthful behavior is the foundation stone of the actor's art.

Notable stage and film actor Al Pacino appeared as the moneylender Shylock in a post-millennial version of Shakespeare's *The Merchant of Venice* with Lily Rabe as Portia; New York Shakespeare Festival/Public Theatre; Broadway.

At the outset, we can state what acting is not. Acting is not showing, narrating, illustrating, or exhibiting. Acting is not dressing up and displaying emotions. Acting is a creative process as old as the first actor who entered the ancient Greek festivals. As a creative artist, the actor (1) selects *sensory* responses (both physiological and emotional) in the search for (2) *selected* behavior pertinent to a character's needs within the (3) *given circumstances*, or human problems, contained within the play.

Acting does not begin with appearing onstage before an audience. It begins with an individual's talent, imagination, discipline, need to express, and process of observation through the sensory organs (eyes, ears, skin, tongue, nose). To prepare a role, the actor selects from memory and personal experience what he or she has seen, heard, felt, and experienced over a lifetime. "At its most rewarding," says British actor Ian McKellen, "acting involves an intense combination of intellect, imagination, and hard work, belying the popular distorted image of dressing-up, booming voices, and shrieking exhibitionism."[2]

Acting also involves other aptitudes that require flexibility. The actor must be capable of taking requests from the director or playwright and be able to absorb and relate to the needs of others onstage. It is imperative that he or she, when called upon, work with and support other collaborating artists, particularly designers and technology artists. In all instances, the actor must show respect to supporting crew members, including the stage manager, backstage dressers, properties crew, and others providing technical support.

Thornton Wilder's *Our Town*
From the original Broadway production of Thornton Wilder's *Our Town*.

THE ACTOR'S REALITY

Reduced to its simplest terms, the actor's goal is to tell the character's circumstances in the play's story as truthfully and effectively as possible. Those *circumstances* are the essential conditions in the play's world that include time (when), place (where), surroundings (what), and others (who) in the situation. In rehearsals, the actor works to discover the truth of an individual's behavior in the circumstances existing among the play's characters and events. The actor must concentrate on the *truth* of the character's behavior—psychological motives, sensory responses, and objectives—within the context of the play, not within the context of "giving" a performance.

Through meticulous "homework," the actor comes to believe in the reality of what he or she is doing onstage from moment to moment. To understand better the actor's truth or reality, let us compare the situation in a play with that in an event on the sports field. Like baseball, for example, a play has its own rules and regulations, the set dimensions of the playing area, a set number of persons on the field, and a coach. The interactions among the players are real, vital, and intense. For the playing time, the field is the players' whole universe. The game, like a stage play, has its own reality that is frequently "more real" and vibrant than everyday reality. Likewise, the actor is given a story, an identity, clothing, circumstances, relationships, motives, obstacles, activities, and environs. The play sets the number of persons; the director and designer set the dimensions of the playing area; the playwright sets the circumstances under which the actor-as-character appears in the story. The play has its own reality that the actor finds in the exploration of the play's life and in the character's circumstances and needs.

Anton Chekov's *The Cherry Orchard*
Dianne Wiest as Madame Ranevskaya in Chekhov's *The Cherry Orchard*, directed by Andrei Belgrader, Classic Stage Company, Off Broadway.

Eugene O'Neill's *The Iceman Cometh*
Brian Dennehy and Nathan Lane in Eugene O'Neill's *The Iceman Cometh*, The Goodman Theatre, Chicago.

The creative process that brings the actor to the "field of play," like Nathan Lane as Hickey in Eugene O'Neill's *The Iceman Cometh* or Dianne Wiest as Madame Ranevskaya in *The Cherry Orchard*, is demanding and complex. Throughout stage history, actors have honed both internal belief and external technique to create the character's reality onstage. *Technique* and *belief* are the fundamentals of the actor's craft. Sometimes, however, in the history of the profession one has been favored over the other.

External Technique

External technique is that activity by which an actor chooses, imitates, or outwardly illustrates a character's behavior. The mimetic actor approaches a role through a deep and passionate study of human behavior *in all its outward forms*, with an eye toward reproducing them in a disciplined and sensitive way.

The eighteenth-century British actor David Garrick approached acting as an imitation of life—he called acting *mimical behavior*. To prepare for the role of King Lear, for example, he studied the appearance and behavior of a friend who had been driven mad by his child's death. By his detailed reproduction of such behavior onstage, Garrick introduced what some called *naturalistic* acting into the English theatre. He believed that the actor could produce emotions by a convincing imitation and skilled projection of those emotions being imitated. He did not believe that the actor should actually experience anger or sadness or joy to project these emotions to an audience.

Courtesy Theatre Museum/ V & A Images, London/Art Resource, NY

Garrick's *Macbeth*

David Garrick played Macbeth in a contemporary military uniform. He was famous for the dagger scene; his contemporaries praised him for his ability to project the fact that he was "seeing" the dagger before him. It has been said that Garrick's "face was a language unto itself."

Ascribed to him is the comment "that a man was incapable of becoming an actor who was not absolutely independent of circumstances calculated to excite emotion, adding that for his own part he could speak to a post with the same feelings and expression as to the loveliest Juliet under the heaven."[3] In this external or purely technical approach, actors (such as David Garrick) aim for a calculated, yet seemingly truthful, *presentation* of a character's life onstage.

Many actors in Great Britain and Europe have followed Garrick's approach, thereby creating one school of thought on the matter of what distinguishes great acting. Throughout stage history, actors have been celebrated for their exceptional charisma, their theatrical skills, the bravado of their startling choices, and their ability to *illustrate* many different characters during a long career. Laurence Olivier is included among the ranks of actors notable for working from the "outside in." Celebrated in his lifetime as Great Britain's greatest actor, Olivier admitted being uncomfortable working in any other way. No one can deny the brilliance of Olivier's career, but he was often criticized for being "too technical." He defended his methods in interviews and autobiographical writings. One night, after Olivier had played in John Osborne's

The Entertainer, his friends rushed backstage to congratulate him on a spontaneous and deeply moving performance. He admitted the spontaneity but said, "I don't like that kind of acting; I didn't know what I was doing."[4]

Today's actors, such as Al Pacino, Cherry Jones, Ralph Fiennes, and Viola Davis, strive to find the physical reality of the character, to walk and talk like the king, beggar, housewife, or spinster they are playing. But they also reach into the truthful subtleties of the character's psychology and wholly embody the role, filling it with breath, blood, impulses, desires, and emotions so that we believe Ralph Fiennes when, as Hamlet, he says, "The time is out of joint. Oh, cursed spite/That ever I was born to set it right!"; or, when Al Pacino as Shylock argues, "Hath not a Jew eyes? hath not a Jew hands, organs, dimensions, senses, affections, passions?" We forget that we are watching working actors and become absorbed in the life and trials of Denmark's Prince or the vengeance of Venice's Merchant.

Internal Belief

A second school of thought on acting emerged with those actors who astonish audiences with a creative process that is intuitive, subconscious, and subjective. Actors Ellen Burstyn, Denzel Washington, Cherry Jones, and Al Pacino work "from the inside out" to select behavior pertinent to the character's needs within the play's imagined circumstances. These "realistic" actors allow personal behavior to develop out of the playwright's prescribed circumstances, knowing that their actions will involve a moment-to-moment subjective experience.

© T. Charles Erickson

Cherry Jones in *The Heiress*
Cherry Jones is a graduate of the actor-training program at Carnegie Mellon University, Pittsburgh. She is seen here as Catherine Sloper in the Broadway revival of *The Heiress*; she played the role for 371 performances.

A great deal of the actor's work is a searching within for emotional impulses from personal experience to give reality to the new existence or role. When, at the age of eighteen, Uta Hagen played the young, would-be actress Nina in Chekhov's *The Sea Gull*, she understood Nina as a naive, middle-class girl from the country who is drawn into the life of her neighbor, a famous actress of whom she is in awe, and the actress's lover, a noted writer whom Nina hero-worships.

Onstage with Lynn Fontanne as Madame Arkadina, Hagen found it easy to use her awe of the famous actress and her celebrated husband, actor Alfred Lunt. She said, "I was in awe of Miss Fontanne and hero-worshipped Mr. Lunt. These particular character relationships were mirrored in my own, and I used their reality directly for my role."[5]

Most modern theories of actor training address methods of working "from the inside out." Konstantin Stanislavski's "Method" became the most famous and influential in modern times, especially among American actors.

THE ACTOR'S TOOLS

©Joan Marcus

Stephen Sondheim's *Follies*
Jane Houdyshell as Hattie Walker singing "Broadway Baby" in Sondheim's *Follies*, Broadway.

The actor's tools are the body, voice, impulses, emotions, energy, concentration, imagination, improvisations, and intellect. Actors must be flexible, disciplined, and expressive to communicate a wide range of attitudes, traits, emotions, feelings, and behaviors. The range of demands on the actor's abilities during a career is enormous. Actors must be adequate to re-creating classical and modern roles, such as Medea or Hamlet or Blanche DuBois or Shelly Levene. Toward this goal, actors must learn how to maintain a healthy, flexible and energetic voice and body. In training and rehearsals, the actor works to understand the body and voice: how to control them; how to release psychological tensions and blocks that inhibit them; how to increase powers of imagination, observation, and concentration; and how to integrate them with the demands of the script and director. By using these tools, the actor combines inner belief with external technique.

Successful actors need not be classically beautiful, slim, or define the profile of current fashion. They must, however, possess the "It" factor—defined as the power of apparently effortless embodiment of contradictory qualities simultaneously: strength *and* vulnerability, innocence *and* experience, and singularity *and* typicality among them.[6]

THE ACTOR'S TRAINING

For many years, European and American actors were trained in the theatre itself, beginning their careers as apprentices. A young man or woman who showed ability would be hired to play small parts in a provincial stock company. The older actors would coach the young person, prescribing voice and body exercises that had been handed down for generations. This kind of external training developed a voice capable of being heard in large theatres, exaggerated gestures, and skill in speaking verse. If actors showed talent, they would be given longer parts and eventually be invited to join the company.

When *realism* came into fashion late in the nineteenth century, this "large" style of acting seemed exaggerated and unconvincing. As the stage came to be thought of as a recognizable place with a reality that corresponded to what ordinary people observed around them, scene design, stage decor, and acting styles changed. The play's world—the environment and characters—was represented as directly and in as lifelike a way as possible. A middle-class street, house, and living room represented onstage had to look like middle-class streets, houses, and living rooms outside the theatre. Actors also dressed like bankers or menial laborers that audiences encountered outside the theatre. So, too, actors were called upon to set aside declamation and artificial gestures for the speech, walk, and behavior of recognizable human beings. To capture onstage and before an audience this sense of life being lived as it actually is, new methods for training actors had to be developed and new approaches arrived at for preparing a role.

Preparing the Role

Stanislavski's "Method"

At the turn of the nineteenth century, Konstantin Stanislavski, the Russian actor-director, set about developing a systematic approach to training actors *to work from the inside outward*. Today, his premises, developed over a lifetime, are accepted as the point of departure for most contemporary acting theories and practices.

Stanislavski laid down the basis for a psychological understanding of acting and fused it with a deep sense of aesthetic truth. "The fundamental aim of our art," Stanislavski wrote in *An Actor Prepares*, "is the creation of [the] inner life of a human spirit and its expression in an artistic form."[7] To arrive at this truth, Stanislavski proposed that actors understand how men and women actually behave physically and psychologically in given circumstances. Stanislavski's approach asked the actor to study and experience subjective emotions and feelings and to manifest them to audiences by physical and vocal means. He also stressed that personal truth in acting had to be balanced by attention to the playwright's text, to imaginative realities outside the actor's immediate experience. The actor was called upon to enter "the imagined world of the play," not just to attend only to his or her part.

Vandamm Theatre Collection/New York Public Library for the Performing Arts

Stanislavski the Actor
Stanislavski as Gaev in the 1904 Moscow Art Theatre production of Chekhov's *The Cherry Orchard*.

Over the years, Stanislavski developed a system for training actors (his followers in America called it "the Method") whereby they not only would create a subjective reality of their own—an inner truth of feeling and experience—but also would represent the "outer" truth of the character's reality in the surrounding world of the play. Speaking of the "external" acting that he had seen and abhorred in his time, Stanislavski said that "the difference between my art and that is the difference between 'seeming and being.'"[8]

What distinguished Stanislavski's theory (and his lasting influence) was the actor's discovery of the purpose and objectives of his or her character's behavior and the successful "playing" of those goals within the world of the play.

©Sara Krulwich/The New York Times/Redux

Gore Vidal's *The Best Man*
James Earl Jones as former President Arthur Hockstader in *Gore Vidal's The Best Man*, directed by Michael Wilson, Broadway.

Stanislavski developed rehearsal methods by which the actor would "live life" onstage. He developed a set of exercises and principles designed to help the actor call on personal feelings and experiences, and the body and the voice, in the creation of the role. This aspect of his training was called the "psychotechnique." Through the development of self-discipline, observation, memory, relaxation, and total concentration, his actors learned to recall emotions from their own lives that were analogous to those experienced by the characters they played. What mattered to Stanislavski was the *actor's truth*: What the actor feels and experiences internally expresses itself in what the character says and how the character reacts to the play's given circumstances.

The Magic If

Stanislavski called "the magic if" the method by which the actor thinks, "If I were in Othello's *situation*, what would I do?" Not, "If I were Othello, what would I do?" By "being" in the situation, the actor can give a performance that is a truthful, living experience, not merely the imitation of the experience.

Recalling Emotions

How does the actor create a reality of emotions in performance night after night? One of the early methods developed by Stanislavski was "emotional recall," or "affective memory," which became a subject of considerable dispute among his American followers. Lee Strasberg interpreted emotional recall as the actor's conscious efforts to remember circumstances surrounding an emotion-filled occasion from the past in order to stimulate impulses and emotions that could be used onstage. For example, the actor uses a relative's death, or another sad event, to evoke memories that bring tears of sorrow. Actress Meryl Streep has said, "Acting is not about being someone different. It is finding the similarity in what is apparently different, then finding myself in there."[9]

FOCUS ON THEATRE

Uta Hagen "Preparing" the Role of Blanche DuBois

Uta Hagen, actress and teacher, described her preparations for performing the role of Tennessee Williams's heroine as a hunt for understanding the character's needs and desires for perfection, gentleness, beauty, romantic love, and protection against the world's ugliness and brutality.

In order to bridge the enormous distance between the actress's nature and the role, Hagen called upon sensory and psychological responses to animate her actions as Blanche DuBois. She called them *substitutions*.

The actress remembered personal experiences that could be readily substituted for Blanche's desire for civility in her life. Hagen substituted personal responses to beautiful music, poetry, opera, and elegant dinner parties. In the absence of actually having lived in a plantation house in Mississippi, Hagen substituted her memories of visits to other mansions and found ways to build from her own experiences the impact of the cramped Kowalski apartment and the cacophonous New Orleans street noises on Blanche's frayed sensibilities.

For Hagen, substitutions were central to the actor's creativity and craft in the building of a role. But, the actor does not stop there. The character's emotional life must be reproduced in the theatre night after night with precise timing, on cue, and with a minimum of conscious thought.

In 1947, as artistic partner and teacher, Hagen joined the professional actor-training school HB Studio in New York City; her books *Respect for Acting* (with Haskel Frankel) and *A Challenge for the Actor* remain important sources on the acting process.

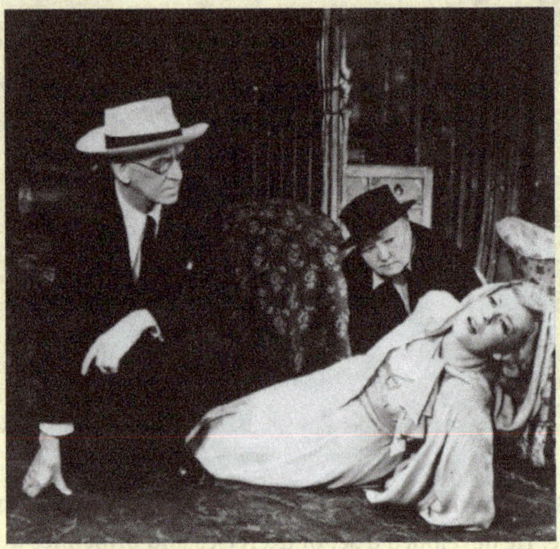
Eileen Darby Images

Uta Hagen as Blanche DuBois
She succeeded Jessica Tandy as Blanche DuBois on Broadway in *A Streetcar Named Desire*.

Psychophysical Actions

During the last ten years of his life, Stanislavski revised his understanding of emotional recall. Concerned about the actor's reliance on recalling emotions every night of the performance, he turned to physical actions, or what he called the "physical score," as a means of triggering emotional memory in a more spontaneous and truthful way. Combined with an understanding of the objectives of the character and the play, the actor could repeat physical actions night after night and organically trigger emotional memory. Stanislavski gave a name to this new dimension of his work with actors: "psychophysical actions," that is, an inner psychological understanding combined with physical actions. The goal remained the same: the actor's truthful behavior within the play's given circumstances.[10]

TRENDS IN TRAINING AMERICAN ACTORS

Today's acting programs evolved in studios and universities across the United States. The theory and practice of modern actor training ranges from the Neighborhood Playhouse, The Stella Adler Conservatory of Acting, and The William Esper Studio (to name only three) to degree programs in some 1,600 colleges and universities. Trends in American actor training, from Stanislavski-based approaches to the "practical aesthetics" of David Mamet and the "Viewpoints" of Anne Bogart, are profiled here, beginning with the Actors Studio and the teachings of Lee Strasberg.

FOCUS ON THEATRE

Lee Strasberg and the Actors Studio

Courtesy Lee Strasberg Theatre Institute

Lee Strasberg (1901–1982), one of the best-known acting teachers in America, transformed Stanislavski's system of acting into an American "Method." Stella Adler, Robert Lewis, and Sanford Meisner also famously devised their own variations on Stanislavski's research to influence actor training in the United States.

In 1947, Elia Kazan, Robert Lewis, and Cheryl Crawford, members of the Group Theatre (an ensemble of actors, directors, and playwrights), started the Actors Studio as a workshop for professional actors (directors and playwrights were later added) to concentrate on their craft away from the pressures of the commercial theatre. The studio is located today in a former church at 432 West Forty-fourth Street in New York City, where Lee Strasberg assumed leadership in 1951. (A second studio, Actors Studio West, was later opened in Hollywood.) As a teacher and acting theorist, Strasberg revolutionized American actor training and engaged such remarkable performers as Marlon Brando, Julie Harris, Paul Newman, Geraldine Page, Joanne Woodward, Dustin Hoffman, Ellen Burstyn, Robert de Niro, and Al Pacino.

Strasberg demanded great discipline of his actors, as well as great depths of psychological truthfulness. He once explained his approach in this way:

"The human being who acts is the human being who lives. That is a terrifying circumstance. Essentially the actor acts a fiction, a dream; in life the stimuli to which we respond are always real. The actor must constantly respond to stimuli that are imaginary. And yet this must happen not only just as it happens in life, but actually more fully and more expressively. Although the actor can do things in life quite easily, when he has to do the same thing on the stage under fictitious conditions he has difficulty because he is not equipped as a human being merely to playact at imitating life. He must somehow believe. He must somehow be able to convince himself of the rightness of what he is doing in order to do things fully on the stage."[11]

After Strasberg's death in 1982, the Actors Studio has been lead by copresidents Ellen Burstyn, Harvey Keitel, and Al Pacino, along with a series of artistic directors (most recently Ellen Burstyn). Strasberg's thoughts on the "Method" were published posthumously as *A Dream of Passion: The Development of the Method*. In 1994, the studio initiated a three-year Master of Fine Arts degree program with New York's New School in lower Manhattan and James Lipton has created a popular television show, *Inside the Actors Studio*, in which he interviews actors, director, and authors.

Sanford Meisner's Foundations

Creating another American approach to actor training, Sanford Meisner began teaching at The Neighborhood Playhouse School of the Theatre in New York City in 1935 and became head of the Playhouse the following year. As actor and teacher, Meisner evolved a "foundation" technique for training actors that sets out an approach to the creation of truthful behavior within the imaginary circumstances (the human problems) contained within the play.

As a founding member of the Group Theatre, Meisner was exposed to the ideas of Konstantin Stanislavski in the 1930s and emerged from the Group Theatre along with Lee Strasberg, Stella Adler, and Robert Lewis as a preeminent teacher of the "Method." Each developed his or her own approach to training actors. Meisner's foundations aim to ignite the actor's imagination and provide means for achieving truthful behavior onstage. These techniques are built upon what Meisner calls "the reality of doing." His system of exercises provides actors with the means for calling upon inner impulses and instinctive behavior, freeing the imagination and strengthening concentration, to achieve a "reality of doing." For Meisner, this "reality of doing" is the *foundation* of acting.

Meisner summarized his approach in this way: "My approach is based on bringing the actor back to his emotional impulses and to acting that is firmly rooted in the instinctive. It is based on the fact that all good acting comes from the heart."[12]

"Practical Aesthetics" with David Mamet and William H. Macy

Practical aesthetics as an acting technique evolved out of a series of workshops given by playwright David Mamet and actor William H. Macy in the early eighties. These workshops mixed the beliefs of ancient Stoics ("treat the endeavor with respect") with Stanislavski's principles on acting ("to work truthfully within the play's given circumstances") as a "gateway to truthful performance."[13]

FOCUS ON THEATRE

Atlantic Theatre Company

Atlantic Theatre Company, an award-winning Off Broadway theatre, was formed in 1985 when playwright David Mamet urged a group of students to form a company to serve the play, new and established playwrights, and society in powerful and truthful ways. Today, the company has a home in a Revival-style historic landmark building in Manhattan's Chelsea district; its actor-training school, located on Sixteenth Street, is affiliated with New York University. Neil Pepe is the company's artistic director.

The goal of "practical aesthetics" is to provide the actor with tools to perform with the freedom to be completely involved with the play as it unfolds. The focus of the training is on things *within the actor's control*: voice, body, concentration, script analysis.

The training is based upon acting as a craft with a definite set of learned skills and tools combined with will, courage, and common sense to help the actor bring a living humanity to the playwright's circumstances. The actor's homework focuses on physical actions (opening a window, for example) that the actor is called upon to accomplish and analysis of the playwright's intentions and words (script analysis). Exercises in repetition are added to heighten the actor's awareness of living truthfully moment to moment onstage. Moreover, rehearsals are treated as part of a work ethic that fosters habits for achieving a concrete, doable objective in a scene, thus freeing the actor to pursue the emotions and inflections that complete the character's moment of truth.

As set forth in *A Practical Handbook for the Actor*, practical aesthetics is a process of making acting tools habitual in order to free the actor in rehearsals and performance to live truthfully and fully within the play's circumstances. In a letter to the company, David Mamet said that "a good actor sticks to his objective, no matter what. Emotion comes, sure, but it's a by-product of the larger action. It's all about serving the play."[14]

ANNE BOGART'S "VIEWPOINTS"

Influenced by dancer-choreographer Mary Overlie's "Six Viewpoints," an approach to dance/stage movement, director Anne Bogart applied Overlie's vocabulary of time and space to her work with actors in the shaping of stage space and reinventing older plays. Her work has been described as "dance done by actors in the service of dramaturgy."[15]

In *Anne Bogart: Viewpoints*, she explained her version as a postmodern approach to acting and directing. Unlike Aristotle's elements, her six elements (later expanded to nine) are not conceived as a hierarchy of components. Listed as Space, Time, Shape, Movement, Story, and Emotion, these names given to basic principles of movement make up a vocabulary and strategy for director and actor. Primarily rehearsal techniques, they apply to tempo, space, duration of movements, repetitions, physical gestures, spatial relationships, and the physical stage.

How are Viewpoints an actor's tool? Essentially replacing the Stanislavski vocabulary of "emotional recall" and "sense memory" in actor training, Bogart's emphasizes a *physical* (or a movement-based) approach to rehearsal and performance; most of her recent work bears the imprint of Viewpoints staging and has influenced artists working in postmodern forms of nonnaturalistic theatre.

> **"The Viewpoints give actors the ability to develop presence while resisting the temptation to 'explain themselves.'"**[16]
>
> —KEVIN KUHLKE, DIRECTOR, NEW YORK UNIVERSITY'S EXPERIMENTAL THEATRE WING

FOCUS ON PEOPLE IN THEATRE

DIRECTOR–TEACHER

Anne Bogart

© Andrew Savulich/NY Daily News Archive/Getty Images

Anne Bogart (1953–) graduated from Bard College in Annandale-on-Hudson, New York. While studying in a master's program at New York University's Tisch School of the Arts in the late seventies, she began writing and directing her own works for the stage. As *New York Times* theatre critic Mel Gussow pointed out, "Depending on the point of view [Anne Bogart] is either an innovator or a provocateur assaulting a script."[17]

Bogart has won Obie (Off Broadway) Awards for direction of her own *No Plays, No Poetry* and for Paula Vogel's *The Baltimore Waltz*. She served briefly as artistic director of Trinity Repertory Company (RI) and in 1992, cofounded with Japanese director and acting theorist Tadashi Suzuki (creator of a rigorous physical and vocal discipline for actors called "the Suzuki Method") the Saratoga International Theatre Institute (SITI), based in Saratoga, New York. Their goal was to put into practice their artistic theories and "revitalize the theatre from the inside out." Beginning as a summer training program for actors, SITI eventually established a year-round base in New York City. Since the company's beginning, SITI has performed throughout the world. At present, Bogart serves as head of the Directing program at Columbia University's School of Theatre, New York City.

Work directed by Bogart divides roughly into four categories: new plays (*The Baltimore Waltz* by Paula Vogel and *In the Eye of the Hurricane* by Eduardo Machado); her own theatrical portraits of well-known cultural figures, such as Bertolt Brecht (*No Plays, No Poetry*), Andy Warhol (*Culture of Desire*), and Robert Wilson (*Bob*); iconoclastic interpretations of classic and popular plays (*A Streetcar Named Desire* set in a German club with ten Stanleys and twelve Blanches, one of them a man); and original performance pieces that examine the history of popular entertainment in the United States—her trilogy *American Vaudeville* (1992), *Marathon Dancing* (1994), and *American Silents* (1997).

Bogart's recent works include Bizet's opera *Carmen*, Euripides's *Trojan Women* adapted by Jocelyn Clarke, Charles Mee's *Under Construction*, and Sarah Ruhl's *Dead Man's Cell Phone*.

©Photo by Richard Termine

Anne Bogart's *War of the Worlds*
Anne Bogart staged *War of the Worlds*, based on the life of Orson Welles.

ACTORS AT WORK

Acting is a demanding profession, requiring at all times dedication, sacrifice, and stamina. Following years of training in studios and/or universities, the actor begins his or her real work. The actor's entrée into the professional world is the *audition*—the gateway to roles and rehearsals, to the challenges and rewards of performance, and to membership in Actors' Equity Association (AEA).

AUDITIONS

In her book *Auditioning: An Actor-Friendly Guide*, actor and casting director Joanna Merlin opines that acting is a hazardous profession.[18] Not only is the audition process unpredictable, but actors frequently encounter creative and emotional obstacles as they try to present themselves.

Whether auditioning for the stage or camera, actors encounter their first obstacles in a variety of audition spaces (a small office, rehearsal room, or large stage), distractions (the presence of many auditors, including casting director, director, producer, playwright, and composer), atmosphere (welcoming, impersonal, or rushed), and the cold reading (a scene to be read without prior notice). Finally, in the waiting room, there are many actors, all seemingly suitable for the role. All of these components lend themselves to an actor's loss of confidence in his or her suitability for the role.

Audition coaches (and there are many) recommend basic preparations for auditioning, beginning with preparing the resumé with professional headshot; accessing the "sides" (as an audition scene is called) from "Sides Express"; reviewing the character description from the cast breakdown sent out by Breakdown Services, a company that provides these lists to agents; and reading the script or play, if available. Actors also use *Backstage*, a weekly publication, that announces casting calls for theatre, film, and television. In preparation for the audition, actors apply all of the tools of their actor-training (concentration, truthfulness, spontaneity, energy, humor, and skill) in anticipation of the few minutes of the audition.

Callbacks follow the preliminary audition. Actors are advised to wear the same clothes as a badge of identification because directors see a lot of actors over several days of auditions. Actors are also advised to repeat in the callback the same approach to the scene, but with a deeper understanding of the character. Following callbacks, there is usually a waiting period before actors are notified of their success. If the news is not favorable, the search and preparation begin for the next audition. (For a discussion of the Alliance for Inclusion in the Arts, formerly, the Non-Traditional Casting Project, see Chapter 13 "Image Makers: Producers.")

IMPROVISATIONS, EXERCISES, AND GAMES

Improvisation

Improvisation is useful in actor training and in rehearsals to free the actor's imagination and to strengthen concentration. Defined as "spontaneous invention," improvisation may be used with a group as warm-up exercises before classes or rehearsals. In rehearsal,

FOCUS ON THEATRE

Open Calls

Open casting calls are usually the exception, not the rule. Within limits, an *open call* allows interested actors the opportunity to audition. Educational theatres often hold general auditions for theatre majors only; and community theatres open auditions to the community at large. Actors' Equity Association requires periodic open calls (known as EPAs, for Equity Principal Auditions) of professional regional theatres and Broadway/Off Broadway productions and touring companies. EPAs are restricted to Equity members and are held in New York, Los Angeles, or Chicago, and also locally if there are Equity members in the area where the regional theatre is located.

In a short amount of audition time (usually three minutes for EPAs), casting directors see professional actors, note their suitability for future roles, and file resumés for future reference. In university theatres, directors attend open calls as part of the educational process and as an aid in planning seasons for student actors.

improvisation may be used to establish rapport between actors; to solve acting problems; to spur spontaneity and release inhibitions; or to encourage new, instinctive responses to overly familiar circumstances.

Exercises

Improvisation engages the actor's mind and body. Some *exercises* ask the actor to substitute his or her own words for the words in the script. As actors improvise arguments between two characters using their own words rather than the playwright's, the content of a difficult scene, its emotions and tensions, can be made clearer. The actor's newly found, inner emotional material can then be reapplied to the circumstances of the playwright's scene.

Many improvisations involve physical interactions that release energy and focus strong feelings and gestures as verbal exchanges take place. The improvised physical activity may appear, at first, to have little relation to the written dialogue. However, the intensity of the physical work can support the equally intense verbal exchange required by the script.

FOCUS ON THEATRE

Jewel Walker

Jewel Walker, an inspiring movement teacher who initiated programs at the University of Wisconsin, Milwaukee, and currently at the University of Delaware, Newark, explained to an interviewer in baseball terms: "Suppose I hit a line drive over the head of the second baseman. I'm off running right away. And I'm watching the ball, and there comes the possibility I can get to second base on this hit. My body knows without looking where first base is, and I need to watch only the ball and the fielder. If I have to look down at my feet, I've lost. That's like being on stage—you have to be super aware."[19]

Games

There are many kinds of improvisational games. One such game is the repetition between two actors of the same word or phrase (for example, "What time is it?"). Some are based on invented, or nonsensical, words. This made-up language spurs communication between actors. Some games are invented stories in which one actor begins with a single word or sentence and other actors add to the developing story line. In all, actors learn to concentrate, to react instinctually, and to work moment-to-moment with real feelings with other actors.

Games and exercises condition actors to immerse themselves in the play's circumstances and to find new impulses and behavior that lead to real emotion. They also encourage a sense of play, collaboration, and ensemble. The end product of improvisation is freeing the actor's creativity, honing concentration, and spurring commitment to finding the truth of behavior. These newfound instincts and impulses can be used in support of the demands of the text.

©Joan Marcus

Ron Liebman in *Angels in America*

Ron Liebman as Roy Cohn, chief counsel to Senator Joseph R. McCarthy's investigative subcommittee on Communist activities in the United States during the 1950s and member of the Reagan administration's Justice Department, in Tony Kushner's *Angels in America: A Gay Fantasia on National Themes. Part One: Millennium Approaches.*

Movement and Voice Training

Movement Training

Modern movement training provides actors with a wide range of physical choices in the creation of character. It is not simply a matter of physically demonstrating a pompous valet or a nervous debutante. In movement training ("stage movement" is the older term), the emphasis is on developing the actor's body as a more open, responsive, physical instrument by first eliminating unnecessary tensions and mannerisms. Movement training today is not the imposition of arbitrary positions or alignments, as it was when young actors copied the gestures of leading actors. Rather, it is more a matter of sensitizing actors to the variety of possibilities of human movement *as an expressive signal* of character and intentions.

In recent years, movement training in the United States has changed in two fundamental ways. First, the influence of psychology has given insight into the actor's inner world and consequently into how that world can be expressed through the body's motion. Second, numerous approaches to movement or physical training from different cultures and traditions have been *integrated* and have had an enormous impact on actor training over the last decade. They range from techniques in martial arts, fencing, yoga, tai chi, juggling, clown and circus arts, stage combat, and mask and mime training (influenced by Étienne Decroux and Jacques Lecoq) to Laban movement analysis, the Suzuki Method, Feldenkrais and Alexander somatic techniques, and a growing array of physical-training options. The best movement teachers are familiar with and aim for increased integration of physicality in the classroom.

©Sara Krulwich/The New York Times/Redux

Lynn Nottage's *Ruined*
Lynn Nottage's *Ruined* takes place in a Congolese brothel where actress Saidah Arrika Ekulona as Mama Nadi, a latter-day variant on Brecht's Mother Courage, struggles to keep the terrors of civil war outside the walls of her establishment. Manhattan Theatre Club, NYC.

Today's movement teachers use physical-training options to find ways for actors to broaden their skill sets to make fresh, often startling, physical choices—for movement grows from the urge to move as an expression of something that, until one critical moment, is hidden. The violent encounter between Stanley Kowalski and Blanche DuBois in *A Streetcar Named Desire* is an expression of Stanley's pent-up hostility and unconscious fear of his sister-in-law. He provokes a physical encounter—a fight and sexual assault—to express his fear and rage at the intruder who has disrupted his household and violated his sense of masculine authority. Blanche, on the other hand, fights for her dignity and sanity in what is clearly a rape encounter.

Truly expressive onstage movement, such as the duel in *Hamlet* or Mama Nadi's defensive gesture with the knife in *Ruined*, begins with the character's inner needs. When those needs are well understood, it is possible to create physical realities that are compelling—such as Kevin Spacey's physically challenged Richard III (in Shakespeare's play) or James Earl Jones's Troy Maxson (in *Fences*), whose physical stance is that of an aging athlete.

To be convincing, the actor's physical movements must *embody* the character's attitudes or needs. In performance, all physical and vocal choices must serve those needs.

Voice Training

The voice is our means of communicating to others, presenting ourselves, and expressing our personality, thoughts, and feelings. The function of the actor's speech, as with our own day-to-day expressions, is to communicate the character's needs and motives. However ordinary, stylized, or heightened (as in poetry) stage language is, when the actor speaks lines from the dramatic text, he or she must root those lines in the *need* to speak in a particular fashion and with a particular choice of words.[20]

Voice training today involves the actor's entire being—the physical and the psychological. Vocal exercises practiced in the classroom are aimed at "freeing" the voice. These exercises involve relaxation, breathing, and increased muscularity of lips and tongue. These are followed by particular exercises on texts (Shakespeare's verse, for

David Auburn's *The Columnist*
John Lithgow as the super-articulate columnist and pundit Joseph Alsop in David Auburn's *The Columnist*, Manhattan Theatre Club, NYC.

example) that stretch the voice, making it more responsive to the demands of the character.

The primary objective in voice training is to open up the possibilities of the voice—its energy, its instinctive responses to what the actor has to say. Correcting one's speech (a regional accent, for example) is not as important in voice training today as it once was, although standard or "neutral" speech is encouraged by the profession. The aim of vocal exercises is to keep the essential truth of the actor's own voice, yet make it large and malleable enough for projecting feelings to a large auditorium or modulating to the intimacy of a television studio. To get this balance between the size of the voice and its malleability, the actor involves both technique and imagination in vocal work. Unlike the singer's voice, whose "sound" is the message, the actor's voice is an extension of the person (and the character). Its possibilities are as complex as the actor's persona. Because actors deal with words that come off a printed page, they continually have to find ways to make those words their own.

Voice training aims at establishing an ongoing process for the actor to become as sensitive as possible to the physical makeup of the voice in relation to the body (breath, diaphragm, ribs, head, neck). The goal is to merge techniques learned in voice exercises with the actor's imagination to communicate the character's needs through the words of the text. Hamlet's instructions to the Players on the use of the voice and the body—"Suit the action to the word, the word to the action"—remain timeless in the actor's process.

FOCUS ON THEATRE

Four Pillars of Voice Training

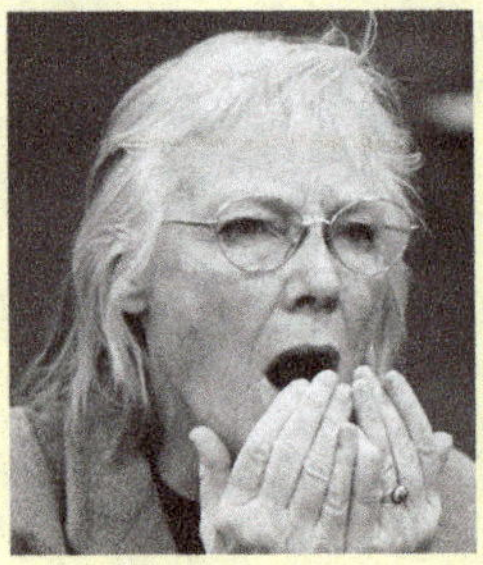

Provided by Cicely Berry/RSC

Cicely Berry, Britain's Royal Shakespeare Company's Voice Director, in workshops on speaking Shakespeare insists, "There is no right or wrong way" in the speaking of Shakespeare's verse. "We want to hear Shakespeare as if it were being spoken in today's world, whilst honouring its heightened language, and this takes a lot of skill—like walking a tightrope."

Photo ©Terry O'Connell, courtesy Catherine Fitzmaurice, www.fitzmauricevoice.com

Catherine Fitzmaurice, founder of Fitzmaurice Voicework, prescribes a regime of finding freedom, release, and transcendence in workshops and classes that can culminate in a two-year certificate program.

©Photo by Matthew Dunivan

Kristen Linklater, head of voice training at Columbia University's School of Theatre, New York, in her work with actors and neuroscience, says, "Words themselves if embodied from the start and neurally wired into memory and emotion will naturally engender action. Voice and text work, well understood and practiced with sensitivity, can make a critical contribution to the creative arena of acting."

©Clive Totman Photography

Patsy Rodenburg, head of voice at London's Guildhall School of Music and Drama, says of voice training: "The ideal to strive for is a naked voice, powered by breath and free of tension, so that when the actor speaks, we can all listen."[21]

Rehearsals and Performance

The work of rehearsals, which may last from two to ten weeks, is to condition the actor's responses so that during performance, emotions flow from the actor's concentration on the character's objectives and the play's psychological and physical circumstances. Rehearsals also bring the cast together with the director to "set" interpretation and physical movement. Not until dress rehearsal, as a rule, is an actor able to work with a complete set of properties, furniture, scenery, costumes, makeup, sound, and lighting. However, rehearsal furniture is provided by stage management, and special rehearsal clothes and properties (eyeglasses, fans, walking sticks, long skirts, and capes) are also provided if these differ significantly from ordinary dress and handheld objects.

On each night of a play's run, the actor brings a living humanity with physical actions and the playwright's words and given circumstances to the stage. Everything the actor has analyzed, memorized, and made personal in rehearsals—objectives, mannerisms, vocal intonations, movements—stays (or should stay) much the same. But the actor's

Tyne Daly in *Master Class*
Tyne Daly, as opera singer Maria Callas, conducts a master class in Terrence McNally's *Master Class*, Broadway.

John Douglass Jones in *The Emperor Jones*
John Douglass Jones as the "Emperor" in Eugene O'Neill's *The Emperor Jones*, Irish Repertory Theatre, Off Broadway.

creativity continues within the boundaries set in rehearsal: This is the actor's freedom and art. Each performance requires the actor to give fresh life to the character's physical actions, responses, desires, and goals—to concentrate anew on the character's speech, behavior, physical movements, and theatrical effectiveness.

Acting with the Camera

Most actors today work in theatre, film, and television. Film acting requires the same discipline, preparation, and attention to relaxation, memory, concentration, and truthful behavior that actors bring with them to a stage performance. Neither the outdoor locations nor the vast hordes of technicians and onlookers during the shooting of a scene make the actor's work in film different from work in the theatre. The essential

Mary-Louise Parker in *Proof*
Mary-Louise Parker as Catherine in *Proof* by David Auburn, Manhattan Theatre Club, NYC.

FOCUS ON THEATRE

Actors' Equity Association

Actors' Equity Association (AEA) is the independent union representing actors and stage managers who work in the professional theatre and dancers who work in a Broadway show. Equity contracts are provided for Broadway, Off Broadway, and Off Off Broadway; in Resident Theatre and Stock and Dinner Theatre; and for Special Contracts.

Screen Actors Guild (SAG) is the independent union representing actors who work in film and television.

difference is *the presence of the camera.* The camera listens to and records everything the actor does and says. The actor's credibility before this ever-present "eye" is what separates the successful film actor from the talented stage actor.

In his entertaining book on acting in film, Michael Caine says that "behaving realistically and truthfully in front of a camera is an exacting craft, one that requires steadfast discipline and application."[22] Hidden microphones pick up the smallest vocal nuance, close-ups record the slightest hesitation or uncertainty, scenes are shot out of sequence, and hordes of technicians (and often sightseers) provide distractions. The actor must learn to work with green screen, CGI, and other virtual technologies when scenery or scene partners (aliens or monsters) are not present.

The Everett Collection

Sleuth
Michael Caine in the film *Sleuth.*

Despite distractions, the actor must concentrate on "being" rather than "performing" because the camera transmits subtleties of emotion and reveals in close-ups the character's thoughts. Film audiences see what the camera sees, so the actor must be mentally prepared and thinking from moment to moment. The camera catches the smallest hesitation, failure of concentration, or verbal slip. The actor's *readiness*—preparation, relaxation, concentration, knowing lines, and familiarity with set, properties, and placement of the "mark" (where the actor must stand to be filmed)—makes the difference between staying in the film business or not.

The vocabulary of film acting has much in common with that of the theatre, but its purposes are often not the same. The film actor's *audition* is the "screen test," where the actor's potential before the camera is assessed. In the theatre, actors and directors use rehearsals to explore character, relationships, and interpretation. In film, rehearsals are most often for the director and cameraman to set blocking for the camera. Films are often made without an opportunity for actors to discuss the role with the director, with no time to meet others in the cast, and without rehearsals on the set. Given these conditions, the actor must be fully prepared to perform a scene when called upon and to repeat that scene over and over again until the director calls for "a wrap."

In film acting, the actor's relationship to other actors is different as well. The actor works only with those actors necessary to a scene. Backstage camaraderie often does not exist. Scenes are repeated many times, and the actor must listen and react as freshly as though each time were the very first. In this facet of the film actor's business, the best advice, according to Michael Caine, is to be completely in charge of "your craft, material, and yourself." At no time must the actor forget that the business of filmmaking is to make the film. Anything that slows down the film's schedule (the temperamental, unprepared, or late actor) will result in cost overruns and probably the quick end of a promising film career.

TRANSITION

Actors bring living presence to the stage. Their search for new depths of creative energy and truthful behavior keeps their performances fresh and lively night after night.

In turn, directors collaborate with actors and other artists to interpret the playwright's text or to create theatrical pieces of their own. As captains of the production's theatrical ship, directors are the final arbiters of choice in the *creative* process.

In the final days of the nineteenth century, the director emerged as a transforming force in the theatre, and has remained so.

Theatre: A Way of Seeing Online

Visit the CourseMate for Theatre: A Way of Seeing 7th Edition for quick access to the digital study resources that accompany this chapter, including links to the websites listed below, Theatre Workshop, digital glossary, a chapter quiz and more.

Websites

The *Theatre: A Way of Seeing* CourseMate includes links for all the websites described below. Simply select "Web links" from the Chapter Resources for Chapter 9, and click on the link that interests you. You'll be taken directly to the site described.

Actingbiz
Online resources for actors, with articles on every aspect of the business.

Acting Workshop On-line
A site for beginners to learn about acting and actors.

Actors' Equity Association
The union representing professional actors and stage managers who work in the theatre, and dancers in a Broadway show.

The Actors Studio
Presented by TheatrGROUP, including a brief history of the Actors Studio, a lecture by Lee Strasberg, audition policies, and links to books about the Actors Studio.

***Alliance for Inclusion in the Arts* (formerly the Non-Traditional Casting Project)**
Works to increase participation of artists of color, women, and artists with disabilities in theatre, film, and television.

Arts International, Inc.
Organization that promotes global connections in the visual and performing arts by providing support to artists and information services.

HOLA: Hispanic Organization for Latin Actors
Serves as a link between Hispanic actors and the entertainment industry. It sponsors a referral service, touring programs, and showcases.

The Lee Strasberg Theatre Institute
Provides information on the institute, services, and training in New York City and Los Angeles.

Screen Actors Guild
The union representing professional actors who work in film and television.

VASTA: Voice and Speech Trainers Association

10

IMAGE MAKER: THE DIRECTOR

The theatre of the future, if it is to hold us, will have to shake off a belief it has held only a relatively short time—the belief that it is showing us "a real room with real people." For the theatre's role is to present life not in its literal exactness but rather through some kind of poetic vision, metaphor, image—the mirror held up as 'twere to nature.[1]

—Alan Schneider, Director

PREVIEW

In collaboration with playwrights and other artists and assistants, directors interpret and shape performances as theatrical metaphors of our world.

FORERUNNERS

During the 1860s in Europe, the practice of a single person guiding all aspects of the production process began to take hold. Before that time, leading actors, theatre managers, and sometimes playwrights "staged" the play, thereby setting actors' movements, dictating financial matters, and making decisions on casting, costumes, and scenery. During the first half of the nineteenth century, actor-managers (following the tradition of James Burbage in England and Molière in France) resembled the modern director in some respects. But the actor-manager was first of all an actor and considered the production from the perspective of the role he or she played. In the eighteenth century, David Garrick was one of England's most successful actor-managers. Although the theatre between 1750 and 1850 was immensely popular in Europe, most actor-managers—Garrick was an exception—maintained inferior artistic standards in their pursuit of large box-office receipts.

This practice began to worry a growing number of theatre people, who reexamined the production process. With the formation in 1866 of Georg II, Duke of Saxe-Meiningen's company in Germany (known as the Meiningen Players), the director in the modern sense began to emerge. He exercised a central artistic discipline over the company—serving as producer, director, and financial backer. By controlling

Director Peter Brook speaking to the cast of *The Mahabharata* during rehearsals of the three-part cycle of plays adapted from the ancient Hindu epic, Théâtre des Bouffes du Nord, Paris, France.

design, he introduced a unified look in costumes and settings. The duke's efforts to define the director's role were followed by those of André Antoine in France and Konstantin Stanislavski in Russia. Under their influence, the modern stage director's identity took shape in Europe: someone who understood all theatrical arts and devoted full energies to combining them into a unified, artistic whole.

FOCUS ON PEOPLE IN THEATRE

ACTOR-MANAGER

Caroline Neuber

Caroline Neuber, the co-founder with Johann C. Gottsched of the modern German-speaking theatre. Lithograph by Carl Loedel from a painting by Elias Gottlob Hausmann.

Caroline Neuber (1697–1760) was one of Europe's earliest female actor-managers. Together with her husband, actor Johann Neuber, she formed an acting company in 1727 in Leipzig, Germany. Shortly thereafter, they joined with dramatist Johann Gottsched, the leading German intellectual of his day, to work together to reform stage practice. Caroline Neuber's efforts were directed toward raising the artistic level of theatrical productions. She replaced the older plays that featured clowns as leading figures with serious drama in imitation of French neoclassical writers. She also instituted reforms in the staging practices of her day: plays were staged with careful rehearsals and without improvisational material; actors were assigned added duties, such as painting scenery or sewing costumes; and the actors' personal lives were monitored in an effort to overcome moral prejudices against them.

Caroline Neuber's company had residencies in such cultural centers as Leipzig, Hamburg, Vienna, and St. Petersburg. At her death, her production techniques were being adopted by other companies, and serious drama was being performed throughout Germany's theatrical centers.

FOCUS ON PEOPLE IN THEATRE

PRODUCER–DIRECTOR

Georg II, Duke of Saxe-Meiningen

Georg II, Duke of Saxe-Meiningen (1826–1914), transformed the Duchy of Meiningen's court theatre in Germany into an example of scenic historical accuracy and lifelike acting. As producer-director, the duke designed costumes, scenery, and properties for historically authentic style and worked for ensemble acting. The duke was assisted by Ludwig Chronegk (1837–1891), an actor responsible for supervising and rehearsing the company. The Meiningen Players were noted throughout Europe for their crowd scenes, in which each member of the crowd had individual traits and specific lines. In rehearsals, actors were divided into small groups, each under the charge of an experienced actor. This practice was in keeping with the company's rule against actors being stars and was the beginning of the new movement in the 1870s toward unified production under the director's control. Saxe-Meiningen's example of the *single creative authority* in charge of the total production influenced Antoine and Stanislavski.

FOCUS ON PEOPLE IN THEATRE

PRODUCER–DIRECTOR

André Antoine

Album Felix Potin, 1902

André Antoine (1858–1943) was founding producer-director of the Théâtre Libre, or "Free Theatre," in Paris. Beginning as a part-time actor, Antoine founded a theatre in 1887 and a naturalistic production style that became world famous. The Théâtre Libre was a subscription theatre, one open only to members and therefore exempt from censorship. It became a showcase for new, controversial plays (Ibsen's *Ghosts* was one) and new realistic production techniques. Seeking authentic detail, Antoine set about reproducing exact environments. In one play he hung real beef carcasses onstage. In 1897, he opened his Théâtre Antoine, a fully professional theatre; and in 1906, he was appointed director of the Odéon Théâtre, a state-subsidized theatre in Paris.

In his efforts to stage "real" life, Antoine developed three important principles that influenced the direction of the European theatre: realistic environments, ensemble acting, and the director's authority.

FOCUS ON PEOPLE IN THEATRE

PRODUCER-DIRECTOR

Konstantin Stanislavski

Culver Pictures, Inc.

Konstantin Stanislavski (1863–1938) was producer-director-actor and co-founder of the Moscow Art Theatre. As a director, Stanislavski aimed for ensemble acting and the absence of stars. He established such directorial methods as intensive study of the play before rehearsals began, the actor's careful attention to detail and truthful behavior, and extensive research by visiting locales and museums to re-create the play's milieu. The Moscow Art Theatre's reputation was made with Anton Chekhov's plays, depicting in realistic detail the lives of the rural landowning class in provincial Russia.

Moscow Art Theatre, 1904

Anton Chekov's *The Cherry Orchard*

A scene from the 1904 Moscow Art Theatre production of *The Cherry Orchard*, directed by Konstantin Stanislavski.

Stanislavski is remembered for his efforts to perfect a "truthful" method of acting. His published writings—*My Life in Art* (1924), *An Actor Prepares* (1936), *Building a Character* (1949), and *Creating a Role* (1961)—provide a record of the "Stanislavski System" as it evolved.

DIRECTOR AS ARTIST

The director collaborates with playwrights, actors, designers, and technicians to create onstage a carefully selected vision of life—a special mirror. Alan Schneider described the *theatre's* role from a director's viewpoint as presenting "life not in its literal exactness but rather through some kind of poetic vision, metaphor, image."

Depending upon the size of the theatrical organization, the director can assume several roles, ranging from attending to budgets and box-office details to creative interpretation of the playwright's text. In all cases, the director is the controlling artist responsible for unifying the production elements, including text, music, scenery, costumes, properties, sound, and visuals.

Although each director has his or her way of working creatively, in general three types of directors have evolved over the years. On the first day of rehearsal, most directors give a speech to the company describing the play and the approach to be taken to interpret and stage the text. One type of director treats actors and designers as "servants" to the director's concept; they are expected to deliver the "look" and "meaning" of the play's world as conceived by the director. Another type reverses this approach and acts as the creative coordinator of a group of actors and designers, thereby limiting his or her vision to the suggestions, criticisms, and encouragements of the group.

Eileen Darby/New York Public Library for the Performing Arts

A Street Car Named Desire
Jessica Tandy as Blanche DuBois (right) with Marlon Brando as Stanley Kowalski and Kim Hunter as Stella in *A Streetcar Named Desire*. Original production staged by Elia Kazan.

The third type functions as a guide, who senses at the outset the direction that the production will take but proceeds in rehearsals and design conferences to provoke and stimulate the actors and designers. This director creates an atmosphere in which actors dig, probe, and investigate the whole fabric of the play. Rehearsals are used to search out ("to harrow" in the original sense of the word *rehearse*), to listen, and to yield to suggestions. The "directorial conception" is what Alan Schneider refers to as the director's "poetic vision," and it precedes the first day's work. Nevertheless, the "sense of direction" crystallizes into a consistent stage image only as the process nears an end.

Unlike questions asked by theatre critics, a director's questions do not deal so much with "What's the event about?" as with the event's *potential*. This is the reason a director chooses one sort of theatrical material over

FOCUS ON THEATRE

Elia Kazan's Notebook for *A Streetcar Named Desire*

The following is taken from Elia Kazan's *Notebook* (dated August 1947), kept before and during rehearsals of *A Streetcar Named Desire*:

A thought—directing finally consists of turning Psychology into Behavior.

Theme—this is a message from the dark interior. This little twisted, pathetic, confused bit of light and culture puts out a cry. It is snuffed out by the crude forces of violence, insensibility and vulgarity which exist in our South—and this cry is the play.

Style—one reason a "style," a stylized production is necessary is that a subjective factor—Blanche's memories, inner life, emotions, are a real factor. We cannot really understand her behavior unless we see the effect of her past on her present behavior.

This play is a poetic tragedy. We are shown the final dissolution of a person of worth, who once had a great potential, and who, even as she goes down, has worth exceeding that of the "healthy," coarse-grained figures who kill her.

Blanche is a social type, an emblem of a dying civilization, making its last curlicued and romantic exit. All her behavior patterns are those of the dying civilization she represents. In other words her behavior is *social*. Therefore find social modes! This is the source of the play's stylization and the production's style and color. Likewise, Stanley's behavior is *social* too. It is the basic animal cynicism of today. "Get what's coming to you! Don't waste a day! Eat, drink, get yours!" This is the basis of his stylization, of the choice of his props. All props should be stylized: they should have a color, shape and weight that spell: style.

An effort to put poetic names on scenes to edge me into stylizations and physicalizations. Try to keep each scene in terms of Blanche.

1. Blanche comes to the last stop at the end of the line.
2. Blanche tries to make a place for herself.
3. Blanche breaks them apart, but when they come together, Blanche is more alone than ever!
4. Blanche, more desperate because more excluded, tries the direct attack and makes the enemy who will finish her.
5. Blanche finds that she is being tracked down for the kill. She must work fast.
6. Blanche suddenly finds, suddenly makes for herself, the only possible, perfect man for her.
7. Blanche comes out of the happy bathroom to find that her own doom has caught up with her.
8. Blanche fights her last fight. Breaks down. Even Stella deserts her.
9. Blanche's last desperate effort to save herself by telling the whole truth. The truth dooms her.
10. Blanche escapes out of this world. She is brought back by Stanley and destroyed.
11. Blanche is disposed of.

The style—the real deep style—consists of one thing only: to find behavior that's truly social, significantly typical, at each moment. It's not so much what Blanche has done—it's how she does it—with such style, grace, manners, old-world trappings and effects, props, tricks, swirls, etc., that they seem anything but vulgar.

And for the other characters, too, you face the same problem. To find the Don Quixote character for them. *This is a poetic tragedy, not a realistic or naturalistic one. So you must find a Don Quixote scheme of things for each.*

Stylized acting and direction is to realistic acting and direction as poetry is to prose. The acting must be styled, not in the obvious sense. (Say nothing about it to the producer and actors.) But you will fail unless you find this kind of poetic realization for the behavior of these people.[2]

another—because of its potential. This realization of a play's or production's potential motivates directors to find space, actors, and forms of expression. Like hunters or explorers, directors intuit that a potential exists within a work (or text) and explore interpretative and staging possibilities with a sense of expectation and a deepening commitment to leading the creative team.

Imagine the potential of an untried script called *A Streetcar Named Desire* and the excitement of its first director, Elia Kazan, searching to find what he called the *spine* (or the through-line) of the play's action. In his notebook, he defined the play's *spine* as the "last gasp" of a dying civilization: "This little twisted, pathetic, confused bit of light and culture ... snuffed out by the crude forces of violence, insensibility and vulgarity which exist in our South—and this cry is the play."[3]

Consider a director such as Peter Brook, who sets out, over a number of years, to explore an ancient Hindu epic (*The Mahabharata*). Brook's nine-hour theatrical realization presents humanity's greatest dilemma: human beings caught up in the conflict between divine and demonic forces. The story line of this theatrical epic is essentially the quest for morality: how to find one's way in an age of global destruction. As director, Brook—with the assistance of collaborators, including writers, designers, musicians, and actors—guided the creation of a theatrical epic out of the ancient, sacred poem. In the case of *A Streetcar Named Desire*, Elia Kazan *interpreted* Tennessee Williams's text. Both Brook and Kazan, as directors using different approaches and texts, created theatrical "mirrors" that held up to human nature its many forms, varieties, and expressions.

FOCUS ON PEOPLE IN THEATRE

DIRECTOR

Elia Kazan

©Popperfoto/Getty Images

Elia Kazan (1909–2003) was educated at Williams College and Yale University. As a member of the Group Theatre, he acted in its productions of Clifford Odets's *Waiting for Lefty, Paradise Lost*, and *Golden Boy*.

He is best known today for his direction of plays by Tennessee Williams and Arthur Miller: *A Streetcar Named Desire* (1947), *Death of a Salesman* (1949), *Cat on a Hot Tin Roof* (1955), *Sweet Bird of Youth* (1959), and *After the Fall* (1964). Kazan also directed films of *A Streetcar Named Desire, On the Waterfront*, and *East of Eden*.

Along with designer Jo Mielziner, Kazan established *selected realism* as the dominant American theatrical style during the 1950s. This style combined acting of intense psychological truth with simplified but realistic scenery. Marlon Brando as Stanley Kowalski embodied the acting style for which Kazan's productions were famous. Kazan described his working methods in his autobiography, called *A Life* (1988).

The Everett Collection

A Streetcar Named Desire
Marlon Brando as Stanley (left) prepares to throw his cup and plate to the floor during Blanche's birthday party in *A Streetcar Named Desire*, directed by Elia Kazan. Jessica Tandy as Blanche (center) and Kim Hunter as Stella (right) are seated at the table.

PETER BROOK AND *THE MAHABHARATA*

"A [theatre] is like a small restaurant whose responsibility is to nourish its customers.... There is only one test: Do the spectators leave the playhouse with slightly more courage, more strength than when they came in? If the answer is yes, the food is healthy."[4]

— PETER BROOK, *THREADS OF TIME*

In a rock quarry in southern France in 1985, Peter Brook first staged the twelve-hour performance of *The Mahabharata*, a cycle of three plays (*The Game of Dice, The Exile in the Forest*, and *The War*) adapted by Jean-Claude Carrière in French from the Sanskrit poem dating from 400 BC. The epic poem compiles the myths, legends, wars, folklore, ethics, history, and theology of ancestral India, including the Hindu sacred book the *Bhagavad Gita*. From high in the quarry's rock wall, the piercing fanfare of the nagaswaram, an instrument that is half trumpet and half pipe, announces the approach of the first play. Brook's multinational company of twenty-one players lends diverse qualities of physical virtuosity, intelligence, humor, and culture.

In staging this epic struggle between two opposing sets of cousins in an ancient Indian dynasty, Brook begins with the narrative voice of the symbolic poet Vyasa, who is writing a poem about the history of his ancestors (and by inference, the story of humankind). His story is recorded by the elephant-man Ganesha, who is also the god Krishna, the supporter of the good and the brave. Throughout, there is the innocence of the young boy who, just as the spectators, listens to the storyteller, watching, questioning, searching. What begins as an austere bargain and a lesson in the right way of life proceeds through adventures that carry an inconsolable sense of loss but ends with a vision of paradise as a gentle place of music, food, cool waters, pleasant conversation, and harmony. At the close, the blind can see, the wounded and slaughtered are restored, and all animosity is forgotten.

Martha Swope/The New York Public Library

Circle of Fire
Peter Brook's staging of *The Mahabharata*, based on the Hindu epic, emphasizes the elements—fire, water, earth, and air.

FOCUS ON PEOPLE IN THEATRE

DIRECTOR

Peter Brook

Peter Brook (b. 1925) is founder of the International Centre for Theatre Research in Paris. Born in London and educated at Oxford University, he began his directing career in the 1940s. As codirector of England's Royal Shakespeare Company in the sixties, he directed acclaimed productions of *King Lear, The Tempest, Marat/Sade*, and *A Midsummer Night's Dream*. His later activities with the Centre include *Orghast* for the Shiraz Festival in Persepolis (Iran), *The Ik* (based on Colin Turnbull's book *The Mountain People*), and *The Mahabharata* (based on a Sanskrit sacred text). His most recent works (*The Death of Krishna, Tierno Bokar*, and *The Grand Inquisitor*) examine religion and power. Brook's influential books on theatre are: *The Empty Space*; *The Shifting Point: Theatre, Film, Opera 1946–1987*; *The Open Door: Thoughts on Acting and Theatre*; and his memoir, *Threads of Time*.

Brook enjoys an enormous international reputation. Since founding the Centre, Brook has experimented with actor training and developed theatrical texts from case histories, myths, anthropology, and fables.

The Archery Contest
Peter Brook's production of the Hindu Epic, *The Mahabharata* toured the United States in 1987–1988.

Brook achieves the stylization of this global war by minimal, yet spectacular, choices. He makes dramatic use of the elements (earth, fire, and water) along with brightly patterned carpets, swirling fabrics of red and gold, and masks to transform actors playing half-animal or half-divine creatures. Staging techniques are adopted from Eastern theatre—a billowing cloth represents newborn children, and a single, large wooden wheel stands for Krishna's chariot. Battles are conveyed by acrobatic displays of Eastern martial arts; dozens of white arrows fly through the air; and, with the flutter of a hand, a god creates a solar eclipse.

The common ground shared by *The Mahabharata* and Western literature derives from those associations with Oedipus found in the wanderings of the blind prince Dhritarashtra, with the Old Testament in the forest exile of Pandavas, with Shakespeare in the wars of ruling dynasties, and with the *Iliad* and *Odyssey* in the moral struggle of ideal heroes representing divine forces of good arrayed against demonic ones.

Brook's production of *The Mahabharata* represents a culmination of his lifelong search for theatrical expression of humankind's greatest dramas and deepest dilemmas. His efforts to transform Hindu myth into universalized art, accessible to any and all cultures, are triumphant. Embedded in the ancient text are eternal

FOCUS ON THEATRE

The Mahabharata

The Mahabharata is a cycle of three plays: *The Game of Dice*, *The Exile in the Forest*, and *The War*.

Part I introduces the main characters, their mythic origins, their characteristics and aims, the role of the gods (especially Krishna), and the growing discord between the Pandavas and the Kauravas, two branches of the Bharata clan. In a game of dice, which the Pandava leader loses to his cousins, the Pandavas forfeit all their property and worldly possessions and are exiled to a forest.

In Part II, the Pandavas live a primordial existence in the forest, while procuring arms for the inevitable battle to come.

In Part III, the devastating war that threatens the entire universe is unleashed—a war foreordained and controlled by the god Krishna. After a gruesome massacre, Pandava regains his rights and is later reconciled with his enemies in heaven. Vyasa, the storyteller, warns that this is "the last illusion," referring to earth and/or the play. According to Hinduism, life is God's dream and, as rendered by God, is an illusion.

At the cycle's end, the actors, dressed in pure white, drop their personae, eat delicacies, and exit, signaling that the game and the performance are over.

Martha Swope/The New York Public Library

The Game of Dice
The dice players toss to determine the fate of the Pandavas in *The Mahabharata*, directed by Peter Brook, at Théâtre des Bouffes du Nord, Paris.

philosophical questions on the paradox of the human condition: Why do people lust for power? What are the causes of humankind's destructiveness? Will humanity survive Armageddon? Does the individual have a choice? What is God's game, and are we pawns?

"Of course, the basic themes are contemporary," Brook says. "One of them is how to find one's way in an age of destruction. What is brought out in *The Mahabharata* is that there is a certain world harmony, a cosmic harmony, that can either be helped or destroyed by individuals.... We, too, are living in a time when every value one can think of is in danger."[5]

In a world of clashing religions and cultures, Brook's intention is not to make older texts appear modern and relevant. Rather, he sets out to connect the stage and the world around him. In an interview, Brook reflected: "A theatrical act cannot influence the political world. But theater allows us to open up to something beyond the daily horrors; it allows us to reinforce something positive inside each of us."[6]

DIRECTORS AT WORK

EARLY RESPONSIBILITIES

In general, a director has six responsibilities: (1) selecting or creating a script, or agreeing to direct an offered script; (2) deciding on the text's interpretation and, with the designers, on the "look" and configuration of the stage space; (3) holding auditions and casting actors in the various roles; (4) working with other theatre artists,

FOCUS ON THEATRE

Stage Vocabulary

Traditional stage vocabulary is a kind of shorthand that has developed over the years between director and actor to allow them to communicate quickly (and without explanation) to one another in rehearsals. *All directions are to the actor's left or right.*

Upstage means toward the rear of the acting area. *Downstage* means toward the front. *Stage right* and *stage left* refer to the performer's right or left when he or she faces the audience. The stage floor is frequently spoken of as though it were divided into sections: *up right, up center, up left, down right, down center, down left.*

Body positions are also designated for work largely on the proscenium stage. The director may ask the actor to *turn out*, meaning to turn more toward the audience. Two actors are sometimes told to *share a scene*, or to play in a profile position so that they are equally visible to the audience. An actor may be told to *dress the stage*, meaning to move to balance the stage picture. Experienced actors take directions with ease and frequently make such moves almost automatically.

Audiences are almost never aware that the actor is taking a rehearsed position. But the actor's speech and movements, along with lighting and sound, often control what we see and hear onstage.

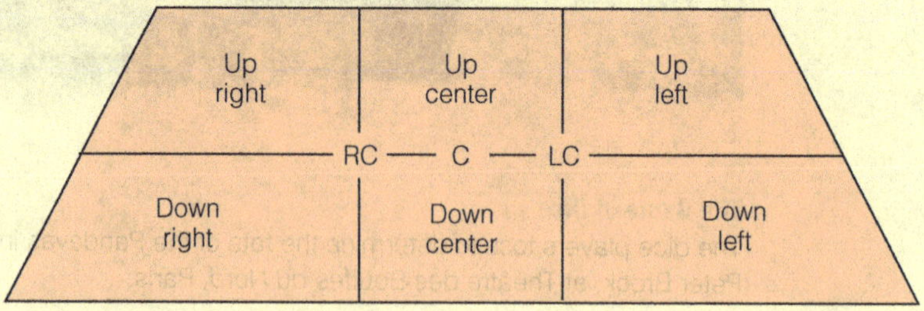

technicians, and managers to plan and stage the production; (5) rehearsing the acting company; and (6) coordinating all design and production elements into a unified performance.

None of the director's process is cut and dried. It is as variable as the names, faces, and talents of the director and the creative team.

T. Charles Erickson

Stage design for *A Streetcar Named Desire*
The agreed-upon space, set, and lighting design for *A Streetcar Named Desire*, directed by Michael Wilson, with designers Jeff Cowie and Michael Lincoln, Alley Theatre, Houston.

Auditions and Casting

Casting, from the director's viewpoint, is matching an actor to a role. During auditions (and often with the help of a casting director), the director looks for actors whose age, physical appearance, personality, and acting ability flesh out the director's idea of the characters. In college and university theatres, auditions are more or less standardized. Copies of the play (scenes or "sides") are made available, and audition notices are posted. With the assistance of stage management, the director holds general auditions or private interviews, or a combination of the two. The director usually asks actors to come to the audition prepared to illustrate their talent and ability by performing selections either from plays of their own choosing or from material assigned for the audition.

Beginning with the leading roles, the director narrows the choices for each part. If time and circumstances warrant, he or she calls back a final group of actors—the potential cast. This group reads together from the play so that the director can see how they relate to one another, how they work together, and how they complement one another in physical appearance and in vocal and emotional quality. Once the director decides on the members of the cast, the casting notice is posted, and rehearsals often begin within a short period.

Design Conferences

Usually six months before casting and rehearsals, the director selects a design team for the production. Julie Taymor and Robert Wilson serve as their own designers, but the majority of directors creates a team of designers and works with them on a regular basis. In colleges and universities, directors and designers are often faculty members whose artistic work is part of their faculty appointment.

In the six-month time frame, director and designers confer in face-to-face conferences, by telephone, and by email to set a production concept and schedules for designs and drawings. The early work is largely between director and designers of sets and costumes, during which time the playing space is shaped and costumes (period or modern garments) suggested. Unless there are unusual requirements (such as an expressionistic play that requires garish colors of changing light throughout), lighting and sound design are often brought into the discussions later in the design process.

In early design meetings, the director suggests his or her approach to the space (a living room or neutral space), placement of windows and entrances (doors or stairs), costumes (historical, modern, or eclectic), and lighting possibilities. After time has been allowed for designers to conceive their designs, there are fuller discussions of the excitement and practicality of the designs. Personnel, budget, time, and safety constraints are brought into the discussions. (See Chapters 11, "Image Makers: Designers—Scenery, Costumes, Masks, Wigs, and Puppets," and 12, "Image Makers: Designers—Lighting and Sound," for fuller discussions on the design process.)

Once designs for scenery, costumes, lighting, and sound are agreed upon to everyone's satisfaction, designers then work independently until they are brought together again as a team during technical rehearsals. With this phase of the preproduction process satisfactory, the director turns to casting and rehearsing the play.

The Ground Plan

The typical rehearsal space (or room) is seldom the stage where performances will take place. Therefore, directors and scene designers agree upon a *ground plan* that defines the size and shape of the future performance space, including walls, windows, furniture, doors, stairs, platforms, and so on. Some areas will have greater access for movement than others. Other areas will restrict and isolate. As actors physically inhabit the ground plan, they discover physical relationships that further the emotional life and meaning of the text. As actors add storytelling details of gesture and speech, the characters' emotional truths come alive visually and vocally and the living quality of the play takes shape in a defined space.

Improvisation

For directors, *improvisation* or game playing is primarily a *rehearsal* tool, not a performance technique. How much improvisation is used in rehearsal depends upon the director's skill with it and the actors' needs.

Improvisational exercises are oftentimes an actor's road to spontaneity and freedom. They are exercises designed to free an actor's imagination and body for spontaneous storytelling. Often directors use improvisations early in rehearsals to release inhibitions and spark the actors' imaginations, behaviors, reactions, and moods as they begin working together. In later rehearsals, improvisations can be used to increase concentration, discover new actions, clarify character relationships, and develop good working relations among actors.

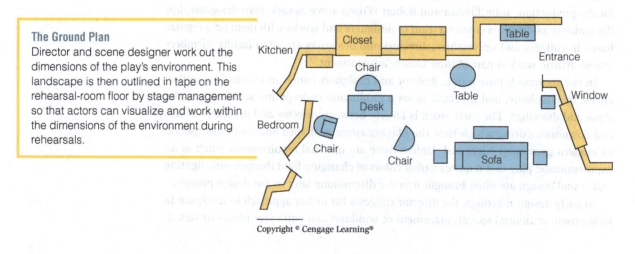

The Ground Plan
Director and scene designer work out the dimensions of the play's environment. This landscape is then outlined in tape on the rehearsal-room floor by stage management so that actors can visualize and work within the dimensions of the environment during rehearsals.

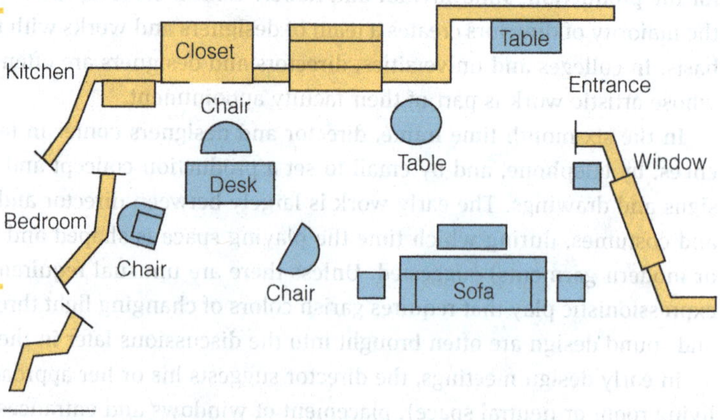

Royal Shakespeare Company

A Midsummer Night's Dream

Peter Brook used circus tricks and techniques borrowed from puppet theatre and English music halls in his acclaimed production of Shakespeare's comedy. Trapezes and a feathered bower create the magical forest as Titania makes love to Bottom, who wears a clown's red nose. The Royal Shakespeare Company, Stratford-upon-Avon, Great Britain.

While rehearsing *A Midsummer Night's Dream*, Peter Brook's actors practiced circus tricks each day along with comic improvisations to encourage inventiveness and playing for the sake of playing. With the "rude mechanicals," Brook organized realistic improvisations to give the actors as working-class men in the story a down-to-earth reality.[7]

Director's Assistants

To prepare a play within a three-to-ten-week rehearsal period, modern directors need assistants. The *assistant director* attends production meetings, coaches actors, and rehearses special or problem scenes. With the introduction of computers and iPads into the rehearsal room, *stage managers* compile a promptbook (in its final form the promptbook is a hardcopy of the script with rehearsal notes); prepare rehearsal schedules; record stage business, blocking, lighting, sound, and other cues; take notes during rehearsals; coordinate rehearsals; and run the show after it opens. The *voice* and *dialects coach* works with actors in rehearsal to ensure audibility and clarity of meaning. The *movement coach* and/or *fight coordinator* works with actors for safety and expressive physical work. In musicals, the composer, musical director, and choreographer are also part of the director's team. In nonprofit theatres, the *production dramaturg* is also an integral part of the production team.

FOCUS ON THEATRE

Society of Stage Directors and Choreographers

Society of Stage Directors and Choreographers (SDC) is an independent national labor union representing professional stage directors and choreographers who work in theatres throughout the United States. There are SDC contracts for Broadway, Off Broadway, national tours, resident theatres, and stock and dinner theatres, along with special contracts for members working in college/university theatre programs and in community theatres.

The dramaturg's position was created in the eighteenth-century German theatre when playwright and critic Gotthold Ephraim Lessing joined the staff of the new Hamburg National Theatre in 1767. He declined the position of resident playwright but served instead as in-house critic, advising on selection of plays and the company's productions, and publishing a journal of reviews and theories on drama. Thereafter, the position of dramaturg was firmly established in German and European theatres. In America, the dramaturg was introduced in the nonprofit theatres in the 1960s and has since become a permanent member of the production staff in most.

How do dramaturgs serve the production? Early in the process, they may select the version of the text to be performed (a Shakespeare or a Brecht text, for example), prepare a translation or adaptation, and cut and rearrange the script that is to be the production script. They usually research background on a playwright's life and his or her other plays and writings, explore the surrounding period or culture, and offer script analysis. In brief, they increase understanding of the play, the writer, and the society that shaped both.

In rehearsals, dramaturgs serve as a critical "eye" for directors and provide feedback on how well the author's and director's intentions are being realized onstage. Nonprofit theatres also ask dramaturgs to manage outreach programs to educate audiences: hold "talk back" sessions with audiences, prepare materials for school programs, and prepare other materials (playbill inserts and newsletters) that elaborate on script interpretation and production values.

In all, dramaturgs serve productions and their creative teams in advisory and critical ways to ensure that both playwright's and director's intentions are complementary and meaningful to audiences.

STAGING: APPROACHES AND STYLES

As creative artists, some directors serve the playwright by translating the script as faithfully as possible into theatrical form. Elia Kazan, for example, interpreted Arthur Miller's and Tennessee Williams's plays with a faithful concern for the playwright's "intentions." Many directors seek out a controlling idea, image, or sound to

FOCUS ON THEATRE

Directors on Directing

©Getty Images

Robert Falls, artistic director of Chicago's Goodman Theatre notable for recent revivals of Eugene O'Neill's *Desire Under the Elms* and *The Iceman Cometh* and new works by Lynn Nottage and Regina Taylor allowed: "I have been doing highly interpretive productions that tried to integrate the acting with design and with the director's hand very much apparent. . . . I believe in the power of theater to change lives. I keep changing, listening, evolving."[8]

©Getty Images

Mike Nichols made his Broadway debut with Neil Simon's *Come Blow your Horn* and *Barefoot in the Park*, followed by recent revivals of *Death of a Salesman* and Harold Pinter's *Betrayal*. Reflecting on the relevance of Arthur Miller's play to millennial America, he said, "Great plays are like life: they are complicated, and you can choose your themes. . . . I wanted it to be about the central American relationship, which is father and son. That is a very American thing."[10]

©Paula Court

Elizabeth LeCompte, called the materfamilias of American experimental theatre, was the founding artistic director of the Wooster Group in 1980 with a mission to entertain and subvert. Of her reinventions of works by Spalding Gray (*Sakonnet Point*), Rodgers and Hammerstein II (*South Pacific*), Tennessee Williams (*Vieux Carré*) and Shakespeare (*Hamlet*), she has said: "This is what I do—bring things together. I take something, I copy it, and maybe something's revealed that's not in the original. I go for that. It's a way of passing on a tradition by reinventing a play."[9]

©Getty Images

Dan Sullivan (recently staged *Twelfth Night, The Merchant of Venice*, and *As You Like It* in New York's Shakespeare in the Park for the Public Theater) said: "I think directors get typed just like actor's get typed. . . . I always try to make the play belong to the actor. That's the goal finally. The only way you have to get that is to push the actor forward, not yourself. . . . I can shape the actor's work, but I can't create it."[11]

define the production's emotional and political meaning. Mike Nichols, in directing Neil Simon's comedies, searches for what he calls the "Event"—the truthful moment or series of moments that will illuminate the author's meaning and reveal "real people living their lives." In contrast, the Wooster's Group's Elizabeth LeCompte, often seen as an iconoclastic director, seeks mystery and danger as she "renovates" texts in her search for imaginative ways to renew theatrical experience in the new millennium.

Many directors today, taking their cues from such great experimental directors as Vsevolod Meyerhold, Bertolt Brecht, and Peter Brook, fashion the script into a wholly new and directorially original work of art. In this role, the director alters the play—changes the historical period, cuts the text, rearranges the scenes—and practically takes over the role of author.

©Sara Krulwich/The New York Times/Redux

As You Like It
Set in the American South and directed by Dan Sullivan, for the 50th anniversary season of New York's Shakespeare in the Park/Public Theater. André Braugher (center left) and Lily Rabe (center right).

At the most basic level, the director helps the actor find the character's inner life and project this life vocally and visually to the audience. Many directors preplan the actor's movements in each scene (called *blocking*) and, like a photographer composing a group photograph, arrange the actors in the stage space to show their physical

©Royal Shakespeare Company

A Midsummer Night's Dream
Peter Brook took Shakespeare's play out of period costumes, painted scenic backdrops, and green forests. The actors performed the text in a white box while balancing on trapezes, juggling plates, hurling streamers, and walking on stilts.

Hubert Witt, ed., Brecht: As They Knew Him (New York: International Publishers, 1974): 126. Reprinted by permission.

FOCUS ON THEATRE

Artistic Directors in Today's Regional Theatres

A regional or resident theatre in the United States is a professional or semiprofessional theatre company that produces its own seasons. The term *regional theatre* most often refers to a professional theatre outside of New York City. Those artists who helm these theatres, many of them women, hold the title *artistic director* or *producing artistic director*.

***Susan V. Booth*, Alliance Theatre, Atlanta,** brings leadership to a theatre located in a Southern city that celebrates, in Booth's words, "a particular polyglot of cultures and transplants and internationalism." As the theatre's leader she gives attention to "conversations with our community" in new works by Pearl Cleage, Marsha Norman, Alice Walker, and others.[12]

***Martha Levy*, Steppenwolf Theatre Company, Chicago,** helms a theatre that is home to modern classics (*Who's Afraid of Virginia Woolf?*) and new works (*August: Osage County*), says that her objective is to "conduct a multigenerational conversation" with audiences. She describes Steppenwolf as "artist-driven" and her job as artistic director is to navigate the company's varied artistic interests.[13]

***Emily Mann*, McCarter Theatre Center, Princeton (NJ),** set out as artistic director to create a "theatre of testimony" engaged in dialogue with the world around it—and one that pays tribute to the enduring power of the human imagination and spirit. Her commitment to multicultural diversity is found in new works by Nilo Cruz, Christopher Durang, John Guare, Athol Fugard, and Theresa Rebeck.

***Diane Paulus*, American Repertory Theatre, Cambridge (MA),** known for the Broadway revival of *Hair*, became artistic director in 2008, and set out to involve audiences in new and different ways. The reimagined production of the musical *Porgy and Bess* (retitled *The Gershwins' Porgy and Bess*) solidified for Boston and Broadway audiences a sea change in the ART's style, choice of works, and artists who work there.

***Carey Perloff*, American Conservatory Theatre, San Francisco,** has championed new and classic works in the newly renovated Geary Theatre (partially destroyed in the 1989 earthquake). She set about producing new plays by José Rivera, Nilo Cruz, Philip Kan Gotanda and modern classics by Samuel Beckett, Harold Pinter, and Tom Stoppard. Of her multifaceted job as artistic director and chief administrator of A.C.T, she has said, "Although you have the burden of keeping the whole place afloat, and that's very stressful, it also allows you to create the ecology in which you work."[14]

***Olga Sanchez*, Miracle Theatre Group, Portland, Oregon,** is head of the Pacific Northwest's preeminent Hispanic theatre. Working as an actor, educator, and director, Sanchez found a home with the Miracle Theatre Group that merged her professional theatre work with her commitment to Latino arts. Expanding the company's reach to Spanish-speaking audiences, the group now presents English, Spanish, and bilingual plays. "Theatre is often elitist and inaccessible in many immigrants' home countries," Sanchez says while explaining the Group's mission "to make theatre a part of people's everyday lives."[15]

***Molly Smith*, Arena Stage, Washington, DC,** was invited to reenergize one of the nation's oldest regional theatres, cofounded in 1950 by Zelda Fichandler. Smith has since renovated Arena's existing theatre spaces as the Mead Center for the American Theater, and refocused the theatre's repertory on American classics and new American works. Reflecting upon her role as artistic director, she told an interviewer, "You have to make the choice that this is something you really want, because it's hard. People can make it look easy, but it's hard to do all this work."[16]

and psychological relationships. Not unlike the photographer, some directors compose pictures with actors onstage to show relationships and attitudes. Others collaborate with actors to discover the possibilities of the text and the stage space. In all instances, directors concern themselves with conveying truthful human behavior and telling the playwright's story.

© Eric Y. Exit/The Goodman Theatre

***A Moon for the Misbegotten* by Eugene O'Neill**
With Gabriel Byrne, Roy Dotrice (center), and Cherry Jones. Directed by Daniel Sullivan, Goodman Theatre, Chicago.

Preplanned Approach

Some directors use early rehearsals to *block* the play. In blocking rehearsals, the director goes through each scene, working with actors on when to enter or exit, where to stand or sit, and which lines to move on. As they go through the scenes, the actors write down this information in their scripts along with stage business (specific actions, such as answering a telephone or turning on a table lamp).

Directors vary a great deal in their approach to rehearsals. Some give full directions immediately; others leave much of the detail to be worked out later as actors try out their lines and reactions to one another. All directors make adjustments in later rehearsals as director and actors discover better ways of moving and reacting and generally shaping their work into a meaningful performance.

Collaborative Approach

A second approach, which many directors favor, is the *collaborative* approach. This method involves director and actors working together in rehearsals to develop movement, gestures, character relationships, stage images, and line interpretations. Rather than enter the rehearsal period with entirely preset ideas, the director watches, listens, suggests, and selects as the actors rehearse. At some point in the rehearsal period, the director sets the performance by selecting from what has evolved in rehearsals.

©Martine Franck/Magnum Photos, Inc.

Shakespeare's *Richard II*
Ariane Mnouchkine removed Shakespeare's play from a traditional Western performance style. As conceived with her company, Mnouchkine's version of *Richard II* relies on Kabuki traditions of setting, costumes, props, makeup, and movement. Théâtre du Soleil, Paris, France.

DIRECTOR AS AUTEUR

JULIE TAYMOR, MARTHA CLARKE, ROBERT LEPAGE

Different creative approaches govern the stagings of many contemporary artists. Julie Taymor is influenced by Eastern puppetry and storytelling; Martha Clarke and Robert Lepage are grounded in nonnarrative traditions. These three artists share in common their intense collaborations with puppeteers, composers, designers, choreographers, dancers, singers, and actors.

Julie Taymor's *Juan Darién*

Julie Taymor and her collaborator, composer Elliot Goldenthal, tell the story of a jaguar cub transformed into a boy in a theatre piece about faith and superstition, compassion and revenge, civilization and savagery. *Juan Darién* is a compelling narrative based on the Latin American story by Uruguayan writer Horacío Quirogà. Taymor's production utilizes puppets, masks, movement, and a musical score sung in Latin and

FOCUS ON PEOPLE IN THEATRE

CREATOR

Julie Taymor

©Walter McBride/Retna Ltd.

Julie Taymor (b. 1952) grew up in a suburb of Boston. She traces her initial interest in puppetry and masks to the École du Mime de Jacques Le Coq in Paris, where she studied before attending Oberlin College in Ohio. She traveled to Eastern Europe, Japan, and Indonesia, where she lived for four years. In Indonesia, she formed her own international company, Teatr Loh (*loh* means "the source" in Javanese), with performers skilled in traditional dance, tai chi, improvisation, shadow puppetry, mask making, acting, and singing. Her first major work, *Way of Snow*, used masks and puppets to take spectators on a cross-cultural journey from the tale of an Eskimo shaman into the modern world of speeding buses and telephone operators.

Returning to the United States in 1979, she designed sets, costumes, puppets, and masks for productions in regional theatres and received a MacArthur Foundation "genius" grant in 1991. Her various projects include *The Tempest*, *Liberty's Taken*, *Tirai*, *The Taming of the Shrew*, *Titus Andronicus*, *Visual Magic*, *Juan Darién*, *The King Stag*, a revised *Juan Darién*, *The Green Bird*, and *The Lion King*; *Fool's Fire* (television); *Oedipus Rex*, *The Magic Flute*, *Salomé*, and *The Flying Dutchman* (operas); and *Titus* (feature film).

Taymor's current credits on Broadway are for the controversial *Spider-Man: Turn Off the Dark*. Dismissed by producers, Taymor sued to protect her rights and royalties as cocreator of the musical.

©Richard Feldman

Juan Darién

A carnival scene from *Juan Darién* with the skeleton puppet Mr. Bones.

Julie Taymor's "Tiger Tales"
The interludes (called "Tiger Tales") in Julie Taymor's *Juan Darién.*

Spanish. Her subjects include maternal love and bereavement, the primitiveness of the natural world and the malevolence of the human one.

Opening images display the play's themes: The deteriorating walls of a mission church are overtaken by giant jungle leaves, while the distant voices of a Latin chorus singing the *Agnus Dei* are drowned out by the buzzing of dragonflies. Taymor describes *Juan Darién* as "a visual dance of images that have a clear story line, with music—not language—motivating the action."[17]

Juan Darién tells the story of a young jaguar transformed by motherly love into a boy, then cruelly executed by superstitious and vengeful villagers, and finally retransformed into the feared jaguar of jungle lore. Understanding the fear of jaguars by people living at the edge of civilization, Julie Taymor says, is paramount to understanding this instance of human savagery.[18]

Interludes between scenes, called "Tiger Tales," reinforce the culture's obsession with the jaguar as enemy. The "Tales" are a series of shadow-puppet plays depicting struggles between humans and beasts presided over by Mr. Bones, the master of ceremonies, a life-size skeleton puppet topped with a black bowler hat. These tales serve to break the linear flow of the story, interrupt the tension, and introduce crude jokes. In one instance, a jaguar eats a baby who then drives the animal mad with its loud and ceaseless crying. The jaguar tries to stop the sound within his stomach by covering his various orifices and finally blows his head off, whereupon the baby emerges giggling and gurgling. These interludes range from the sublime to the ridiculous.

Juan Darién is also a story of transformation. The boy is transformed five times. First, he appears as a jaguar cub (a rod-and-string puppet); second, he becomes an infant (a hand-manipulated doll) cradled by a mother who has lost her own child to disease; at age ten, he transforms into a four-foot-tall Bunraku puppet with realistic features; upon the death of his mother, he becomes a flesh-and-blood child. This is the pivotal moment. From this point on, Juan is the only human (unmasked) actor in the play. When he is accused by the villagers of being a dangerous jaguar, we realize that everyone around him wears a mask and appears not quite human. The final transformation occurs when the child is burned alive on the Bengal lights (fireworks) and metamorphoses into a jaguar once again.[20] The final lesson is that human beings, through abominable acts of torture and murder, unwittingly make beasts of others.

"A puppet is a sort of poetic abbreviation, a distillation to a character's essence. It is more archetype than individual, an ideogram for Vulgarity, Brutality, Helplessness, Despair."[19]

— Julie Taymor

Taymor's work is a blend of Eastern and Western theatre: puppetry, masks, performance styles, and minimal scenery. The stage is transformed into a poetic realm of myth, dreams, nightmares, and childlike storytelling, where puppets and actors concentrate meaning on universal issues that extend beyond specific cultures.

Martha Clarke's Dance-Theatre Pieces

Martha Clarke connects hundreds of imagistic fragments in her theatrical works. First, she asks singers and dancers to move to music and develop fragmentary scenes. Later in the collaborative process among the various artists, she superimposes other parts onto the scenes. If the pieces connect, she then weaves them into the fabric of the

The Lion King
Taymor mixed Javanese rod puppetry, Balinese headdress, African masks, American and British music (much of it written by Elton John) with African music (from Soweto with songs written by Lebo M.) and the click language of Xhosa performed by Tsidii Le Loka (center), from South Africa.

"I'm a very instinctive person and I feel my way around like someone blind-folded in the attic. I stumble the piece into shape and often don't get a vision until late in the process. Then I take out my scissors and my paste and in the very last moments before a first preview it falls together."[21]

— MARTHA CLARKE

total work that is shaped and reshaped in six months or more of rehearsal. *The Garden of Earthly Delights* is Clarke's theatrical interpretation of painter Hieronymus Bosch's fifteenth-century triptych. A one-hour evocation of the Garden of Eden and the netherworld, *The Garden* is inhabited by ten dancers and musicians who at times are earthbound, and at other times are celestially somersaulting through the air on cables.

Clarke is the chief creator of her theatre pieces, which are not narrations of a story line but expressions of her subconscious. They link the points between inspiration and a volatile inner emotional life. Commenting on her collaborative process, she says:

> If you watched a rehearsal of mine, you would see that nine-tenths of it is in such disarray. I flounder.... I'm foggy a lot of the time. And the actors and dancers have to search as much as I do. We're all children dropped on another planet at the beginning of this process and, tentatively, hand-in-hand, we find our way through this mire to whatever. The day-by-day process couldn't be more collaborative.[22]

Martha Clarke's *Belle Epoque*

A scene from Martha Clarke's performance piece, *Belle Epoque*, re-created from a painting by Toulouse-Lautrec.

FOCUS ON PEOPLE IN THEATRE

DIRECTORS-CHOREOGRAPHERS

Martha Clarke and Robert Lepage

Martha Swope/The New York Public Library

Born in Baltimore, Maryland, in 1944, **Martha Clarke** entered the theatre through dance training at the Juilliard School, New York City, and as a member of Anna Sokolow's dance company and later the Pilobolus Dance Theatre. The New York-based Music Theatre Group funded Clarke to develop her own theatrical form. The result was a series of increasingly complex works: *The Garden of Earthly Delights, Vienna: Lusthaus, Endangered Species*, and *Dammerung*. Awarded a MacArthur "genius" grant in 1990, she has since worked on *Alice's Adventures Underground* for the Royal National Theatre, London, and created a new work about the women painted by Toulouse-Lautrec, called *Belle Epoque*.

©Redux Images

Canadian by birth, international artist **Robert Lepage** (b. 1957) studied at Québec City's Conservatoire d'Art Dramatique and became artistic director of the National Arts Centre's Théâtre français in Ottawa where he staged productions of *The Dragons' Trilogy, Coriolanus, Macbeth, The Tempest*, and *A Midsummer Night's Dream*. In 1994, as artistic director, he founded Ex Machina, a multidisciplinary production company, and toured productions to international acclaim. As a gifted opera director, he has staged operas for the Metropolitan Opera Company, New York; Sadler's Wells Theatre, London; the Canadian Opera Company, Toronto; the Brussels Opéra de la Monnaie; and in other venues. In 2005, he was invited by Cirque du Soleil to create a permanent Las Vegas show named *Kà* at the MGM Grand Hotel and also the recent *Totem*. Lepage is featured in a 2012 documentary about the staging of the Metropolitan Opera Company's *Der Ring des NibeLungen* (known familiarly as *The Ring*) and titled *Wagner's Dream*.

©Topham/The Image Works

The Blue Dragon

Choreographer Tai Wei Foo performs in *The Blue Dragon*—a story written by Robert Lepage and Marie Michaud as a critique of two cultures (Modern China and Western capitalism) with three possible endings. In Lepage's 1985 fable, revised and presented in London in 2011, neither Eastern nor Western values emerge unscathed, Barbican Theatre, London.

Unlike directors who faithfully interpret the playwright's world or enrich the text with an idea or concept to better connect the stage and the world around us, the theatre's new *auteurs*, such as Julie Taymor, Martha Clarke, Robert Lepage, Robert Wilson, and Elizabeth LeCompte, develop their own texts or reconceive older texts for postmodern sensibilities. Of ultimate importance to these creators is the act of imparting an *artistically created vision* with a sense of its visual significance and excitement in the staging of new realities.

©Stephanie Berger Photography

Robert Wilson's *The Days Before: Death, Destruction & Detroit III*
Robert Wilson's two-hour exploration of the process of destruction and reconstruction is interwoven with narrative, philosophy, and memory. Featuring actress Fiona Shaw as the narrator, with music by Ryuichi Sakamoto and text based on a novel by Umberto Eco and "Tone Poems" by Christopher Knowles.

TRANSITION

Before the emergence of the director in the nineteenth century, leading actors, managers, and playwrights ran the theatres, dictated production elements, and took care of financial matters. A coordinating specialist—the director—became necessary with advancing technology and changing subject matter brought about by new currents in social, aesthetic, and political thought.

Today's audiences experience theatrical works guided by the director's imagination and intellect, often to such a degree that the modern director has become, at times, almost as distinct a creative force as the playwright.

Other indispensable artists—set, costume, lighting, sound, and graphics designers—entered the theatre in the last century and continue to transform the theatrical experience with their creative energies and skills.

Theatre: A Way of Seeing Online

Visit the CourseMate for Theatre: A Way of Seeing 7th Edition for quick access to the digital study resources that accompany this chapter, including links to the websites listed below, Theatre Workshop, digital glossary, a chapter quiz and more.

Websites

The *Theatre: A Way of Seeing* CourseMate includes links for all the websites described below. Simply select "Web links" from the Chapter Resources for Chapter 10, and click on the link that interests you. You'll be taken directly to the site described.

The Director's Guild of America (DGA)
An organization that represents directors of theatrical, industrial, educational, and documentary films, as well as television (live, filmed, taped), radio, videos, and commercial films.

The Drama League
Provides training, assistant directorships, and Equity production opportunities for early-career directors through its national Directors Project.

Literary Managers and Dramaturgs of the Americas (LMDA)
A national membership organization, that serves literary managers, dramaturgs, and other professionals through conferences, a job phone line, and an early-career dramaturg program.

New York Public Library for the Performing Arts
Includes the Theatre on Film and Tape Archive, containing a collection of theatrical productions on video; also documents on popular entertainment, including scripts, promptbooks, photographs, reviews, books, and personal papers.

Society of Stage Directors and Choreographers (SDC)
An independent national labor union representing professional directors and choreographers.

What Is a Dramaturg?
A description of position and responsibilities.

©Paul Kolnik

11

IMAGE MAKERS: DESIGNERS

SCENERY, COSTUMES, MASKS, MAKEUP, WIGS, AND PUPPETS

Stage-designing should be addressed to [the] eye of the mind. There is an outer eye that observes, and there is an inner eye that sees.[1]

— ROBERT EDMOND JONES, *THE DRAMATIC IMAGINATION*

Designers collaborate with directors (and playwrights) to focus the audience's attention on the actor in the theatrical space. They create three-dimensional environments for the actor and make the play's world *visible* and *interesting*. Sometimes one person (the scenographer) designs scenery, lighting, and costumes. But in most instances today, scenery, costumes, lights, and sound are designed by individual artists working in collaboration.

THE SCENE DESIGNER

BACKGROUND

The scene or set designer entered the American theatre more than 200 years ago. The designer's nineteenth-century forerunner was the resident *scenic artist*, who painted large pieces of scenery for theatre managers. Scenery's main function in those days was to give the actor a painted background and to indicate place: a drawing room, garden, etc. Scenic studios staffed with specialized artists turned out scenery on demand. Many of these studios conducted a large mail-order business for standard backdrops and scenic

Robert Edmund Jones, The Dramatic Imagination: Reflections and Speculations on the Art of the Theatre (New York: Methuen Theatre Arts Books, 1987): 26. Reprinted by permission.

PREVIEW

Designers of theatrical sets, costumes, masks, puppets, hair, and wigs realize the production in visual terms. They are visual artists who transform space and materials into an imaginative world for actors engaged in human activity.

The larger than life horse puppets (Joey and Topthorn), each manipulated by three puppeteers, created by the South African Handspring Puppet Company in association with London's National Theatre of Great Britain for the production of *War Horse*. Projections of drawings (above) on what appears to be an outsize strip of paper convey shifts of time and setting. Lincoln Center Theater, New York City.

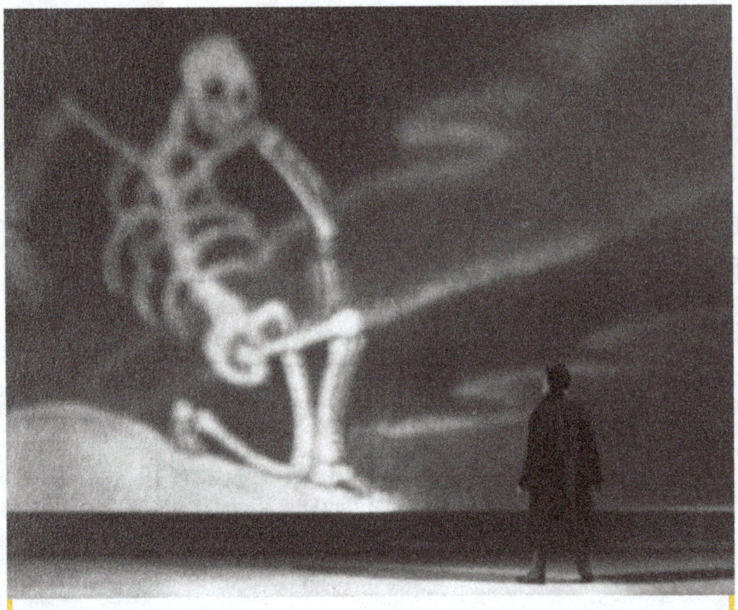

Billy Rose Theatre Collection, The New York Public Library for the Performing Arts, Astor, Lenox and Tilden Foundations

Expressionistic Design
The skeleton scene in the 1922 New York production of German playwright Georg Kaiser's *From Morn to Midnight*, designed by Lee Simonson, is an example of expressionistic design and production style, which stressed imaginative lighting (a tree has been transformed into a human skeleton), symbolic decor on an almost empty stage, and the distortion of natural appearances. The actor is dwarfed by the huge projection.

pieces. By the middle of the nineteenth century, realism had come into the theatre, and the job of making the stage environment look lifelike became a challenge.

By the late nineteenth century, theatre was dominated by a naturalistic philosophy that insisted life could be explained by the forces of environment, heredity, economics, society, and the psyche. This being the case, theatre had to present these forces as carefully and effectively as possible. If environment (including economic factors) really did govern people's lives, then it needed to be shown as audiences actually experienced it. The demands of realism called for the stage to look like actual places and rooms. The responsibility for creating this recognizable stage environment shifted from the scene painter to the set designer.

Realism has been the dominant convention of the theatre in our time. However, many new and exciting movements in the modern theatre came about as reactions to the direct representation of reality, which pretends that the stage is not a stage but someone's living room and the audience is really not present in the dark auditorium. Leaders of many new movements in stage design argued in the early twentieth century that the stage living room and box set (with three walls) were themselves unnatural. They set about pioneering other kinds of theatrical reality for the stage under such names as expressionism, symbolism, and selected realism.

Courtesy KaiDib Films International, Glendale, CA

Sophocles's *Oedipus the King*
Designed by Josef Svoboda and directed by Miroslav Machacek at the National Theatre, Prague, in 1963. The setting was a vast flight of stairs, starting in the orchestra pit and reaching almost out of sight. The stairs were punctuated by platforms that thrust out from the stairs themselves. The actor playing Oedipus appears on a platform. At the end Oedipus was left alone. Virtually all the flat levels disappeared. He climbed an endless staircase made of acoustically "transparent" material (the orchestra was located beneath the risers), into sharp counterlighting.

FOCUS ON PEOPLE IN THEATRE

DESIGNERS

Appia and Craig

Music and Stage Setting, 1899

Adolphe Appia (1862–1928) and **Edward Gordon Craig** (1872–1966) built the theoretical foundations of modern expressionistic theatrical practice. For the Swiss-born Appia, *artistic unity* was the basic goal of theatrical production. He disliked the contradiction in the three-dimensional actor performing before painted two-dimensional scenery, and he advocated the replacement of flat settings with steps, ramps, and platforms. He thought the role of lighting was to fuse all visual elements into a unified whole. His *Music and Stage Setting* (1899) and *The Work of Living Art* (1921) are early source books for modern stage-lighting practices.

Hulton Archive/Getty Images

Edward Gordon Craig was born into an English theatrical family (he was the son of actress Ellen Terry and architect and scene designer Edward Godwin) and began his career as an actor in Henry Irving's company. The 1902 exhibit of his work as a stage designer created controversy throughout Europe. He thought of theatre as an independent art that welded action, words, line, color, and rhythm into an artistic whole created by the single, autonomous artist. Many of his ideas on simplified decor, three-dimensional settings, moving scenery, and directional lighting prevailed in the new stagecraft that emerged after the First World War.

©Edward Gordon Craig/Courtesy the Victoria & Albert Museum, London UK/Art Resource, NY

Edward Gordon Craig's *Hamlet*

Edward Gordon Craig's design models for the famous setting of *Hamlet* for the 1912 Moscow Art Theatre production. Craig designed huge white screens to be sufficiently mobile that the scene could be changed without closing the front curtain. Unfortunately, the screens did not function with the efficiency he envisioned.

Before the First World War in Europe, Adolphe Appia and Edward Gordon Craig, self-proclaimed prophets of a new movement in stage design and lighting, assaulted the illusion of stage realism and led the way to rethinking theatrical art as *expressive*. Today, in the same spirit, modern designers have extended the traditional media of wood, canvas, and paint to include steel, plastics, pipes, ramps, platforms, steps, and computer-generated images to *express* the play's imaginative world. Prominent among the new generation were Jo Mielziner, the designer of *Death of a Salesman*, *A Streetcar*

FOCUS ON THEATRE

Designs for Brecht's *Mother Courage and Her Children*

In an era before computer-aided technology, Bertolt Brecht's favorite designers—Teo Otto, Caspar Neher, and Karl von Appen—avoided illusions of real places. Instead, they provided background materials (projections on a rear cyclorama, placards, signs, and such set pieces as Mother Courage's wagon) to comment on the play's historical period and the characters' socioeconomic circumstances. The setting itself (an open theatrical space with revolving stage) was used to make the dramatic action and individuals appear strange or unfamiliar. Brecht did not disguise the fact that all was taking place in a theatre under exposed lighting instruments, creating "white light," and before an audience.

Berliner Ensemble/Bertoldt Brecht Archive/Akademie der Kunst, Berlin

The Berliner Ensemble's 1949 production of Brecht's *Mother Courage and Her Children* in (former) East Berlin was originally designed by Teo Otto. In this final scene, Mother Courage's wagon is the main set piece, which actress Helene Weigel as Courage, alone in the harness, pulls toward yet another war.

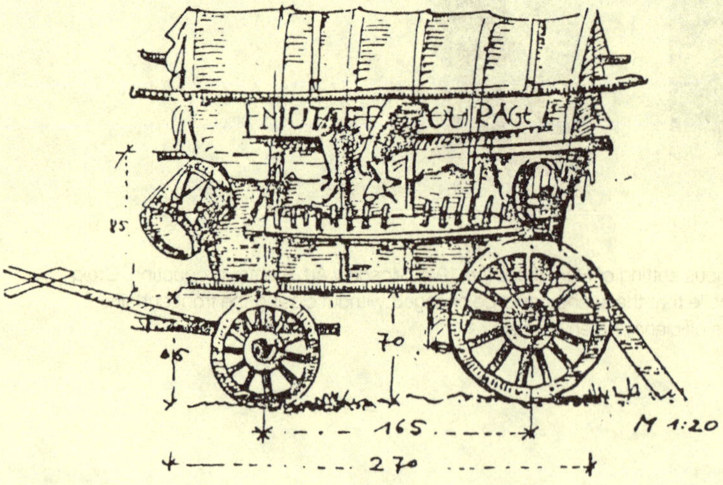

Akademie der Kunst, Berlin

For the Berliner Ensemble's production of *Mother Courage and Her Children*, Brecht used the set model designed by Teo Otto with wagon (see sketch) and movable screens placed on a revolve, or turntable, as the main set pieces of the design.

Named Desire, and *The King and I*; Boris Aronson, the designer of *Cabaret*, *Company*, and *Pacific Overtures*; and Oliver Smith, designer of *Brigadoon*, *The Sound of Music*, and *Plaza Suite*.

Stage Design—as Visual Story-Telling

Many think of designers as detectives who uncover the visual clues that reveal the inner life of the play, its characters, and the environment in which they live.[2] As a member of a collaborative team, including director and other designers, the set designer assembles an imaginative world out of words, images, notes, sketches, photographs, paint chips, three-dimensional models, computer renderings, and so on.

Although there are no hard-and-fast rules about approaches to stage design, designers usually begin by studying the script in much the same way as the director visualizing details of place, texture, movement, mood, metaphor, architecture, and objects in space. They ask questions in intellectually rigorous and artistically supple ways. What are the requirements of the script and the director? How will the director approach the staging? Is there a director's concept? What is the play's historical period? How does the play proceed in time? What kinds of actions are required of the characters? What elements from life are essential to the play's world? Are there multiple sets? Will there be wagons (traveling pieces of scenery) combined with flying scenery? What exits and entrances are needed? Are backdrops or projections needed for the exterior and interior worlds? Are properties and furniture required? Is the audience part of the stage space?

> **"When I sit alone in a theatre and gaze into the dark space of its empty stage, I'm frequently seized by fear that this time I won't manage to penetrate it. And I always hope that this fear will never desert me. Without an unending search for the key to the secret of creativity, there is no creation. It's necessary always to begin again. And that is beautiful."[3]**
>
> —Josef Svoboda, The Secret of Theatrical Space

An Inspector Calls
A revival of J. B. Priestley's play, designed by Ian MacNeil, with spectacular moving scenery that literally unfolds onstage to disclose a realistic interior that collapses at the play's end.

FOCUS ON THEATRE

Mielziner's Design for *Death of a Salesman*

Jo Mielziner pioneered "selective realism" in scenic design. Of his type of design, Mielziner said, "If you eliminate nonessentials, you've got to be sure that the things you do put in are awfully good. They've got to be twice as good, because they stand alone to make a comment.. . . I got to feel that even realistic plays didn't need realistic settings necessarily."[4]

For Arthur Miller's *Death of a Salesman* in 1949, Mielziner designed the salesman's house on several levels (kitchen, sons' bedroom, porch, and forestage). The actors' movements with area lighting were the only scene-change devices. The large backdrop upstage was painted to depict tenement buildings looming over Willy Loman's house in the play's present time. When lighted from the rear, the buildings washed out to be replaced with projections of trees with leaves, suggesting Willy's remembered past with its bright sunshine and cheerful ambience.

Harry Ransom Center, University of Texas, Austin, TX

Jo Mielziner's original design for *Death of a Salesman*, by Arthur Miller, Broadway, 1949.

As the set designer analyzes the play's world and visualizes the space, sketches, models, and computer-aided drawings are shared with the director and the collaborative team. Rough pencil drawings or sketches are made in the early period when both director and designer are visualizing the theatrical space. When their ideas reach some degree of concreteness, they agree on a ground plan (the shape and dimension of the playing area as seen from above). For some designers, models (in scale) are valuable tools to show the visual transformations (shapes, colors, backdrops, furniture, etc.) of the stage space and the way the story will be told.

FOCUS ON PEOPLE IN THEATRE

DESIGNERS

Ming Cho Lee and John Lee Beatty

©China Foto Press/Getty Images

Ming Cho Lee, born in Shanghai and educated at Occidental College and UCLA, designed his first Broadway show, Eugene O'Neill's *A Moon for the Misbegotten*, in 1962. Since then, he has designed scenery for Broadway, Off Broadway, regional theatres, and opera and dance companies. Speaking of his methods, Ming Cho Lee says, "I generally read the script once just to get an impact from which I will try to form some kind of visual concept. . . . I always design for the total play and let the specifics fit in. The total play demands some kind of expression through materials, and this is something I always first ask a director. . . . And then, I would make the choice as to whether it is a realistic play that requires very literal settings or if it's a play that requires a nonliteral approach and essentially you present it on a platform—you create a framework on which to hang your visual statement."[5]

©Joe Corrigan/Getty Images

John Lee Beatty grew up in Palo Alto, California, and attended Brown University (RI) and the Yale University School of Drama, where he studied with designer Ming Cho Lee. Beatty's set designs include Broadway's *Ain't Misbehavin'*, *Chicago*, *An American Daughter*, *The Heiress*, *The Royal Family*, *A Delicate Balance*, *A View from the Bridge*, and *Twelfth Night* in New York's Central Park. Known for designs of poetic realism and playful theatrical settings, Beatty says of his process: "My job as a designer is to design the scenery and to give a designer's point of view. . . . Coming up with the design is what is hard. I normally do a group plan and a rough sketch first. . . . I usually show a fairly simple sketch to a director. . . . It's important to let the director know it's a work in process."[6]

©T. Charles Erickson

John Lee Beatty's Design for *The Heiress*

The Heiress, the Broadway revival of the play by Ruth and Augustus Goetz, directed by Gerald Gutierrez, with sets by John Lee Beatty and costumes by Jane Greenwood. Beatty created an upper-class, richly appointed 1850s, parlor with large windows, chandeliers, lamps, fireplace, and staircase rising to the upper level of the large house on Washington Square, New York.

©Joan Marcus/Arena Stage

Ming Cho Lee's Design for *K2*

The elevations for this rock and ice face resembled a government geological survey map. Fifty thousand board feet of plastic foam were used to build the wall over a wooden frame armature. Finishing touches included an oil fog mist and nightly avalanche of snow from a theatrical supply house. (*K2* opened at Arena Stage, Washington, D.C., and moved to Broadway.)

FOCUS ON THEATRE

Women Designers

Women were late entrants into theatrical design. In the second half of the twentieth century, they took their place, first, as costume and lighting designers and then as set designers. Heidi Ettinger and Anna Louizos are among the recent generation of women set designers.

Heidi Ettinger, a former student of Ming Cho Lee who has also worked under her married name Heidi Landesman, designed the magical large-scale sets for *Big River*, the whimsical setting for *The Secret Garden*, and the folksy landscape for *The Adventures of Tom Sawyer*. Her Broadway career began with the design for the Pulitzer prize-winning *Night, Mother* by Marsha Norman and has since included work as coproducer for the Sondheim/Lapine musical hit *Into the Woods*.

Anna Louizos, who studied with Oliver Smith at New York University's Tisch School of the Arts, has designed sets for musicals *Avenue Q*, *High Fidelity*, *In the Heights*, *Curtains*, and *Irving Berlin's White Christmas*. She served as art director for multiple episodes of the television series *Sex and the City* and has designed numerous regional and Off Broadway premieres, including *Sons of the Prophet*. She received Tony Award nominations for best scene design of the musicals *High Fidelity* and *In the Heights*.

©Joan Marcus

In the Heights
Anna Louizos, set designer for the rap-salsa-pop musical *In the Heights*, has suggested that finding a stylistic framework for the story about a struggling and optimistic Dominican neighborhood in New York's Washington Heights proved her greatest challenge.[7]

The design process takes several months of discussion, research, and analysis. For example, if the play is set in a historical period, decisions must be made on appropriate architecture, furniture, and décor. Once director and set designer arrive at the look and details of the space, the designer's computer-aided drafting is transmitted to the theatre's production manager and technical staff for the final steps in the transformation from the script's words to the production's physical world.

©Sara Krulwich/The New York Times/Redux

The Normal Heart

The final scene from the Broadway revival of Larry Kramer's *The Normal Heart* with the actors surrounded by projections (designed by Batwin + Robin) in which casualties from AIDS are projected on the stage walls.

ADVANCES IN STAGE TECHNOLOGY

Advanced technologies in computer software are available to assist in technical areas of theatrical design and production with speed and efficiency. Computer-aided drafting provides complete visualizations of the set designer's concepts. One advantage the new technology offers designers is rapid communication with the director, other members of the design team, and shop managers. Images of the designs-in-progress are shared in an instant with others in faraway locations.[8]

With advances in technology, projected scenery has become integral to stage design. When used in an organic way, as in *War Horse*, *Sunday in the Park with George*, and *The Normal Heart*, projections (or filmic reality) fill in the scenic background with projected images of Georges Seurat's paintings, or juxtapose images of the peaceful village in *War Horse* as counterpoint to the encroaching war, or add walls of names of individuals lost to AIDS at the close of *The Normal Heart*.

THE COSTUME DESIGNER

Costume design has been compared by designer Patricia Zipprodt to a car trip in which unpredictables of life pop up—unavailable fabric, inadequate budget, temperamental actor. The designer, like the car's driver, remains in a constant state of problem solving.

THE COSTUME

Costumes include all of the character's garments and accessories (handbag, cane, jewelry, hat, handkerchief), all items related to hairdressing, and everything associated with face and body makeup, including masks.

Costumes tell us many things about the characters and about the nature, mood, and style of the play. As visual signals, they add color, style, and meaning to the play's environment. Costumes establish period, social class, economic status, occupation, age, geography, weather, and time of day. They help clarify the relationships and relative importance of various characters. Ornament, line, and color can tie together members of a family, group, faction, or party. Changes in costumes can indicate alteration in relationships among characters or in a character's psychological outlook. Similarities or contrasts in costumes can show sympathetic or antagonistic relationships. Hamlet's black costume, for instance, is usually contrasted with the bright colors worn by the court and speaks eloquently of his altered attitude toward the court. Designer Lucinda Ballard's costumes for *A Streetcar Named Desire* express Blanche DuBois's self-image of Southern gentility.

Costume by Designer Lucinda Ballard
Blanche DuBois's famous party costume, what Stanley Kowalski calls Blanche's "wornout Mardi Gras outfit," was created by Lucinda Ballard for the 1947 Broadway production of *A Streetcar Named Desire*. Tennessee Williams described the dress as a "somewhat soiled and crumpled white satin evening gown and a pair of scuffed silver slippers with brilliants set in the heels." A rhinestone tiara, bracelet, and faded corsage completed the costume.

Years ago, the leading actor, manager, or person in charge of stage wardrobe was responsible for costumes. But modern stagecraft has required designers trained to select and control these important visual elements with great attention to detail. Designers are involved in costume research and in sketching, preparing costume plates, assessing color choices, choosing fabrics, and sometimes overseeing construction. Depending upon the size of a school's or regional theatre's budget, there can be many assistants involved in cutting, sewing, fitting, and making shoes, boots, hats, and accessories.

Today, costume design and construction have become a major industry. Professional designers work in film, fashion, theatre, opera, television, dance, commercials, and extravaganzas (ice shows, nightclubs, circuses, and dance revues). Large costume houses located in New York City, Los Angeles, and Toronto rent and build costumes on demand. Some costume houses also rent to nonprofit regional, community, and university theatres. A visit to these collections is not only an exciting adventure in itself but also serves as a tour through the history of theatrical design.

FOCUS ON PEOPLE IN THEATRE

COSTUME DESIGNERS

Jane Greenwood and William Ivey Long

©Joseph Marzullo/Retna, Ltd.

Jane Greenwood is one of the American theatre's premier costume designers. British by birth, she designed her first professional costumes at the Oxford Playhouse (Great Britain) and worked in Canada at the Stratford (Ontario) Shakespeare Festival for three seasons. Relocating to New York City, she made her Broadway debut in 1963 with *The Ballad of the Sad Café* and has since designed over 100 productions, including Broadway's *The Prime of Miss Jean Brodie, Master Class, Passion, Same Time Next Year, Driving Miss Daisy, The Sisters Rosensweig*, and revivals of *Waiting for Godot* and *Harvey*. Her costumes are

©Paul Kolnik

seen in films, the Alvin Ailey and Martha Clarke dance companies, and also appeared in the world premiere of the opera *The Great Gatsby*. Among her many awards are Antoinette Perry "Tony" Award nominations, the Irene Sharaff Award for Lifetime Achievement, and the American Theatre Wing Design Award. She teaches costume design at the Yale University School of Drama.

William Ivey Long studied history at The College of William and Mary (VA) and set design at the Yale University School of Drama with Ming Cho Lee. Known today as a costume designer, his credits include musical revivals of *Chicago, 1776, Guys and Dolls, Cabaret, Annie Get Your Gun*, and *The Music Man*; and the new musicals *Contact, Seussical, The Producers, Hairspray*, and *Rodger and Hammerstein's Cinderella*. He has also designed costumes for a Siegfried and Roy Las Vegas Show, for the Rolling Stones, and ballets for the Peter Martins, Paul Taylor, and Twyla Tharp dance companies.

©Paul Kolnik

Hairspray

Costumes by William Ivey Long. Directed by Jack O'Brien, with choreography by Jerry Mitchell, Broadway.

FOCUS ON PEOPLE IN THEATRE

COSTUME DESIGNER

Theoni V. Aldredge

Courtesy Theoni V. Aldredge

Theoni V. Aldredge, one of theatre's most gifted and respected designers, produced more than 1,000 costumes in her career and designed costumes for five hit musicals that ran simultaneously on Broadway: *A Chorus Line*, *42nd Street*, *Dreamgirls*, *La Cage aux Folles*, and *The Rink*. She also designed costumes for other Broadway shows, including *The Secret Garden*, *Annie Warbucks*, *The Flowering Peach*, and *Annie*. Her film credits include *Ghostbusters*, *Addams Family Values*, and *The Great Gatsby*, for which she received an Academy ("Oscar") Award for costume design.

About the designer's creative process, she said: "To me, good design is design you're not aware of. It must exist as part of the whole—as an aspect of characterization. Also, a designer must be flexible and extremely patient. . . . A performance will suffer if an actor doesn't love his costume, and it's your job to make him love it."

For *A Chorus Line*, the story of a Broadway audition, Aldredge closely observed the personalities of the dancers and singers and the outfits they wore to rehearsals. Of this long-running musical she said, "I took millions of snapshots of what the kids came in wearing, and adapted what they had on for my costumes. I didn't depart too much, because it's what made each of them so unique. The only real transformation came with the golden chorus line at the end of the show, which, incidentally, Michael [Bennett] had wanted it to be a red chorus line. But I felt red was too definite a color. I thought it should be a fantasy number. I told him it ought to be the color of champagne—of celebration—and that's what we did."[9]

John Gruen, "She is One of Broadway's Most Designing Women," New York Times (8 April 1984): II, 5, 14. Copyright © 1984 by The New York Times Company. Reprinted by permission.

George E. Joseph/New York Public Library for the Performing Arts

A Chorus Line
A closing musical number of *A Chorus Line*, conceived by Michael Bennett and costumed by Theoni V. Aldredge.

The Designer's Process and Conferences

Set and costume designers work with directors to make visible the world in which the play's characters live. They explore verbally and with rough sketches many different approaches and creative ideas to bring that world into theatrical focus onstage. Designers reinforce with visual elements the director's concepts and, in so doing, often inspire the director to think in a different way about the play. Award-winning designer Theoni V. Aldredge said: "The costumes are there to serve a producer's vision, a director's viewpoint, and an actor's comfort."

Peter Brook, Threads of Time: A Memoir (London: Methuen Publishing Ltd., 1999): 149–150. Reprinted by permission.

Like the director and the set designer, the costume designer begins by studying the script and taking note of the story, mood, characterization, visual effects, colors, atmosphere, geography, period, and season. Later in the process, the designer asks practical questions: How many costumes (including changes) and accessories are required? What physical actions must the actor undertake that will affect the construction or wear of the costumes? What is the costume budget?

FOCUS ON PEOPLE IN THEATRE

COSTUME DESIGNER

Susan Hilferty

©Nielson Barnard/Getty Images

Susan Hilferty, a set and costume design student at the Yale University Drama School, was assigned to design for South African playwright Athol Fugard's *A Lesson from Aloes* and thus began a thirty-year relationship with the playwright.

Relocating to New York City, Hilferty has since designed costumes for dance, opera, and theatre, including for *Spring Awakening, Assassins, Into the Woods*, and the revival of *Annie*. She chairs the Department of Design for Stage and Film at New York University.

She has said that "costume designers actually have the most dangerous job in the world because we change people. . . . We make people walk a different way. We change their bodies. We give them teeth or noses or busts. . . . So the relationship with an actor is usually a one-on-one, trusting relationship. They trust you to see them naked and help make them into something else."[10]

©Joan Marcus

Milky White from *Into the Woods*
Susan Hilferty's costume design for Milky White, *Into the Woods*, Broadway.

Design Conferences

The overall plan of the production is worked out in design conferences. The costume designer brings sketches, color plates, costume charts, accessory lists, and fabric swatches to these meetings to make his or her visual concept clear to the director and set designer. The costume designer must be specific to avoid later misunderstandings and costly last-minute changes.

Sometimes a brilliant costume design develops through trial and error. While designing the costumes for the Broadway production of the musical *Pippin*, Patricia Zipprodt and director Bob Fosse had difficulty deciding on the right look for the strolling players. The musical is performed by a group of actors costumed as some kind of theatrical caravan, who relate the story of Charlemagne's eldest son, Pippin, an idealist journeying through courts, battles, and love's intrigues. The script said, "Enter strolling players of an indeterminate period." Zipprodt remembers:

> Now, to me, this meant exactly nothing. I did a lot of sketches, which everybody seemed to like. On the day I was supposed to present finished sketches, time ran short. Instead of fully coloring the costumes of the strolling players as was planned and expected, I just painted beige and off-white washes so that Fosse could read the sketches more easily. I put the whole group of 14 or 15 in front of him and was just about to apologize for not getting the color done when he said, "That's just brilliant, exactly the colors they should be. How clever of you." The minute he said it, I knew he was right.[11]

But, more often, final designs are selected after numerous alternatives have been explored.

COSTUME CONSTRUCTION

After approving sketches and plans, the director turns full attention to rehearsals, and the costume designer arranges for construction, purchase, or rental of costumes and schedules measurements and fittings with the actors. If the costumes are being constructed in the theatre's shop (as is most often the case in college, university, and regional theatres) actors are measured, patterns cut, fabric dyed and painted, garments constructed, and accessories built or purchased. After fittings with the actors, the costumes are ready for the *dress parade*, during which designer and director examine the costumes on the actors before the dress rehearsal begins.

The designer coordinates with assistant designers, shop supervisors, cutters, drapers, seamstresses, wigmakers, milliners, and other assistants to cut, sew, dye, and make hats, footwear, masks, and wigs. Often in small costume shops this personnel doubles up on the responsibilities. In the commercial theatre, the construction of costumes is jobbed out to costume construction businesses, where designs are turned into costumes and delivered to the Broadway companies.

FOCUS ON THEATRE

Costume Construction at Tricorne Studios, New York City

Katherine Marshall is part of a trio of founding owners of Tricorne Studios in New York City that has become one of the top costume construction houses in Manhattan. She studied at the University of Illinois, Urbana, and began her professional career at the Guthrie Theater, Minneapolis. Moving to New York City to work with Barbara Matera, Ltd., once considered the best in the business, Marshall founded Tricorne, Inc., in 2000. Tricorne is now a full-service costume house, constructing stage clothes with a couture-level of fit and finish while supporting the designer's vision through the creative teamwork of the many hands at Tricorne. Recent projects include *Mamma Mia, The Producers, Spamalot, Nine, Wicked*, and the San Francisco Ballet's *The Nutcracker*, and many more.

Dress Rehearsal and Wardrobe Personnel

The dress parade and dress rehearsal (where costumes, makeup, and masks are worn onstage with full scenery and lights) usually take place a week before opening night. It is not unusual to discover that the color of a fabric doesn't work under the lights or against the scenery. In this event, the designer may redesign the garment, select another fabric or color (or both), and have the costume reconstructed or dyed almost overnight and ready for the next rehearsal or opening performance.

Once costumes and accessories are finished, the costumes leave the shop and the wardrobe crew takes charge of them during dress rehearsals and performances. The crew's responsibility is to mend, press, clean, and maintain the costumes for the length of the play's run. Although in the professional theatre there is a clear-cut division between these two groups, in college and university theatres the construction and wardrobe crews may be many of the same people.

Before dress rehearsals begin, the wardrobe supervisor (long ago called the wardrobe master or mistress), or crew head, makes a list of the costumes and accessories worn by each actor. These lists are used by crew members and actors to check that each costume is complete before each performance. The "running" crew helps each actor dress, make quick changes, and is responsible for costumes before, during, and after each performance. Wardrobe routines are established during the dress rehearsal period and are strictly followed during production. The crew is also responsible for "striking" the costumes when the production closes. Costumes are cleaned, laundered, and returned to the rental houses or placed in storage along with accessories such as hats, wigs, handbags, shoes, and jewelry.

Costume Preparations
The costume technician's tools—industrial sewing machines and irons, worktables, dress forms, movable racks, and storage cabinets—are available in the modern costume shop.

"The clothing worn by an actor on stage is a result of the collaboration between the designer and costume maker. The designer provides the vision. The costume maker utilizes the elements of design, the knowledge of period silhouette, and construction techniques to emphasize character and implement the design."[12]

— JUDY ADAMSON, COSTUME DIRECTOR, PLAYMAKERS REPERTORY COMPANY (NC)

MAKEUP, WIGS, MASKS, AND PUPPETS

Makeup

Makeup enhances the actor and completes the costume. It is essential to the actor's visibility. In a large theatre, distance and lighting make an actor's features without makeup colorless and indistinct. Like the costume, makeup helps the actor reveal character by giving physical clues to age, background, ethnicity, health, personality, and environment.

In the ancient Asian and Greek theatres, actors used a white-lead makeup with heavy accents, or linen or cork masks. Today, basic makeup in Western theatre consists of a foundation and color shadings to prevent the actor from looking "washed out" beneath the stage lights. Pancake makeup has replaced greasepaint, or oil-based makeup, as the foundation for the actor's basic skin color and, like everyday makeup, is applied with a damp sponge. Color shadings with rouge, lipstick, liner, mascara, and powder are applied with pencils and brushes. A well-equipped makeup kit (which can be purchased inexpensively from theatrical supply houses) includes standard foundations and shading colors plus synthetic hair, glue, solvents, wax, and hair whiteners.

Martha Swope/The New York Public Library

Cats

The "cats" in the musical wore costumes and makeup designed by John Napier and wigs designed by Paul Huntley.

Straight, Character, and Fantasy Makeup

Makeup is classified as *straight* and *character*. Straight makeup highlights an actor's features and coloring for distinctness and visibility. Character makeup transforms the actor's features to reveal age or attitude. Noses, wrinkles, eyelashes, jawlines, eye pouches, eyebrows, teeth, hair, and beards can be added to change the actor's appearance. Character (sometimes called *illustrative*) makeup can make a young actor look older or can give the actor playing Cyrano a large nose. Actors must know, then, the basics of stage makeup and how to work with hair and wigs.

Makeup is normally applied by the actor and approved by the designer. In fantasy productions, such as the musicals *Cats* and *Beauty and the Beast*, makeup, hair, wigs, and masks are the final responsibility of the designer.

WIGS

Wigs and Hair Design

The creation of theatrical wigs starts with a meeting between the wig designer (or maker) and the costume designer to determine the needs and style of hair and wig.

A discussion of color follows, along with questions about use of the hair and wig. Will a hat be worn, for example? Will the hair be let down for a bedroom scene? This meeting is followed by another for measurement of the actor's head.

The base of the wig is then made of lace, and the hair is prepared. The next step is to "ventilate" the wig (or knot the strands of hair in place). Designer Paul Huntley says that a good wig has very little hair, so it has better balance and is lighter.

FOCUS ON PEOPLE IN THEATRE

WIG AND HAIR DESIGNER

Paul Huntley

©Bruce Gilkas/Getty Images

Paul Huntley's career as a designer spans thirty years. Starting out as an actor in Great Britain, he developed an interest in theatrical hair, wigs, and makeup and went to work for Wig Creations, where he learned the history and traditions of hairstyles throughout the ages. "It's really very good for the wigmaker to know about dressing hair," he said, "... you start as a wigmaker and then you become a hairdresser. In other words, you learn to *address* the hair."[13]

Huntley came to New York City in 1971 to make wigs for director Mike Nichols's film *Carnal Knowledge*. He then launched a Broadway, film, and television career that has included wigs and hair for *Cats*; *Amadeus*; *My Fair Lady*; *42nd Street*; *Evita*; *Dreamgirls*; *Kiss Me, Kate*; *Jekyll and Hyde*; *The Scarlet Pimpernel*; *Chicago*; *Cabaret*; and *Contact*.

Although the wigs for *Amadeus* and *Jekyll and Hyde* are stylized, Huntley prefers designing "natural wigs," such as the wig he created for Mia Farrow in the Woody Allen film *Broadway Danny Rose*.

©Nigel Teare/AP Images

Paul Huntley's wigs and hair for *Cats*
The yak-hair wigs for *Cats* were first ventilated and then dyed. Additional, bolder coloring was required for some wigs to stand out under the theatrical lighting.

Illustration of Pantalone from Jacques Callot's etchings, c. 1622, of commedia actor

The Commedia Dell'arte Mask
All characters in Italian commedia, with the exception of the young lovers, wore masks. Unlike classical masks and those of China and Japan, commedia masks did not express any particular emotion, such as joy or sorrow. Instead, they gave a permanent expression to the character, such as cunning or avarice. The mask's expressiveness varied with the angle from which it was seen. Pantalone, one of the chief commedia characters, was a miserly merchant. His mask, brown with a hooked nose, gray, sparse moustache, and pointed white beard, has a fixed expression of crafty greed.

Masks

Ancient and Modern Masks

In early theatres, masks had many uses. They enlarged the actor's facial features to make the character's image visible at great distances. Greek masks expressed basic emotions: grief, anger, horror, sadness, pity. Most important for us today, the masked actor creates an altogether different *presence* onstage than the actor without a mask. Although the masked actor may lose something in subtlety of expression, the presence of the actor-with-mask can be stately, heroic, comical, sinister, or mysterious. Nor is the masked actor totally deprived of the facial subtlety available to the actor whose facial muscles move and change expression. By changing the mask's position (if the mask is made with this effect in mind), by angling the head and catching the light, different emotional responses can be evoked.

Mask making is an ancient art dating from early cultures in which masks were objects of fear; they were thought to have supernatural powers. Masks have been used in the Greek and Roman theatres, by the commedia dell'arte in Renaissance Italy, in Japanese Noh, and in the modern theatre. In addition to having an artful exterior, a mask must

©Joan Marcus

The Green Bird
Director/designer Julie Taymor designed the masks for *The Green Bird* (Broadway) based on an eighteenth-century Italian play by Carlo Gozzi, who championed commedia dell'arte traditions.

be comfortable, strong, light, and molded to the contours of the actor's face. Today, in educational and regional theatres, the costume designer often creates masks as part of the costume, designing for color, durability, and expressiveness.

PUPPETS

The London and American productions of *War Horse*, adapted for the stage by Nick Stafford, from Michael Morpurgo's children's book, in association with the Handspring Puppet Company, based in Cape Town, South Africa, brought renewed interest from audiences, familiar with *Punch and Judy* shows and the children's television program *Sesame Street*, in the magic of puppetry. The magnificent horse-like puppets, known to audiences as "Joey" and "Topthorn," are the show's stars. Each is manipulated by three visible puppeteers (two within the horse controlling body and legs and the third standing outside manipulating the neck and head). A fractious puppet goose and two crows enliven early scenes in the Devonshire village where the play begins.

The plight of the war horses and their humans is central to the universal story about innocent victims of war's savagery where the use of horses in France between 1914 and 1918 was a cruel anachronism in a war fought with machine guns, trenches, mortars, barbed wire, and, toward the war's end, a new mobile weapon—the tank.

The puppeteers and the horse-like puppets created by the Handspring Puppet Company explore a new theatrical language, without words. Based on familiar images, manipulated in time and space, the puppeteers move their "charges" from village to cavalry regiment in a story at once poignant and inhumane.

War Horse
The horse puppets (Topthorn and Joey) lead the charge in *War Horse*, created by Adrian Kohler with Basil Jones for the Handspring Puppet Company. Lincoln Center Theater, 2011–2012 New York season.

TRANSITION

All good theatrical design enhances the actor's presence and supports the director's interpretation of that world—developing, visualizing, illuminating, and enriching it. Lighting and sound designers complete the roster of theatrical designers and find essential support for their endeavors among the theatre's production personnel and technology.

Theatre: A Way of Seeing Online

Visit the CourseMate for Theatre: A Way of Seeing 7th Edition for quick access to the digital study resources that accompany this chapter, including links to the websites listed below, Theatre Workshop, digital glossary, a chapter quiz and more.

Websites

The *Theatre: A Way of Seeing* CourseMate includes links for all the websites described below. Simply select "Web links" from the Chapter Resources for Chapter 11, and click on the link that interests you. You'll be taken directly to the site described.

The Costume Gallery Research Library
A central location to study costume and fashion.

Costume Institute of the Metropolitan Museum of Art, New York City
Website of the Costume Institute, which houses more than 75,000 costumes and accessories covering seven centuries and five continents. The holdings include dress accessories (hats, shoes, gloves, buttons), eighteenth-century men's wear, twentieth-century haute couture, and contemporary fashions.

The Costumer's Manifesto
Advice on the "how to" of costuming.

The Costume Site
Online costuming sources for historical, science fiction, and fantasy costumers.

Entertainment Design
An online magazine about the art and technology of show business, featuring profiles of designers, products, and projects. Scroll down the page to see the articles about current projects.

Museum of the City of New York
The Theatre Collection of the Museum of the City of New York, covers theatrical activity in New York City from the late eighteenth century to the present day. The collection includes original scenery and costume renderings, elevations, and set models by such notable designers as Jo Mielziner, Robert Edmond Jones, and Patricia Zipprodt; original scripts by Eugene O'Neill and others; more than 5,000 costumes and props; significant drawings and photographs; and a major Yiddish theatre collection. The *Costume & Textiles* collection includes Broadway theatre costumes and all aspects of New York City costume history, including clothing and inaugural gowns.

United Scenic Artists, L.U. 829 (USA)
The union for designers and artists for the entertainment industry, with links to web pages displaying their works.

United States Institute for Theatre Technology (USITT)
The association of design, production, and technology professionals in the performing arts and entertainment industry.

12

IMAGE MAKERS: DESIGNERS LIGHTING AND SOUND

I feel that light is like music. In some abstract, emotional, cerebral, nonliterary way, it makes us feel, it makes us see, it makes us think, all without knowing exactly how and why.[1]

—Jennifer Tipton, Lighting Designer

THE LIGHTING DESIGNER

Stage lighting is a powerful theatrical tool to focus an audience's attention, enhance understanding, and give aesthetic pleasure. It is sometimes surprising to learn that the "lighting" designer emerged in the theatre well before the invention of electricity.

Background

The Greeks called their theatres "seeing places." These were outdoor theatres, and performances took place chiefly during daylight hours, but not without some attention to lighting effects. Playwrights, who were also the earliest directors, called for dramatic effects with torches, fires, and even sunlight. Aeschylus in *Agamemnon*, which tells the story of the King's return at the close of the Trojan War, begins with a Watchman standing atop the palace to watch for beacons shining from distant mountaintops that will signal Agamemnon's return to Argos. Most interpreters think that the Watchman's speech begins virtually in the early morning mist and that his recognition of the signal flames coincides with the actual sunrise over the Theatre of Dionysus. Although the material of legend, the theatrical use of natural light would be spectacular in this

Red Beads, a performance poem created and staged by Mabou Mines, conjures with the magic of stage technology. Stage hands with blowers work beneath the fabric to lift and move it in coordination with the suspended actress (Clove Galilee); lighting by designers Jennifer Tipton and Mary Louise Geiger illumines the shimmering fabric from above, Off Off Broadway, New York.

PREVIEW

In today's theatre, lighting, sound, and computer technologies affect what we see, how we see, how we hear, how we feel, and often what we understand. As areas of theatrical design, lighting and sound, along with the new "machines," are essential to the modern stage's theatrical effectiveness.

instance. Because the plays lasted throughout the day, it is also logical that the red rays of sunset in the Attic sky simulated the destructive flames of the burning Troy, and, in the last rays of sunlight, the cessation of military or personal struggles.

Again, in the medieval outdoor theatres, torches, cauldrons of flame and smoke, and reflecting metals focused the audience's attention on important events in Biblical stories. As productions of morality plays during the late Middle Ages moved indoors within manor houses and public halls, oil lamps, candles, and reflecting colored glass provided illumination and effects.

By the time of the Renaissance, Italian painters and architects in Italy and France were creating general illumination with tallow or wax candles in chandeliers and wall sconces; spectacular effects with oil lamps, panes of colored glass illuminated from behind, colored lanterns, and transparent veils of cloth; and astonishing outdoor displays of fireworks to climax festival events in Florence or Versailles with incendiary brilliance.

Between 1660 and 1800 in England, the general practice was to light the onstage candles before the curtain opened and to snuff them out when the play ended. Chandeliers above the auditorium remained lighted from start to finish. The playhouse was not darkened, so spectators continued to attend theatres as much to be seen as to give attention to the actors and the plays. Diarist Samuel Pepys, in the mid-seventeenth century, complained of candle wax dripping onto spectators and of the candlelight hurting his eyes.

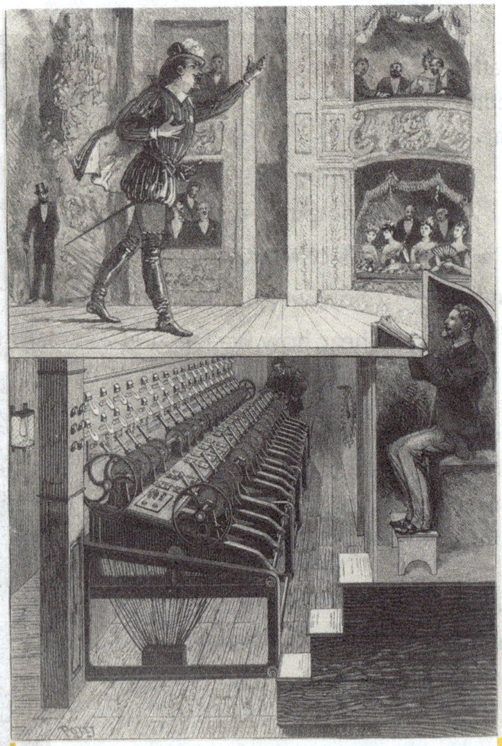

L'Illustration, June 18, 1887/Mary Evans Picture Library

An Early Lighting Control Board

An early lighting control board at the Paris Opera, 1893, with the operator beneath the stage. Note also the prompter seated at the front of the stage.

There were other inventions such as footlights, placed along the apron of the stage around 1672 to give increased illumination to the actors standing there. In 1785, Argand, or "patent," oil lamps produced brighter and steadier light and replaced candles. But the introduction of gas, the "gas table," and limelight (or calcium or Drummond light, the prototype of the spotlight or follow spot) in the mid-1880s provided for the first time better general illumination and more realistic lighting effects on European and American stages. A single operator at a gas table, comparable to a modern control console, could adjust a valve and increase or decrease the intensity of a single lamp or control all lights from a single position in the same manner as a modern dimmer system.

Nevertheless, gas lighting had its drawbacks, not the least of which were unpleasant fumes, intense heat, and the danger of live flame onstage, not infrequently resulting in the burning down of such theatres as the Drury Lane in London. In addition, the heat, smoke, and carbon pollution from gaslights caused the deterioration of scenery and costumes and affected the eyes of actors and spectators alike. The incandescent lamp, invented by Thomas Edison in 1879, was almost immediately adopted as the means of lighting the entire stage. It was an answered prayer to end the disastrous theatre fires caused by open gas flames.

Electricity transformed overall possibilities for lighting design in the theatre. It made possible complete control of a range of intensities and colors; it provided the ability to lighten or darken different areas of the stage; it provided a source of mood for the actor and atmosphere for the play; and it also made possible spectacular effects. In 1881, London's Savoy Theatre was the first to be fully lighted with electricity.

Enter the modern lighting designer. At the turn of the twentieth century, Swiss designer Adolphe Appia understood the artistic possibilities of lighting for the theatre. In *Music and Stage Setting* he argued that light should be the guiding principle of all design and set down modern stage lighting practices. He believed that light could unify or bring into harmony all production elements, including two- and three-dimensional objects, actors, and inanimate objects, shapes, and things. Appia established light as an artistic medium for the theatre and defined the role of the modern lighting designer.

FOCUS ON PEOPLE IN THEATRE

LIGHTING DESIGNER

Jennifer Tipton

©George E. Joseph

Jennifer Tipton, born in Columbus, Ohio, grew up in Knoxville, Tennessee, where she briefly studied dance with Martha Graham and José Limón. A graduate of Cornell University, she eventually found her way with the help of designer Thomas Skelton into a career as a lighting designer for choreographers Paul Taylor, Robert Joffrey, Jerome Robbins, and Twyla Tharp.

Throughout the late sixties, she worked as a lighting designer for regional theatres, for dance and opera companies, and on Broadway. In 1976, she won the Drama Desk Award for lighting design in Ntozake Shange's *for colored girls who have considered suicide/when the rainbow is enuf* and Antoinette Perry "Tony" Awards for *The Cherry Orchard* at Lincoln Center and later for *Jerome Robbins' Broadway*. She designed lighting for Robert Wilson's *the CIVIL warS* at the American Repertory Theatre, Cambridge, Massachusetts, and for the revival of Eugene O'Neill's *The Hairy Ape*, starring Willem Dafoe, for the Wooster Group, New York City. In 1989, she again received the Drama Desk Award for lighting design in *Jerome Robbins' Broadway*, *Long Day's Journey into Night*, and *Waiting for Godot*. She made her directing debut at the Guthrie Theater, Minneapolis, with *The Tempest* in 1991. She is Professor of Design at the Yale University School of Drama.

Tipton's use of light is characterized by "textured and sculptured space" and by use of a palette based on white. She summarizes the essence of the lighting designer's art, saying, "While 99.9 percent of an audience is not aware of light, 100 percent is affected by it."[2]

George E. Joseph/New York Public Library for the Performing Arts

Agamemnon

Stage lighting controls what we see and often what we hear. Jennifer Tipton's lighting design for the production of *Agamemnon* at Lincoln Center Theater, New York City, creates a somber atmosphere while focusing attention on the bodies of Agamemnon and Cassandra lying before the palace doors.

©Joan Marcus

Gypsy
With Bernadette Peters, revival directed by Sam Mendes, sets and costumes by Anthony Ward, and lighting by Jules Fisher and Peggy Eisenhauer.

The Art of Light

Pioneering American designer Jean Rosenthal defined lighting design as "imposing quality on the scarcely visible air through which objects and people are seen."[3] One rule of lighting maintains that *visibility* and *ambience* (the surrounding atmosphere) must be inherent to the total theatrical design, including scenery and costumes. The light designer's tools, other than the instruments themselves, are form (the shape of the lighting's pattern), color (the mood achieved by filters—thin, transparent sheets of colored plastic, gelatin, or glass—or by varying degrees of intensity, or by both), and movement (the changes of forms and color by means of dimmers, motorized instruments, and computerized control consoles).

The Designer's Process

The lighting designer's first step in the design process is to read the script, giving attention to visual images and noting the practicals, such as table lamps to be turned on or chandeliers to be used overhead. The next step is to meet with the director and to confer with the set and costume designers. In these conferences, there are basic questions about lighting to be asked: What degree of reality does the director want to suggest? Where are the important scenes, or areas, within the stage? What restrictions are there? What forms, moods, colors, and movements are required by the play and/or director? Are there special effects needed? Are there backdrops? What practicals are required?

FOCUS ON THEATRE

Jennifer Tipton

Jennifer Tipton says that the directors who have meant the most to her are the ones who urged her to use darkness. Andrei Serban, who directed the revival of Chekhov's *The Cherry Orchard* for which Tipton won her first Tony Award, insisted on "darkness." He said, "No, darker, darker, darker, darker." "And it got very dark, so people were almost invisible," Tipton said, "which made voices ring out even more clearly than when the lights were on. The fact that he [Serban] had made me go that dark at that moment meant that the whole composition over time changed. . . . Because the darkness was there, the brightness had to be brighter, and there had to be other darker moments. Serban didn't tell me to do that. I just did it. It had to be. Any one thing you do, any change you make, affects everything in the whole production."[4]

FOCUS ON PEOPLE IN THEATRE

LIGHTING DESIGNERS

Jules Fisher, Peggy Eisenhauer, and Natasha Katz

©The Everett Collection

Jules Fisher and **Peggy Eisenhauer** are among American theatre's leading lighting designers. Educated at Pennsylvania State University and Carnegie Institute of Technology, Fisher has designed lighting for Broadway's *Hair*, *Pippin*, *Jesus Christ Superstar*, *Chicago*, *La Cage aux Folles*, and *Grand Hotel*, among others. Since 1986, he and Peggy Eisenhauer (educated at Carnegie-Mellon University) designed numerous productions jointly, including *Victor Victoria*; *Ragtime*; *Jane Eyre*; *Bring in 'da Noise, Bring in 'da Funk*; and *Gypsy*. Eisenhauer also designed the lighting for the recent revival of *Cabaret*. In the music industry, her concert production designs have been seen internationally in twenty-six countries.

Jules Fisher provided the lighting design and production supervision for the 1975 *Rolling Stones* tour. Today, he is a principal of a theatrical consulting firm, Fisher Dachs Associates, and also partner in an architectural lighting firm, Fisher Marantz Stone.

©Getty Images

Natasha Katz says that stage lighting is "both a pragmatic craft and an art. Pragmatically, lighting functions simply to tell us where to look. At its loftiest, it creates mood, unconscious feelings, musicality, and subliminal emotions."[5] Educated at Oberlin College, her first lighting-design job on Broadway was for *Pack of Lies*. Since then, she has designed lighting for thirty-eight Broadway plays and musicals, including *The Addams Family*, *Follies*, *Aida*, *The Little Mermaid*, *The Coast of Utopia*, and *Once* for which she received the 2012 Tony Award for Best Lighting Design of a Musical.

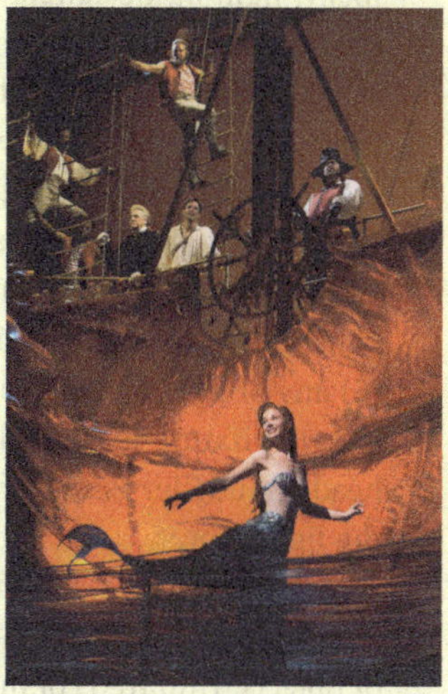
©Joan Marcus

The Little Mermaid
A musical based on the animated 1989 Disney film and Hans Christian Andersen's story, with lighting design by Natasha Katz, Broadway.

When directing the Broadway revival of *Gypsy* with Bernadette Peters as Rose, the indomitable mother, Sam Mendes asked designers Jules Fisher and Peggy Eisenhauer to light the musical "like a play"—to make the scenes and songs (musical numbers) all of a piece. The only time the lighting was to have a "show-business" look was during the vaudeville scenes.[6] Then, these scenes exploded with light, color, and theatricality.

Armed with information about the production gleaned from the design conferences, the lighting designer creates a design and a light plot. Basically a map, a light plot shows the shape of the stage and auditorium, as seen from above, with the location of the lighting instruments to be used, including type, size, wattage, wiring, and connection to appropriate dimmers or circuits. There are no set rules. Any particular instrument may or may not be used in any location. The only limitations in lighting design are those imposed by the director, by the physical nature of the theatre, by the theatre's available technology, and by safety concerns.

FOCUS ON THEATRE

Mary Louise Geiger

Designer **Mary Louise Geiger** has said that artistic director Lee Breuer of the Mabou Mines freed her to take on a more linear version of storytelling with light. "I like ways of telling the story," she said, "that can operate on a more subliminal level. And take advantage of what live theatre can do that film cannot, which is provide a live story that is not necessarily realistic."[7] Her lighting design is represented in the production of *Red Beads* (page 266).

The Designer's Working Methods: Plotting, Focusing, and Cueing

Today, lighting designers spend, on average, four and a half weeks lighting a show, from early conferences through technical and dress rehearsals. Digital imaging on iPads and smart screens shortens the amount of time lighting designers need to create light plots and also allows designers to preview the effectiveness of the design and share it (along with changes) with the creative team.

A finished light plot shows (1) the location of each lighting instrument to be used; (2) the type of instrument, wattage, and color filter; (3) the general area to be lighted by each instrument; (4) circuitry necessary to operate the instruments; and (5) any other details necessary for the operation of the lighting system. For example, if a wall fixture is needed onstage so that an actor can "turn on" a light, or an overhead chandelier is required, the position and circuitry of the fixtures are shown on the light plot.

Once the lights specified by the designer are hung in the theatre they are then focused—that is, pointed—in a precise direction to illuminate areas, actors, backdrops, or objects. Hundreds of instruments of different types and wattages, as well as colored gels and dimmers, may be necessary to achieve the desired effects in production. During technical rehearsals, the lighting will be fine-tuned to account for the changing presence of the actors-in-costume and movable scenery.

After the instruments are hung, circuited, angled, and focused, the lighting designer is ready to "cue" the show. A computer-generated cue sheet (or chart of the control console indicating instrument settings and color, with each cue numbered and keyed to the script) is provided in advance to the operators at the control console. During technical rehearsals, the designer asks for various intensities of light and makes changes until satisfied. With each change of lighting, a notation (the light cue) is made that tells how to set the control board and at what point in the stage action to change intensity and color. In the past, these changes were performed manually during each performance. Computers now permit preprogrammed cues (timed changes) to happen smoothly and light cues (often hundreds) for the entire show to be programmed. All is achieved in consultation with the director.

FOCUS ON THEATRE

Robert Wierzel's Lighting for *The Cherry Orchard*

In this scene, designed for a thrust stage, the house is open, the window shades are raised, and the lighted chandelier indicates that it is evening.

Courtesy Bill Clarke Designs

Robert Wierzel designed the lighting for the PlayMakers Repertory Company's production of Chekhov's *The Cherry Orchard* in Chapel Hill, N.C., for a thrust stage, with set design by Bill Clarke.

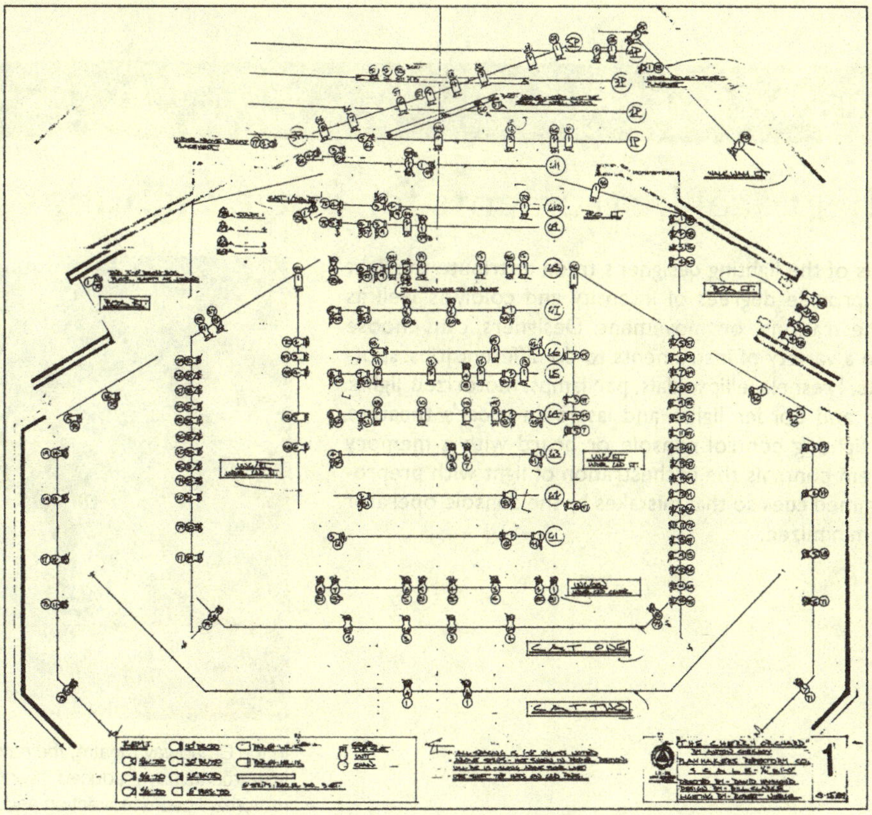

The light plot illustrates the positioning of 250 instruments around three sides of the thrust stage, as well as the overhead chandelier and backlighting behind the rear doorways.

Courtesy Will Owens/PlayMakers Repertory Company

Special Lighting Effects

Special lighting effects range from the simple to the complex, from mirror balls, searchlights, and lightning to projections, holograms, fireworks, and Tinkerbell's moving light in *Peter Pan*. The plan, budget, and rehearsal with equipment and staff are essential to preparing special effects. The most frequently seen special effects relate to the use of *gobos* (a slide inserted into the gate of an instrument) to project images of trees, clouds, water, windows, abstract shapes, and so forth; rear projections to throw images on backdrops and screens; color wheels to produce changing color effects; twinkling star effects on backcloths; and moon effects perfected in the Victorian theatre with a box with lights inside. More complicated and costly effects are related to projections, holograms, and lasers.

Commercial devices can be purchased to achieve most effects but require designers and technicians to ensure that they are credible, effective, and safe.

Both lighting and sound designers are usually involved where explosions, fireworks, and sudden apparitions of Shakespeare's ghosts and witches are needed. Today's effects in the theatre and film are notable for their emotional impact on audiences rather than, with some exceptions, the quantity of the "magic."

FOCUS ON THEATRE

Theatrical Instruments for Stage Lighting

Tools of the lighting designer's trade distribute the light and provide degrees of intensity and color, as well as orchestrations, or movement. Designers can choose from a variety of instruments to do different jobs: spotlights, Fresnels, ellipsoidals, par lamps, motorized lights, strip and border lights, and lasers. In today's theatres, the lighting control console or board with a memory system controls the orchestration of light with preprogrammed cues so that mistakes by the console operator are minimized.

Courtesy of High End Systems

In the Broadway theatre, the new automated lighting instruments have reduced inventory (and rental costs). The motorized beam redirection and color changers solve many of the problems of limited space for hanging instruments in the older New York theatres.

The Designer's Assistants

The professional lighting designer usually has an assistant designer to help prepare light plots, compile instrument schedules, act as liaison with the theatre's stage electrician and other technicians, and locate special equipment. The assistant designer also aids in supervising the installation of the instruments, compiling cue sheets, and programming the light design.

Most theatres have a master electrician on staff (or a lighting crew head) who works closely with the designer when equipment is installed and instruments are adjusted. This individual oversees safety issues, checks and maintains equipment before each performance, and deals with all lighting issues during the run. In the professional theatre, the master electrician and lighting crew are members of the International Alliance of Theatrical Stage Employees union (IATSE).

Courtesy Narelle Sissons

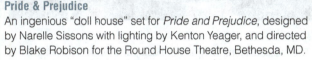

Pride & Prejudice
An ingenious "doll house" set for *Pride and Prejudice*, designed by Narelle Sissons with lighting by Kenton Yeager, and directed by Blake Robison for the Round House Theatre, Bethesda, MD.

In all types of theatres, the lighting crew installs, operates, and generally maintains all lighting equipment and shifts any electrical equipment that must be moved during the performance. The control board operator executes the lighting cues during performances and maintains the designer's work. All backstage technicians are responsible to the production stage manager during the performance.

Successful stage lighting complements and unifies the whole without calling attention to itself unless for special effects, for example, or to give greater emphasis to a stage area or to illuminate the ghost of Hamlet's father. It contributes to the play's interpretation with visibility and ambience—controlling what we see (and even hear) and how we see what is taking place onstage.

THE SOUND DESIGNER

The Art of Theatrical Sound

Sound has always been a part of the theatrical event. In earliest times, music (pipes, drums, lyres), choral chanting, and actors' voices provided the chief sound effects. Until the use of disc recordings in the 1950s and more recently, samplers and CD or MD players, sound effects in the theatre were produced live offstage; many—such as gunfire, doorbells, and door slams—still are. In Elizabethan times, "thunder machines" (a series of wooden troughs for cannonballs to rumble down), "thundersheets" (suspended sheets of tin that when rattled made a rumbling sound), and "thunder runs" (sloping wooden troughs for rolling cannonballs down with a large crashing sound at the end) were used to simulate tremendous storms, such as the storms in *Twelfth Night*, *The Tempest*, and *King Lear*. A cannon was fired from the roof of Shakespeare's

© Joan Marcus

Rent
The musical Rent, with book, music, and lyrics by Jonathan Larson, with actors wearing visible wireless microphones, Broadway.

theatre to convince audiences of fierce battles taking place, and musicians with trumpets sounded "flourishes," and so forth.

With the invention of electricity, most theatres since 1900 have used electric telephone or doorbell ringers (a battery-powered bell mounted on a piece of wood) and a door slammer (a small door frame and door, complete with knob and latch) to simulate real-life sounds. Assistants usually created or supervised these manual "sound effects." With the development of audio recording, playback technologies, and sound systems, a virtual revolution in sound creation emerged along with a new theatre artist: the *sound designer*.

Theatres today have the capability for both live and recorded sound. Augmented sound, including the actor's voice, is routinely used even in nonmusical performances. Microphones are placed across the front of the stage, or actors wear miniature wireless microphones (usually concealed in their hair or beneath wigs). In the musical *Rent*, there is no attempt to conceal the wireless microphones that the actors wear, and in effect, they become part of the "rock" costumes.

There is much debate today over the electronic amplification of speaking and singing voices in Broadway musicals and nonmusical plays by those who prefer a "more natural" sound. The sound-mixing board has become a permanent fixture in the rear of the orchestra rows of most Broadway theatres and a visual reminder that sound technology is an important part of enhancing the "aliveness" of the theatre.

The use of live or recorded sounds serves many purposes, for example,

Information	location
Establishment of locale	foghorns
Time of day	chimes on the hour
Time of year	birds in springtime
Weather conditions	rain or thunder
Street sounds	car horns, screeching brakes
Realism	ambulance siren, toilet flushing, television sounds
Mood	ominous sounds for scary moments
Onstage cues	telephones, door bells
Special effects	the "breaking string" at the end of *The Cherry Orchard*, the helicopter sequence in *Miss Saigon*, or the sound of "a terrifying CRASH" as the angel descends through the ceiling at the end of *Angels in America: Millennium Approaches*

FOCUS ON PEOPLE IN THEATRE

SOUND DESIGNER

Abe Jacob

©Carol Rosegg

Abe Jacob pioneered today's theatrical sound design in American theatre, along with the sound credit on the title page of playbills. He got his start mixing sound for rock-and-roll stars in San Francisco in the 1960s, working with Jimi Hendrix; The Mamas and the Papas; and Peter, Paul, and Mary. His Broadway career began with a preview performance of *Jesus Christ Superstar,* canceled because of technical problems. Director Tom O'Horgan, who had worked with Jacob on a West Coast production of *Hair*, asked him to help. His Broadway work continued with Bob Fosse on *Pippin*, *Chicago*, and *Big Deal*; Michael Bennett on *Seesaw* and *A Chorus Line*; Gower Champion on *Mack and Mabel* and *Rockabye Hamlet*. He credits these directors with being among the first supporters of sound design as a legitimate art form. More recently, he championed the cause to acquire union representation for sound designers and technicians in the Broadway theatre within Local 922 of the International Alliance of Theatrical Stage Employees (IATSE).

Jacob also pioneered sound design in opera, serving as sound consultant for the New York City Opera Company. Acknowledging that the opera world is unfriendly to sound designers, he said, "When I started in theatre, it was almost immediate that the critics started making comments about the sound in the theatre, and how it was going to bring about the death of the American musical as we knew it, and they've been saying it ever since. And now they're saying it about opera, so I guess," he laughs, "I have the distinction of being able to destroy both art forms."[8]

Music also serves many purposes, such as evoking mood, establishing period, heightening tension, intensifying action, and providing transitions between scenes and at endings. Today, music is often composed by sound designers for a production and played "live" during the performance, or music is derived from copyrighted recordings (the use rights must be acquired by the theatre and licensing fees paid) and then played through the theatre's sound system. The sound designer oversees the implementation of all of these elements. Sometimes the sound designer is also the musical composer and holds copyright to the music he or she writes for the production. For example, John Gromada was both sound designer and composer for the production of *Camino Real* at Hartford Stage and wrote music and lyrics for actress Betty Buckley to sing.

©Richard Feldman

Olly's Prison
Resident sound designer David Remedios creating sound for *Olly's Prison* at the American Repertory Theatre, Cambridge, Mass.

FOCUS ON THEATRE

Sound Effects with Cue Sheet

Cue #	Page	Tape 1	Tape 2	Tape 3	Tape 4
1	61	Magic noise			Storm background
2	61		Thunder #1		
3	61			Thunder #2	
4	61	Wind blast			
5	61		Wave crash		
6	62			Thunder #3	
7	62	Thunder #4			
8	62		Ropes crash		
9	62			Bosun cry!	
10	62	Wave crash 2			
11	62		Thunder #5		
12	62	Wave crash 3		Big crash	
13	63		Thunder #6	Voices	
14	63	Split #1	Split #2		
15	63	Rocks crash	Wave #4		
16	63			Magic noise	
17	63	Distant storm	Rumble		
18	63			Waves	

Sound Cue Sheet for *The Tempest*

A sound cue sheet listing sound effects cues, locations on tape, and the page number of the script for a production of Shakespeare's *The Tempest*.

FOCUS ON PEOPLE IN THEATRE

SOUND DESIGNER

Jonathan Deans

Courtesy Jonathan Deans

Jonathan Deans is involved in the development of the use of digital sound-processing technology for mixing live (real-time) performances and automation (timed) performances. He has designed more than 120 musicals, plays, operas, Las Vegas spectaculars, and theme park attractions. Recent credits include *Ragtime, Fosse, Priscilla Queen of the Desert, Young Frankenstein, Spider-Man: Turn Off the Dark*, and *Cirque du Soleil* at the Bellagio Hotel and *Mystère* at Treasure Island Hotel in Las Vegas.

©Walter McBride/Retna

Fosse on Broadway

Fosse, a musical based on the choreography of Bob Fosse, with set and costume designs by Santo Loquasto, lighting by Andrew Bridge, and sound by Jonathan Deans.

Whatever the source or quality of the sound, sound designers and technicians are responsible for it: music, abstract sounds, gunshots, rain and thunder, airplanes passing overhead, trains in the distance, telephones and doorbells ringing, sounds of nature (bird calls, crickets chirping), even military bands marching offstage, as Chekhov requires at the end of *The Three Sisters*.

In consultation with the director, the sound designer plots the effects required by the script (and often added by the director). New digital technology permits operators to program dozens of individually recorded sounds onto the control board, where each can be instantly recalled and played individually or in combination. Today, theatrical sound systems include speakers of high quality and versatility placed throughout the auditorium, a patch bay (a means of connecting tapes and microphones to any outlet), and a control board. Almost any sound can be programmed into a sampler with the exception of gunshots—which are still performed "live" with blanks because they are too loud for most sound systems. The use of guns on or offstage must meet precise conditions specified by fire and safety authorities.

The Designer's Working Methods

Like the lighting designer, the sound designer studies the script, noting aural images and effects implied or detailed in the text (and the practicals, such as a telephone ring or a toilet flush); holds discussions with the director, other designers, the composer, and technicians; researches sound-effects libraries; records sounds and music; prepares a sound track; develops a cue sheet indicating the placement of each sound in the script, the equipment involved, sound levels, control levers, and timing of sounds; and determines placement of speakers and microphones. The sound designer also has assistants to help with preparations and crews to run the show.

Special Effects with Sound

Special sound effects capture the audience's attention for a theatrical moment and/or increase the emotional impact of a scene. A sound effect may be an offstage noise such as the sound of a car door shutting as preparation for an actor's entrance or departure. Or it may be recorded music underscoring an emotional scene onstage. Whatever the sound effect, it grows out of a preconceived need on the part of playwrights, directors, and designers to enhance the storytelling.

Sound effects in the theatre date from the use of music and human voices to enhance the storytelling in the classical Greek theatre. Shakespeare wrote sound effects into his plays. They are mostly battle-and-storm sounds that could be re-created with percussion instruments and simple backstage devices such as thunder and wind machines. The English theatre during the Victorian era built other machines to reproduce the sounds of weather, horse-drawn carriages, trains, and disasters. These mechanical effects were handled by the property master rather than a sound engineer. In the modern theatre, such sounds as telephones ringing, gunshots, door slams, doorbells, and breaking dishes are still created manually backstage by a member of the crew. Less than thirty years ago, the introduction of electronic amplification followed by recording and playback systems, microphones and loudspeakers, and digital audio technology created the need for a "sound designer."

Abe Jacob introduced the sound designer into the American musical theatre, and now all Broadway, Off Broadway, and regional theatres hire sound designers and/or sound technicians to create this element of theatrical design.

FOCUS ON THEATRE

Laurie Anderson and *Moby Dick*

Frank Micelotta/Image Direct/Getty Images

Laurie Anderson and *Moby Dick*
Laurie Anderson in a virtual voyage aboard Captain Ahab's ship *The Pequod* in *Songs and Stories from Moby Dick*, directed by Anne Bogart (Next Wave Festival at the Brooklyn Academy of Music).

Performance artist Laurie Anderson created a virtual voyage called *Songs and Stories from Moby Dick* with a custom-built MIDI-controlled "talking stick," prerecorded musical tracks (vocals and keyboards), in-ear monitoring system plugged into a wireless microphone system, loudspeakers, mixing console, and digital playback devices. There are no literal whale sounds in the show. Anderson's sound track is basically an abstract landscape of sounds. The visuals, designed by Anderson herself, project images such as the opening of pages of a book, large gold coins, underwater bubbles, and various abstractions. At one point, Anderson, with short spiky hair, black clothes, and red shoes, sits in a huge armchair, a lone voice in a vast sea. Sound, images, and lighting provide the audience with a road map into her interpretation of Herman Melville's famous novel.

COMPUTER-AIDED DESIGN FOR SCENERY, COSTUMES, LIGHTING, SOUND

For centuries, theatrical designers worked with the same tools as other visual artists: drafting table, paper, charcoal, pencils, colored paints, rulers, squares, and slide rules. Not until personal computers became readily available did theatre artists and technicians gain a remarkable new tool of far-reaching potential. In the mid-1980s, computer-aided design (CAD) and computer-aided manufacture (CAM) were widely adopted by the industry and became the fastest-growing technology for the stage.

This "machine" with its developing software has the capacity for configuring (and reconfiguring) spaces, angles, shapes, colors, perspectives, and measurements in response to the designer's imagination, research, and artistic choices. Computer-aided design is a remarkable asset in the design studio. First, computers reduce the drudgery of the set designer's drawing mechanics. With the click of a mouse, the designer reconfigures spaces, changes colors, lengthens lines, adds walls, raises platforms, inserts windows, reconfigures instruments on the lighting grid, and redesigns or resizes costumes. A click of the "mouse" also edits a text, adds director's notes, and inserts sound cues. Indeed, the computer saves many hours of painstaking drafting, copying, researching art collections, and creating final designs (and in color).

Vast visual and aural databases are literally at the designer's fingertips. Virtual libraries of art, sound effects, and music are found on CD-ROMs; and virtual catalogues of sculpture, decorative arts, chandeliers, and clothing and wardrobe collections from historical and modern periods have been digitized for computer retrieval. Reuse of another artist's theatrical designs can be subject to legal copyright considerations and always requires investigation.

Three-dimensional models of scenery can be created with computerized scenographic modeling. Computer models provide perspectives from above and from the left, right, and center of the house. Although computing equipment for such modeling is expensive, it is often cheaper than rebuilding scenery when a director or designer decides at the last minute to move a door.

The use of computers has made possible "integrated computer design" whereby a design team can present with the click of a "mouse" the scenic model, computerized costume renderings, colored lighting from calibrated lighting positions, and music and sound effects.

Computerized inventories of clothing, hats, wigs, shoes, and accessories have also revolutionized costume management and shops. For the costume designer, the advantage of the new tool is the freedom to cut, paste, and combine elements of clothing before actually purchasing and cutting the cloth. With the computer, a designer can change sleeves on a garment or shorten the skirt without sewing a single stitch. Through the use of the actor's photo and measurements, a "virtual actor" can be dressed in the entire costume design before fabric is cut and sewn. By the same token, the wig designer can "virtually" change color and styles before the first fitting with the actor.

In all cases, the reality of computers is instantaneous communications. Designs can be sent instantly across the United States by digital electronic transmission, reducing travel costs and conference time. However, as designer Jennifer Tipton warns, "Technology . . . is only as good as the person using it." The designer's creativity and imagination are not imperiled by the new technology, as some have argued. Greater experimentation and innovation are made possible by the ease and speed of computer-enhanced design.

TECHNICAL PRODUCTION

Without the *production team*—managers, technicians, craftspeople, and crews—no theatre has the capacity to organize the production; build and install scenery; create sound, light, and costumes for production; and run the show from start to finish. Depending upon the size of the theatre's organization, these individuals often outnumber the director, designers, and actors, and they shoulder responsibility for the production night after night.

THE PRODUCTION TEAM

Just as with any complex organization, the theatre has an established hierarchy of production managers and technicians charged with responsibility for supervising a large number of specialists: electricians, carpenters, stagehands, properties artisans, cutters, drapers, stitchers, milliners, wigmakers, shoemakers, wardrobe, dressers, makeup artists, light and sound operators, and running crews. A backstage hierarchy of management and technical practices—of what works and what does not—has evolved over centuries.

Until the twentieth century, technical crafts were learned through apprenticeships in the theatre. Today, the "technical arts," called *technical production* and *costume production*, are taught in college's and university's theatre departments, and students serve their "apprenticeships" within university theatre shops—the scene shop, the costume shop, the props shop, the sound and light studios. Each of these specialty shops serves as a working unit of the theatre as well as a laboratory for instruction. Key professional personnel command these shops and contribute through their expertise to the artistic enterprise as a whole—the production.

Production Manager

The technical production team is led by the *production manager* (PM) and seconded by the *technical director* (TD). The position of PM has grown in importance over the last two decades, especially in professional regional theatres.

The PM coordinates the staffing, scheduling, and budgeting of every element in the production, including building, installation ("load-in"), and operation ("running") of all design and technical elements. The PM is sensitive to the artistic needs of director, designers, and technicians throughout the production process and struggles with the complex problems of integrating the many disparate elements of production, including the needs of the theatre's shops. Safety procedures, accounting policies, legal codes and union practices, and time management are part of the PM's knowledge and expertise.

FOCUS ON THEATRE

International Alliance of Theatrical Stage Employees (IATSE)

International Alliance of Theatrical Stage Employees (IATSE) is the union that serves production managers, technical directors, and technicians in theatre, opera, film, and television, and employees in some sound studios. Sound designers are also represented by IATSE.

Technical Director

The TD has charge of the management of the scene shop and the construction and operation of scenery and stage machinery, such as hydraulics for moving scenery or trapdoors for special effects or entrances. Following the build period, which requires conferences with the set designer, the TD oversees the moving of scenery into the theatre, plans adequate "stage time" for the various scenery and paint crews to complete their jobs, and establishes policies and directives for scene shifting, special effects, and "strike" (the final removal of scenery from the theatre or into storage at the close of the production). The TD coordinates the build, the "put-in," and "strike" schedules in tandem with the other units of the theatre. In small theatres, lighting and sound installation and operation, for example, are often the responsibility of the TD as well.

Costume Shop Manager

The *costume shop manager* has a function parallel to that of the TD, with responsibility for the management of the costume shop, its inventory and budgets; the buying of fabrics; and building, buying, and/or renting of costumes and accessories, including hats, wigs, and shoes. Following a comparable build period during which conferences are held with the costume designer and craftspeople, the shop manager is responsible for

The Production Team in a Non-Profit Theatre

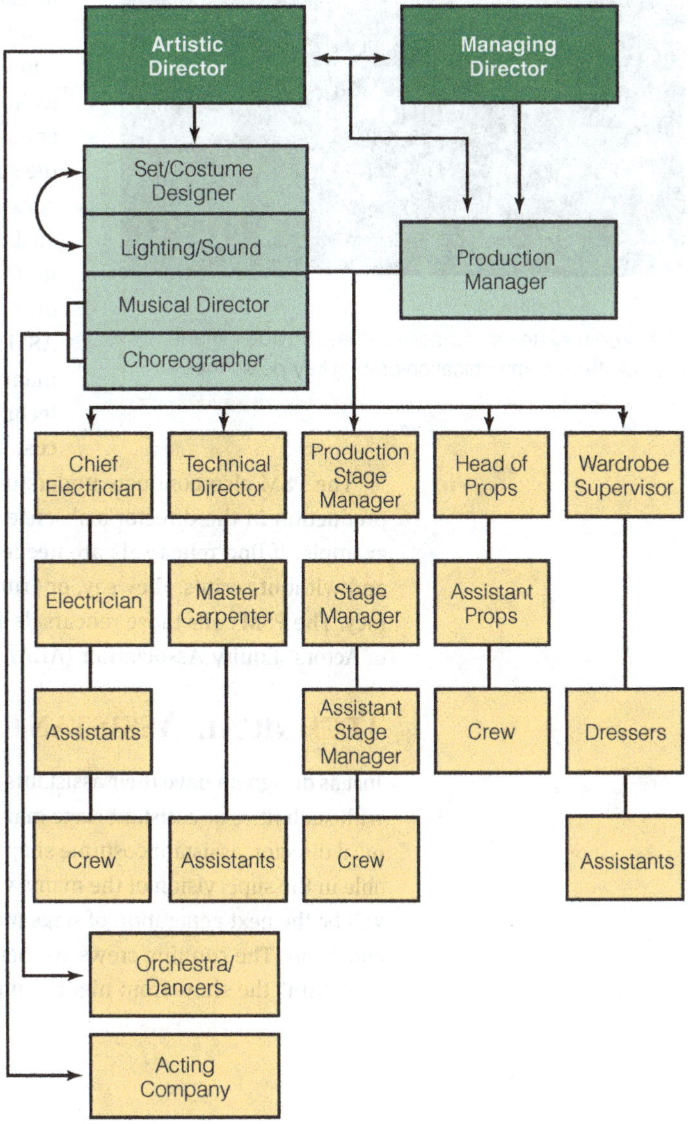

Courtesy of Clear Com

Backstage Communication
Intercom systems and accessories provide instant backstage communication among key personnel.

the scheduling of the tasks of the various personnel and crews in order to complete the costumes, maintain them during the run, and "strike" them according to the theatre's policies at the close of the show.

Production Stage Manager

As we come to the role of the *production stage manager* (PSM)—formerly known as the *stage manager* (SM)—and the *assistant stage manager* (ASM), we find a highly responsible and artistically sensitive position. The PSM coordinates the director's work in rehearsals with the actors and the technical departments. For example, the use in rehearsals of furniture, props, and clothing will be coordinated by stage management. At the beginning of rehearsals, the PSM organizes and schedules calls and appointments, records the blocking of actors, anticipates technical concerns for quick costume changes and scenery shifts, and organizes and annotates the "calling" of the show—that is, the system by which actors' entrance cues and lighting, sound, and scene-shift cues are initiated. During performance, the PSM has full responsibility for the running of the show and has final authority over the entire onstage and backstage operation. The ASM is usually positioned backstage during the performance with responsibility for the smooth operation of technical systems and the actors' exits, entrances, and costume changes.

The PSM also conducts understudy rehearsals and maintains the precision of the production in the director's absence during the run of a professional production. For example, if line rehearsals are needed, the cast is brought together and, while seated and without scripts, they say, or "run," their lines of dialogue with attention to accuracy. The PSM calls those rehearsals as well. Professional stage managers are members of Actors' Equity Association (AEA).

Technical Assistants and Running Crews

Just as designers have their assistants, key technical management people have assistants with such titles as assistant stage manager, assistant production manager, assistant technical director, assistant costume shop manager, and so on. These individuals are invaluable in the supervision of the many, varying elements within a production. In turn, they will be the next generation of stage managers, production managers, technical directors, and so on. The running crews, as their name implies, are the technicians and personnel who "run" the show from night to night.

TRANSITION

All design elements in the theatre serve the play and enhance the storytelling quality of the theatre. In collaboration with the director, designers (in tandem with actors) transform the "empty space" into the living world of the production. The theatre's production and stage managers, along with the many technicians, provide the technical support system without which no theatre can open its doors.

Theatre: A Way of Seeing Online

Visit the CourseMate for Theatre: A Way of Seeing 7th Edition for quick access to the digital study resources that accompany this chapter, including links to the websites listed below, Theatre Workshop, digital glossary, a chapter quiz and more.

Websites

The *Theatre: A Way of Seeing* CourseMate includes links for all the websites described below. Simply select "Web links" from the Chapter Resources for Chapter 12, and click on the link that interests you. You'll be taken directly to the site described.

Arts, Crafts, and Theater Safety
A nonprofit organization concerned with artists' health and safety, including safety laws in the United States and Canada.

Glossary of Technical Theatre Terms
Searchable glossary of more than 1,500 theatre terms.

World Lighting Links
A categorized index of some of the best (and most useful) lighting sites on the Internet today. These links include sites related to theatre, entertainment, and much more.

Professional Lighting and Sound Association (PLASA)
Information for lighting and sound professionals in the worldwide entertainment industry.

The Theatre Design and Technical Jobs Page
Source of a free list of job openings for all behind-the-scenes jobs in the live entertainment industry. Also includes a listing of freelance designers, directors, and technicians sorted by geographic area.

Theatre Sound Design Directory
Hundreds of links to sound design resources throughout the United States and worldwide.

United States Institute for Theatre Technology
The association of design, production, and technology professionals in the performing arts and entertainment industry

©Paul Kolnik

13

IMAGE MAKERS: PRODUCERS

There's no business like show business.

—Irving Berlin, Composer and Lyricist

Many contribute to the making of theatre, a highly complex, collaborative art form. The producer is that anomalous person who, in the highly competitive and risky business of theatre, deals with plays, investors, artists, theatre owners, trade unions, agents, contracts, taxes, rentals, deficits, grosses, and the bottom line. The producer is rarely an artist but rather an astute businessperson with creative judgment who knows the demands of the commercial theatre and nonprofit theatre. In answer to the question "What exactly do you do?" producer Cheryl Crawford said, "I find a good play or musical, I find the money required to give it the best physical form on a stage, I find the people to give it life, I find a theatre and try to fill it."[1]

PRODUCING ON BROADWAY

The Broadway Producer

There are forty Broadway theatres at the present time. At least sixteen are owned by the Shubert Organization of major New York producers. Because of the high cost of producing on Broadway—more than \$5 to \$15 million for a musical; \$2,500,000 or more for a dramatic play—many

PREVIEW

Producers are responsible for financing productions, for hiring and firing the artistic and managerial personnel. Producers are frequently all things to all people: money machine, mediator, friend, tyrant, boss, enemy, gambler, investor, consultant. In a word, the producer's job is to make the play happen.

Nathan Lane and Matthew Broderick, as wannabee producers, perform a vaudeville-style dance number to celebrate their producing triumph in *The Producers*, Mel Brooks's stage adaptation from his 1968 film with direction and choreography by Susan Stroman, Broadway.

Broadway producers are seasoned veterans and collaborate more frequently with one another in their producing efforts. (*Spider-Man: Turn Off The Dark* holds the record today for costs at $75 million.) As costs of producing on Broadway continue to skyrocket, producers commingle their know-how and assets. They employ general managers, accountants, and lawyers to assist with the business of financing a Broadway play from option to opening.

Why is theatre, and especially the commercial Broadway theatre, so costly? Analysts agree that theatre is a service business in which most of the cost of the product is labor—actors, dancers, directors, choreographers, designers, musicians, production managers, stagehands, ushers, press reps (and, if needed, aerial supervisors and physical trainers), and so on. As wages rise with general living standards across the country, most businesses turn to technology (projection and sound technology and equipment, digital imaging, integrated computer systems) rather than to people to blunt the cost of inflation. However, in the theatre, the opportunities for saving Laborcosts are still limited, even with the current use of new technologies. It takes just as long for actors to play an uncut *Hamlet* in the new millennium as it did in Shakespeare's day, and almost as long to design and build *The Cherry Orchard* set as it did in Chekhov's. Unlike the film industry, the multimillion-dollar theatre production cannot be put in a "can" and distributed to tens of thousands of moviehouses to offset the original costs. One solution is the creation of national touring companies of *The Lion King*, *Mamma Mia!*, and *Wicked*, for example, as a means of broadening distribution.

©newscom

Duffy Square Ticket Booth (TKTS)
The TKTS booth, located on Broadway's Duffy Square at Forty-seventh Street, sells discounted tickets on the day of the performance for Broadway and Off Broadway shows.

THE BROADWAY OPTION

Once a play is written, the playwright's agent contacts producers, who may eventually option the play. The *option*—a payment advanced against royalties to the playwright—is the starting point on that long road to opening night. It is an agreement that grants producers the right to produce a play or musical within a specified period of time in exchange for a fee paid to the writer or to the composer/lyricist. The amount paid, the length of the option, and what the money buys are all negotiable.

©Andy Kropa/Redux

Broadway's Foxwood Theatre
The Foxwood Theatre on West Forty-second Street announcing on the marquee *Spider-Man: Turn Off The Dark.*

Another approach is to send the script directly to the artistic director of a regional theatre in the hope that there will be interest in the play. Regional and Off Broadway theatres produce new plays and musicals, and today many Broadway hits are first seen elsewhere. For example, *Newsies* was staged at the Papermill Playhouse, New Jersey, before transferring to Broadway. The same has been true of the musical *Once* (New York Theatre Workshop), *Clybourne Park* (Playwrights Horizons, New York City), and the Mark Taper Forum Theatre, Los Angeles), and the revival of *The Iceman Cometh* (Goodman Theatre, Chicago).

All plays produced on Broadway by an American author are optioned by producers under the Dramatists Guild contract. There are separate contracts for musicals, dramatic productions, stock tryouts, and collaborations.

When a commercial producer options the exclusive rights to a play for Broadway, the playwright works on the script during workshops, rehearsals, out-of-town tryouts, and previews. On the basis of critical notices and audience response during this period, the play is reworked and sometimes completely rewritten before the official New York opening.

An initial option usually lasts for one year from the date of delivery of the completed script. There are permissions for extending the option (if a star is unavailable for six months, for example, or if there is a wait of four to six months for an available Broadway theatre).

Producer-director Jed Harris used an unusual strategy to open *Our Town* on Broadway in 1938. Convinced that

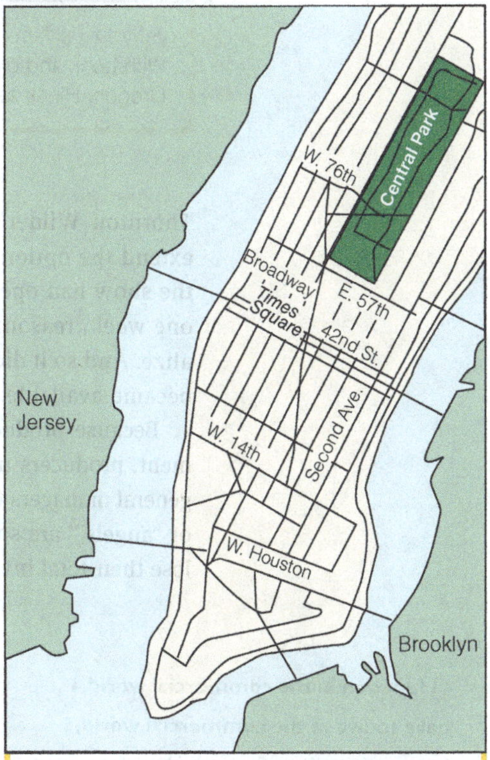

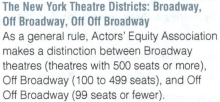

The New York Theatre Districts: Broadway, Off Broadway, Off Off Broadway
As a general rule, Actors' Equity Association makes a distinction between Broadway theatres (theatres with 500 seats or more), Off Broadway (100 to 499 seats), and Off Off Broadway (99 seats or fewer).

Martha Swope/The New York Public Library

Jelly's Last Jam
With book and direction by George C. Wolfe and music by Jelly Roll Morton, featured Gregory Hines as the legendary jazz musician with masks/puppets by Barbara Pollitt.

Thornton Wilder's play could not open in just any theatre, but not wanting to extend the option, Harris gambled on a suitable theatre becoming available once the show had opened. He opened the play in a theatre that was available for only one week, reasoning that if the play was a success, another theatre would materialize. And so it did. When the play proved to be a hit, the favored theatre magically became available.

Because producing a Broadway show is a multimillion-dollar, high-risk investment, producers usually seek assistance from coproducers, associate producers, and general managers in raising the money and in handling other business details. Backers, or "angels," are sought to invest in the show, with the full knowledge that they can lose their total investment.

"I function in the commercial world, I have to live in the commercial world, I have to finance the productions I do—not by writing a check on what Mr. Ziegfeld left me because he knew I was coming, but by going out and hustling to get the money to produce plays on Broadway."[2]

—Alexander H. Cohen, Producer

Associations and Craft Unions

The Broadway producer deals with a variety of organizations. The Broadway League, an association of producers and theatre owners, oversee the common interests and welfare of theatre owners, lessees, operators, and producers. The League's primary function is to act as a bargaining representative for theatre owners and producers with the many unions and associations, ranging from ticket sellers to press agents.

FOCUS ON PEOPLE IN THEATRE

PRODUCERS

Jeffrey Richards and Daryl Roth

©FilmMagic/Getty Images

Jeffrey Richards and **Daryl Roth** are producers with different backgrounds but common interests in new playwrights and established talent. A graduate of Columbia University's School of Journalism, Richards became a Broadway press agent who later turned Broadway producer. He has had success with a variety of productions, including such dramatic plays as *Gore Vidal's The Best Man* and August Wilson's *Radio Golf,* David Ives's farce *Venus in Fur,* a musical version of *Spring Awakening,* and *The Gershwins' Porgy and Bess.* He is described as a professional theatre man with a "scary" amount of industry knowledge, likened to baseball fans who can rattle off batting averages of obscure players.

©newscom

As an independent producer, Daryl Roth has produced an unprecedented six Pulitzer Prize-winning plays: *August: Osage County, Proof, Wit, How I Learned to Drive, Anna in the Tropics,* and Edward Albee's *Three Tall Women.* She has consistently produced plays that deal with serious issues and taboo subjects. "My criteria is to do things that instinctively say something to me," she has said. "That's all I have to go by. If I hear something, and it touches me, then I think it will touch other people of like mind." Commenting on her choice of plays with very serious subjects, she says that "theatre is basically a very safe place yet we are able to experience something that isn't very safe within its confine."[4]

Both producers have production companies (Jeffrey Richards Associates and Daryl Roth Productions) to serve their interests in dramatic plays that explore new territories and musicals with strong character-driven stories.

©Sara Krulwich/The New York Times/Redux

August: Osage County

Tracy Letts's *August: Osage County*, a Steppenwolf Theatre Company (Chicago) production, transferred to Broadway with the backing of fifteen producers, including Jeffrey Richards and Daryl Roth.

FOCUS ON THEATRE

Actors' Equity Association Contracts

Actors' Equity Association, the union for actors, stage managers, and dancers in Broadway musicals, has three basic contracts: a standard minimum contract for actors and stage managers, a standard minimum contract for chorus members, and a standard run-of-play contract. (All of these are spelled out in the Actors' Equity *Rules Handbook*.) Once assembled for rehearsals, the cast elects a *deputy* to represent Equity members in dealing with the producer over any breach of agreements and other employment issues. Chorus singers and dancers have separate deputies.

Casting

Casting in the professional theatre (commercial and nonprofit) is conducted by *casting directors* in association with producers, directors, playwrights, and composers (for new musicals).

At the outset, the casting director receives a "breakdown" of roles to be cast and those qualities needed for each part. This information is posted with agents through Breakdown Services and audition space reserved. Agents then submit actors' names and resumés to the casting director, who selects those actors to audition based on their training and past work. The casting director also searches office files for actors he or she may have seen for past projects and who might be appropriate for the current one. (Special auditions may also be held to "screen" unknown actors before the main audition.) Then, the casting director schedules actors for the audition, emails them scripts and "sides," and also the place and time of the audition.

During auditions, the casting director sits with the show's director and producer and may also be part of the discussion to select the final cast. The director and producer make the *final* casting decisions. If it is a new work, the creators (playwright and composer of a musical) also have casting approval. The choreographer also has approval of dancers. Most casting directors are located in New York City or Los Angeles, although

©Newscom

The Book of Mormon
The marquee for *The Book of Mormon* at Broadway's Eugene O'Neill Theatre, West Forty-ninth Street

©Carol Rosegg

Shakespeare's *Othello*
The National Asian-American Theater Company produced Shakespeare's *Othello* with American actors of Asian descent, including Korean, Chinese, Japanese, and Filipino. Joshua Spafford as Othello and Joel de la Fuente as Iago, Off Off Broadway.

large nonprofit theatres, such as Lincoln Center Theater and the Mark Taper Forum Theatre, have casting directors as part of the theatre's permanent staff. Names and addresses of casting directors, who are also members of the Casting Society of America (CSA), are listed in the *Ross Reports*.

Inclusive Casting

Inclusive casting (formerly *nontraditional casting*) involves casting actors in roles for which they might not have been considered in the past for reasons of ethnicity, gender, or physical impairment. Another term, *colorblind casting*, ignores race or ethnicity, casting actors solely on the basis of talent and suitability to a role.

Conceptual casting alters the race or ethnicity of characters to bring about a new perspective on the play. *Othello* produced by the National Asian-American Theater Company altered the historical obsession with racial and class differences in Shakespeare's text and substituted a nonracial contest between a great warrior and a confederate of boundless evil.

Casting inversions involve issues of injustices to minority actors by denying them ethnic roles. Although it is no longer the practice to cast Caucasian actors in nonwhite roles, the issue erupted into an international controversy when Actors' Equity Association objected to the casting of British actor, Jonathan Pryce, as the Eurasian narrator in *Miss Saigon*. Pryce had played the role in the successful London musical, but as it was transferred to Broadway, the union took issue with producer Cameron Mackintosh and called for an Asian actor in the role. Eventually, Actors' Equity gained other concessions and permitted Pryce to play the lead on Broadway.

FOCUS ON PEOPLE IN THEATRE

PLAYWRIGHTS' AGENT

Audrey Wood

The New York Times Pictures/Redux

Playwrights' agent **Audrey Wood** (1905–1985) represented and guided the careers of Tennessee Williams, William Inge, Robert Anderson, Clifford Odets, Carson McCullers, Preston Jones, Arthur Kopit, and many other writers.

Wood discovered Tennessee Williams through his entry in a playwriting contest sponsored by the Group Theatre. It took her eight years to sell the script of *The Glass Menagerie*, but when she did, it launched Williams's international career. When "her" playwrights were young and struggling, she found them work and grants and often loaned them money. She was known for her extraordinary devotion to her clients and was tireless in her calls on their behalf to producers and influential people. Moreover, she was the first agent in the American theatre to be given billing in playbills: "Mr. Williams' Representative—Audrey Wood." In her autobiography, *Represented by Audrey Wood*, she said, "The theater is a venture (one hesitates to call it a business) built on equal parts of faith, energy and hard work—all tied together with massive injections of nerve."[5]

Audrey Wood with Max Wilk, Represented by Audrey Wood (Garden City, NY: Doubleday and Company, 1981): 7.

The Agent

When asked "What does an agent do?" Audrey Wood, possibly the most famous playwrights' agent of the last fifty years, answered: " . . . my work involves locating talented playwrights . . . to encourage them to write . . . to create for the professional theater. If they accept me as their representative, I will attempt to guide their careers and see to their business affairs. Hopefully, together, we will both enjoy a long and rewarding future."[6]

An agent, whether for playwright, translator, director, actor, or designer, acts on behalf of that artist to find theatre, film, television, commercials, and publishing contracts. For a percentage, the agent looks after the livelihood of the artist, negotiates contracts and royalties, and writes checks. The agent is as much a part of the artist's professional life and success in the commercial theatre as the director or producer, because it is through the agent that the actor or playwright is usually seen and heard by directors and producers. As the artist's lifeline into the commercial theatre, the agent is frequently friend, mentor, parent, psychiatrist, and valued counselor.

Previews and Out-of-Town Tryouts

Until recently, almost every Broadway show had a trial run in New Haven, Boston, or Philadelphia before its New York opening. The purpose was to get audience response and to "fix" the script and casting problems before subjecting the production to the scrutiny of Broadway critics. Today, out-of-town tryouts, as they were conceived in the

©Sara Krulwich/The New York Times/Redux

The Gershwins' Porgy and Bess
Adapted by Suzan-Lori Parks and Diedre L. Murray from the original book and music for the American Repertory Theatre, Cambridge, Mass. Directed by ART's artistic director Diane Paulus.

past, are so expensive that many producers use other options, such as the Broadway *preview* (usually of one to three weeks); another is transferring with commercial producers a play or musical that has had a successful debut in a regional theatre directly to Broadway (*The Gershwins' Porgy and Bess*); or transferring the successful commercial London production (*The Phantom of the Opera* or *Mary Poppins*).

Broadway Openings and After

Those late opening-night parties at Sardi's or other restaurants in the Broadway district, where everyone connected with the show waits to learn the critics' verdicts, are legendary. Will the show have a run, or won't it? Tension mounts as those involved with the show wait to learn their fate. Usually, the show's press agent or publicity manager downloads the reviews from the internet onto an iPad. They are read aloud to the assembled group of cast and well-wishers.

The morning after an opening, there is a customary meeting among producers, press agent, and general manager (and sometimes an attorney). If the show receives rave reviews, as did *The Lion King* and *The Book of Mormon*, the job of planning advertising

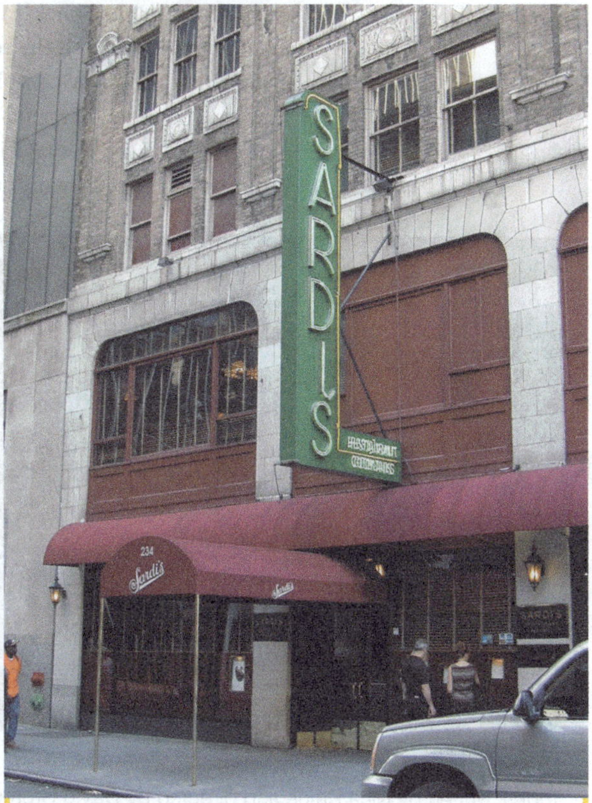

©Walter McBride/Retna Ltd.

Sardi's Restaurant
This restaurant on Broadway's West Forty-fourth Street is famous for its opening-night theatre parties.

A Chorus Line
With marquee and crowds of ticket-buyers and theatregoers in front of the Shubert Theatre on West Forty-fourth Street.

expenses is an easy one. If the reviews are "pans," the decision to close is painful but justifiable. However, if the reviews are mixed, decisions are difficult. There's always a chance that the show can play long enough to recover its investment, but calculating how much money to spend to keep it running until expenses can be made is tricky.

Neither is it an easy decision to close a show if the possibility exists of developing business at a later date or mounting a tour. So many jobs, from stage electricians to actors, depend on this decision. Advance sales to theatre parties have to be weighed against current box-office sales. Generally, when a show is panned, it has little chance of making its costs, much less returns on investments.

Off Broadway's *Tribes*
Tribes, written by Nina Raine and directed by David Cromer, was produced Off Broadway at the Barrow Street Theatre to critical acclaim for the story about a hearing-impaired son in a competitive intellectual family.

PRODUCING OFF BROADWAY

Once a haven from the high costs of Broadway contracts and union wages, Off Broadway is a smaller, less expensive version of its namesake. The Dramatists Guild and Actors' Equity have developed Off Broadway contracts, which apply to the smaller theatres (100 to 499 seats) and the smaller box-office potential.

Coproducers and associate producers also appear on the Off Broadway scene. A coproducer enters into a joint venture (or limited partnership, as it is called) to assist the producer in raising money for the production. Today, there is little difference, other than the scale of the production and the amount of the investment, between producing on and off Broadway. The language is the same, contracts similar, key personnel identical, and risks ever-present.

PRODUCING IN REGIONAL THEATRES

In regional theatres—sometimes called *resident theatres* or *companies*—an artistic director or producing director (the titles vary from theatre to theatre) helms the theatre. As the theatre's leader, this person defines the theatre's artistic and social mission and deals with a board of directors or trustees, corporations, foundations, federal and state agencies, patrons, subscribers, and general audiences. Together with the company's managers, he or she plans the theatre's season, hires the artists, and is the "face" of the theatre.

Although Broadway remains the mecca for America's commercial theatre, nonprofit professional theatres have proliferated beyond Broadway and throughout the United States. Beginning in the late fifties, the regional theatre movement by 2011 had established a network of more than 1,876 nonprofit theatres in cities and communities across the country. Some formed a national alliance known as the League of Resident Theatres (LORT) that negotiates contracts with theatre unions, including Actors' Equity, under which all nonprofit professional theatres operate. It is unusual to find a major city that does not have one or more professional resident theatres.

The terms *resident* and *regional* are used interchangeably to describe nonprofit professional theatres located from coast to coast. In a 2011 survey, these companies gave more than 177,000 performances and attracted more than 34 million people to the theatre. Most schedule seasons of five to ten months, generally to subscription

Albee's *The Play about the Baby*
Written and directed by Edward Albee, this play had its American premiere with Earle Hyman and Marian Seldes at the Alley Theatre, Houston.

Some of the 1,200 nonprofit theatres

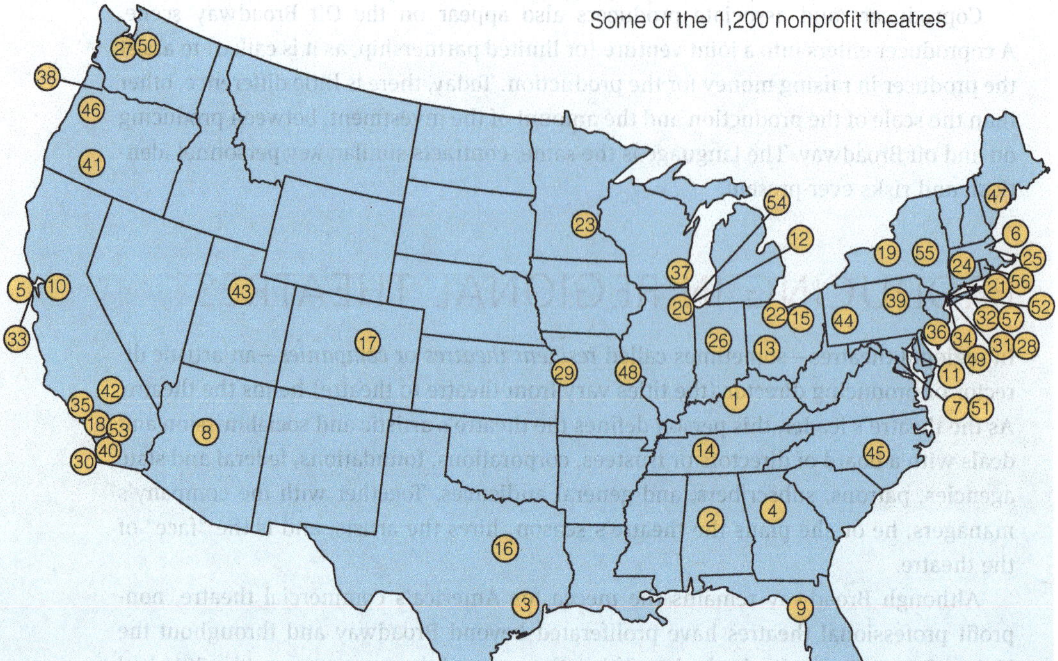

Theatre	City
1 Actors Theatre of Louisville	Louisville, KY
2 Alabama Shakespeare Festival	Montgomery, AL
3 Alley Theatre	Houston, TX
4 Alliance Theatre Company	Atlanta, GA
5 American Conservatory Theatre	San Francisco, CA
6 American Repertory Theatre	Cambridge, MA
7 Arena Stage	Washington, D.C
8 Arizona Theatre Company	Tucson, AZ
9 Asolo Theatre Company	Sarasota, FL
10 Berkeley Repertory Theatre	Berkeley, CA
11 Center Stage	Baltimore, MD
12 Chicago Shakespeare Theatre	Chicago, IL
13 Cincinnati Playhouse in the Park	Cincinnati, OH
14 Clarence Brown Theatre Company	Knoxville, TN

	Theatre	City
15	The Cleveland Playhouse	Cleveland, OH
16	Dallas Theatre Center	Dallas, TX
17	Denver Center Theatre	Denver, CO
18	Geffen Playhouse	Los Angeles, CA
19	GeVa Theatre	Rochester, NY
20	Goodman Theatre	Chicago, IL
21	Goodspeed Opera House	East Haddam, CT
22	Great Lakes Theater Festival	Cleveland, OH
23	Guthrie Theater	Minneapolis, MN
24	Hartford Stage Company	Hartford, CT
25	Huntington Theatre Company	Boston, MA
26	Indiana Repertory Theatre	Indianapolis, IN
27	Intiman Theatre Company	Seattle, WA
28	The Joseph Papp Public Theater/ New York Shakespeare Festival Theatre	New York City
29	Kansas City Repertory Theatre	Kansas City, MO
30	La Jolla Playhouse	La Jolla, CA
31	Lincoln Center Theater	New York City
32	Long Wharf Theatre	New Haven, CT
33	Magic Theatre	San Francisco, CA
34	Manhattan Theatre Club	New York City
35	Mark Taper Forum	Los Angeles, CA
36	McCarter Theatre Center for the Performing Arts	Princeton, NJ
37	Milwaukee Repertory Theatre	Milwaukee, WI
38	Miracle Theatre Group	Portland, OR
39	New York Theatre Workshop	New York City
40	Old Globe Theatre	San Diego, CA
41	Oregon Shakespeare Festival	Ashland, OR
42	The Pasadena Playhouse	Pasadena, CA
43	Pioneer Theatre Company	Salt Lake City, UT
44	Pittsburgh Public Theatre	Pittsburgh, PA
45	Playmakers Repertory Company	Chapel Hill, NC
46	Portland Center Stage	Portland, OR
47	Portland Stage Company	Portland, ME
48	Repertory Theatre of St. Louis	St. Louis, MO
49	Roundabout Theatre	New York City
50	Seattle Repertory Theatre	Seattle, WA
51	The Shakespeare Theatre	Washington, D.C.
52	Signature Theatre	New York City
53	South Coast Repertory	Costa Mesa, CA
54	Steppenwolf Theatre Company	Chicago, IL
55	Syracuse Stage	Syracuse, NY
56	Trinity Repertory Company	Providence, RI
57	Yale Repertory Theatre	New Haven, CT

audiences. Many have school touring programs. Others have outreach programs for audiences of all ages that are models for community-wide social and cultural organizations. All offer employment opportunities for playwrights, directors, designers, actors, and management and technical staff.[7]

At the outset, regional theatres have had a mandate to develop new works. Because New York productions have high staging costs, astronomical ticket prices ($85 to $400 for a single ticket), and mercurial critics, writers increasingly prefer to have their works initially produced by regional companies. There, during a guaranteed rehearsal period and a four- to six-week run, writers have time to make changes without the threat of closing notices being posted on opening night.

Regional theatres have developed such writers as Pearl Cleage, Rebecca Gilman, Tracy Letts, Bruce Norris, Marsha Norman, Lynn Nottage, Sarah Ruhl, Sam Shepard, Paula Vogel, and Cheryl L. West, among others. Even established playwrights (Edward Albee, Tony Kushner, David Mamet, and Terrence McNally) have unveiled their plays in regional theatres.

The producer's job in the regional theatre is both similar to and different from the Broadway producer's job. The artistic or producing director oversees not a single play but a season of plays. This individual is in charge of planning a season of plays, sometimes in two or more theatres, including classical and modern works, musicals, lesser-known European works, and new plays. The artistic director may direct one or more plays within a season and hire other directors to complete the season. The regional theatre producer approves a projected budget to cover all contingencies:

- artistic salaries and fees
- administrative salaries and costs
- travel and housing (for casting and artists)
- marketing and development costs
- production and personnel expenses
- equipment, facilities maintenance, and services

In this milieu, producing is also precarious. Although there is usually continuity of administrative and artistic leadership within regional theatres, no continuous financial support system exists from season to season, although some theatres have developed endowments to offset annual operating costs. Regional theatres and their producers depend on a delicate balance of federal and state dollars, foundation and corporation money, contributed income, and subscribers' dollars. Producers must at all times juggle the season's budgeted expenses against real and projected income. Although most theatres hire permanent administrative staff and artistic leadership, few have been able to fund a resident acting company for the entire season, as is the practice in Britain, France, and Germany. At best, a small core of actors returns year after year, playing a variety of roles. They are matched with other performers who are hired on a show-by-show basis. The artists themselves often support the theatre by accepting minimal salaries until they grow tired and move into film and television, or leave the business entirely. New actors replace them, and the cycle begins again. This talent drain is wearing at best and discouraging at most.

A Moon for the Misbegotten
Cherry Jones and Gabriel Byrne in Eugene O'Neill's *A Moon for the Misbegotten* at the Goodman Theatre, Chicago. Directed by Daniel Sullivan.

Despite the lack of permanent funding and resident companies, the regional theatre movement is strong. One way a number of producers have chosen to counterbalance the fiscal difficulties has been to reestablish connections with the New York commercial theatre. In the last decade, Broadway has been enlivened by shows that established themselves first with regional audiences (a variation on the out-of-town tryout) and then moved with added capital (and coproducers) onto Broadway. A short list includes *The Gershwins' Porgy and Bess* from the American Repertory Theatre in Cambridge, *Angels in America* from the New York Shakespeare Festival/Public Theatre, *The Iceman Cometh* from the Goodman Theatre in Chicago, and *Once* from the New York Theatre Workshop.

Broadway producer Alexander H. Cohen said that the commercial and nonprofit theatre share something in common: "*What's good succeeds.*"

> If the material is good—if it addresses the nature of our society—then it will succeed in either the commercial or nonprofit theatre, or, in both, as the case may be. There's a great deal of trial and error in choosing material and producing it. But finally the dross sinks beneath its own undistinguished weight and the meaningful, imaginative, and exciting continue on our stages.[8]

Out of the commercial and nonprofit theatres and visionary risk-taking by producers have come such American classics as *A Streetcar Named Desire, Death of a Salesman, A Raisin in the Sun, Who's Afraid of Virginia Woolf?, A Chorus Line*, and *Angels in America: A Gay Fantasia on National Themes.*

FOCUS ON PEOPLE IN THEATRE

FOUNDING ARTISTIC DIRECTOR

James Houghton

©newscom

Since 1991, Founding Artistic Director of the Signature Theatre Company James Houghton has created a new home for the Signature in a newly-designed theatre by Frank Gehry on Forty-second Street and Tenth Avenue, New York City. The Signature exists to celebrate playwrights and has devoted entire seasons to the works of Edward Albee, María Irene Fornés, Horton Foote, Adrienne Kennedy, Tony Kushner, Sam Shepard, Paula Vogel, and August Wilson. Houghton has recently introduced the "Legacy Program" that invites past playwrights-in-residence to return either with well-known or new works.

©T. Charles Erickson

The Orphans' Home Cycle
The Orphans' Home Cycle by Horton Foote is a three-part cycle of nine plays staged by Michael Wilson and coproduced by Hartford Stage Company, CT, and the Signature Theatre, 2009–2010 season.

In addition to leading the Signature Theatre, Houghton serves as Dean of the Juilliard School of Drama where he oversees the professional training of actors and directors.

©Maurice Meredith/Courtesy of St. Louis Black Repertory Company

Ain't Misbehavin'
The musical by Murray Horwitz and Richard Maltby Jr., with J. Samuel Davis and Eddie Webb, produced by the St. Louis Black Repertory Company.

STAGING DIVERSITY

Beginning in the early seventies, small and ethnically diverse theatre companies emerged throughout the United States with dynamic artistic leadership. Many took their names from the ethnicity that was the sounding board of their founders, writers, artists, communities, and political coalitions. Today, these *producing organizations* mirror America's ethnic diversity; frame the overriding political, economic, and social issues of minority cultures; and, in turn, are radically changing American culture, society, and theatre.

AFRICAN AMERICAN COMPANIES

As producing organizations, the New Federal Theatre and St. Louis Black Repertory Theatre are measures of the successful emergence of the African American experience onto the

FOCUS ON THEATRE

Literary Management and Literary Managers

In the United States, *literary managers* are most often found in professional, nonprofit theatres. Although the literary manager's responsibilities may vary from one company to the next, the essential job is to find and read new scripts and develop the most promising. Almost every professional theatre receives a large number of unsolicited scripts each season. Many companies read only those scripts submitted by agents or brought to them by known writers and other professionals.

Literary management most often includes new-play development. This is a highly sensitive and lengthy undertaking because it involves working with playwrights to realize the full potential of their scripts. In this capacity, the function of the literary manager merges with that of the dramaturg. Oftentimes, the process is taken over by a director, but usually late in the developmental process. Director Daniel Sullivan suggested "substantial changes" to Rebecca Gilman's *Spinning into Butter* (already "developed" at the Goodman Theatre) before its New York premiere at Lincoln Center Theater.

In the process of developing new plays, the literary manager talks with and advises playwrights to clarify intentions and shape the action. Then, readings and workshops test the stage-worthiness of the new piece. Many established writers have voiced concerns about well-intentioned literary managers (and dramaturgs) "rewriting" their plays.

In recent years, there have been legal disputes over "authorship." Perhaps the most publicized dispute involved the late playwright Jonathan Larson and dramaturg Lynn Thomson, who, together, developed the popular musical *Rent*. There was no contractual arrangement between Larson and Thomson at the moment of his untimely death. She sued the playwright's estate for a percentage of the royalties on the grounds of her contributions to the project as co-collaborator. The court ruled in favor of the estate based on the absence of a contract. Despite the notoriety of this case, legal disputes between collaborators are rare owing to contractual arrangements exercised by theatres with playwrights.

Some theatres are known for their new-play development programs. In this category are the South Coast Repertory Theatre (Costa Mesa, CA), Actors Theatre of Louisville (KY), and Playwrights Horizons (New York City).

national stage. The creation of African American theatre companies paralleled the civil rights movement of the sixties. Amiri Baraka (LeRoi Jones) formed Spirit House in Newark, New Jersey, in 1966 to create a black "separatist" theatre "by us, about us, for us." The New Lafayette Theatre, founded in 1967 by Robert Macbeth, became a Harlem cultural center with Ed Bullins as resident playwright, associate director, and editor of *Black Theatre* magazine. The magazine functioned as an information service for black artists. Disagreements within the company brought about its dissolution in 1973. The Free Southern Theater (New Orleans), founded in 1963 by Gilbert Moses and John O'Neal as an extension of the civil rights movement in the South, has also dissolved. (See Chapter 3, "Alternative Theatrical Spaces.") The Negro Ensemble Company (NEC), created by Douglas Turner Ward in 1968 in New York City, produced works about the black experience. The company's most influential works were *A Soldier's Play*, *Ceremonies in Dark Old Men*, *The Sty of the Blind Pig*, and *River Niger*.

The works of Lorraine Hansberry, Amiri Baraka, Ed Bullins, and August Wilson shaped the writing of serious plays about the black experience in mid-twentieth-century America and into the new millennium.

FOCUS ON THEATRE

Hip-Hop Expressions

With origins in modern African American cultural innovations (rapping, DJ turntablism, break dancing, and graffiti), hip-hop has become synonymous with artistic innovation, social analysis, and democratic participation. It has reached into subcultures of young people and disenfranchised populations. "Hip-Hop Theatre," coined by poet Eisa Davis in *The Source* magazine in 2000, describes the work of artists ranging from dance-theatre choreographers to playwrights and ensemble and solo artists. Solo artist Danny Hoch and writer Kamilah Forbes are co-artistic directors of New York City's Hip-Hop Theatre Festival and its satellite festivals in San Francisco and Washington, D.C.

As no other recent theatrical experiment, Hip-Hop Theatre has touched a youth audience in the breakdown of separation between performers and audiences. It has encouraged a new etiquette that is participatory and new audiences that are passionate about its rebellions and complacencies.

Outside the mainstream of traditional American theatre, hip-hop has emerged as a new genre with jazz rhythms, in-your-face language, use of open mikes to encourage talk back, freestyle improvisations, streetwise urban behavior, media-savvy rap music, and DJ samplings. Hip-hop plays, such as *Def Poetry Jam* and Forbes's *Rhyme Deferred*, confront cultural and social issues in a style and language that attack American consumerism, discrimination, and violence. Crossing lines of race, class, and ethnicity, hip-hop gives voice to individual expressions and community narratives. Its artists have also adopted civil rights-era agendas, such as education reform, Laborpractices, immigrant rights, and prison reform. In a surge of democratic participation that throws time-honored audience etiquette to the four winds, hip-hop has influenced and polarized—it has influenced performance forms, media, visual art, literature, fashion, and language; and it has also polarized those who fear or dislike its innovations, virtuosity, in-your-face style, and social messages.

The New Federal Theatre, founded by producer-director Woodie King Jr. in 1970 in New York City, is among the most successful companies to achieve artistic and financial stability as a producing organization. Now in its fortieth season, the New Federal Theatre serves minority audiences in New York's Lower East Side and sponsors a variety of ethnic theatre groups and events.

The St. Louis Black Repertory Theatre, founded in 1976 by Ronald J. Himes, is committed to producing works by African American and Third World writers. It has ongoing arts programs, expanded seasons to include six productions and touring shows, and workshops and residences, to heighten the community's social, cultural, and educational awareness. Charles Fuller, Wole Soyinka, Laurence Holder, August Wilson, and Cheryl L. West are among the writers featured in the company's seasons.

Almost 200 African American theatre companies exist today throughout the United States. The outcome of the growing availability of companies and stages dedicated to the American black experience has been the increase in opportunities for African American playwrights, actors, directors, and designers over four decades. Such names as Tazana Beverly, Clinton Turner Davis, Ossie Davis, Ruby Dee, Gloria Foster, Allen Lee Hughes, Derek Anson Jones, Marion I. McClinton, Novella Nelson, Lloyd Richards, Seret Scott, Paul Tazewell, Regina Taylor, Tazewell Thompson, Jane White, and George C. Wolfe have led a pantheon of African American artists, many of whom have found their way into mainstream commercial theatres.

Asian American Companies

Asian workers were imported into the United States in the mid-nineteenth century to build railroads. Many workers and their families remained clustered in neighborhoods within major port cities, such as San Francisco, New York City, Chicago, Los Angeles, and Seattle. Many communities developed their own entertainments that featured Asian players, and many Asians were featured in films, although chiefly as racial stereotypes. The inscrutable detective "Charlie Chan" and the "Dragon Lady" were two among many stereotypical characters in films, but this was to change. The Korean and Vietnam wars increased the number of Asian immigrants to the United States, and the plight of Vietnamese boat people developed further awareness of Asian culture and traditions. International theatre artists such as Antonin Artaud and Bertolt Brecht drew heavily on Asian theatrical traditions. They were followed by Jerzy Grotowski, Peter Brook, Ariane Mnouchkine, Harold Prince, Andrei Serban, and Julie Taymor, whose work owes a great debt to Asian stage and puppet traditions.

In the late sixties and early seventies in the wake of the civil rights movement, Asian American artists formed small theatre companies in major cities to tell their stories with authentic voices. Among the earliest Asian American companies were the East West Players in Los Angeles; the Asian Exclusive Act, later renamed Northwest Asian American Theatre Company; the Asian American Theatre Workshop in San Francisco; Ping Chong and Company, founded by current artistic director Ping Chong in New York City; Pan Asian Repertory Theatre, founded by current artistic director Tisa Chang; and the Ma-Yi Theatre Ensemble in New York City. These companies nurtured such writers and artists as Tisa Chang, Daryl Chin, Frank Chin, Ping Chong, Tim Dang, Philip Kan Gotanda, David Henry Hwang, Maxine Hong Kingston, Fabian Obispo, Han Ong, Jon Shiroto, Diana Son, Ching Valdes-Aran, B. D. Wong, and Laurence Yep.

The East West Players, founded in 1965, is the oldest of the present group of Asian American companies producing in the United States today. Created as a California-based home to promote Asian Pacific American works, the company first operated out of a storefront facility on Santa Monica Boulevard in Silver Lake. In 1996, it moved into the Union Center for Arts in downtown Los Angeles and performs to 40,000 annually. Under the leadership of actor-director Mako, the group

Courtesy Ping Chong and Company

Kwaidan
Directed and adapted by Ping Chong from the novel by Lafcadio Hearn, *Kwaidan* was presented by Ping Chong and Company, New York City.

Peter Brook, Threads of Time: A Memoir (London: Methuen Publishing, Ltd., 1999): 149-150. Reprinted by permission.

Golden Child
David Henry Hwang's play was produced by the East West Players and directed by Chay Yew. Los Angeles.

©Michal Daniel

concentrated on plays by Asian Americans and showcased Asian American actors in classical plays. Today, under the artistic leadership of Tim Dang, the company features about four plays a season by such influential writers as David Henry Hwang, Philip Kan Gotanda, Jon Shirota, and Euijoon Kim; and it also produces American classics (*The Zoo Story, A Chorus Line, Follies, The Fantasticks*) with Asian casts.

Founded by performance artist, choreographer, writer, director, and designer Ping Chong in 1975, the Ping Chong and Company exists at the intersection where race, culture, history, art, and technology meet. The clash of these forces is the source of Ping Chong's artistic investigations that have earned an international reputation for the company. Resisting being "ghettoized as an Asian-American artist," he has said, "I am an American artist. I believe that it is important to be inclusive; a free society should allow for a multiplicity of views." Ping Chong views his company's work as "an ongoing dialogue." He creates about four pieces a season with the company; notable creations include *Throne of Blood, Blind Ness, Cathay: Three Tales of China*, and the ongoing series *Undesirable Elements.*

Latino/Hispanic/Mexican American Companies

Theatre historians record that the first play to be staged in the United States was performed by Spanish soldiers in 1598 near what is now El Paso, Texas. In the late nineteenth century, Spanish-language theatre was commonly found, first in California, then in Texas, and by the early twentieth century in the territories bordering Mexico. By 1918, Los Angeles had five professional Spanish-language theatres, but the economic depression of the 1930s, along with the popularity of film, ended these professional troupes.

The political unrest of the 1960s again brought attention to U.S. Latino/a theatre. Luis Valdéz' El Teatro Campesino ("The Farmworkers' Theatre"), a bilingual company, formed in 1965 in Delano to call attention to the plight of migrant farmworkers in California. Other groups followed, including Repertorio Español (New York City),

Thalia Spanish Theatre (Sunnyside, NY), and such cultural centers as the INTAR Hispanic American Arts Center (New York City), Bilingual Foundation of the Arts (Los Angeles), and GALA Hispanic Theatre (Washington, D.C.). Their agendas serve to bring attention to their Hispanic heritage and new works by emerging Latino/a playwrights.

El Teatro Campesino, San Juan Bautista, founded by Luis Valdéz under the wing of the United Farm Workers to dramatize the plight of agricultural workers in California, subsequently devoted itself to plays focused on broader issues of Mexican American culture, consciousness, and pride.

At first, Valdéz staged improvised, didactic *actos* to dramatize the exploitation of farmworkers by their bosses; these short plays were in themselves political acts and performed in Spanish and in English, on flatbed trucks, on farms, in marketplaces, and at political rallies. About these *actos*, Valdéz said, "Our theatre work is simple, direct, complex and profound, but it works."

During the 1970s, the work broadened to include Mexican American issues on education, culture, and religion. A vivacious performance style informed the *carpa* (itinerant tent shows), *corridos* (narrative ballads), and *mitos* (myths). The long history of the group's collective work ended in 1980. Luis Valdéz, a prolific writer, has since written a number of full-length plays about the heritage and lives of contemporary Mexican Americans. *Los Vendidos*, *Corridos*, *Zoot Suit*, *I Don't Have to Show You No Stinking Badges*, and *Bandito* have been performed throughout California and on national and European tours. Valdéz' film work, especially *La Bamba*, has also brought him and his theatre international acclaim.

Founded in 1973 in Los Angeles by Margarita Galban (artistic director), Estela Scarlata, and Carmen Zapata (producing

Courtesy El Teatro Campesino

La Conciencia del Esquirol
Founding artistic director and playwright Luis Valdéz (right) plays the *Esquirol*, or Scab, in one of El Teatro Campesino's early actos presented at nightly rallies of the United Farm Workers.

Margarita Galban/Courtesy Bilingual Foundation of the Arts

Blood Wedding
Suzanna Guzman and María Bermudez in Frederico García Lorca's *Blood Wedding*, directed by Margarita Galban, and produced by the Bilingual Foundation of the Arts, Los Angeles.

director), the Bilingual Foundation of the Arts aims to present the rich diversity of Hispanic history, traditions, and culture in classic and contemporary plays written in Spanish and in English. BFA provides an "artistic doorway," writes Margarita Galban, "through which the rich diversity of Hispanic literature may be experienced by people of all cultures." The company operates three theatres and produces year-round.

The Gala Hispanic Theatre, Washington, D.C., was founded in 1976 by producing director Hugo J. Medrano and Rebecca Read Medrano, to promote Hispanic culture by presenting bilingual theatre. Since its beginnings, GALA has produced more than 100 plays and other arts programs in Spanish and English. With associate producing director Abel Lopez, a professional company of actors performs an average of four classic and contemporary plays a season. A recent season included classics by Pablo Neruda and Tirso de Molina and new works by Rudolfo Walsh and Alberto Pedro Torriente.

Native American Companies

There are only a handful of Native American theatre companies in existence. Their theatrical heritage is rooted in the outdoor dance performances of Native Americans based on inherited myths and traditions to unite communities and reinforce traditional beliefs. What plays there are aim to sustain that heritage and build pride among Native American peoples. Many of these Western-style dramas have found productions in established producing organizations, such as the Denver Center Theatre, the Great American History Theatre (St. Paul), the Mixed Blood Theatre Company (Minneapolis), the Montana Repertory Theatre (Missoula), and the Perseverance Theatre (Douglas, AK).

The Native American Theatre Ensemble (originally called the American Indian Theatre Ensemble), founded by writer-director-choreographer Hanay Geiogamah in 1972, was the first all-Native American repertory company to present plays based on traditional myths and contemporary life for Native American audiences. Their aim was to promote ethnic pride. In recent years, Geiogamah transformed the company into the American Indian Dance Theatre, which performs an intertribal repertory with members drawn from a dozen tribes. *Kotuwokan*, by Geiogamah, is a dance-drama about a Native American boy's efforts to find his way in the contemporary world.

Power Pipes
A production by Spiderwoman Theatre, *Power Pipes* with Lisa Mayo, Muriel Miguel, and Gloria Miguel premiered at the Brooklyn Academy of Music.

Spiderwoman Theatre (named after the Hopi Goddess of Creation) was founded in 1975 by three Kuna-Rappahannock sisters—Muriel Miguel, Gloria Miguel, and Lisa Mayo—to promote both Native American and feminist concerns. The three women worked with the Minnesota Native American AIDS Task Force as teachers and artists. As artistic director of Spiderwoman, Muriel Miguel developed more than twenty shows in the late seventies. The success of the first piece, *Women in Violence*, led to an invitation to perform at the World Festival Theatre in Nancy, France, and elsewhere in

Europe. Their work reveals a story-weaving technique—spinning together words and movement. These loosely structured pieces range from satires on sexuality and violence against women adapted from Aristophanes and Chekhov (*Lysistrata Numbah*, *The Three Sisters from Here to There*) to explorations of the Native American heritage, spirituality, racism, and politics (*Sun Moon and Feather* and *Power Pipes*). Spiderwoman Theatre is unique in its blending of Native American ritual traditions and myths and modern feminist concerns. It is one of the most important Native American theatre groups performing today in the United States and Canada.

TRANSITION

The producer's job, as the title implies, is to *produce*. Many business people are attracted to "show biz" and to investing for a variety of reasons, many of them wrong reasons, such as the glamour of associating with Broadway and "stars," and the get-rich-quick dream of an overnight "hit."

In fact, producing means making a lot of difficult, educated decisions about art, people, and money—and carrying them out. It is not for the dilettante or the faint of heart. Producing is frequently painful. It can mean firing your favorite actor, director, or designer who turns out not to be right for the show. A producer has to have the personality and experience to influence people, raise money, hire, dismiss, mediate disputes, encourage and assist, option wisely, soothe bruised egos, and be all things to all people. Most important is the ability to extract money from investors—in brief, *to produce the show.*

In American theatre, the Broadway musical is the pièce de résistance of producing—the costliest, the most lucrative, and the most popular of the theatrical arts.

Theatre: A Way of Seeing Online

Visit the CourseMate for Theatre: A Way of Seeing 7th Edition for quick access to the digital study resources that accompany this chapter, including links to the websites listed below, Theatre Workshop, digital glossary, a chapter quiz and more.

Websites

The *Theatre: A Way of Seeing* CourseMate includes links for all the websites described below. Simply select "Web links" from the Chapter Resources for Chapter 13, and click on the link that interests you. You'll be taken directly to the site described.

Actors' Equity Diversity
Actors Equity's EEO and Diversity policies, committees, and events.

Alliance for Inclusion in the Arts
An advocate for diversity and inclusion in film, theatre, and television.

Back Stage
Covers the entertainment world of theatre, film, and television for the performer with an emphasis on casting, job opportunities, and career advice.

Broadway and Off Broadway Theatre
Up-to-date information about U. S. and International theatre, including shows, reviews, ticket prices, and spotlights on theatre in various cities.

Curtain Up
The Internet theatre magazine of reviews, features, and annotated listings.

DiverCity
Site of NBC Universal's Talent Diversity Initiative.

The League of Broadway Producers
The national trade association for the Broadway theatre industry made up of theatre owners, producers, presenters, and general managers.

League of Chicago Theatres
Composed of members from the commercial, nonprofit, and educational theatres. The League promotes the Chicago theatre industry.

The New York Theatre Experience
A thorough website connecting real audiences to real New York theatre in a virtual world. Includes links to reviews from 1997 on, to interviews with actors and celebrities, to a list of coming attractions, and more.

The Off Off Broadway Review
Links to listings and reviews for Off Off Broadway productions.

Playbill
Hundreds of links to theatre news, plays, show times and dates, and ticket resources.

Theatre Facts
Special Annual Report published in *American Theatre* magazine detailing an annual analysis of the fiscal state of the American not-for-profit theatre.

Theatre Reviews Limited
Online source for theatre reviews around the United States.

© Joan Marcus

14

THE AMERICAN MUSICAL

MUSICAL BOOKS, COMPOSERS, LYRICISTS, CHOREOGRAPHERS, AND MEGAMUSICALS

"When Broadway history is being made, you can feel it. What you feel is a seismic emotional jolt that sends the audience, as one, right out of its wits."[1]

— FRANK RICH ON, *DREAMGIRLS*

PRECEDENTS

Musical theatre, America's most popular theatrical form, dates from the colonial period. English touring companies presented ballad operas (plays with spoken dialogue interspersed with lyrics set to popular tunes) and encouraged imitations. Following the American Revolution, entrepreneurs, composers, and writers created their own comic operas. Many of them imitated the French *opéra comique*, a type of performance that alternated spoken dialogue with verses set to popular tunes, similar to English ballad operas. By the 1840s, permanent theatres in urban centers and other types of musical venues contributed to the growth of musical theatre in America. Melodrama (plays with musical passages to heighten emotional effects), burlesques (send-ups of serious themes), and musical spectacles with lavish scenery and costumes imported from Europe were soon adapted to American subjects and idioms. John Brougham's popular burlesque *Po-ca-hon-tas; or the Gentle Savage* (1855) parodied plays written about Native Americans.

Meanwhile, minstrel shows that combined sentimental ballads, comic dialogue, and dance interludes performed by actors in blackface, ostensibly based upon life in the American South, developed as a uniquely

PREVIEW

Broadway has been described as a shifting, even chimerical phenomenon.[2] The forty-two-block neighborhood around Times Square, identified as New York's central theatre district, has been home to great plays and musicals since the mid-nineteenth century.

A revival of *Follies* starring actress Bernadette Peters singing "Losing My Mind," with music and lyrics by Stephen Sondheim and book by James Goldman, Broadway.

The Everett Collection

The Jazz Singer
Al Jolson, singer and comedian, in the "blackface" of the minstrel shows where he received his early training. Here he appears in a poster for *The Jazz Singer,* 1927.

American form of musical theatre. Widely influential, white-and black-owned companies toured minstrel shows that perpetuated exaggerated fictions of black life. The shows included music (played on the banjo, tambourine, violin, and a rhythm instrument called *bones*), stereotypical characters (shifty lazybones, the urban dandy, loyal uncle, warmhearted mother), jigs and other folk dances, and female performers (in black companies). Many outstanding performers, including Eddie Cantor, Al Jolson, and Bert Williams, owe a great deal to the minstrel tradition, even though the idea today strikes modern audiences as racist and offensive.

The American Civil War interrupted the expansion of musical theatre, but after the war, minstrelsy and burlesque both remained popular. In 1866, *The Black Crook*, with music by Thomas Baker, was the most influential event cited as the starting point of modern American musical theatre. A combination of melodrama and spectacle, the show used music, dance, spectacular scenery and costumes, and scantily clad chorus girls in the telling of an uncomplicated story. But the American premiere of W. S. Gilbert and Arthur Sullivan's *HMS Pinafore* in 1879 made British operetta the dominant musical form until the turn of the twentieth century. Moreover, American composers Victor Herbert (*Naughty Marietta*) and Sigmund Romberg (*The Student Prince*) capitalized on the success of the light operatic entertainments.

AN AMERICAN MUSICAL IDIOM

At first, musical librettos (the story line, called the *book*) were constructed to allow for interpolations of unrelated songs, dances, and specialty acts. This format of loosely connected stories and themes led to the development of the *revue*, a musical form featuring songs, dances, comedy sketches, and elaborate production numbers. The first American revue was *The Passing Show* (1894) and resulted in the early twentieth-century's Florenz Ziegfeld's *Follies of 1907*, the first of a series of annual revues (*The Ziegfeld Follies*) that featured scantily clad chorines known famously as "Ziegfeld's girls," star comedians and singers, including Fanny Brice, Bert Williams, W. C. Fields, and Will Rogers. Today, the revue format can be found in such seasonal extravaganzas as the Radio City Music Hall shows in New York City.

At the dawn of the twentieth century, revues or topical extravaganzas, comic operettas (Franz Lehar's *The Merry Widow*), and George M. Cohan's series of musical comedies with contemporary characters and settings, wisecracking humor, and patriotic sentiments dominated the musical stage. Cohan's first musical was *Little Johnny Jones* (1904), best remembered for the songs "Give My Regards to Broadway" and "The Yankee Doodle Boy" ("I'm a Yankee Doodle Dandy"); it was followed by *Forty-five Minutes from Broadway* and *Seven Keys to Baldpate*. His song "Over There," written in 1917, won Cohan a Congressional Medal of Honor.

During the First World War, significant innovations in musical style took place on American stages, most notably *ragtime*. Introduced by black musicians, ragtime was first heard on musical stages as individual songs interpolated into shows. In 1914, composer and lyricist Irving Berlin, who became an international sensation with his popular song "Alexander's Ragtime Band," composed his first complete ragtime score for the revue *Watch Your Step*. The success of the work brought ragtime (or pseudo-ragtime rhythms) to the forefront of musical styles for the legitimate stage. His songs ("What'll I Do?" and "All Alone") and later shows, such as *Annie Get Your Gun*, showed his ability to bring to the musical stage the thoughts, feelings, and aspirations of average Americans.

In the first quarter of the twentieth century, Broadway's musical stage remained a mix of ragtime, operettas, and musical revues. Black book musicals (Noble Sissle and Eubie Blake's *Shuffle Along*, 1921) reappeared and popularized a form of jazz that replaced ragtime as the dominant musical comedy style.

Originally a vaudeville act featuring their own songs, Sissle, a singer and lyricist, and Blake, a pianist and composer, created the first black musical to play a major Broadway theatre during the regular season and introduced "I'm Just Wild About Harry," which became Harry Truman's campaign song in 1948. *Shuffle Along* and other black book musicals and revues introduced new dance steps, such as the Charleston, and a number of African American performers, including Bill Robinson and Florence Mills. Sissle and Blake songs became popular again on Broadway in the seventies with *Bubbling Brown Sugar* and *Eubie*.

Meanwhile, in the late 1920s, composer Jerome Kern along with librettists Guy Bolton and P. G. Wodehouse created the intimate musical for small casts and orchestras and simple settings. Known as the Princess musicals (named for the Princess Theatre, a small playhouse on West Thirty-ninth Street where they were staged), *Very*

Good Eddie and *Irene* launched their careers. By 1927, Kern had pioneered a new style of musical theatre with his score for *Show Boat*, based on Edna Ferber's popular novel about relationships between the races, with lyrics by Oscar Hammerstein II. The musical depicted the lives of a riverboat family, their deck crew, and a troupe of showboat performers from the 1880s to 1920s. *Show Boat* changed the tone of musical theatre by incorporating serious themes (miscegenation, "passing," and addiction), and with such memorable songs as "Ol' Man River," "Make Believe," "Can't Help Lovin' Dat Man," and "Why Do I Love You?" pointed the way to the serious musical plays of the 1940s and 1950s.

In the 1920s, a jazz-influenced style of musical theatre evolved with the creative team of the brothers George and Ira Gershwin as composer and lyricist. *Lady, Be Good!* with

FOCUS ON THEATRE

Vaudeville

Vaudeville, originally a variety show, was an entertainment with song-and-dance routines, jokes, and comic business. Early variety shows were found in saloons with singing waiters and dancing girls performing for all-male audiences. Tony Pastor decided to lure family audiences with promises of clean amusement and took the variety show out of the saloon and into a legitimate New York theatre in 1881.

By 1900, vaudeville had become polite entertainment featuring comedians and specialty acts, ranging from mimes and ventriloquists to trained-animal acts and miniature musicals. An entertainment in two parts featured a "dumb act," with acrobats and animals opening the first part and proceeding through ten-to twenty-minute routines to the intermission; in the second part, headliners, or star performers, appeared and closed the show. Organized by booking agencies (the Keith-Albee circuit dominated the eastern United States), vaudevillians toured the country playing a well-defined circuit of small houses across America. By 1910, there were twenty-two vaudeville theatres in New York City.

© Mirrorpix/The Everett Collection

Sugar Babies

A vaudeville recreation, *Sugar Babies* was a modern musical revue created by Ralph G. Allen starring two popular entertainers, Mickey Rooney and Ann Miller, and played for 1,208 performances on Broadway. Mickey Rooney performs here with the "Sugar Babies."

Vaudeville spawned many leading comedians, singers, and dancers, including Eva Tanquay, Eddie Cantor, Al Jolson, Bert Williams, George M. Cohan, Bill "Bojangles" Robinson, Will Rogers, Ethel Waters, and the team of George Burns and Gracie Allen. Most of these artists then moved onto the legitimate stage and into film, radio, and later, television.

The decline of vaudeville was brought about by increased ticket prices that proved a hardship for families, nightclubs with songsters and bands that attracted more sophisticated crowds bored with vaudeville's material, and finally, the universal popularity of the new cinema. By the mid-1920s, many vaudeville houses were converted to cinemas, but the symbolic ending of vaudeville is traced to the closing in 1932 of New York's Palace Theatre, the legendary mecca for vaudeville performers. Historians regard this date as the official death of vaudeville as a significant form of entertainment.

***Porgy & Bess* by George and Ira Gershwin**
Directed by Tazewell Thompson for New York City Center Opera, Lincoln Center.

Fred and Adele Astaire established the ascendancy of jazz-based lyricism and included the songs "Fascinating Rhythm" and "Oh, Lady Be Good!" In the 1930s, the Gershwins followed with the satirical musicals *Strike Up the Band* and *Of Thee I Sing*, the first musical book to be awarded the Pulitzer Prize for Drama. The Gershwins' folk opera, *Porgy and Bess*, based on the play *Porgy* by DuBose and Dorothy Heywood in 1935, whose magnificent score includes "Summertime" and "It Ain't Necessarily So" sung by the residents of Catfish Row in Charleston, South Carolina, has proved to be the their most enduring work. The Gershwin Theatre on Broadway was renamed for them in 1983.

The 1927–1928 season was a high point in the history of the Broadway stage—some 250 shows were produced. (Today's average is thirty-seven.) However, events outside the theatre district brought about a decline in productions. The advent of "sound" in films drew audiences and artists to another form of popular entertainment; and the stock market crash of 1929, followed by the Depression years, resulted in a smaller number of productions on Broadway. Moreover, musicals began to reflect the country's growing unemployment, economic despair, and social unrest. Nevertheless, the Second World War interrupted musical theatre experiments in political and social commentary because audiences wanted escapism in story and song.

POST–SECOND WORLD WAR MUSICAL THEATRE

Richard Rodgers and Oscar Hammerstein II's *Oklahoma!*

The unprecedented popularity of *Oklahoma!*, the first musical by the new partnership of Richard Rodgers and Oscar Hammerstein II, affirmed the simple values of an earlier America. Based on the Lynn Riggs play *Green Grow the Lilacs*, the musical pioneered many firsts for Broadway: a book that allowed a murder to take place onstage and a "dream ballet" choreographed by Agnes de Mille, depicting the heroine's troubled dream. Everything about the show was different. There was no opening chorus number.

Oklahoma!
A revival of the musical *Oklahoma!*, directed by Molly Smith for Arena Stage, Washington, D.C.

Lerner and Loewe's *My Fair Lady*
With Julie Andrews as Liza Doolittle and Rex Harrison as Professor Henry Higgins, was created by the musical team of Alan Jay Lerner (book and lyrics) and Frederick Loewe (music), Broadway.

Instead, the lone cowboy, Curly, sings "Oh, What a Beautiful Mornin"; he has come to ask his sweetheart, Laurey, to ride with him in a surrey ("The Surrey with the Fringe on Top") to a social gathering. The villain, a farmhand named Jud Fry, was truly menacing, not just some cardboard cutout of a mustache-twirling villain. At the end, the two men fight over Laurey, and Curly inadvertently kills Jud but is acquitted by a jury of townspeople. The couple, now married, ride off on their honeymoon as the neighbors sing "Oklahoma!"

In 1943, *Oklahoma!* set a new standard for integration of story and song and introduced a dramatic ballet to advance the story line. When it closed after 2,212 performances, it was the longest-running musical in Broadway history.

Rodgers and Hammerstein repeated their success with *Carousel* (1945), with Billy Bigelow and Julie Jordan as the star-crossed lovers; *South Pacific* (1949), taken from James A. Michener's *Tales of the South Pacific*, with Nellie Forbush (Mary Martin, who sings "I'm Gonna Wash That Man Right Outa My Hair") and a rich French planter (Ezio Pinza, who sings "Some Enchanted Evening") as the unlikely couple; and *The King and I* (1951), starring Gertrude Lawrence as the English schoolteacher and Yul Brynner as the King of Siam. The musical is a perennial favorite, including such songs as "I Whistle a Happy Tune," "Getting to Know You," "We Kiss in a Shadow," and "Shall We Dance?"

FOCUS ON PEOPLE IN THEATRE

COMPOSER AND LYRICIST

Richard Rodgers and Oscar Hammerstein II

As a postwar creative team, **Richard Rodgers** (1902–1979) and **Oscar Hammerstein II** (1895–1960) were among the greatest of all Broadway composers and lyricists. Their style consisted of well-integrated songs and book, with songs reflecting the characters' personalities in words and music. At the time they entered into collaboration, both were in need of a creative partner. Lorenz Hart's personal problems had broken up the successful team of Rodgers and Hart, known for playful, lighthearted shows (*Poor Little Ritz Girl*). Hammerstein, with *Show Boat* and *The Desert Song* to his credit, thought he was washed up as an artist as he looked at a string of failures. The team transformed the play *Green Grow the Lilacs* into *Oklahoma!* and the rest is Broadway history.

Rodgers and Hammerstein took liberties with musical comedy traditions. They dispensed with the opening chorus number sung by leggy chorines. Instead, a lone figure singing "Oh, What a Beautiful Mornin'" walked onto an empty stage. They added a sinister villain uncommon to musical comedy, an onstage murder, and a psychological dream sequence of balletic importance.

Composer Richard Rodgers (left) at the piano with lyricist Oscar Hammerstein II.

Oklahoma! was followed by a string of successes: *Carousel*, *South Pacific*, *The King and I*, *Flower Drum Song*, and *The Sound of Music*. The 1965 film version of *The Sound of Music* with Julie Andrews became one of the top-grossing films of all time.

With Hammerstein's death, Rodgers sought other creative partners. He teamed up with Arthur Laurents to adapt *The Time of the Cuckoo* into the musical *Do I Hear a Waltz?* and worked with Martin Charnin and Sheldon Harnick on *Two by Two*. So great was Rodgers's influence on Broadway that the Richard Rodgers Theatre on Forty-sixth Street is named for him.

MUSICAL THEATRE AT MID-CENTURY

Despite the innovations, dark themes, and magical appeal of the Rodgers and Hammerstein musicals, two basic threads of musical theatre remained unchanged at mid-twentieth century. Operetta and musical comedy flourished, and a large number of musical stars became household names: Mary Martin (*South Pacific* and *The Sound of Music*), Alan Alda (*Guys and Dolls*), Rosalind Russell (*Wonderful Town*), Julie Andrews and Rex Harrison (*My Fair Lady*), Zero Mostel (*Fiddler on the Roof*), Ethel Merman (*Gypsy*), Carol Channing (*Hello, Dolly!*), Judy Holliday (*Bells Are Ringing*), Gwen Verdon (*Pajama Game*), Joel Grey (*Cabaret*), and Carol Lawrence (*West Side Story*).

The stars were matched by the new teams of writers and composers that shaped the musical stage: Alan Jay Lerner and Frederick Loewe, Betty Comden and Adolph Green with Leonard Bernstein, Richard Adler and Jerry Ross, John Kander and Fred Ebb, Arthur Laurents, Stephen Sondheim and Jule Styne, Sheldon Harnick and Jerry Bock, Abe Burrows and Frank Loesser, Leonard Bernstein and Stephen Sondheim. They varied traditional formulas by exploring new settings and subjects untried on the

FOCUS ON PEOPLE IN THEATRE

CHOREOGRAPHER

Agnes de Mille

Agnes de Mille (1905–1993), a noted modern dancer and influential choreographer, had her greatest successes in musical theatre, and, with the Rodgers and Hammerstein team, worked to stretch the conventions of musical comedy and operetta. Born into a theatrical family (her father, William C. de Mille, was a playwright; and her uncle, Cecil B. DeMille, the noted film director and producer), she studied dance in London with Anthony Tudor and returned to New York to dance and choreograph for several seasons. Her inspired choreography in *Oklahoma!* popularized modern ballet styles in musical theatre and showed how ballet could further and deepen the story.

De Mille's choreography was also seen in *One Touch of Venus, Carousel, Brigadoon, Gentlemen Prefer Blondes,* and *Paint Your Wagon*; at the American Ballet Theatre; and at the Heritage Dance Theatre, which she founded in 1973. She was associated with other great Broadway choreographers, including Jerome Robbins and Michael Kidd. Of the three she wrote, "To the classic base we have accordingly added colloquialism. We have come down to earth; we have put our feet on the ground."[3]

© The Everett Collection

Photofest

Choreography created by Agnes de Mille for the original *Oklahoma!*

West Side Story
Jerome Robbins filming *West Side Story* in the streets of New York City. Music and lyrics by Leonard Bernstein and Stephen Sondheim and choreographed by Jerome Robbins.

musical stage. *Gypsy* was based on the life of stripper Gypsy Rose Lee; *Fiorello!* followed the checkered career of New York mayor Fiorello La Guardia; *How to Succeed in Business Without Really Trying* satirized corporate infighting; *The Pajama Game* looked at management-labor strife in a pajama factory; *Guys and Dolls* was about gamblers and their perennial girlfriends. Writers turned to adaptations of older plays, novels, and stories to inject new vibrancy onto musical stages: George Bernard Shaw's *Pygmalion* became *My Fair Lady*; Cervantes' novel, *Don Quixote*, became *Man of La Mancha*; Damon Runyon's short stories about raffish gamblers became *Guys and Dolls*; Christopher Isherwood's stories about Berlin in the thirties became *Cabaret*; and the 400-year-old legend of star-crossed lovers in Shakespeare's *Romeo and Juliet* became *West Side Story*.

Bernstein and Sondheim's *West Side Story*

This ambitious work of creators Leonard Bernstein, Arthur Laurents, Stephen Sondheim, and Jerome Robbins combined the many successful threads of established musical comedy in the service of a book musical about gang warfare in the streets of New York City. Instead of the Capulets and Montagues, we have the Sharks and the Jets, rival street gangs, fighting for supremacy among the tenements and bridges of Manhattan's lower West side. To re-create a modern-day *Romeo and Juliet*, the creators of *West Side Story* did not gloss over urban violence that draws young men and women into its streets and brutally kills them in senseless acts. Bernstein's music captured the shrill beat of life in the streets, and Robbins's energetic choreography re-created the wildness and ecstasy of youthful passions.

Book musicals, handsomely produced with star performers, have dominated the Broadway theatre since the days of *Annie Get Your Gun* with Ethel Merman, *My Fair*

Lady with Julie Andrews, and *Fiddler on the Roof* with Zero Mostel. Today, book musicals and their stars remain the most popular entertainments for audiences who crowd into theatres to see *Hairspray* (with Harvey Fierstein), *Wicked* (with Kristin Chenoweth), and *The Book of Mormon* (with Josh Gad and Andrew Rannells).

SIXTIES ALTERNATIVES TO BROADWAY MUSICALS

The antiwar defiance of the Vietnam era brought new sounds onto musical stages—rock—and new subjects. The alternative theatre pieces (alternatives to the established musicals of Rodgers and Hammerstein, for example) were created Off Broadway and Off Off Broadway in modest, often improvised spaces. Megan Terry's *Viet Rock* and experimental musicals by composer-lyricist-librettist Al Carmines, who collaborated with María Irene Fornés on *Promenade,* addressed in musical terms an unpopular war and found new audiences made up of antiwar protesters, students, and aging radicals.

Nevertheless, Broadway producers with an eye to new audiences took note of two slightly traditional Off Broadway shows—*The Fantasticks* and *Hair.*

MacDermott, Ragni, and Rado's *Hair*

The pop-rock lyricism of *Hair* with its hippie protesters, four-letter words (*love* included), frontal nudity, and free-flowing references to homosexuality, miscegenation, and antipatriotism was a revelation to Broadway's audiences. Robin Wagner's junk-art setting (a blank stage replete with broken-down truck, papier-mâché Santa Claus, jukebox, and neon signs) and Nancy Potts's tattered and colorful costumes matched the irreverence of Tom O'Horgan's staging. Audiences flocked to see *Hair* whose essential message was tolerance and love, expressed in such songs as "Aquarius" and "Good Morning, Starshine."

© Redux

Hair
A revival of the "tribal" love-rock musical with original book and lyrics by Gerome Ragni and James Rado and music by Galt MacDermot. Directed by Diane Paulus, Broadway.

FOCUS ON THEATRE

Bob Fosse's *Chicago*

With original direction and choreography by Bob Fosse, *Chicago* has had several Broadway incarnations along with a 2002 film starring Catherine Zeta-Jones and Renée Zellweger. The tale of murder, greed, corruption, violence, exploitation, adultery, and treachery in 1920s Chicago is also a stylish concept musical displaying a series of con games and vaudeville turns. The leggy showgirls, called Roxie Hart and Velma Kelly, sing and dance through a pastiche of songs by John Kander and Fred Ebb, including "Razzle, Dazzle" and "Cell Block Tango."

Conceived in the minimalist style of vaudeville, the focus is on the performers. The orchestra, seated center stage on a bandstand, allows space for Fosse's finger-snapping choreography, which begins with slow, silky routines building into a burst of show-stopping energy. *Chicago* is all about seduction and performing, and audiences are taken in by the razzle-dazzle of show business.

Chicago
The revival with Bebe Neuwirth as Velma Kelly. Choreography by Ann Reinking in the style of Bob Fosse, Broadway.

Bob Fosse (1927–1987) choreographed and directed many of Broadway's finest musicals: *How to Succeed in Business Without Really Trying*, *Sweet Charity*, and *Pippin*, but *Chicago* has become his most enduring legacy.

The alternative musicals of the sixties demonstrated anew that elaborate spectacles, sizable orchestras, and large choruses were not necessary components of the musical stage. Modest musicals (*The Fantasticks*, for example), with their authentic voices and new musical sounds, paved the way for the concept musicals of Stephen Sondheim, the minimalist improvisations of Michael Bennett's *A Chorus Line*, the sinuous jazz movements of Bob Fosse's *Chicago*, and the electric rock-Motown-reggae-amplified sounds of Jonathan Larson's *Rent*.

NEW DIRECTIONS

The Concept Musicals

Stephen Sondheim's *Company* and *Follies*

Stephen Sondheim popularized the "concept musical" loosely tied around a theme without elements of traditional storytelling. In 1970, *Company*, with music and lyrics by Stephen Sondheim, was essentially plotless (a birthday party for an emotionally detached bachelor surrounded by his married friends), and, in a series of vignettes and songs, reveals the flaws in their marriages along with the emptiness of their urban social world. *Company* pointed the way for other Broadway musicals to take up issues of contemporary urban life with wit and compassion in intricate rhythms and melodies.

FOCUS ON PEOPLE IN THEATRE

COMPOSER-LYRICIST

Stephen Sondheim

© Getty Images

Stephen Sondheim (b. 1930) came to the attention of the musical world with lyrics for *West Side Story* and *Gypsy*. *A Funny Thing Happened on the Way to the Forum* in 1962 was his first opportunity to write music *and* lyrics for a Broadway show. He turned to writing a series of stylish scores with intricate rhythms and melodies that became the Sondheim trademark.

Company, Follies, A Little Night Music, Pacific Overtures, Sweeney Todd, Merrily We Roll Along, Sunday in the Park with George, Into the Woods, Assassins, and *Passion* have distinguished Sondheim as the most influential composer-lyricist in the musical theatre since the early seventies. Moreover, the eclecticism of his themes is startling. *Pacific Overtures* employed the conventions of Kabuki theatre and an all-Asian cast to tell of the opening of Japan to the West; *Sweeney Todd* adapted Victorian melodrama to reveal the tormented soul of the "demon barber of Fleet Street"; *Sunday in the Park with George* brought to life the works of French painter Georges Seurat; and *Into the Woods* explored the darker Freudian aspects of classic fairy tales.

Called "a brilliant, if brittle look at the road not taken,"[4] *Follies* introduces a bittersweet reunion of former Follies performers on the stage of the Weismann Theatre under demolition. Designed by Boris Aronson, the scenes take place during the reunion party in the present where memory-figures of their younger selves appear to jolt recollections. The final sequence takes place in "Loveland," a rose-colored fantasyland of unrealized loves, dreams, and desires.

© Joan Marcus

Follies
The 2011 Broadway revival of *Follies*, featuring "Loveland." With music and lyrics by Stephen Sondheim and book by James Goldman.

Michael Bennett's *A Chorus Line*

Martha Swope/The New York Public Library

A Chorus Line

Conceived, choreographed, and directed by Michael Bennett, with costumes by Theoni V. Aldredge, Broadway.

Director-choreographer Michael Bennett added another kind of concept musical to Broadway history five years later. He conceived, choreographed, and directed the innovative musical *A Chorus Line*—a dance audition for a Broadway show, with music by Marvin Hamlisch.

Seventeen hopeful dancers have survived the first cut for the chorus line in a Broadway musical and are lined up in the "rehearsal hall" before the director. The "gypsies" of a chorus line, as Broadway show dancers are called, introduce themselves one by one, revealing their hunger for the job, their sex lives, and their failures with schools and parents. Donna McKechnie, the chorine who walked out on a relationship with the director but has returned to try to win a way back into the chorus line; Priscilla Lopez is the histrionic dropout; and Robert LuPone is the uptight director. One by one, the director asks a dancer to step out of the line and talk about personal things: the girl who flunked Stanislavski motivation in a high school acting class, the boy who discovered he was homosexual, and the girl who wanted to be a ballerina. Once chosen, they dance Michael Bennett's inspired choreography in two numbers: the mirror dance for Donna McKechnie and the Busby Berkeley-inspired finale in golden costumes by Theoni V. Aldredge. Called an "intimate big musical," *A Chorus Line*, a success with Off Broadway audiences, moved to Broadway's Shubert Theatre, where it set a record 6,137 performances.[5]

Rock Opera—Jonathan Larson's *Rent*

© Joan Marcus

Rent

With music, book, and lyrics by Jonathan Larson, *Rent* starred Adam Pascal and Daphne Rubin-Vega in the original cast. Directed by Michael Greif, Broadway.

Jonathan Larson's landmark rock opera, based on Puccini's nineteenth-century opera *La Bohème*, features a marginal band of artists living under the shadow of death by AIDS in Manhattan's East Village. Like *Hair*, *Rent* has a cast of genial, disheveled musicians, originally helmed by Adam Pascal and Daphne Rubin-Vega. They give voice to their generation's confusion and anarchic pleasure-seeking while defying the evidence of mortality that lingers over Mimi Marquez (Daphne Rubin-Vega). Unlike Puccini's tubercular heroine, Larson's Mimi is HIV-positive; others of the group also

FOCUS ON THEATRE

Recent American Choreographers-Directors

Following in the notable footsteps of Jerome Robbins and Bob Fosse, recent choreographer-directors continue to shape the American theatre with multifaceted approaches to staging.

Susan Stroman, an innovative choreographer, made her entrance as a director-choreographer with *Contact*, an original dance drama that she cocreated for Lincoln Center Theatre. She has choreographed revivals of traditional musicals, *Oklahoma!* and *The Music Man*. Taking over the staging and choreography of *The Producers* from her late husband, director Michael Ockrent, she received Tony Awards for Best Direction and Best Choreography; she followed with *Crazy for You*, *The Scottsboro Boys*, and *Young Frankenstein*.

Casey Nicholaw started out as a performer and understudy in *Crazy for You*, *Victor/Victoria*, and *Saturday Night Fever*, and began his career as a choreographer with *Spamalot*. He became a choreographer-director with *The Drowsy Chaperone* for which he won Tony Awards in both categories. He has continued these dual roles with *The Book of Mormon* for which he won Tony Awards for Best Direction of a Musical and Best Choreography.

carry the virus and are candidates for death. Altogether, they sing the show's credo: "Seize the day."

Larson, who died at age thirty-five of an aortic aneurysm just weeks before *Rent* opened, captured in musical terms the feelings of fear and defiance of young people living with the inevitability of death.

BRITISH MEGAMUSICALS

In the first half of the twentieth century, London's stages featured, with few exceptions, American musicals, until the recent megamusicals of Cameron MacIntosh and Andrew Lloyd Webber. During the Second World War, theatres shut down in the commercial district, called the West End, in anticipation of German bombing sorties but opened soon after because of a high demand for live entertainment. During the war years, operetta-style revivals, satirical musicals by Ivor Novello and Noël Coward, and a few restaged American musicals held British musical theatre in a time-warp. Postwar American imports (*Carousel; South Pacific; Kiss Me, Kate*) flooded West End theatres because British producers preferred proven Broadway shows to the financial risks of producing unknown British ones. However, this situation was soon to change.

In the last quarter of the twentieth century, two influential British producers, Cameron Mackintosh and composer Andrew Lloyd Webber, brought "larger-than-life" musicals to London's West End and to Broadway: *Cats*, *The Phantom of the Opera*, *Les Misérables*, and *Miss Saigon*. Called *megamusicals* (a term that described the phenomenon of sung-through musicals in which set design, choreography, and special effects were as important as the music) the shows dazzled with furry junkyard creatures (*Cats*), a falling chandelier (*The Phantom of the Opera*), the barricade (*Les Misérables*), and the helicopter (*Miss Saigon*). The theatricality of the aural and visual elements combined with stories about social injustice, human suffering, and redemption—plus the sumptuous music—appealed to audiences of all ages.

Cameron Mackintosh's *Miss Saigon*

Set in the final year of the Vietnam War, *Miss Saigon* conveyed a number of sociopolitical messages about the terrible consequences of war on populations in faraway countries. The photographic images of children in wartime and the onstage helicopter re-creating the American military's final exit from the war-torn country, accompanied by sounds of rotors beating in the air and thundering orchestrations, reinforced the musical's antiwar and humanitarian messages.

Miss Saigon had the potential to be perceived as anti-American, but the spectacle of the sung-through musical, lavish musical sounds, and the love story that echoed with the star-crossed lovers of *Romeo and Juliet* overwhelmed the political content. The musical, loosely adapted from Puccini's opera *Madama Butterfly* by the creative team for *Les Misérables,* revisited a love story enlarged by the geopolitics of the late twentieth century and by the fusion of drama and music in the larger-than-life megamusical.

With echoes of the East-meets-West motifs of Rodgers and Hammerstein's *South Pacific* and *The King and I, Miss Saigon*, named for the Vietnamese girl who is reduced to working as a prostitute in Saigon in the final days of the war, looked squarely into the face of America's abandonment of ideals and, ultimately, Vietnam's people. The story of Kim and Chris was enlarged by the geopolitics of the late twentieth century and by the fusion of drama and music in the larger-than-life style of the megamusical.

In the new millennium, there is no longer a one-directional flow of creativity, artistry, and diversity between the British and the American musical theatre. The rich tradition of English-language theatre continues to be seen in the work of creative artists on both sides of the Atlantic who combine music, words, dance, and other theatrical elements into a greatly loved musical genre that entertains and enchants audiences throughout the world.

Manuel Harlan Photography

Matilda: The Musical Adapted from Roald Dahl's short story and imported from London, *Matilda: The Musical,* brings to Broadway the story of a child prodigy unwanted by her odious parents who prevails over adversity at home and school.

FOCUS ON THEATRE

Musical Theatre Creators: Cameron Mackintosh and Andrew Lloyd Webber

© Camera Press/Redux

Photofest

Cats
Cameron Mackintosh produced the long-running Andrew Lloyd Webber musical on Broadway.

The creative forces behind the late twentieth-century musical genre, called the megamusical, are British producer Cameron Mackintosh and composer-producer Andrew Lloyd Webber.

Born in 1946 in Enfield, North London, **Cameron Mackintosh** is a leading producer in the commercial theatre on both sides of the Atlantic—on London's West End and on Broadway. His name is synonymous with such award-winning musicals as *Cats, Les Misérables, The Phantom of the Opera, Miss Saigon, Whistle Down the Wind, The Witches of Eastwick,* and the London revival of *Oklahoma!* Knighted in 1996 for "services to the British theatre," Mackintosh owns seven theatres in London's West End.

The Everett Collection

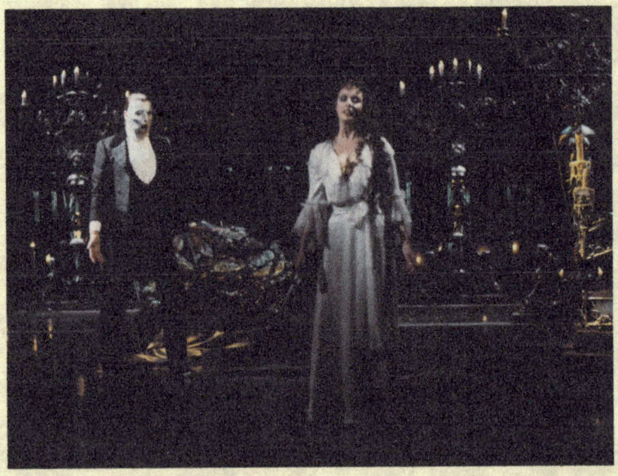

© Topfoto/The Image Works

The Phantom of the Opera
Composed by Andrew Lloyd Webber, with Michael Crawford and Sarah Brightman, directed by Harold Prince, Broadway.

Born in 1948, **Andrew Lloyd Webber** began composing at the age of seventeen. At one time he had four musicals playing simultaneously on London's West End: *Cats, Starlight Express, The Phantom of the Opera,* and *Whistle Down the Wind.* Webber's musicals deal by and large with religious/historical figures and healing and redemption and include *Joseph and the Amazing Technicolor Dreamcoat, Jesus Christ Superstar, Evita, Sunset Boulevard, Aspects of Love,* and *The Beautiful Game.*

BROADWAY'S AUDIENCES

Today's audiences are all ages. With individual theatre tickets ranging from $85 to more than $400, the typical Broadway audience in the new millennium is a mix of well-to-do baby boomers, tourists, and students with discount tickets. As counterweight to the large, expensive musicals, small-scale musicals with reduced costs and serious social themes of a bipolar parent (*Next to Normal*), Spanish-speaking urban dreamers (*In the Heights*), and folk-rock resignation to life's disappointments (*Once*) are attracting audiences interested in recognizable people engaged in familiar struggles.

The blocks surrounding Times Square are the heart of New York's theatre district, where thousands converge for matinee and evening performances, including families, couples, out-of-towners, and actors hurrying to their respective stage doors. Patrons no longer necessarily wait in line at box offices to buy tickets that are readily available through computerized ticket sales (Telecharge and Ticketron sell tickets by telephone or the Internet with a surcharge for the service) and at the TKTS booth in Broadway's Duffy Square, where discounted tickets are sold on the day of performance (see page 290). Available shows are placed on a billboard at the front of the TKTS booth, and, in all kinds of weather, lines form around the square several hours before performances.

According to one report, the TKTS booth, operated by the Theatre Development Fund, sells about 25 million theatre seats annually for both Broadway and Off Broadway shows, as well as seats for dance and music performances. Moreover, Internet discount tickets are available on a variety of websites maintained by theatre owners, industry groups, and corporate producers to almost all events.

Once
Inspired by an Irish film, *Once*, with book by Enda Walsh and music and lyrics by Glen Hansard and Marketa Irglova, is a modest musical by Broadway standards. The ensemble functions as the show's band and the cast of characters to tell a familiar story of longing and heartache, Broadway.

The crowds crisscrossing Times Square come from almost every nationality and ethnic background, every age, and every walk of life. America's melting-pot reputation is expressed in the energy, exuberance, and chatter of Broadway's audiences and in the musicals that fill the majority of theatres in the famous theatrical district.

© Joan Marcus

The Lion King
With music and lyrics by Elton John and Tim Rice and others, costumes by Julie Taymor, masks and puppets by Julie Taymor and Michael Curry. Directed by Julie Taymor, Broadway.

TRANSITION

The final chapter adds the perspective of the theatre critic to our understanding of "seeing" theatre. Called "Viewpoints," this concluding chapter deals with theatre criticism—the critic's role, perspective, and vocabulary—and the ways in which critical perspectives often shape our enjoyment of productions and performances. Theatre criticism adds another dimension to our discovery of theatre, its artists, forms, and styles.

Theatre: A Way of Seeing Online

Visit the CourseMate for Theatre: A Way of Seeing 7th Edition for quick access to the digital study resources that accompany this chapter, including links to the websites listed below, Theatre Workshop, digital glossary, a chapter quiz and more.

Websites

The *Theatre: A Way of Seeing* CourseMate includes links for all the websites described below. Simply select "Web links" from the Chapter Resources for Chapter 14, and click on the link that interests you. You'll be taken directly to the site described.

Musicals101.com
The cyber encyclopedia of musical theatre, TV, and film, featuring links to the history of musicals and particular productions, reviews and essays, and a how-to guide for staging your own musical.

National Alliance for Musical Theatre
The only national service organization dedicated to musical theatre. Its mission is to nurture the creation, development, production, presentation, and recognition of new musicals and classics; provide a forum for sharing resources and information about professional musical theatre; and advocate for the imagination, diversity, and joy unique to musical theatre.

Blackface Minstrelsy
A history of minstrel shows as reflected by Mark Twain's *Huck Finn,* including two dialogues typical of minstrel shows during the nineteenth century and links to notices and ads for minstrel shows.

Ragtime History
A history of ragtime, plus links to related sites.

Musical Comedy Is Born
An article at TheatreHistory.com that examines the early development of American musical comedy, specifically the contributions of George M. Cohan.

Rodgers and Hammerstein
A Time magazine profile of composer Richard Rodgers and librettist Oscar Hammerstein II.

Bob Fosse
Yahoo! biography of Bob Fosse, including dozens of links to information about his work and associates.

Sondheim.com
A website of all things Sondheim, including links to FAQs, chats, and reviews. Be sure to click on the "Features" link.

Broadway Theatre
Websites for up-to-date information on Broadway musicals performed in New York City, including shows, cast lists, reviews, and ticket prices.

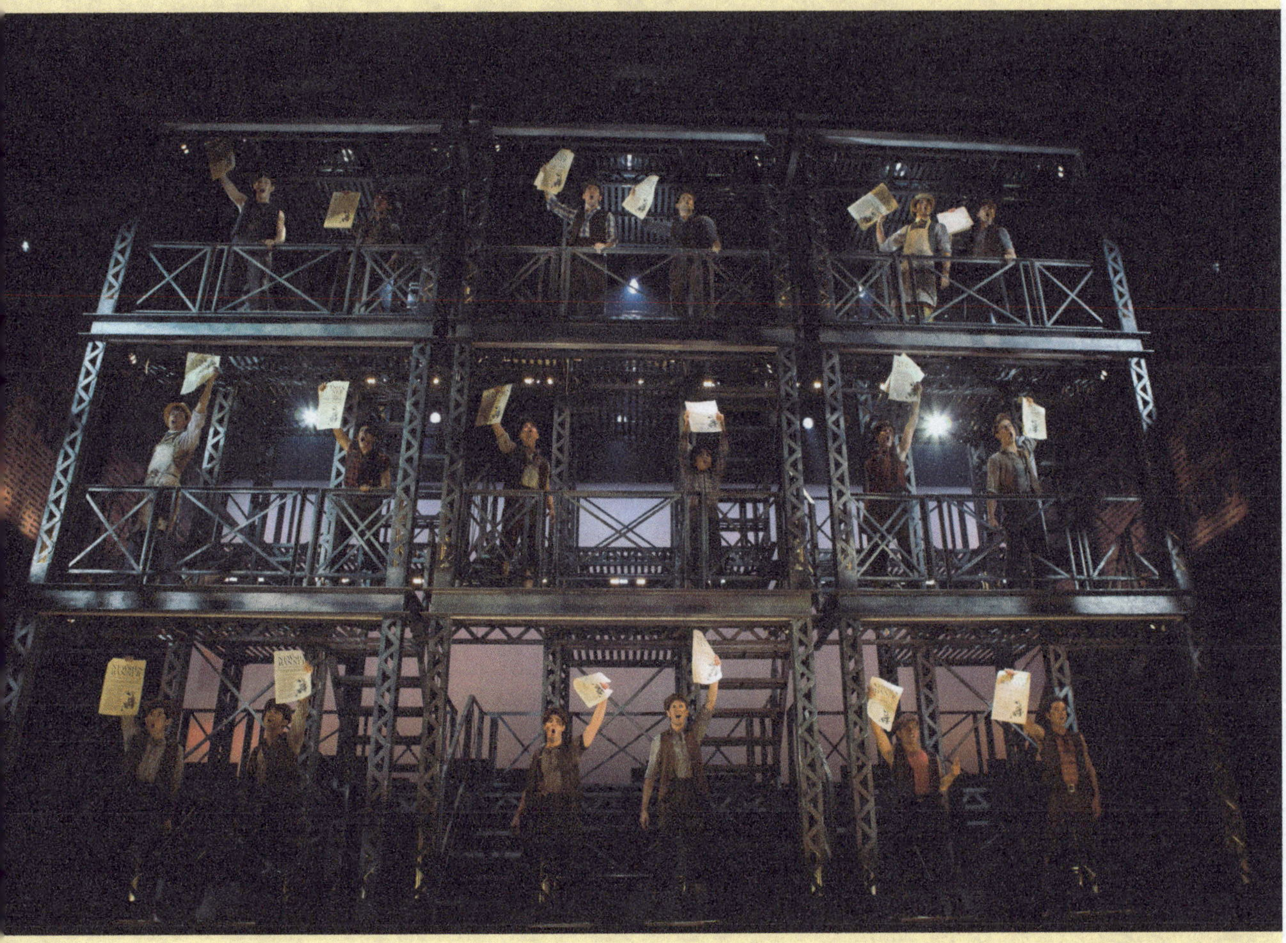

T. Charles Erickson

15

VIEWPOINTS

"A critic; nay, a night-watch constable."

— WILLIAM SHAKESPEARE, *LOVE'S LABOUR'S LOST*

CRITICISM

There are two kinds of criticism for the theatre. *Drama criticism* comments on the written text from a literary and cultural-historical-theoretical perspective. *Theatre criticism* gives us a professional assessment of what we see onstage. Theatre criticism, or theatre reviewing, most often deals with plays-in-performance.

Present-day theatre criticism found in newspapers, magazines, online chat forums, eblasts, blogs, and think-tanks reflects the fact that we live in a consumer-oriented society. The business of professional reviewers writing for the *New York Times*, the *Los Angeles Times*, the *Chicago Tribune*, the *Washington Post*, *Variety*, and online publications is to appraise productions found on Broadway, Off Broadway, and in civic and regional theatres. Other reviewers who work on the staffs of local newspapers in cities and towns throughout the country also cover college, community, and touring productions.

Theatre criticism is more than appraisal. It is also an economic force (although many critics deny this fact). In the commercial theatre, theatre critics often determine whether a play will continue for months or close after opening night. It is a fact that the critic for the *New York Times* has the power to close a Broadway play or keep it running for months. It is,

PREVIEW

Critics often add fresh dimensions to our awareness and appreciation of theatre. They acquaint readers and audiences with both good and bad productions. At best, they hope to connect the truly good work with audiences and to preserve it for future generations.

Newspaper "boys" selling their newspapers in *Newsies: The Musical,* adapted from the 1992 Disney film. The newsboys go on strike against a newspaper magnate, thus limiting the dissemination of newspapers to buyers. Originated by the Papermill Playhouse, Millburn, New Jersey, and restaged for Broadway.

therefore, important to consider how the critic's viewpoint affects the quality of our national theatre and the plays that we see. It is also interesting to reflect on our own roles as critics in which we are cast by simply attending a show.

SEEING THEATRE

Audience as Critic

A well-performed and meaningful play remains in our thoughts and emotions long after the curtain falls. After the curtain comes down and the applause is over, we often go with friends to our favorite restaurant or diner or chat with one another online to talk about the production we have just seen. It's hard to shut our minds to a powerful performance of a play, whether we've just experienced Blanche DuBois' dependence on "the kindness of strangers" or the Orgon family's triumphant return to a peaceful house after their ordeal with Tartuffe. It's also difficult to rid our memories of those abiding questions raised by great plays. Is the world a stage? What's in a name? Must "attention be paid" to the Willy Lomans of the world? Can we depend on the kindness of strangers? And so on.

We also talk about the production—about the acting, the directing, the costumes, scenery, lighting, and sound effects. These conversations generally bring us to questions about the truthfulness of the acting. Were we aware of the actors "playing" their parts, or did they convince us that they were the Loman family? Were the costumes appropriate, or did Blanche's Mardi Gras gown seem new rather than old and worn? Were the sound effects too loud, calling unnecessary attention to themselves as effects?

After the curtain call and applause for the actors, we pick up our playbills, leave the theatre, and discuss the performance with friends. In other words, we become critics.

The Curtain Call
For *The Book of Mormon*, Broadway.

All audiences are critics by virtue of seeing a play performed and expressing opinions. We may like the play and not the performance; or like the performance and not the play; or like neither or both. We may even praise certain strong scenes or single out powerful performances by certain actors. It is generally agreed that audiences bring at least four viewpoints to their theatregoing experience: We relate to a play's human significance, its social significance, its artistic qualities, and its entertainment value, but not necessarily in any particular order.

Courtesy Utah Shakespeare Festival

Utah Shakespearean Festival
Audiences seated before the outdoor festival stage in Cedar City, Utah.

Audience Viewpoints—Human Significance, Social Significance, Aesthetic Significance, and Entertainment

Human Significance

Playwrights and other theatre artists connect audiences with a common humanity. Great plays confront us with life's verities, conveying the hope, courage, despair, compassion, violence, love, hate, exploitation, and generosity experienced by all humankind. They show us ways of fulfilling ourselves in relationships; they also show us the possibility of losing our families and property through accidents or catastrophes of war. The best plays explore what it means to be human beings in special circumstances. These circumstances can be bizarre, such as the witches' fortuitous appearances before Macbeth, or recognizable, such as an unwanted relative appearing at a New Orleans multiple dwelling. Theatre is an extraordinary medium that links us as audiences with actors as characters. They become reflections of ourselves, or what potentially could be ourselves. Theatre's best achievements lead us to discoveries and reflections about our own personalities, circumstances, desires, choices, and anxieties.

> **"I have looked at some of my earlier stuff and said, 'I can't believe how harsh this was, and how unforgiving it was, and how I was so concerned with artistic principles that I forgot that there was any kind of humanity involved.'"[1]**
>
> —Frank Rich, *former theatre critic for the New York Times and current Writer-at-large for New York Magazine.*

Social Significance

Of all the arts, theatre has an inherent relationship to society; by definition, an audience is an assembled group of spectators, a social unit. We become part of a community as we experience theatre. Communities vote, express themselves at town council meetings, and respond to local, national, and international events. So, too, audiences share collectively in the social meanings of the play's world and relate them to the people and world surrounding them.

FOCUS ON THEATRE

Arthur Miller's *Death of a Salesman*

Linda Loman reprimands her sons (and the world) for not paying attention to the worthiness of an average man such as Willy Loman. Arthur Miller's celebrated play *Death of a Salesman* calls attention to the *human significance* of average people in this world.

LINDA LOMAN: I don't say he's a great man. Willy Loman never made a lot of money; his name was never in the paper; he's not the finest character that ever lived. But he's a human being, and a terrible thing is happening to him. So attention must be paid. He's not to be allowed to fall into his grave like an old dog. *Attention*, attention, must be finally paid to such a person.[2]

©Charles Sykes/AP Images

Linda Emond

Miller's *Death of a Salesman*
Actress Linda Emond as Linda Loman in a revival of Arthur Miller's *Death of a Salesman*. Directed by Mike Nichols with Philip Seymour Hoffman and Linda Emond as Willy and Linda Loman, the 2012 revival was reviewed by *New York Times* theatre critic Ben Brantley who wrote: "The curtain rises, and the floodgates open. How could it be otherwise? Because suddenly it's all there before you: that set, that music and, above all, that immortal silhouette—the shadowed figure of a stooped man with sample cases, heavy enough to contain a lifetime's disappointments."[3]

Since the days of the classical Greek theatre, the playing space has served as an arena wherein to discuss social and political issues, popular and unpopular. Euripides and Aristophanes were often scorned because of their unpopular pacifist beliefs in a time of great nationalistic fervor among Athenians. The modern theatre likewise deals with controversial issues. The theatre section of any Sunday edition of the *New York Times* lists plays that deal with almost every imaginable social issue: drug addiction, abortion, racism, gay rights, sports scandals, investment fraud, family strife, discrimination, financial hardship, incest, terminal disease, mental illness, capital punishment, political chicanery, and so on. The best plays present social issues as fuel for thought, not as propaganda.

Playwrights focus our attention, compassion, and outrage on social injustices, political corruption, and human evil. *Tartuffe* celebrates triumph over chicanery and injustice, and *Macbeth* deplores subversion and murder by evil forces and personal ambition. The aim of great playwriting is to give us new perspectives, to expand our consciousness, on old and new social issues and human behaviors.

Aesthetic Significance

Each of us has aesthetic standards. We know what we like and what we don't like. We have seen a lot of television shows and many films. As we attend more and more plays, we quickly come to recognize honesty in acting and writing. We see the gimmicks for what they are—tools for manipulating our emotions. We sense the miscasting and the awkward moments.

There is no reliable checklist for what makes one performance more effective, provocative, or moving than another, but there are a number of questions we can ask

FOCUS ON THEATRE

Tony Kushner's *Angels in America, Part Two: Perestroika*

At the end of Part One of *Angels in America: A Gay Fantasia on National Themes,* titled *Millennium Approaches,* the central figure, Prior Walter, is visited by an angel with spreading silver wings in a shower of unearthly light and sounds of triumphal music. The Angel announces that "The Great Work Begins." At the close of Part Two, Prior, seated before New York City's Bethesda Fountain in Central Park with its stone angel commemorating the Union navy's war dead rising above him, delivers Kushner's "coda" on the world's ills and its salvation.

PRIOR: This disease will be the end of many of us, but not nearly all, and the dead will be commemorated and will struggle on with the living, and we are not going away. We don't die secret deaths anymore. The world only spins forward. We will be citizens. The time has come.

Bye now.
You are fabulous creatures, each and every one.
And I bless you: *More Life.*
The Great Work Begins.[4]

© Joan Marcus

Kushner's *Angels in America: A Gay Fantasia on National Themes*
With Ellen McLaughlin as the Angel and Stephen Spinella as Prior Walter in *Part Two: Perestroika,* directed by George C. Wolfe, Broadway.

ourselves about any play or performance. Does the play, as performed, excite or surprise us? Does it barely meet our expectations, or worse? Does it stimulate our thoughts and emotions? Are the actors convincing? Or are they more than just convincing—are they mesmerizing? Does the performance seem wooden or lively? Does what we are seeing seem in any way original? Are we caught up in the characters' lives, or are we simply looking at our watches and waiting for the play to end?

As we see more and more theatre, we develop a more sophisticated awareness of sights, words, characters, actions, actors, sounds, and colors. We appreciate balance and harmony—beginnings, middles, and ends. We admire situations that defy our expectations, amuse, and speak to our sense of the bizarre and ridiculous in human behavior. We also appreciate stage performances that exceed our expectations—that reveal issues and viewpoints that we did not know existed, and present them in theatrical ways we did not anticipate.

Entertainment

Great theatre is always amusing or diverting in one or more ways. Although we think of theatre as entertaining often because of the foolish behavior, the clever lines, the laughable gags, and the pratfalls in comedy and farce; even tragedy jolts our emotions and moves us in unusual ways. Aristotle called the tragic way *catharsis*, or the

© Sara Krulwich/The New York Times/Redux

Albee's *Who's Afraid of Virginia Woolf?* In the Steppenwolf Theatre Company's revival with (left to right) Amy Morton as Martha, Tracy Letts as George, Madison Dirks as Nick, and Carrie Coon as Honey, Chicago and Broadway.

cleansing of the emotions by exciting pity and fear. In addition, tragedy has its share of just plain thrills. *Hamlet* and *Macbeth* offer ghosts, witches, murders, and duels, but they also please us at a deeper level. By witnessing the trials and hearing the poetic insights of the heroes, we are liberated from despair over the senselessness of human deeds.

Comedy and farce openly entertain us with romance, misunderstandings, wit, and nonsense while assuring us that wishes can be fulfilled (and even if our wishes cannot, farce assures us that it is safe to wish for the unheard of, or for the socially unacceptable). Comedy and farce persuade us that society is really not so bad after all. In effect, they affirm that society will survive humanity's bungling.

In short, theatre is a dependable source of pleasure, laughter, tears, and companionship in an uncertain world. It is a place where we meet friends and join with them (and also strangers) in a collective experience: We laugh together, we cry together, and we applaud together. Theatre entertains by involving us with friends and strangers in a social situation with others onstage and seated around us in the auditorium.

THE PROFESSIONAL CRITIC

THE CRITIC'S JOB

The writing of criticism about theatrical performance takes place after the fact. After the curtain comes down on the opening-night performance, critics begin their formal work—writing the review for publication in the next morning's newspaper or preparing their sound bites for late-night television or quickly disseminating blogs on the

FOCUS ON THEATRE

Tennessee Williams's *The Glass Menagerie*

In 1945, Laurette Taylor stunned audiences with her performance as Amanda Wingfield in Tennessee Williams' first major success (see page 346). The Wingfield family, isolated in their St. Louis apartment, captures Williams's understanding of the "beauty and meaning in the confusion of living." Clinging to her illusions of a more genteel life in the Mississippi Delta, the mother, Amanda Wingfield, incarnates pretensions, pride, disappointment, and desperation. Williams's human "menagerie" displays the oppressed, the fragile, the needful, and the desperate.

Amanda, trying to make a little money selling magazine subscriptions, telephones one of her former subscribers:

AMANDA: [*on the telephone trying to sell magazine subscriptions*] Ida Scott? This is Amanda Wingfield! We *missed* you at the D.A.R. last Monday! I said to myself: She's probably suffering with that sinus condition! How is that sinus condition? Horrors! Heaven have mercy!—You're a Christian martyr, yes, that's what you are, a Christian martyr!

Well, I just now happened to notice that your subscription to the *Companion's* about to expire! Yes, it expires with the next issue, honey!—just when that wonderful new serial by Bessie Mae Hopper is getting off to such an exciting start. Oh, honey, it's something that you can't miss! You remember how *Gone with the Wind* took everybody by storm? You simply couldn't go out if you hadn't read it. All everybody *talked* was Scarlett O'Hara. Well, this is a book that critics already compare to *Gone with the Wind*. It's the *Gone with the Wind* of the post-World-War generation!—What?—Burning?—Oh, honey, don't let them burn, go take a look in the oven and I'll hold the wire! Heavens—I think she's hung up![5]

© T. Charles Erickson

The Glass Menagerie

Judith Ivey as Amanda Wingfield with Keira Keeley as Laura Wingfield in the Long Wharf Theatre production of Tennessee Williams's play, New Haven, CT, and New York City.

Internet. These are the reviews read by producers, managers, or directors during opening-night parties in the Broadway district.

The critic's education, background, experience in the theatre, and analytical skills make it possible for him or her to produce reviews in a short time span for television and the Internet, or to write any number of paragraphs for a newspaper deadline. Those critics writing for weekly or monthly magazines have more leisure and usually write longer reviews. In all instances, the professional critic has deadlines and a specific number of words allotted for the review.

Critic Stanley Kauffmann, formerly of the *New Republic*, gives an interesting viewpoint on the critic's work:

> *[The critic's] Criticism is a body of work obviously related to but still distinct from what the theatre does . . . but no more closely connected than is political science to the current elections. The critic learns that, on the one hand, there is the theatre, with good and bad productions . . . the theatre is the critic's subject, and he ought to be good about its good and bad plays.*[6]

Frequently, artists, producers, and managers resent the critic's power to sit in public judgment on their productions. The resentment is not so much against the individual critic or the review, but against the very practice of theatre criticism itself. Anton Chekhov, according to one report, referred to critics as "horse-flies . . . buzzing about anything." In contrast, Broadway theatres are named for such revered critics as Brooks Atkinson and Walter Kerr, suggesting the industry's admiration for their distinguished service.

Critics actually perform many services for the theatregoing public, its artists, and producers. They recognize and preserve the work of artists and producers for future generations. Plays that receive favorable critical attention are usually published, in turn creating a wider audience. Critics serve as mediators between artists and audiences. They also serve as historians. Analyses of professional productions by Ben Brantley, Benedict Nightingale, Charles Isherwood, John Lahr, Marilyn Stasio, and others provide historical accounts of theatre seasons, theatrical events, and performances. Many, such as Frank Rich, and Robert Brustein, publish collections of their criticism, which serve as social and theatrical records of the times. Finally, critics discover new playwrights and directors and call attention to electrifying performances by artists.

The Critic's Creativity

The most brutal (and dishonest) argument levied against theatre critics is that they are no more than failed artists. As the saying goes, "If you can't do it, you write about it." This is also said of music, opera, and architecture critics. Sometimes first-rate criticism is written by second-rate artists; often the reverse is true. George Bernard Shaw excelled in both. Criticism is a true talent, combining artistic sensibilities, writing ability, performance insights, knowledge of theatre past and present, and the ability to recognize artistic talent and potential. Stanley Kauffmann defines the critic's creativity "[as] the imaginative rendering of experience in such a way that it can be essentially re-experienced by others." Finally, the critic holds a mirror up to theatre's nature, serving in the long run even those who most resent the role of the critic in the theatre.

The Critic's Questions

Theatre criticism evaluates, describes, or analyzes a performance's merits and a production's effectiveness. Since the time of the early nineteenth-century German playwright and critic Johann Wolfgang von Goethe (1749–1832), the theatre critic traditionally has asked three basic questions of the work:

- What is the playwright trying to do?
- How well has he or she done it?
- Was it worth doing?

The first question concedes the playwright's creative freedom to express ideas and events. The second question assumes that the critic is familiar with the playwright, as well as with the forms and techniques of the playwright's time. The third question demands a sense of production values and a general knowledge of theatre. These questions show up in varying degrees of emphasis in reviews.

If critics work with these essential questions (and each usually generates more questions about the performance), they first consider the imaginative material, the concept, and the themes. Second, they judge how well the performance accomplishes the playwright's intentions. Story line, character, acting, directing, sets, costumes, lighting, and sound may be considered, depending on their relative contributions to the effectiveness of the production. Third, the response to the question "Was it worth doing?" is the most sensitive and influential aspect of the review, placing critical standards and the fate of the production on the line. Claudia Cassidy and Brooks Atkinson had the innate good judgment to know that Tennessee Williams had said something significant about human vulnerability in *The Glass Menagerie* and *A Streetcar Named Desire*. Their reviews demonstrate the evaluations that get at the heart and substance of great plays and performances.

Whatever the order of the critic's essential questions about the performance, theatre criticism describes, evaluates, and assesses to one degree or another, depending on the critic's tastes, talents, and preferences. Where the critic places his or her emphasis also depends on the production itself. Is it an old play dressed out in fresh designs and interpretations, as was Peter Brook's production of Shakespeare's *A Midsummer Night's Dream*?

Performance/Production Notes

American Theatre, *The Drama Review*, and *Theatre Journal* publish critical descriptions of distinguished productions in the nonprofit theatre both in the United States and in Europe. These short, critical writings provide, first, a record of productions. The critical viewpoints stress experimental qualities in acting, directing, and design, along with new interpretations that emerged from texts and staging. The critical notes are usually accompanied by photographs to give a visual sense of performance style.

The short writings also offer impressions of trends in avant-garde and regional theatres, as well as familiarity with directors whose tastes and styles are gradually finding their way into the commercial theatre. A glance at a collection of critical program/production notes from recent theatrical seasons turns up such directors' names as Robert Lepage, Mary Zimmerman, Daniel Sullivan, Joe Montello, Sam Gold, and Barbara Gaines; such international companies as Cirque du Soleil, London's Blind Summit Theatre, Lepage's Ex Machina, and the National Theatre of China.

© Sara Krulwich/The New York Times/Redux

Shakespeare's *Measure for Measure*
The New York Shakespeare Festival's production of Shakespeare's *Measure for Measure* with Sanaa Lathan as Isabella and Daniel Pino as Claudio, directed by Mary Zimmerman with scene design by Dan Ostling.

Theatre Scholarship

The majority of scholarly critics in the United States are university teachers and/or professional dramaturgs. They bring a range of intellectual backgrounds to historical, social, and cultural issues. They theorize about large issues of dramaturgy; uncover hidden aspects of a text's meaning; and analyze social, philosophical, and cultural resonances.

Scholarly critics ordinarily write with a comprehensive knowledge of a specific subject. That subject may be a playwright's body of work, performance theories and practices, historical periods, or intercultural and gender studies. Traditional scholarly methodologies have included studies of dramatic character, analyses of play forms, examinations of staging and theatrical styles, and detailed interpretations of texts. The great writers of dramatic criticism in the West have also created literary works of lasting value, beginning with Aristotle's *Poetics* and continuing through Harold Bloom's *Shakespeare: The Invention of the Human*.

In recent years, changing intellectual fashions of academic life have introduced new methodologies that draw heavily upon the fields of linguistics, anthropology, and cultural and critical theory. These new areas include applications of theory and vocabulary from linguistics, semiotics, structuralism, poststructuralism, and deconstructionism. Moreover, theories of feminism, gender, reception, and post-colonialism offer startling insights from multiple perspectives on how we expose and express our prejudices through dramatic forms.

© The New York Times Company/Redux

Brooks Atkinson

Modern Pathfinders Among Theatre Critics

Brooks Atkinson

Educated at Harvard University, Brooks Atkinson (1894–1984) attended George Pierce Baker's Workshop 47 at Harvard. Beginning a career as a reporter on the Springfield (MA) *Daily News*, he moved to the *Boston Daily Evening Transcript* as assistant drama

FOCUS ON PEOPLE IN THEATRE

Brooks Atkinson on Tennessee Williams's *A Streetcar Named Desire*

After opening night at the Barrymore Theatre on December 3, 1947, Brooks Atkinson reviewed "Streetcar Tragedy: Mr. Williams' Report on Life in New Orleans" for the *New York Times*. In an unusual approach, Atkinson wrote two reviews of *Streetcar*. The first appeared after opening night. The second, and more famous, appeared ten days later. In both reviews Atkinson recognized that Williams's play did not address the great social issues of the times, that it solved no problems and arrived at no general moral conclusions. Nor did it deal with "representative" men and women. But, as Atkinson wrote, it was a work of art. Its audiences sat in the "presence of truth."

Organized to deal, first, with *the play's truthfulness* about the human beings portrayed, Atkinson's review then takes up Williams's "poetic language," Elia Kazan's directing, Jo Mielziner's scene details, the actors' performances, and, finally, Williams's career as the author of two Broadway successes in two years: *The Glass Menagerie* and *A Streetcar Named Desire*.

A Streetcar Named Desire
Jessica Tandy as Blanche DuBois with Marlon Brando as Stanley Kowalski in the original New York production of *A Streetcar Named Desire* (1947), directed by Elia Kazan.

Atkinson on Williams's "Character Portrait" in *A Streetcar Named Desire*

. . . Out of nothing more esoteric than interest in human beings, Mr. Williams has looked steadily and wholly into the private agony of one lost person. He supplies dramatic conflict by introducing Blanche to an alien environment that brutally wears on her nerves. But he takes no sides in the conflict. . . . There is no solution except the painful one Mr. Williams provides in the last scene.[7]

critic. In 1922, he became book review editor for the *New York Times* and succeeded Stark Young as the newspaper's theatre critic in 1926.

When the Second World War broke out, Atkinson took an overseas assignment, later receiving a Pulitzer Prize in 1947 for his reports on the Soviet Union. After the war, he returned to reviewing the Broadway theatre and became the most respected theatre critic of his generation. At his retirement in 1960, the Mansfield Theatre was renamed in his honor.

Claudia Cassidy

Earning the nickname "acidy Cassidy," the *Chicago Tribune's* theatre critic Claudia Cassidy (1899–1996) was known for her acerbic reviews. From 1942 to 1965, she wrote the often controversial column "On the Aisle" which became a fixture in the Chicago arts scene. Cassidy was sharply opinionated in her criticism of shows she deemed second-rate. Her prose could be so brutal performers would vow never again to play Chicago. But, Cassidy was also a persuasive advocate for work she admired. She single-handedly championed Tennessee Williams's play *The Glass Menagerie*, thus helping to establish his career in the early forties.

FOCUS ON THEATRE

Claudia Cassidy on Tennessee Williams's *The Glass Menagerie*

Opening in Chicago the night after Christmas in 1944 to a small audience, the producers prepared a closing notice for the show. But, Claudia Cassidy, writing in the *Chicago Daily Tribune*, said that the play had "the stamina of success . . . [it] knows people and how they tick. . . . If it is your play, as it is mine, it reaches out . . . and you are caught in its spell." By the third night, Laurette Taylor as Amanda Wingfield was creating a legend and Cassidy, returning night after night and writing almost daily, summarized in her column, *On the Aisle*, on January 7, 1945: "[*The Glass Menagerie*] gripped players and audiences alike, and created one of those rare evenings in the theatre that made 'stage struck' an honorable word."[8]

By the middle of the month, no tickets were available. One expert recalled that in an unusual example of journalistic salvation, a play, for once, was not lost but kept alive because of *critical support.*

The Glass Menagerie
Julie Haydon and Laurette Taylor as the original Laura and Amanda Wingfield in Tennessee Williams's *The Glass Menagerie*, Chicago and Broadway, 1944-45.

FOCUS ON THEATRE

Edith Oliver on David Mamet's *American Buffalo*

Edith Oliver, introducing a new playwright to readers of *The New Yorker*, maintained her conviction that she was in the presence of a remarkable new writer with an aptitude for lowlife dialects and pawnshop characters. Her review of David Mamet's *American Buffalo* appeared in the February 9, 1976 issue in which she wrote:

> "... The setting is the cluttered pawnshop, presumably in Chicago, of one Donny Dubrow. Before the action starts, a coin collector has been in and paid more than fifty dollars for a buffalo-head nickel that Dubrow had considered worthless, and then departed, leaving his card. The plot is entirely concerned with the plans of Dubrow—aided by a young man who works for him and a crony called Teach—to break into the customer's safe and steal his collection. Dubrow and Teach, we learn, are given to a bit of petty thievery, but they are really innocents of a sort, to put it as kindly as possible, and inexperienced in serious crime.
>
> ....
>
> It is all but inconceivable that these two clucks, however edgy, could turn so ruthless and cruel. Much of the conversation is a matter of obscenities used as casually and wholeheartedly as if they were the only words available.... But the evening belongs to the dramatist. Mr. Mamet ... is original and a true humorist."[9]

Mamet's *American Buffalo*
The production of David Mamet's *American Buffalo* opened Off Broadway with William H. Macy and Philip Baker Hall.

Edith Oliver, "Off Broadway," The New Yorker (February 9, 1976): 81. Reprinted by permission.

Edith Oliver

For thirty-two years, Edith Oliver (1913–1998) reviewed Broadway and Off Broadway for *The New Yorker* magazine. Identified by her "straight-from-the-shoulder" reviews, Oliver could be unsparing with playwrights. She also actively promoted the works of David Mamet, Christopher Durang, and Wendy Wasserstein. She vigorously supported the Off Broadway movement of the sixties and seventies and favored such companies as the Negro Ensemble Company, Café La Mama, and the New Federal Theatre.

FOCUS ON THEATRE

Today's Critics at Work

Ben Brantley and **Charles Isherwood** (*New York Times*) are influential critics in today's theatre. When Isherwood speaks of the state of theatre today, he laments: "In New York, there's this 'Broadway or die' mentality, where you can only get enough attention for a show to be a success if it's on Broadway. So you get a lot of shows that go there and flop and lose money for investors."[10]

Chris Jones (*Chicago Tribune*) has defined the Chicago theatre scene as blue-collar, profane, and prone to violence. Jones estimates that he reviews over 200 shows a year in Chicago's more than 200 venues. He describes the city: "It's a funny town. In the last 10 years, there's been an explosion of storefront and waterfront companies. And there's also been a renaissance of Chicago theatre's reputation in New York. . . . If a show is a hit here, five minutes later you're seeing agents and people on planes going to see it."[11]

Misha Berson (*The Seattle Times*) has been covering the Seattle theatre beat for over two decades. Her experience as a producer, arts administrator, and actor gives her a special appreciation for the actors' process on stage and the challenges of running a theatre company in the Northwest. "It's hard to be an actor in Seattle," she says, "because there's not a lot of ancillary work—film or television production. So the actors who stay here really invest themselves in the community."[12]

Linda Winer (*Newsday*) has been reviewing theatre, music, and dance for over thirty-five years. Of trends in musical theatre she writes: "Putting aside for a moment an anomalous, old-fashioned little throwback called 'Spider-man: Turn off the Dark,' it seems that Broadway's appetite for big-budget, humongous spectacles has been replaced by intimate, much less costly musicals with offbeat subjects, multicultural/multigenerational appeal and an almost indie-film vibe.)[13]

Bruce Norris's *Clybourne Park*
In his review of Bruce Norris's *Clybourne Park* (a revisitation fifty years later to Lorraine Hansberry's small house in *A Raisin in the Sun*, located in the [fictional] Chicago neighborhood of Clybourne Park), critic Frank Rich called the Pulitzer Prize-winning play a "post-racial farce."[16] In doing so, the critic used the two different American eras fifty years apart—1959 (Act I) and 2009 (Act II)—depicted in Norris's play, to comment on changing (and unchanging) cultural and racial forces in America.

© Sara Krulwich/The New York Times/Redux

FOCUS ON THEATRE

Writing the Theatre Review

Although there is no general agreement on criteria for judging a performance, the first step in writing theatre criticism is *the ability to see.* If we can describe what we see in the theatre—our sensory impressions—then we can begin to arrive at critical judgments. The play or production, or both, determines the approach: the organization of the review and the critical priorities. If the staging justifies a detailed account of what we observe, then the review incorporates a great deal of description. However, what we see in the theatre must connect with the play's meaning. For these reasons, *all theatre criticism involves both description and evaluation.*

Because we build critical concepts on the foundation of our perceptions, we can begin the process of seeing theatre critically by learning to describe our perceptions, always keeping in mind Goethe's three basic questions (see page 343). A model for writing a theatre review might follow the points listed below:

1. Heading
2. Substance or meaning of play
3. Setting or environment
4. Acting (actor or character)
5. Language
6. Stage business
7. Directing
8. Costumes
9. Lighting, projections, and sound effects
10. Other significant human details
11. Concluding evaluation

Select and prioritize these elements

In writing any commentary, it is first necessary to identify the production early in the review. Brooks Atkinson identifies both play and playwright in the first paragraph of his review of *A Streetcar Named Desire.* Others identify play, playwright, and actors in the opening paragraphs of the review.

Next, commentary on the play's substance or meaning informs the reader about the playwright's particular perspective on human affairs. Third, the performance involves what J. L. Styan calls "an environment of significant stimuli": sights, sounds, color, light, movement, space.[14] These stimuli can be described by answering questions related to setting, costumes, sound, lighting, projections, acting, and stage business. Is the stage environment open or closed, symbolic or realistic? What are the effects of the stage's shape on the actor's speech, gesture, and movement? Is the lighting symbolic or suggestive of realistic light sources? What role do projections play? What details of color, period, taste, and socioeconomic status are established by the costumes? What use is made of sound, music, or lighting effects? What details separate the actor-at-work from his or her character-in-situation? What do the characters do in the play's circumstances? What stage properties do the actors use? Are they significant? Finally, what visual and aural images of human experience and society develop during the performance? How effective are they?

CRITICAL STANDARDS

It takes years of seeing theatre to develop critical standards. The best professional critics genuinely enjoy going to the theatre and are open and flexible even in their immense knowledge of theatre. George Jean Nathan got at the heart of the matter when he said, "Criticism, at its best, is the adventure of an intelligence among emotions."[15]

After all is said and done, theatre criticism is the encounter of one person's sensibility with the theatrical event. Thus, it is important that the critic tells us about the performance, humankind, society, and perhaps even the universe in the course of evaluating the production. Critic and director Harold Clurman once said that whether the critic is good or bad doesn't depend on his opinions but on the reasons he can offer for those opinions.

Theatre criticism—carefully weighed by the reader—adds a new dimension to our discovery of theatre. To become skilled critics is to hone our perceptions of the *when*, *where*, and *how* of the event taking place before us. As we gain experience seeing theatre, we become skilled in arranging our critical priorities, describing those details that enhance the performance and omitting those that contribute little to it. We develop criteria for judging the play's and the performance's effectiveness. We share our insights with others. In a word, we become *critics*.

For the professional critic, the play-in-performance is the end product of the theatre's creative process. At best, the critic enhances our understanding of the production or theatre event by enabling us to read about the theatrical experience from a perspective other than our own or that of our friends. *Theatre criticism*—carefully weighed by the reader—adds a new dimension to the discovery and understanding of theatre.

Theatre: A Way of Seeing Online

Visit the CourseMate for Theatre: A Way of Seeing 7th Edition for quick access to the digital study resources that accompany this chapter, including links to the websites listed below, Theatre Workshop, digital glossary, a chapter quiz and more.

Websites

The *Theatre: A Way of Seeing* CourseMate includes maintained links for all the websites described below. Simply select "Web links" from the Chapter Resources for Chapter 15, and click on the link that interests you. You'll be taken directly to the site described. Most major newspapers have websites. Listed below are websites for national newspapers noted for their influential critics and theatre reviews.

Boston Globe
Features critics Ed Siegel and Louise Kennedy.

Chicago Tribune
Features critic Chris Jones.

Los Angeles Times
Features critics Rob Kendt and David C. Nichols.

New York Times
Features critics Ben Brantley and Charles Isherwood.

Seattle Times
Features critic Misha Berson.

Variety (Northeast Region)
Features critics Steven Suskin and Marilyn Stasio.

Washington Post
Features critic Peter Marks.

The Daily Digest of Arts, Culture, and Ideas
Collection of current topics on arts-and-culture–related news from around the world covering music, theatre, dance, publishing, and the visual arts. There are also topics on the issues and people that shape the cultural world.

NOTES

Chapter 1

1. Peter Brook, *The Empty Space* (New York: Atheneum, 1968): 9. Copyright © 1968 by Peter Brook. (New York: Atheneum Publishers, 1968) and Granada Publishing Ltd., England.

Chapter 2

1. Excerpt from *The Sacred and the Profane: The Nature of Religion* by Mircea Eliade, copyright © 1957 by Rowohlt Taschenbuch Verlag GmbH, English translation by Willard R. Trask. Copyright © 1959 and renewed 1987 by Harcourt, Inc.

Chapter 3

1. Jerzy Grotowski, *Towards a Poor Theatre* (New York: Clarion Press, 1968): 19–20. Reprinted by permission.
2. Richard Schechner, *Environmental Theater* (New York: Hawthorn Books, 1973): 25. Copyright © 1973 by Richard Schechner. All rights reserved. Reprinted by permission of Hawthorn Books, Inc.
3. Grotowski: 19–20.
4. Grotowski: 19–20.
5. Grotowski: 75.
6. Pierre Biner, *The Living Theatre: A History Without Myths* (New York: Avon Books, 1972): 72.
7. Mel Gussow, "The Living Theater Returns to Its Birthplace," *New York Times* (15 January 1984): II, 6.
8. David Williams, ed., *Collaborative Theatre: The Théâtre du Soleil Sourcebook* (New York: Routledge, 1999): x.
9. Peter Schumann, "The Radicality of the Puppet Theatre," *The Drama Review*, 35, No. 4 (Winter 1991): 75. See also Peter Schumann, "The Bread and Puppet Theatre (Interview)," *The Drama Review*, 12, No. 2 (Winter 1968): 62–73.
10. *The Free Southern Theater by the Free Southern Theater*, ed. Thomas C. Dent, Richard Schechner, and Gilbert Moses (Indianapolis: The Bobbs-Merrill Company, 1969): 3, 9.
11. Elizabeth Sutherland, "Theatre of the Meaningful," *The Nation* (19 October 1964): 254–256.

Chapter 4

1. Tennessee Williams, Afterword to *Camino Real* (New York: New Directions, 1953): xii. Copyright © 1948, 1953 by Tennessee Williams.
2. Carol Lawson, "Caryl Churchill Wins Blackburn Drama Prize," *New York Times* (25 February 1984), 1, 16. Copyright © 1984 by The New York Times Company.
3. David Savran, *The Playwright's Voice: American Dramatists on Memory, Writing and the Politics of Culture* (New York: Theatre Communications Group, 1999): 6.
4. Lillian Hellman, *Pentimento: A Book of Portraits* (Boston: Little, Brown & Company, 1973): 152–153.
5. Amy Lippman, "Rhythm & Truths: An Interview with Sam Shepard," *American Theatre*, 1, No. 1 (April 1984): 12. Permission needed of the Theatre Communications Group Inc.
6. Lippman: 9.
7. "David Mamet," *Contemporary Authors*, Vol. 15, New Revision Series (Chicago: Gale Research Company, 1985): 300.
8. R. C. Lewis, "A Playwright Named Tennessee," *New York Times Magazine* (7 December 1947): 19. Copyright © 1947 by The New York Times Company.
9. August Wilson, *Fences* (New York: NAL Penguin, 1986): 69.
10. Kathy Sova, *American Theatre*, 14, No. 2 (February 1997): 24. Permission of the Theatre Communications Group Inc.
11. Lorraine Hansberry, *To Be Young, Gifted and Black*, adapted by Robert Nemiroff (Englewood Cliffs, NJ: Prentice-Hall, 1969): 133–134. Copyright © 1969 by Prentice-Hall, Inc.
12. Suzan-Lori Parks, "Elements of Style," in *The America Play and Other Works* (New York: Theatre Communications Group, 1995): 6, 8.
13. David Henry Hwang, *Contemporary American Dramatists*, ed. K. A. Berney (Chicago: Gale Research Company, 1994): 285.

14. María Irene Fornés, "The 'Woman' Playwright Issue," *The Performing Arts Journal*, 7, No. 3 (1983): 91. Reprinted by permission.

15. Randy Gener, "Dreamer from Cuba," *American Theatre*, 20, No. 7 (September 2003): 91.

Chapter 5

1. Bertolt Brecht, "A Short Organon for the Theatre," *Brecht on Theatre: The Development of an Aesthetic*, ed. and trans. John Willett (New York: Hill and Wang, 1964): 204.
2. Peter Brook, *The Empty Space* (New York: Atheneum, 1968): 15.
3. Lane Cooper, *Aristotle on the Art of Poetry* (Ithaca, NY: Cornell University Press, 1947): 17.
4. Jack Kroll, "A Seven-Hour Gay Fantasia," *Newsweek* (23 November 1993): 83.
5. "Lillian Hellman, Playwright, Author and Rebel, Dies at 79," *New York Times* (1 July 1984): 20. Copyright © 1984 by The New York Times Company.
6. Eric Bentley, "The Psychology of Farce," in *Let's Get a Divorce! and Other Plays* (New York: Hill and Wang, 1958): vii–xx.
7. Eugène Ionesco, *Notes and Counter-Notes: Writings on the Theatre*, trans. Donald Watson (New York: Grove Press, 1964): 26. Copyright © 1964 by Grove Press, Inc.
8. Excerpt from *Brecht on Theatre*, ed. and trans. John Willett: 121. Translation copyright © 1964, renewed © 1992 by John Willett.
9. Albert Camus, *The Myth of Sisyphus and Other Essays* (New York: Alfred A. Knopf, 1955): 5.
10. Ionesco: 29.

Chapter 6

1. David Mamet, *Writing in Restaurants* (New York: Viking Penguin, 1986): 8.
2. Laurence Olivier, *On Acting* (London: George Weidenfeld & Nicolson Limited, 1986): 192.
3. Francis Fergusson, *The Idea of a Theatre* (Princeton, NJ: Princeton University Press, 1949): 36.
4. For my understanding of climactic and episodic drama I am indebted to material from Bernard Beckerman, *Dynamics of Drama: Theory and Method of Analysis* (New York: Alfred A. Knopf, 1970).
5. Jo Bonney, "Fragments from the Age of the Self: Nine Artists Span the Century of the Soloist," *American Theatre*, 16, No. 10 (December 1999): 32.
6. Deb Margolin, "A Perfect Theatre for One: Teaching 'Performance Composition,'" *The Drama Review*, 41, No. 2 (Summer 1997): 69.
7. John Lahr, "Under the Skin," *The New Yorker* (28 June 1993): 90.
8. Guillermo Gòmez-Peña, "A Binational Performance Pilgrimage," *The Drama Review*, 35, No. 3 (Fall 1991): 22–46.
9. Simi Horwitz, "About Face," *TheaterWeek* (22 June 1992): 25.
10. Gina Kolata, "Through 1 Woman, 20 Views of Life's End," *New York Times* (November 10, 2009): 36.
11. Cathy Madison, "Hearing Voices: Portraits of America at the Public," *Village Voice* (10 December 1991): 106.
12. Robert Wilson, *the CIVIL WARS*, ed. Jan Graham Geidt (Cambridge, MA: American Repertory Theatre, 1985): 6.
13. Robert Wilson and David Byrne, *The Forest* (Berlin: Theater der Freien Volksbühne, 1988): 29–32.

Chapter 7

1. From Appendix I in *Naked Masks: Five Plays* by Luigi Pirandello, ed. Eric Bentley (New York: Penguin Books USA, 1952): 372. Copyright © 1922 by E. P. Dutton. Renewed 1950 in the names of Stefano, Fausto, and Lietta Pirandello. Used by permission of Dutton Signet, a division of Penguin Books USA, Inc.
2. Tennessee Williams, *A Streetcar Named Desire* (New York: New American Library, 1947): 13.
3. From *Six Characters in Search of an Author* by Luigi Pirandello, in *Naked Masks: Five Plays*, pp. 214–215.

Chapter 8

1. Eugène Ionesco, *Notes and Counter-Notes: Writings on the Theatre*, trans. Donald Watson (New York: Grove Press, 1964): 29.
2. Peter Brook, *The Empty Space* (New York: Atheneum, 1968): 12.
3. George Steiner, *The Death of Tragedy* (New York: Alfred A. Knopf, 1961): 275. Copyright © 1963, renewed 1989 by George Steiner.

4. From *The Cherry Orchard* by Anton Chekhov, in *Plays*, trans. Elisaveta Fen (Penguin Classics, 1954). Copyright © Elisaveta Fen, 1951, 1954.

5. Excerpt from "On Gestic Music" from *Brecht on Theatre*, ed. and trans. John Willett. Translation copyright © 1964, renewed © 1992 by John Willett.

6. Bertolt Brecht, *The Caucasian Chalk Circle*, trans. Ralph Manheim, in *Collected Plays*, Vol. 7, ed. Ralph Manheim and John Willett (New York: Random House, Inc., 1975): 226.

7. Antonin Artaud, *The Theater and Its Double* (New York: Grove Press, 1958): 107.

8. David Mamet, *Glengarry Glen Ross* (New York: Grove Press, Inc., 1983), 15–16.

9. Ben Brantley, "That's No Girl Scout Selling Those Cookies," *New York Times* (17 November 2004): B1, 4.

10. Sam Shepard, *Buried Child* (New York: Bantam Books, Inc., 1979), 74–77. Included in *Seven Plays* by Sam Shepard. Copyright © 1979 by Sam Shepard.

Chapter 9

1. Laurence Olivier, *On Acting* (New York: Simon & Schuster, 1986): 192.

2. Lionel Gracey-Whitman, "Return by Popular Demand," *Plays and Players*, No. 367 (April 1984): 21–25. Reprinted by permission.

3. Toby Cole and Helen Krich Chinoy, eds., *Actors on Acting: The Theories, Techniques, and Practices of the Great Actors of All Times as Told in Their Own Words* (New York: Crown, 1959): 132. Reprinted by permission.

4. See Olivier, *On Acting*: 21–34.

5. Uta Hagen, *A Challenge for the Actor* (New York: Charles Scribner's Sons, 1991): 70. See also Jared Brown, *The Fabulous Lunts: A Biography of Alfred Lunt and Lynn Fontanne* (New York: Atheneum, 1986).

6. Joe Roach, *"IT"* (Ann Arbor: University of Michigan Press, 2007), 8.

7. Konstantin Stanislavski, *An Actor Prepares*, trans. Elizabeth Reynolds Hapgood (New York: Routledge, 1989): 14.

8. Konstantin Stanislavski, *An Actor's Handbook*, ed. and trans. Elizabeth Reynolds Hapgood (New York: Theatre Arts, 1963): 100.

9. Meryl Streep, "The Ken Burns Interview," *USA Weekend.com* (December 1, 2002).

10. Lawrence Sacharow, "Enemies: A Russian Love Story," *American Theatre*, 21, No. 1 (January 2004): 34.

11. Robert Hethmon, *Strasberg at the Actors Studio* (New York: Viking Press, 1965): 78.

12. Sanford Meisner and Dennis Longwell, *Sanford Meisner on Acting* (New York: Vintage Books, 1987): 37.

13. Jordan Lage, "Boot Camp with David Mamet," *American Theatre*, 21, No. 1 (January 2004): 39.

14. *New York Times* (7 November 1999): II, 8.

15. Jon Jory, "Foreword," in *Anne Bogart Viewpoints*, ed. Michael Bigelow Dixon and Joel A. Smith (Lyme, NH: Smith and Kraus, Inc., 1995): xv.

16. Steven Drukman, "Entering the Postmodern Studio: Viewpoint Theory," *American Theatre*, 15, No. 1 (January 1998): 32.

17. "Anne Bogart," *Current Biography*, 60, No. 2 (February 1999): 3.

18. Joanna Merlin, *Auditioning: An Actor-Friendly Guide* (New York: Vintage Books, 2001): xix.

19. Quoted in Nicole Potter, "Let's Get Physical: What's Happening Now?," *American Theatre*, 28, No. 1 (January 2011): 50.

20. Cicely Berry, *The Actor and the Voice* (New York: Macmillan, 1973): 121. "Also Quoted in "Pillars of Voice Work," American Theatre, 27, No. 1 (January 2010): 36, 39, 44, 48."

21. Quoted in "Pillars of Voice Work," *American Theatre*, 27, No. 1 (January 2010): 36, 39, 44, 48.

22. Michael Caine, *Acting in Film: An Actor's Take on Movie Making*, rev. ed. (New York: Applause Theatre Book Publishers, 1997): 4.

Chapter 10

1. Alan Schneider, "Things to Come: Crystal-Gazing at the Near and Distant Future of a Durable Art," *American Theatre*, 1, No. 1 (April 1984): 17.

2. Elia Kazan, "Notebook for *A Streetcar Named Desire*," in *Directing the Play: A Source Book of Stagecraft*, ed. Toby Cole and Helen Krich Chinoy (Indianapolis, IN: The Bobbs-Merrill Company, 1953): 364–366.

3. Toby Dole and Helen Krich Chinoy, eds., *Directors on Directing*, 2nd rev. ed. (Indianapolis, IN: The Bobbs-Merrill Company, 1977): 364.

4. Peter Brook, *Threads of Time: A Memoir* (London: Methuen Publishers, 1999): 141.

5. Margaret Croyden, "*The Mahabharata*: A Review," *New York Times* (25 August 1985): 11, 20.
6. Alan Riding, "Peter Brook Considers Matters of Faith and Power," *New York Times* (29 November 2004): E3.
7. Brook, *Threads of Time*: *A Memoir*: 149–150.
8. Chris Jones, "Evolution of Robert Falls: Goodman Theatre's artistic director moves toward minimalism," *Chicago Tribune* (October 3, 2010).
9. Jane Kramer, "Experimental Journey," *The New Yorker* (October 8, 2007): 86.
10. Charles Isherwood, "Making 'Salesman' His own, Despite Kazan's Shadow," *New York Times* (March 16, 2012): C1.
11. Misha Berson, "Dan Sullivan Travels," *American Theatre* (March 2007): 26.
12. Rhona Justice-Malloy, "Susan V. Booth: The Excitement of Risk," *Women in Theatre Magazine* (2011-2012): 36. Reprinted with permission.
13. Whitney Dibo, "Martha Lavey: First Lady," *Women in Theatre Magazine* (2011–2012): 13. Reprinted with permission.
14. Richard Dodds, "The Drama Queen of Noe Valley: Off Stage with ACT's Carey Perloff," *The NOE Valley Voice* (September 1998): 3.
15. Julie Cortez, "Olga Sanchez: A Love Affair with the Theatre," *Women in Theatre Magazine* (2011–2012): 23. Reprinted with permission.
16. Alexis Clements, "Molly Smith: A Woman's Journey," *Women in Theatre Magazine* (2011–2012): 43. Reprinted with permission.
17. Bree Burns, "Breaking the Mold: Julie Taymor," *Theatre Crafts*, 22, No. 3 (March 1988): 49.
18. Miriam Horn, "A Director Who Can Conjure Up Magic Onstage," *Smithsonian* (February 1993): 66.
19. Horn: 66.
20. See "*Juan Darién*: A Carnival Mass," *Theater*, 20, No. 2 (Spring 1989): 52.
21. Arthur Bartow, "'Images from the Id': An Interview," *American Theatre*, 5, No. 3 (June 1988): 56–57. Courtesy of the Theatre Communications Group Inc.
22. Bartow: 17.

Chapter 11

1. Robert Edmond Jones, *The Dramatic Imagination: Reflections and Speculations on the Art of the Theatre* (New York: Methuen Theatre Arts Books, 1987): 26.
2. Randy Gener, "The Designer as Thinker," *American Theatre*, 20, 1 (January 2003): 27.
3. Josef Svoboda, *The Secret of Theatrical Space*, ed. and trans. J. M. Burian (New York: Applause Theatre Books, 1993): 8.
4. Lynn Pecktal, "A Conversation with Ming Cho Lee," in *Designing and Painting for the Theatre* (New York: Holt, Rinehart, 1975): 242.
5. Pecktal, 51.
6. Pecktal, "A Conversation with John Lee Beatty," in *Designing and Painting for the Theatre*, 544–545.
7. See Joan D. Firestone, "A Panel of Designers," *Round Up: A Magazine for the League of Professional Theatre Women*, IX (2008–2009): 23. Reprinted with permission.
8. Designer Bill Clarke shared his thoughts on advances in design technologies with Author in an email, dated August 5, 2012.
9. Patricia Zipprodt, "Designing Costumes," in *Contemporary Stage Design U.S.A.* (Middletown, CT: Wesleyan University Press, 1974): 29.
10. Joseph V. Melillo, "In Conversation with Designer Susan Hilferty," *Round Up: A Magazine for the League of Professional Theatre Women*, IX (2008-2009): 17. Reprinted with permission.
11. John Gruen, "She Is One of Broadway's Most Designing Women," *New York Times* (8 April 1984): II, 5, 14. Copyright © 1984 by The New York Times Company. Reprinted by permission.
12. Courtesy of Judy Adamson (30 January 2005).
13. Ronn Smith, "Paul Huntley: Big on Wigs," *Theatre Crafts* (February 1983): 23.

Chapter 12

1. *New York Times* (11 January 1995). See also *Current Biography*, 58, No. 7 (July 1997): 52–54.
2. *Current Biography*: 52–54.
3. Jean Rosenthal and Lael Wertenbaker, *The Magic of Light* (Boston: Little, Brown and Company, 1972), 115.
4. Elizabeth Stone, "Jennifer Tipton Interview," *New York Times* (14 April 1991).
5. Natasha Katz quoted in, *Curtain Call*: *Celebrating A Century of Women Designing for Live Performance* (New York: The New York Public Library for the Performing Arts and League of Professional Theatre Women, 2008): 99.
6. Ellen Lampert Gréaux, David Barbour, and David Johnson, "Rose's Return," *TCI*, 37, No. 7 (August 2003): 19.

7. Lighting designer Mary Louise Geiger shared her thoughts with the Author on working with Lee Breuer of the Mabou Mines in an Email dated October 1, 2012.
8. "Abe Jacob Profile," *Entertainment Design* (January 2000): 20.

Chapter 13

1. Cheryl Crawford, *One Naked Individual: My Fifty Years in the Theatre* (Indianapolis, IN: The Bobbs-Merrill Company, 1977): 4.
2. Alexander H. Cohen, "Broadway Theatre," in *Producers on Producing*, ed. Stephen Langley (New York: Drama Book Specialists, 1976): 15.
3. Campbell Robertson, "A Broadway Producer Is Bringing Back Drama," *New York Times* (January 16, 2008), E 1.
4. Robin Pogrebin, "Off Broadway's Mom and Angel," *New York Times* (July 26, 1999): 1B.
5. Audrey Wood with Max Wilk, *Represented by Audrey Wood* (Garden City, NY: Doubleday and Company, 1981): 7
6. Wood, 11.
7. See "Theatre Facts 2010," *American Theatre* (November 2011): 36-41.
8. Cohen, 15.

Chapter 14

1. Frank Rich, "Review of *Dreamgirls*," *New York Times* (21 December 1981): C11: 1.
2. Ben Brantley, ed., *The New York Times Book of Broadway: On the Aisle for the Unforgettable Plays of the Last Century* (New York: St. Martin's Press, 2001): x.
3. Ken Bloom, ed., *Broadway: Its History, People and Places: An Encyclopedia*, 2nd ed. (New York: Routledge, 2003): 125.
4. Bloom: 421.
5. Clive Barnes, "Review of *A Chorus Line*," *New York Times* (22 May 1975), 32.

Chapter 15

1. Frank Rich, "A Critic's Summit: Robert Brustein and Frank Rich Talk About Criticism," *American Theatre*, 16, No. 5 (May/June 1999): 18. Permission needed of Theatre Communications Group Inc.
2. Arthur Miller, *Death of a Salesman* in *Arthur Miller's Collected Plays* (New York: The Viking Press, 1958): 56. Copyright © 1949, renewed © 1977 by Arthur Miller. Permission needed of Viking Putnam, a division of Penguin Putnam, Inc.
3. Ben Brantley, "American Dreamer, Ambushed by the Territory," *New York Times* (March 16, 2012), C1.
4. Tony Kushner, *Angels in America. Part Two: Perestroika* (New York: Theatre Communications Group, 1994): 148.
5. Tennessee Williams, *The Glass Menagerie*, Vol.1 (New York: New Directions, 1970): 55.
6. Stanley Kauffmann, *Persons of the Drama: Theater Criticism and Comment* (New York: Harper & Row, 1976): 369–380.
7. Brooks Atkinson, "'Streetcar' Tragedy, Mr. Williams' Report on Life in New Orleans, *New York Times* (14 December 1947): II, 3. Copyright © 1947 by The New York Times Company.
8. Claudia Cassidy, "On the Aisle," *Chicago Daily Tribune* (January 7, 1945).
9. Edith Oliver, "Off Broadway," *The New Yorker* (February 9, 1976): 81.
10. Christopher Isherwood, "Critical Juncture," *American Theatre*, 28, no. 9 (November 2011): 33–34.
11. Chris Jones, "Critical Juncture," *American Theatre*, 28, no. 9 (November 2011): 34.
12. Misha Berson, "Critical Juncture," *American Theatre*, 28, no. 9 (November 2011): 32.
13. Linda Winer, "Are Days of Big Broadway Spectacles Ending?" www.newsday.com (September 21, 2012).
14. J. L. Styan, *Drama, Stage and Audience* (New York: Cambridge University Press, 1975): 33
15. George Jean Nathan, *The Critic and the Drama* (New York: Alfred A. Knopf, 1922): 133.
16. Frank Rich, "Post-Racial Farce," *New York Magazine* (May 21, 2012).

CREDITS

Chapter 1

3: Peter Brook, The Empty Space (New York: Athenum, 1968): 9.

Chapter 2

23: Excerpt from The Sacred and the Profane: The Nature of Religion by Mircea Eliade.

Chapter 3

57: Jerzy Grotowski, Towards a Poor Theatre (New York: Clarion Press, 1968): 19–20. **57–58:** Richard Schechner, Environmental Theater (New York: Hawthorn Books, 1973): 25. **58:** Jerzy Grotowski, Towards a Poor Theatre (New York: Clarion Press, 1968): 19–20. **59:** Jerzy Grotowski, Towards a Poor Theatre (New York: Clarion Press, 1968): 19–20. **61:** Jerzy Grotowski, Towards a Poor Theatre (New York: Clarion Press, 1968): 75. **66:** David Williams, ed., Collaborative Theatre: The Théâtre du Soleil Sourcebook (New York: Routledge, 1999): x. **70:** Peter Schumann, "The Radicality of the Puppet Theatre," The Drama Review, 35, No. 4 (Winter 1991): 75. See also Peter Schumann, "The Bread and Puppet Theatre (Interview)," The Drama Review, 12, No. 2 (Winter 1968): 62–73.

Chapter 4

80: Tennessee Williams, Afterword to CAMINO REAL. By Tennessee Williams, from CAMINO REAL, copyright ©1953 by The University of the South. Reprinted by permission of New Directions Publishing Corp. **83:** Amy Lippman, "Rhythm & Truths: An Interview with Sam Shepard," American Theatre, 1, No. 1 (April 1984): 9. **84:** Amy Lippman, "Rhythm & Truths: An Interview with Sam Shepard," American Theatre, 1, No. 1 (April 1984): 12. **87:** R. C. Lewis, "A Playwright Named Tennessee," New York Times Magazine (7 December 1947): 19. **93:** Kathy Sova, American Theatre, 14, No. 2 (February 1997): 24.
94: Lorraine Hansberry, To Be Young, Gifted and Black, adapted by Robert Nemiroff (Englewood Cliffs, NJ: Prentice-Hall, 1969): 133–134.
95: Suzan-Lori Parks, "Elements of Style," in The America Play and Other Works (New York: Theatre Communications Group, 1995): 6, 8.

Chapter 5

104: Lane Cooper, Aristotle on the Art of Poetry (Ithaca, NY: Cornell University Press, 1947): 17.
116: Lillian Hellman, Playwright, Author and Rebel, Dies at 79," New York Times (1 July 1984): 20.
126: Albert Camus, The Myth of Sisyphus and Other Essays (New York: Alfred A. Knopf, 1955): 5.

Chapter 6

132: Laurence Olivier, On Acting (London: George Weidenfeld & Nicolson Limited, 1986): 192. **143:** Jo Bonney, "Fragments from the Age of the Self: Nine Artists Span the Century of the Soloist," American Theatre, 16, No. 10 (December 1999): 32. **147:** Deb Margolin, "A Perfect Theatre for One: Teaching 'Performance Composition,'" The Drama Review, 41, No. 2 (Summer 1997): 69. **152:** Robert Wilson, the CIVIL warS, ed. Jan Graham Geidt (Cambridge, MA: American Repertory Theatre, 1985): 6. **154:** Robert Wilson and David Byrne, The Forest (Berlin: Theater der Freien Volksbuhne, 1988): 29–32.

Chapter 7

157: From Appendix I in Naked Masks: Five Plays by Luigi Pirandello, ed. Eric Bentley (New York: Penguin Books USA, 1952): 372. **158–159:** By Tennessee Williams, from A STREETCAR NAMED DESIRE (New York: New American Library, 1947): 13. Copyright ©1947 by The University of the South. Reprinted by permission of New Directions Publishing Corp. **169:** From Six Characters in Search of an Author by Luigi Pirandello, in Naked Masks: Five Plays, pp. 214–215.

Chapter 8

175: Eugène Ionesco, Notes and Counter-Notes: Writings on the Theatre, trans. Donald Watson (New York: Grove Press, 1964): 29. **175:** Reprinted with the permission of Scribner, a Division of Simon & Schuster, Inc., from THE EMPTY SPACE by Peter Brook. Copyright © 1968 by Peter Brook; copyright renewed 1996 by Peter Brook. All rights reserved. **176:** George Steiner, The Death of Tragedy (New York: Alfred A. Knopf, 1961): 275. **183:** From The Cherry Orchard by Anton Chekhov, in Plays, trans. Elisaveta Fen (Penguin Classics, 1954). **183:** Excerpt from "On Gestic Music" from Brecht on Theatre, ed. and trans. John Willett.

Translation copyright © 1964, renewed © 1992 by John Willett. **185:** Bertolt Brecht, The Caucasian Chalk Circle, trans. Ralph Manheim, in Collected Plays, Vol. 7, ed. Ralph Manheim and John Willett (New York: Random House, Inc., 1975): 226. **187:** Excerpt from "Glengarry Glen Ross" by David Mamet, copyright © 1982, 1983 by David Mamet. Used by permission of Grove/Atlantic, Inc. Any third party use ofthis material, outside of this publication, is prohibited.

Chapter 9

194: Lionel Gracey-Whitman, "Return by Popular Demand," Plays and Players, No. 367 (April 1984): 21–25. **197:** Toby Cole and Helen Krich Chinoy, eds., Actors on Acting: The Theories, Techniques, and Practices of the Great Actors of All Times as Told in Their Own Words (New York: Crown, 1959): 132. **203:** Sanford Meisner and Dennis Longwell, Sanford Meisner on Acting (New York: Vintage Books, 1987): 37. **208:** Quoted in Nicole Potter, "Let's Get Physical: What's Happening Now?," American Theatre, 28, No. 1 (January 2011): 50. **210:** Cicely Berry, The Actor and the Voice (New York: Macmillan, 1973): 121. **214:** Michael Caine, Acting in Film: An Actor's Take on Movie Making, rev. ed. (New York: Applause Theatre Book Publishers, 1997): 4.

Chapter 10

219: Alan Schneider, "Things to Come: Crystal-Gazing at the Near and Distant Future of a Durable Art." American Theatre, 1, No.1, (April 1984): 17. **223:** Toby Dole and Helen Krich Chinoy, eds., Directors on Directing, 2nd rev. ed. (Indianapolis, IN: The Bobbs-Merrill Company, 1977): 364–366. **225:** Peter Brook, Threads of Time: A Memoir (London: Methuen Publishers, 1999): 141. **228:** Margaret Croyden, "The Mahabharata: A Review," New York Times (25 August 1985): 11, 20. **233:** Chris Jones, "Evolution of Robert Falls: Goodman Theatre's artistic director moves toward minimalism," Chicago Tribune (October 3, 2010). **233:** Jane Kramer, "Experimental Journey," The New Yorker (October 8, 2007). **233:** Misha Berson, "Dan Sullivan Travels," American Theatre (March 2007): 26.

Chapter 11

250: Lynn Pecktal, "A Conversation with Ming Cho Lee," in Designing and Painting for the Theatre (New York: Holt, Rinehart, 1975): 51. **251:** Lynn Pecktal, "A Conversation with Ming Cho Lee," in Designing and Painting for the Theatre (New York: Holt, Rinehart, 1975): 242. **251:** Lynn Pecktal, "A Conversation with Ming Cho Lee," in Designing and Painting for the Theatre (New York: Holt, Rinehart, 1975): 544–545. **257:** Joseph V. Melillo, "In Conversation with Designer Susan Hilferty," Round Up: A Magazine for the League of Professional Theatre Women, IX (2008–2009): 17.

Chapter 13

289: Cheryl Crawford, One Naked Individual: My Fifty Years in the Theatre (Indianapolis, IN: The Bobbs-Merrill Company, 1977): 4. **292:** Alexander H. Cohen, "Broadway Theatre," in Producers on Producing, ed. Stephen Langley (New York: Drama Book Specialists, 1976): 15. **293:** Robin Pogrebin, "Off Broadway's Mom and Angel," New York Times (July 26, 1999): 1B. **296:** Audrey Wood with Max Wilk, Represented by Audrey Wood (Garden City, NY: Doubleday and Company, 1981): 11. **299:** See "Theatre Facts 2010," American Theatre (November 2011): 36–41. **303:** Alexander H. Cohen, "Broadway Theatre," in Producers on Producing, ed. Stephen Langley (New York: Drama Book Specialists, 1976): 15.

Chapter 15

337: Frank Rich, "A Critic's Summit: Robert Brustein and Frank Rich Talk About Criticism," American Theatre, 16, No. 5 (May/June 1999): 18. **338:** Arthur Miller, Death of a Salesman in Arthur Miller's Collected Plays (New York: The Viking Press, 1958): 56. **338:** Ben Barntley, "American Dreamer, Ambushed by the Territory," New York Times (March 16, 2012), C1. **339:** Tony Kushner, Angels in America. Part Two: Perestroika (New York: Theatre Communications Group, 1994): 148. **341:** Tennessee Williams, The Glass Menagerie, Vol.1 (New York: New Directions, 1970): 55. **342:** Stanley Kauffmann, Persons of the Drama: Theater Criticism and Comment (New York: Harper & Row, 1976): 369–380. **346:** Claudia Cassidy, "On the Aisle," Chicago Daily Tribune (January 7, 1945). **348:** Linda Winer, "Are Days of Big Broadway Spectacles Ending?," www.newsday.com (September 21, 2012). **348:** Chris Jones, "Critical Juncture," American Theatre, 28, no. 9 (November 2011): 34.

GLOSSARY

Absurdism A post-Second World War movement in Europe, absurdism grew out of existentialism as a philosophical viewpoint. The absurdist begins with the assumption that the world is irrational. Such writers as Samuel Beckett and Eugène Ionesco show the irrationality of the human experience without suggesting remedies. The sense of absurdity in their plays is heightened by nonsensical events, ridiculous effects, and language that fails to communicate rational meaning.

Aesthetic distance The term implies a detachment (or "distance") between the work of art and the spectator. In order to experience a play as a work of art and not as life, there must be some sort of "psychical distance" between the viewer and the theatre event or art object itself. If we become too involved in a play for personal reasons (perhaps the subject matter is too painful based on a recent experience), then we may be able to view the play only as a real-life experience and not as art.

Aesthetic distance does not mean that we are unmoved by a play, a performance, or a painting. It means we are aware of ourselves as receptors and can experience with a new interest the work of art as something that is like life, but is not life. Simply put, aesthetic distance is the emotional and intellectual distance between the spectator and the work of art.

Agon A Greek word meaning contest or debate between opposing characters and viewpoints in Greek tragedy and comedy. The fierce debate between Oedipus and Teiresias in *Oedipus the King* is called an agon.

Alienation effect (*Verfremdungseffekt*) Bertolt Brecht called his theory and technique of distancing or alienating audiences from emotional involvement with characters and situations an "alienation effect." Brecht wanted a thinking audience rather than an emotionally involved audience. To break down emotional involvement, Brecht used theatrical effects such as white light, placards, loudspeakers, projections, loosely connected scenes, songs, and music to make things onstage appear unfamiliar, even strange, so audiences would observe and think about what they were seeing.

Allegory A narrative in which abstractions, such as virtue, charity, and hope, are made concrete for the purpose of communicating a moral. In a drama, such as *Everyman* (written around 1500), characters are personified abstractions, a device typical of a morality play for teaching lessons to audiences. In *Everyman,* the most famous dramatic allegory of its time, we find Good Deeds, Beauty, Five Wits, Death, and so on represented onstage by actors.

Amphitheatre Today, the term refers to an open-air structure with tiers of seats around a central area, such as a stadium, arena, or auditorium. The term originated to describe a Roman building of elliptical shape, with tiers of seats enclosing a central arena, where gladiatorial contests, wild beast shows, and staged sea battles took place. The first amphitheatre was probably built by Julius Caesar in 46 BC. The most famous is the Colosseum in Rome, which was completed in AD 80 and is a tourist attraction today.

Anagnorisis (Recognition) Aristotle introduced *anagorisis* in the *Poetics* as a simple recognition of persons by such tokens as footprints, clothes, birthmarks, and so on. The term also has a larger meaning to include the tragic hero's self-understanding. All of Shakespeare's tragic heroes have great moments of recognition wherein they realize who they are, what they have done, and what their deeds mean for others as well.

Antagonist The character in a play who commonly opposes the chief figure, or *protagonist.* The agon in Greek tragedy is usually centered on the debate between protagonist and antagonist; for example, in *Oedipus the King* the great antagonists to Oedipus in various debates are Teiresias, Creon, Jocasta, and the Shepherd.

Apron A large forestage used in proscenium theatres in England and Europe built in the late seventeenth century. In England, theatres such as Covent Garden and Drury Lane had two doors, called proscenium doors, that opened onto the apron, allowing actors to exit and enter with greater ease.

Arena stage See **Stages.**

Aside A short statement made by a character directly to the audience to express a personal attitude or to comment upon another character or event. The convention is that the aside cannot be overheard by another character.

Audition The opportunity for actors to "try out" for a role. The date, place, and time are announced, and "sides" (parts to be read) are provided by the theatre or the casting director. During the audition a reader assists the actor by reading dialogue with him or her. In the professional theatre, the casting director schedules auditions for actors through their agents.

Avant-garde A term appropriated by artists and critics to signify original and startling experiments and innovations in theatrical writing, ideas, performance styles, designs, and staging within a particular period. For example, at one time the plays of Eugène Ionesco and Samuel Beckett were considered avant-garde.

B

Black box See **Stages**.

Box set An interior setting, such as a living room or a dining room, using flats to form the back and side walls and often the ceiling of the room. The Moscow Art Theatre settings for Chekhov's *The Three Sisters* and *The Cherry Orchard* used box settings.

Broadway Broadway is one of the longest streets in Manhattan, extending diagonally the length of the island. However, for theatregoers, "Broadway" is the thirty to forty theatres clustered between Forty-first and Fifty-fourth Streets two or more blocks to the west and east of the thoroughfare. Most Broadway playhouses were built at the turn of the century, tending to have small foyers, proscenium stages, and very small dressing rooms. In 1994 the renovation of Broadway (particularly Forty-second Street) began with a production of *Beauty and the Beast*, followed by shows such as *Mary Poppins* and *Hair Spray*. Today the theatre district has been transformed into a "family friendly" tourist destination. Called the "Great White Way" for its glittering lights and lighted marquees, Broadway remains the area where the most important commercial theatre in the world is produced. When it has a dud of a season, it is then referred to as "the fabulous invalid."

Bunraku The doll or puppet theatre *(ningyo shibai)* first came into prominence in Japan during the seventeenth century. As the dolls became more complex with the addition of hands, feet, and movable fingers and eyes, the number of handlers increased from one to three men—all visible to the audience. Chikamatsu Monzaemon, Takedo Izumo, and Chikamatsu Hanji were its most popular playwrights. As interest in doll theatre declined in the late seventeenth century, Uemura Bunrakuken restored its vitality in Osaka, and the name Bunraku is used by present-day doll or puppet theatres.

Today, the future of Bunraku has been secured by the Bunraku Association (formed in 1963) to manage all aspects of the art. In addition to performing in Osaka, the troupe plays four months each year in a small theatre created in 1966 in the National Theatre in Tokyo.

C

Catharsis Aristotle considered *catharsis* to be the release of twin emotions of pity and fear in the audience as it experienced tragedy. Catharsis is thought of as psychologically purgative, for it produces in an audience a purgation (or purification) of the emotions aroused by pity and fear. Thus, an audience comes away from tragedy having felt and even been modified by these emotions. Catharsis, it has been argued, produces a psychologically useful role for tragedy in society.

Character Drama's characters are sometimes divided into two types: *flat* and *round*. Flat characters represent a single trait (for example, a lecherous villain or faithful wife) and are highly predictable. Round characters are more complex, seen as it were from many sides. Like those of Hamlet, Blanche DuBois, and Troy Maxson, their motives, insights, and behavior, though sometimes unexpected, are credible and provocative. See **Stock character**.

Climax A decisive turning point in the plot where tension is highest. The burning of the orphanage in Henrik Ibsen's *Ghosts* is a good example of climax.

Comic relief Humorous episodes in tragedy that briefly lighten the growing tension and tragic effect. Scenes of comic relief often deepen rather than alleviate the tragic effect. The grave digger's scene in *Hamlet* is one such example. Despite its jokes and humor, the scene calls attention to the common end of all humanity—death and the grave.

Commedia dell'arte Professional, improvisational companies of actors, including women, that flourished in Italy in the sixteenth century. An average-sized commedia company had ten to twelve members, divided usually into stock characters of two sets of lovers, two old men, and several *zanni* (the array of comic servants, braggarts, buffoons, tricksters, and dupes). Each character had an unvarying name, such as

Pantalone, costume, mask, and personality traits. Commedia actors worked from a basic story outline (posted backstage), improvising dialogue, action, and stage business (called *lazzi)* from that outline. They performed on temporary outdoor stages. The best companies also performed in the halls and palace theatres of dukes and kings.

Because the commedia dell'arte was improvisational theatre, and even though we have some 700 or more scenarios, or plot outlines, performed by the companies, we are left today with only the bare bones of a theatrical tradition: its characters, events, disguises, *lazzi,* and artists' illustrations of costumes and masks.

Commercial theatre A term from the business (commerce) world relating to theatre that has financial profit as the primary aim. Commercial theatre, as opposed to nonprofit theatre, aims at producing shows to earn profits for investors.

Convention An understanding established through custom or usage that certain devices will be accepted or assigned specific meaning or significance by audiences without requiring that the devices be natural or real. While delivering a soliloquy, the actor speaks to himself or herself so that audiences can "overhear" private thoughts. Because this behavior is accepted as a theatrical convention dating from the English Renaissance, we do not think it odd or unnatural when it occurs.

Criticism *Criticism* (variously called drama or theatre criticism) is critical assessment of a play as a literary text or as a vehicle for performance. *Drama* (or interpretive) *criticism* is usually associated with scholarly articles, books on theatre, and classroom teaching. The drama critic is concerned with the what and how of the play—with historical, social, and cultural surroundings, dramatic theories, ideas, imagery, themes, genres, audience interactions, and staging. Written by journalists, *theatre criticism* is found largely in newspapers and popular magazines. The theatre reviewer evaluates productions of new or revived plays and theatrical events. The *New York Times* remains the most important and powerful newspaper in America to review theatre. The daily critic for the *Times* has the power to make reputations and close shows. Outside New York, critics for dominant newspapers in major urban cities also have gained immense power over theatre in their areas.

Cycle plays (medieval) By the end of the fourteenth century in Europe, lengthy religious cycles, spoken in the vernacular, had replaced liturgical or church drama. The cycles were staged outdoors and performed by laymen during spring and summer months, but chiefly on the feast of Corpus Christi. Most English cycle plays take their names from four towns where they were chiefly staged: York (48 plays), Chester (24), Wakefield (32, sometimes called the Towneley plays), and the *Ludus Coventriae* or *N*—town plays (42, town unknown). Most English cycles covered Biblical material from the Creation to the Last Judgment and were performed on pageant wagons drawn through the towns.

D

Dada Following the First World War in Europe, many artists revolted against traditions of realism in painting and theatre. Switzerland, where dada was launched in 1916, was the refuge for many artists and political dissenters. Tristan Tzara, the principal spokesman for dada, published seven manifestos on the art between 1916 and 1920.

Dada grew out of skepticism about a world that could produce a global war. Convinced that insanity was humanity's true state, the dadaists substituted discord and chaos for logic, reason, and harmony. They composed "sound poems," dances, visual art, and short plays. For a time, the movement thrived in postwar Germany but received its greatest support in Paris. By 1920, interest declined and dada shortly disappeared. The dadaists were one among many forerunners of the Theatre of the Absurd.

Deus ex machina ("god from the machine") In Greek plays, a cranelike device (the *mechane)* used to raise or lower "gods" into the playing space. Euripides used the device to solve a problem in a story, usually the ending. Medea escapes from Corinth on a winged chariot, for example. Hence, in drama and literature, the term has come to mean any unexpected or improbable device used to un-knot a plot and thus conclude the work. The king's officer who arrests Tartuffe and rewards Orgon in Molière's comedy is another example.

Dionysus According to myth, Dionysus was the son of Zeus (the greatest of Greek gods) and Semele (a mortal). For this reason, some refer to him as a demigod. Reared by satyrs (woodland deities represented in classical mythology as part human and part goat), Dionysus was killed, dismembered, and resurrected. As a god, he was associated with fertility, wine, and revelry. The events of his life also link him to recurring patterns of birth, maturity, and death among seasonal cycles and human beings. Because his worshippers sought a mystical union with primal creative urges, he is also associated with the *dithyramb,* drama, and art. On a more practical level, his followers sought to promote fertility in order to guarantee the productivity of human beings, their crops, and their harvests.

It is commonly held that Greek tragedy evolved from choral celebrations (dithyrambic odes) held to honor Dionysus. The Greater Dionysia (or City Dionysia) in Athens was a festival held each year in the god's honor, and the popular dramatic contests took place in the theatre named for him—the Theatre of Dionysus.

Double plot, subplot, simultaneous plots Drama's *plot* is the arrangement of incidents or sequences in the story, that is, the order of events. Aristotle called plot the "soul of tragedy" and "the whole structure of the incidents." He considered it more important than character or the traits of the story's individuals.

The double, or simultaneous plot (sometimes called main plot and subplot or underplot), develops two plots, usually with some sort of connection between them. In the order of things, one will be more important than the other. The secondary plot (the story of Polonius's family in *Hamlet* or the Gloucester plot in *King Lear)* is a variation on the main plot. In *Hamlet,* the main plot and the subplot deal with two families whose children suffer parental loss, grief, and untimely deaths. In repeating themes, problems, and events, the double plot demonstrates the world's complexity by engaging a large number of people, events, and locales in parallel stories.

Dramaturg(e) The dramaturg's profession, which was created in eighteenth-century Germany, has recently been instituted in professional regional theatres in the United States. The dramaturg is a critic in residence who performs a variety of tasks before a play opens. He or she prepares, adapts, and even translates texts of plays for performance; advises directors and actors on questions of the play's history and interpretation; and educates audiences by preparing lectures, program notes, and essays. To accomplish all of this, the dramaturg serves as theatre historian, translator, play adaptor, editor, director's assistant, and resident critic of the work in progress. The term *production dramaturg* describes a full-time member of the production team. Sometimes the work of the dramaturg is confused with that of the *literary manager* (sometimes the duties are combined into one position). The literary manager is also a staff member in the nonprofit regional theatres whose essential job is to find and develop new plays.

E

Ensemble acting (ensemble performance) Acting that stresses the total artistic unity of the performance rather than the individual performance of a specific (or "star") actor. The photos of Stanislavski's productions of *The Three Sisters* and *The Cherry Orchard* show the unity of acting style for which the Moscow Art Theatre was celebrated.

Epic theatre Refers to the twentieth-century theories, writings, and stagings of German playwrights Erwin Piscator and Bertolt Brecht to create anti-illusionistic theatre featuring narration, song, distancing, and blatant theatrical effects to underscore social and political messages.

Epilogue Usually, a concluding address following the play's ending. Many epilogues were written to encourage applause or to feature a popular actor one final time.

Existentialism A philosophical viewpoint espoused in France by Jean-Paul Sartre and Albert Camus—novelists, essayists, and playwrights—in the 1940s. Sartre conceived of a universe without God, fixed standards of conduct, or moral codes. In this absence, Sartre argued, the individual must choose his or her own values and live by them regardless of the choices of others or prevailing ideas. He also believed that people must be politically "engaged" and make choices to determine the direction of events. His plays *(The Flies, No Exit, Dirty Hands)* show characters faced with choices that require them to reassess their beliefs and to forge new personal standards.

Albert Camus' work was of equal importance. He defined the "absurd" as part of the existential outlook. Camus was a journalist and editor of a clandestine newspaper during the German occupation of France. His influence on the theatre came in part from his essay "The Myth of Sisyphus" (1943), in which he supplies the name for the "absurdist" movement that emerged in the early 1950s. Camus argued that the human condition is absurd because of the gap between a person's hopes and an irrational universe into which he or she has been born. The remedy rested in the individual's search for a set of standards that allowed him or her to bring order out of the chaos. Camus rejected Sartre's argument for "engagement" and even denied being an existentialist, although his conclusions about individual choice are similar to Sartre's.

Although Sartre and Camus wrote plays about an irrational universe, they used traditional dramatic forms with a cause-to-effect arrangement of episodes along with discursive language. Their plays were labeled "existentialist drama." The later absurdist playwrights accepted the existentialist's view of the irrationality of human experience but arrived at a dramatic structure that mirrored the chaos of experience and the inadequacy of language to make sense of it all.

Expressionism A term coined in 1901 by the French painter Julien-Auguste Hervé to describe his paintings as "expressing" emotional experiences rather than giving impressions of the physical world. Expressionism became synonymous with nonrealistic works in art and theatre. The rise of theatrical expressionism occurred in Germany between 1907 and the mid-1920s. The movement was led by such writers as Reinhard Sorge *(The Beggar)*, Georg Kaiser *(From Morn to Midnight)*, and Ernst Toller *(Masses and Man)*. Although the production style was antirealistic, employing garish colors, harsh lighting, distorted lines, stairs, treadmills, and bridges, the themes were aimed at a spiritual regeneration of humankind. Often the plays were acts of rebellion against generations, class, sex, and taboo subjects (incest and patricide, for example). Plays were made up of nameless character types, short scenes, telegraphic dialogue, and long rhapsodic speeches in an effort to depict the injustices, warmongering, and materialism suffered by society's powerless. The work of Eugene O'Neill and Sophie Treadwell introduced theatrical expressionism to the United States.

F

Farce A comedy of situation, *farce* (the word derives from the Latin *farsa,* meaning "stuffing") entertains with seemingly endless and raucous variations on a single situation usually having to do with pursuit of bedroom adventures and sexual antics. Farce depends upon broad physical humor for its effects, such as mistaken identities, harmless beatings, pies in the face, doors opening onto awkward situations, and general human ineptitude.

Traced from short medieval plays and the Italian commedia dell'arte, modern forms of farce include vaudeville sketches, silent films, absurdist plays, and farcical plays by Michael Frayn, Alan Ayckbourn, and Neil Simon. Critic Eric Bentley has written perceptively on farce in *The Life of the Drama* (1964).

G

Genre Refers to works of literature and art that fall into distinctive groups with respect to style, form, purpose, and spectator response. Major genres in Western playwriting are tragedy, comedy, tragicomedy, and melodrama.

Green room A room backstage in the theatre where actors wait for their cues to go onstage, relax, drink coffee, eat snacks, receive instructions from stage management, and meet guests after the show.

H

***Hamartia* (hybris, hubris)** A Greek word variously translated as "tragic flaw" or "tragic error." Though Aristotle used *hamartia* to refer to those personality traits that lead heroes to make fatal mistakes, the idea of tragic flaw became simplified over the centuries to mean a single vice, frailty, or even a virtue (for example, pride, ambition, arrogance, overconfidence) that brings about the tragic hero's downfall. When applied to Sophocles's and to Shakespeare's great heroes, *hamartia* becomes a very complex concept related to reasons underlying human choice and action.

Hand properties See **Properties.**

I

Interlude The interlude dates from the Middle Ages, when it was a loose term applied to short plays presented indoors as entertainment for rulers, nobles, and rich merchants. They took place within other events or occasions, for example, between courses of a banquet. The interlude had a variety of subjects (religious, moral, farcical) and included singing and dancing as well. Today, an "interlude" is synonymous in the British theatre with an intermission.

Irony *Dramatic irony* (Sophoclean irony or tragic irony) refers to a condition of affairs that is the tragic reverse of what the participants think will happen but what the audience knows at the outset. Thus, it is ironic that Oedipus accuses the blind prophet Teiresias of corruption and lack of understanding. By the play's end, Oedipus learns (as the audience has known from the beginning) that he himself has been mentally blind (ignorant) and the prophet has had superior sight (knowledge).

Dramatic irony also occurs when a speech or action is more fully understood by the audience than by the characters. Found in both tragedy and comedy, this sort of irony is usually based on misunderstanding or partial knowledge. It is ironic, for example, that Tartuffe thinks the king's officer has come to arrest Orgon when, in fact, he has come to arrest Tartuffe.

K

Kabuki Dating from the sixteenth century, Kabuki has become the principal form of indigenous commercial theatre in urban Japan. The word *Kabuki* derives from the adjective *kabuku*, meaning "tilted or off-center," and came to describe a new and unorthodox form of popular theatrical entertainment. In order to appeal to popular audiences, Kabuki performers were always creating new plays and blending acting and musical styles to appeal to changing times. Actors both speak and dance. The heroic figures *(aragoto)* are performed in a bravura acting style dressed in exaggerated costumes with bold red and black facial makeup. Actors of female roles (*onnagata)* display their charm and skill through solo dances. A Kabuki performance originally lasted ten to twelve hours and matched the moods and emotional states of the seasons: love (in spring) and lament for the spirits of the dead (in summer).

Special theatres were built for Kabuki performances. They are oblong boxes in which stage and audience are physically part of the same space. A ramp or *hanamichi* (meaning "flower path") extended the stage through the left part of the auditorium and permitted actors to exit or enter through the audience or deliver a major speech standing among them. Floor-level revolving stages were installed in the mid-eighteenth century, and elaborate painted scenery and other staging devices were part of a Kabuki performance. In the twentieth century, large theatres (three times the size of traditional theatres) modeled on European opera houses were built to accommodate the commercial appeal of Kabuki. The present Kabuki-za in Tokyo has a ninety-three-foot-wide stage and seats 2,600.

Kathakali A major dance drama from the Kerala state in southern India. Dating from the seventeenth century, *kathakali* (the word literally means "story play") blends dance, music, and acting in a vigorous masculine style of physical movement, vivid emotionalism, and superhuman characters in stories adapted from the *Ramayana* and *Mahabharata* epics. Kathakali blends various theatre and dance forms from regions rich in cultural traditions and in the creation of an indigenous dance drama. Performances take place almost anywhere—in family homes, large halls, temple compounds, and formal stages—and take about two to three hours to complete. Because actors do not speak, the stories and ideas are conveyed through lyrics sung by two singers, by musicians, and by actors' facial expressions, physical movements, and hand gestures.

Kutiyattam The oldest surviving theatre form preserved in sacred temples and unique to Kerala, India. *Kutiyattam* preserves a tradition of performing plays in Sanskrit with fantastical makeup and headdresses, costumes, movements and gestures, chanted speech, and musical instruments of the ancient world.

M

Melodrama Derived from eighteenth-century plays having music as background for dialogue, melodrama is a popular type of serious play that contrives and oversimplifies experience with characters whose goals and morality are clear-cut and the dangers to the innocent and virtuous spectacular. Characters in melodrama are clearly divided between the virtuous and the villainous, the sympathetic and the unsympathetic. After many complications, the villain's destruction brings about the happy ending. Some modern critics have stressed the social and humanitarian features of the genre in which central figures are crushed by external forces rather than by forces within themselves. Modern examples of melodrama include television cop shows, horror films, suspenseful stage thrillers, and realistic plays whose messages ring out with the triumph of the righteous victim over dark social forces. Many of the world's great tragedies have melodramatic elements, including plays written by William Shakespeare and Eugene O'Neill.

Mise-en-scène The arrangement of all the elements in the stage picture either at a given moment or dynamically throughout the performance. Modern directors give careful attention to the mise-en-scène, or total stage picture, integrating all elements of design, acting, and so forth. The mise-en-scène created by director Andrei Serban and designer Santo Loquasto for the 1977 New York production of *The Cherry Orchard* reflects the director's emphasis on the cherry trees and the dying civilization.

Monologue Usually, a long speech delivered by one character that may be heard but not interrupted by others. Or it may refer to a performance by a single actor, called a "solo performance." The term *monologue* has been applied to the soliloquy, a lengthy aside; and to direct address, in which a character steps out of the world of the play and speaks directly to the audience, as Tom Wingfield, both narrator and character, does in Tennessee Williams's *The Glass Menagerie.*

Musical theatre Musical theatre in America dates from the colonial period. As background to today's musical theatre, we find burlesque, spectacles with music and dance, minstrel shows, and comic opera (namely, Gilbert and Sullivan operettas). The revue, such as the *Ziegfeld Follies,* is a musical form featuring songs, dances, comedy sketches, elaborate production numbers, and loosely connected stories and themes, was also highly influential. Irving Berlin introduced another American idiom, ragtime, onto the musical stage in 1914. With *Oklahoma!*, in 1943, Rodgers and Hammerstein introduced a "musical play" with simple American values having broad appeal, a "dream ballet" choreographed by Agnes de Mille, and a story line (called the "book") that allowed a murder to take place onstage. It became the most influential and imitated musical of its day.

The operetta-style musicals produced in the 1960's by Sheldon Harnick include *West Side Story, She Loves Me,* and *Fiddler on the Roof.* Beginning in the 1970s, composer-lyricist Stephen Sondheim introduced a unique sound tempered with rock rhythms and bold, cynical lyrics in *Company, Sweeney Todd, Sunday in the Park with George,* and *Into the Woods.* He popularized the "concept musical" in which a creative team of composer, lyricist, director, and choreographer collaborate to create a show. Director-choreographers such as Bob Fosse, Michael Bennett, and more recently, Ann Reinking and Susan Stroman, dominated the musical theatre with *Pippin, Chicago, A Chorus Line, Dreamgirls, Fosse,* and *Contact.* Also, in the 1980s and 1990s, the London musical connection flourished on Broadway with the restaging of such British successes as *Cats, Miss Saigon, The Phantom of the Opera,* and *Les Misèrables.* In the 2010s many of the musicals produced on Broadway are adaptations of popular films and books such as *The Lion King* and *The Little Mermaid.* Taken as a whole, musical theatre is considered by many to be America's unique contribution to world theatre.

N

Naturalism Like realistic writers, the nineteenth-century naturalists accepted that reality was discoverable only through the five senses. They departed from the realists in their insistence that art must adopt scientific methods in its examination of human behavior. The two most important factors to observe were *heredity* and *environment.* French playwright and novelist Émile Zola became the early spokesman for the naturalistic movement. He argued that artists should select subjects and analyze them in the detached way of a medical doctor to determine the consequences of birth and background. In practice, naturalists emphasized that behavior is determined by factors (heredity, for example) largely beyond our control. Inevitably, human beings appeared as victims of birth and society, and the conclusions for happiness and well-being were pessimistic. In the firm belief that environment was also a determinant of character and choice, naturalists reproduced stage environments as accurate reflections of real locales. The great naturalistic playwrights of the late nineteenth century were Émile Zola, Henrik Ibsen, August Strindberg, Gerhart Hauptmann, and Maxim Gorky.

Neoclassicism The rebirth of classical ideals (called neo-classicism) found expression first in Italy in 1570 and spread to the rest of Europe, where it was to dominate writing and criticism from the mid-seventeenth century until the late eighteenth century. Two classical works influenced the rebirth of "classicism": Aristotle's *Poetics* and Horace's *Art of Poetry.* Aristotle came to be considered the supreme authority on literary (and dramatic) matters. His position was enhanced by three Italian critics: Antonio Minturno, Julius Caesar Scaliger, and Lodovico Castelvetro. They were in agreement on the basic precepts that constituted the neoclassical ideal: (1) *verisimilitude,* or the appearance of truth (events that could happen in real life, violence and death held offstage, and a confidant or trusted companion to receive inmost secrets rather than through a chorus or soliloquy); (2) the demand that drama teach a moral lesson enhanced by *poetic justice* by which the wicked were punished and the good rewarded; (3) the requirement that all drama be reduced to two types—tragedy or comedy—with no intermingling of comic and serious elements; (4) adherence to *decorum* whereby characters were proper to the subject matter; for example, royal persons in tragedy and lower-class people in comedy; and (5) precise conventions of language. The seventeenth-century French playwright Jean Racine is considered the finest writer of neoclassical tragedies. In *Phèdre, Britannicus,* and *Bérénice,* he transcended the limitations of the neoclassical "rules" and wrote remorseless psychological tragedies of human beings vacillating between extremes of duty and desire.

Noh A serious Japanese drama that evolved in the fourteenth century out of songs, dances, and sketches and was first performed by Buddhist priests. There are about 240 extant plays, or "song books," that contain prose and poetry sections. The majority of the text is in verse and sung by the Doer *(shite)*, the Sideman *(waki)*, or Chorus *(ji)*. The plays are categorized into one of five types according to the *shite* role. The Warrior play is one such category. The dignified and aesthetic conventions of Noh performance were set down by the Japanese actor and playwright Zeami during his years in the Kyoto court under the patronage of Shogun Yoshimitsu. These conventions extend to the locations onstage of role types, stage assistants, chorus, and musicians.

Modern-day Noh is performed on traditional outdoor stages maintained by temples and shrines and in contemporary buildings constructed especially for Noh performances. Among the major stages in modern Japan are the National Noh Theatre in Tokyo, the Kanze and Kongo theatres in Kyoto, and the Yamamoto Theatre in Osaka.

O

Off Broadway A term that came into theatrical usage in the 1950s, defined by the Actors' Equity Association minimum contract as theatres located in the Borough of Manhattan outside the Broadway area surrounding Times Square with 100 to 299 seats.

Off Broadway playhouses developed as alternatives to Broadway's commercialism. Today, the term refers to professional (Equity) theatres operating on significantly reduced budgets in comparison with Broadway, but under a financial structure prescribed by the Actors' Equity Association and other unions. David Mamet's plays are often performed Off Broadway, and some popular Off Broadway plays and musicals transfer to Broadway. Michael Bennett's *A Chorus Line* and Terrence McNally's *Love! Valour! Compassion!* are two examples.

Off Off Broadway A term that came into use in the 1960s, referring to experimental theatres and converted spaces located between West Houston Street, Greenwich Village, and the Bowery. These theatres are found in lofts, garages, warehouses, studios, churches, and coffeehouses where experimental workshops and performances take place. As Broadway's commercialism encroached on the Off Broadway theatres, adventuresome producers and artists moved elsewhere, looking for solutions to high production costs and union demands. The Open Theatre, the Wooster Group, and La Mama Experimental Theatre Club are in this category. Off Off Broadway shows include performance art, solo shows, interactive experiences and improvisation/comedy shows.

Open stage See **Stages.**

P

Performance art/solo performance refers to the "doing" of a single (usually) performer in the presence of spectators and applies to such diverse events as Alan Kaprow's "happenings," Merce Cunningham's dance/movements, and Spalding Gray's solo pieces. Performance art often takes place in "found" spaces (environmental theatre) and employs computer-aided forms of performance. A self-created composition (called the solo text) serves as the basis for an improvisatory and confrontational style of performance that shares autobiographical and political material with audiences. Deb Margolin, a performance artist and creator of solo texts, calls solo performance art "a perfect Theater for One."

Postmodern/postmodernism A combination of the prefix *post* (meaning "subsequent to") and the word *modern* ("present or recent") coined to describe in theatrical terms works that have come after the "modern." The works of Robert Wilson and Martha Clarke have been labeled "postmodern," meaning that they follow the "modern" works of Lillian Hellman and Tennessee Williams. In art and theatre, postmodern has been used since the 1980s to identify architecture, artistic style, or mind-set (a point of view) that is often cynical, playful, contradictory, ironic, or despairing. In visual terms, a postmodern style is dominated by repetition, parody, multiple images, synthetic sounds, electronic technology, and deconstruction of past masterpieces.

Producer In the American theatre the person who puts together the financing and management and the publicity and artistic teams to "produce" a show, usually commercial. The producer hires (and even fires) the artistic personnel and in this way may put a kind of stamp on the overall artistic effect. Producers who have significantly affected the Broadway theatre are Roger L. Stevens, David Merrick, Bernard Jacobs and Gerald Schoenfeld (the Shuberts), Alexander H. Cohen, James M. Nederlander, Emanuel Azenberg, Hal Prince, and Rocco Landesman.

Properties There are two categories for properties: *set* and *hand* properties.

Set properties are items of furniture or set pieces; they are placed onstage for design reasons and for accommodating the requirements of the text. The size and structure of set properties, especially furniture, determine the actor's movement in and around them.

Hand properties, such as fans, pistols, swords, or telephones, are required for the actor's use within the play's action. Sometimes the distinction between set and hand props is unclear, but staging is the main function of the set prop; the hand prop first satisfies the needs of the actor using it. The table lamp that Mrs. Alving turns out in the final act of *Ghosts* is a hand prop, one with symbolic significance. As a set prop, the tree in *Waiting for Godot* is part of the playwright's intention and a chief design element. Properties are the initial responsibility of the set designer. There are a property head and crew responsible for acquiring or making props, supplying rehearsal props, handing out and storing props during the production, and repairing and returning props to storage at the production's close.

Proscenium theatre See **Stages.**

Protagonist The major character in a play. The Greek word literally means "first" *(protos)*, that is, the first contender or chief actor in the performance. For example, Oedipus, Hecuba, Hamlet, Macbeth, and Othello are all protagonists. The Greeks labeled the second role the *deuteragonist* and the third the *tritagonist.* The character in conflict with the protagonist is the *antagonist.*

R

Realism Realism developed in Europe about 1860 as a conscious rebellion against Romanticism. The realists set about depicting the world truthfully by what could be verified by direct observation of ordinary people (usually the middle class) and recognizable places. Playwrights and novelists set about emphasizing observed details of contemporary life to present a truthful depiction of the world, using stage language both familiar and appropriate. They introduced new subjects (many considered shocking and controversial) dealing with outcomes of poverty, prostitution, industrial conditions, disease, and social and judicial prejudices and injustices. Many held society responsible for human ills and argued indirectly for social reforms. Influential playwrights pioneering realism in the theatre were Henrik Ibsen and George Bernard Shaw.

Recognition See **Anagnorisis.**

Regional theatres, resident theatres The terms *regional* and *resident* have been used interchangeably for the past fifty years to describe professional nonprofit theatres. Today, there are more than sixty theatres (members of the League of Resident Theatres) in fifty-one cities with operating budgets ranging from $200,000 to $25 million. They produce more than 600 productions yearly to audiences of over 12 million. Most perform seasons of five to eleven months, generally to subscription audiences. Established in the fifties and sixties, these theatres from Seattle to Boston have been heralded as alternatives to the commercialism of Broadway and to the American theatre's centralization in major urban centers. In a society as diverse and as far-flung as that of the United States, these theatres make up a matrix that many call our *national theatre.* Among the most prestigious of the regional theatres are the Guthrie Theater (Minneapolis), American Repertory Theatre (Cambridge, MA), Arena Stage (Washington, D.C.), Mark Taper Forum (Los Angeles), Lincoln Center Theater (New York City), Alley Theatre (Houston), Seattle Repertory Theatre (WA), the Old Globe Theatre (San Diego), and the Goodman Theatre (Chicago).

Revenge play The development of revenge plays was influenced in the Renaissance by the work of the Roman author Lucius Annaeus Seneca (4 BC–AD 65). Seneca's ten extant Roman tragedies, probably written for private readings, were filled with deranged heroes, ghosts, deeds of vengeance and horror, stoical speeches, messengers reporting offstage horrors, and pithy moralisms (called *sententiae).*

Elizabethans read the Roman writers in their classrooms and transposed revenge conventions to the public stage. *Hamlet* has its ghost; its variety of deaths by sword, poison, trickery; and its revengers (Hamlet, Laertes, Fortinbras). In *King Lear,* Gloucester is blinded onstage, and *Titus Andronicus* is a virtual feast of atrocities. The revenge play had its own excitement in its many variations on patterns and conventions (like today's horror films), but some, such as *Hamlet,* achieved greatness in the writing, characters, originality, and universal insights.

Reversal (peripeteia, peripety) A plot reversal occurs when an action produces the opposite effect of what was intended or expected. Reversals occur in tragedy, comedy, and tragicomedy. A complex play may have several reversals before its ending. The reversal that occurs when Tartuffe's true nature is revealed to Orgon in the seduction scene is not at all what the characters anticipate. In fact, this reversal "reverses" their situation in the sense that it only makes it worse. The king's officer brings about the final reversal by restoring Orgon's family to good fortune and by punishing Tartuffe.

Romanticism The roots of Romanticism lie in European philosophical, political, and social movements more so than in artistic ones. In the early days of the nineteenth century, Romantic writers, like political revolutionaries, rejected the rigid neoclassical rules for writing tragedy and comedy. They turned to Shakespeare as a model for avoiding rules and including varieties of experience. Their subjects were inclusive because higher truths were found in nature and the human spirit. They preferred subjects about unspoiled nature or human beings in rebellion against restraints imposed by despotic societies. The most celebrated Romantic novelist and playwright was Johann Wolfgang von Goethe, whose *Faust, Part I,* represented the indomitable human will engaged in an unquenchable searching for experience.

S

Satyr play The fourth play in the series of fifth-century BC classical Greek tragedies functioned as an afterpiece to the tragic trilogy and always had a happy ending. The satyr play usually burlesqued the serious themes or the major characters of the three earlier plays (the trilogy) by showing persons such as Heracles, Dionysus, or Odysseus in ludicrous situations. The piece had a chorus of lewd satyrs (creatures half-man and half-horse or -goat) led by Silenus, who was a regular character. Euripides' *The Cyclops* is the only complete satyr play in existence. It travesties the legend of Odysseus's encounter with Polyphemus.

Scenographer A designer with artistic control over all design elements, including set, lighting, and costume. The recent development of theatre technology, particularly the use of film projections and moving scenery, frequently calls for unified production with one person integrating the various design elements. Although the scenographer works closely with the director, he or she is responsible for the totality of theatrical expression in time and space. Artistic unity is the goal. The idea that one person must have total control over design is derived from the theatrical concepts of the early twentieth-century theorists Adolphe Appia and Edward Gordon Craig.

One of the world's most famous scenographers today is Josef Svoboda, the leading designer of the Prague National Theatre in the Czech Republic. He became known in America through the Czech Pavilion at the 1967 Montreal Exposition, where he orchestrated films and stills, cascading images over surfaces and spectators. The result was a visually kinetic assault on the spectators. Svoboda's stage designs feature moving blocks, projections, and mirrors. The basis of his theory is that all scenic elements must appear and disappear, shift and flow, to complement the play's development.

Set properties See **Properties.**

Simultaneous plots See **Double plot.**

Soliloquy A speech delivered by an actor alone onstage that, by stage convention, is understood by the audience to be the character's internal thoughts, not part of an exchange with another character or even with the audience.

Spine In the Stanislavski method, a character's dominant desire or motivation, which underlies his or her action in the play. For a director, the *spine* is the throughline of a character's action that propels the play forward toward its conclusion. Director Elia Kazan conceived of the spine of Tennessee Williams's character Blanche DuBois in *A Streetcar Named Desire* as the search for refuge from a brutal and hostile world.

Stage business An actor's "business" in a role can be anything from the reading of a newspaper to smoking a cigarette to drinking a cup of coffee while he or she performs the text. Stage business is the actor's "busyness," activities devised by the actor (sometimes at the director's suggestion) to create a sense of character apart from the dialogue.

Stages—proscenium, arena, thrust or open, and black box Throughout theatre history, there have been five types of enclosed theatre buildings and basic arrangements of audience seating: (1) the proscenium, or picture-frame stage; (2) the arena stage, or theatre in the round; (3) the thrust, or open stage; (4) the black box; and (5) created or found space of the kind discussed as environmental theatre in Chapter 3.

The *proscenium,* or picture-frame, stage is the most familiar. Almost all college campuses have proscenium theatres, and our Broadway theatres are proscenium playhouses. The word *proscenium* comes from the wall with a large center opening that separates the audience from the raised stage. In the past the opening was called an "arch" (the proscenium arch), but it is actually a rectangle. The audience faces in one direction before this opening, appearing to look through a picture frame into the locale on the other side. The auditorium floor slants downward from the back of the building to provide greater visibility for the audience; usually there is a balcony above the auditorium floor protruding about halfway over the main floor. Frequently, there is a curtain just behind the proscenium opening (along with a safety curtain) that discloses or hides the event on the other side. The idea that a stage is a room with its fourth wall removed comes from this type of stage; the proscenium opening is thought of as an "invisible wall."

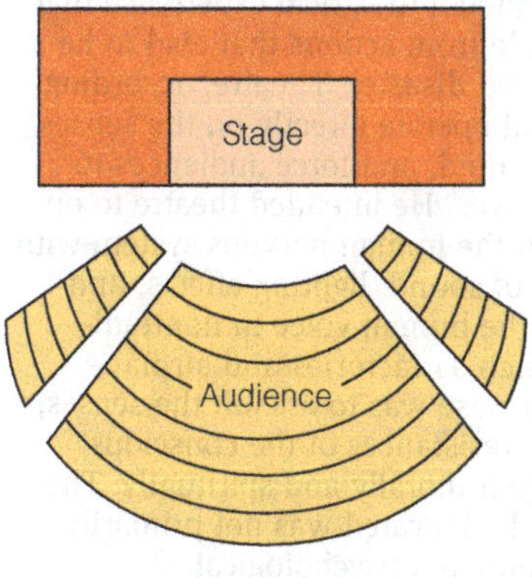

Proscenium Stage

The *arena* stage (also called a theatre in the round) breaks away from the formality of the proscenium theatre. It places the stage at the center of a square or circle with seats for the spectators around the circle or on the four sides. This stage offers more intimacy between actor and audience because the playing space usually has no barriers separating them. In addition, productions can usually be produced on low budgets because they require minimal scenery and furniture to indicate scene and place. Margo Jones (1913–1955) pioneered arena theatre design and performance in America, establishing Theatre 47 in Dallas, Texas, in 1947. Today, Arena Stage in Washington, D.C., founded by Zelda Fichandler and Edward Mangum, is one of the most famous.

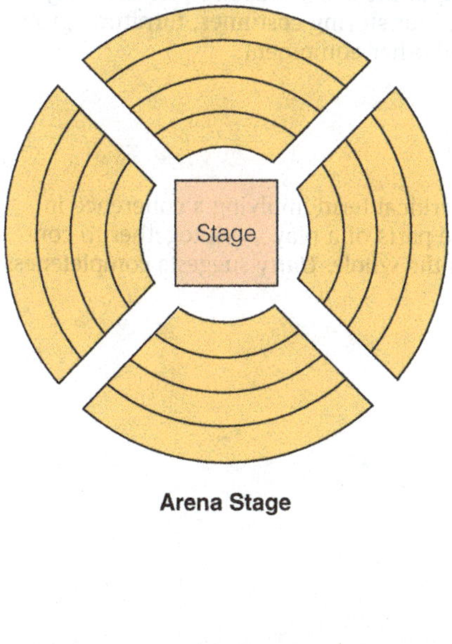

Arena Stage

The *thrust*, or *open*, stage combines features of the proscenium theatre and the arena stage with three-quarter seating for the audience. The basic arrangement has the audience sitting on three sides or in a semicircle around a low platform stage. At the back of the stage is some form of proscenium opening providing for entrances and exits as well as scene changes. The thrust stage combines the best features of the other two stages discussed here: the sense of intimacy for the audience and a stage setting against a single background that allows for scenic design and visual elements. After the Second World War, a number of thrust stages were built in the United States and Canada, including the Guthrie Theater in Minneapolis and the Shakespeare Festival Theatre in Stratford, Ontario.

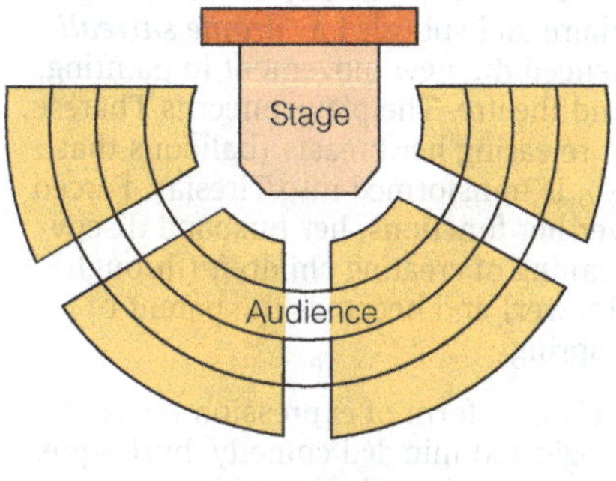

Thrust Stage

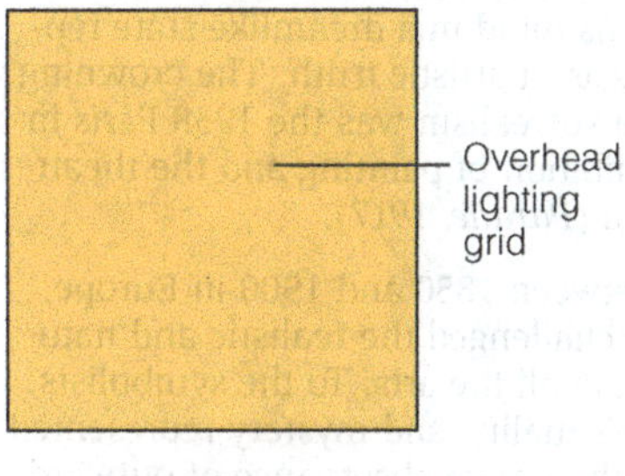

Black Box

The *black box* is a type of minimal performance space developed in the 1960s for experimental work. Essentially a large rectangular room (usually painted a flat black to avoid glare from the overhead lighting instruments), the black-box theatre is usually equipped with a complex overhead lighting grid with instruments and movable seating (approximately ninety to two hundred seats). The movable seating permits experimentation with the shape and size of the performance space. The Cottesloe Theatre at the Royal National Theatre, London, is a black-box theatre with two galleries surrounding three sides of the rectangular space. Designed along the lines of an Elizabethan innyard, the galleries are permanent, but the risers (with seating) positioned along the floor are movable.

Stock character The stock character is not only a "flat" character but a generic type found throughout drama: jealous husband, clever servant, braggart soldier, hypocrite, pedant, cuckold, miser. Though most common to comedy (Molière has a number of stock characters in *Tartuffe,* ranging from hypocrite to clever servant), stock characters are also found in serious plays. In tragedy we find the avenger, the usurper, the tyrant, and so on.

Surrealism In France, *surrealism* followed dada and drew inspiration from the works of Guillaume Apollinaire, Alfred Jarry, and André Breton. The play *The Breasts of Tiresias,* written by Apollinaire and subtitled a *"drame surréaliste,"* influenced the new movement in painting, writing, and theatre. The play concerns Thérèse, who, after releasing her breasts (balloons that float away), is transformed into Tiresias. Forced to take over her functions, her husband discovers the meaning of creating children (through sheer willpower) and becomes the parent of 40,000 offspring.

Apollinaire's new form of expression rejected everyday logic and mingled comedy, burlesque, tragedy, fantasy, and acrobatics with music, dance, color, and light. The critic André Breton defined the movement in his 1924 manifesto: the subconscious mind in a dreamlike state represented the basis of artistic truth. The crowning achievement of surrealism was the 1938 Paris international exhibition of painting and the theatre of Jean Cocteau *(Parade,* 1917).

Symbolism Between 1850 and 1900 in Europe, the symbolists challenged the realistic and naturalistic outlook in all the arts. To the symbolists, subjectivity, spirituality, and mystery represented a truth higher than mere observance of outward appearance. This deeper truth could be evoked only indirectly through symbols, myths, legends, and moods. The French poet Stephane Mallarmé became the principal spokesman for the symbolist movement. In theatre, the movement was led in the 1890s by director Aurélieu-Marie Lugné-Poe at the Théâtre de l'Oeuvre and by dramatists Maurice Maeterlinck *(The Intruder)* and Alfred Jarry *(Ubu Roi).*

T

Theatre of cruelty A phrase coined by French actor and director Antonin Artaud, an avant-garde figure in Paris following the First World War. Artaud formulated a theory of theatre (published as *The Theatre and Its Double,* 1938) in which he advocated a theatrical experience that would free people from actions that lead to hatred, violence, and disaster. Theatre, according to Artaud, would operate directly on the senses, not the rational mind, and force audiences to confront themselves. He intended theatre to operate directly on the human nervous system with bombardments of sound, lighting effects, and dissonances of the human voice in nontraditional spaces such as factories and airplane hangars. His purpose was to assault the senses, break down the resistances of the conscious mind, and purge it morally and spiritually. The "cruelty" Artaud advocated was not primarily physical but moral and psychological.

Thespis Tradition credits Thespis as winner in 534 BC of the first contest for the best tragedy presented at the City Dionysia, Athens. Tradition also credits him with inventing drama as it developed out of improvisations by the chorus leader of dithyrambs. In truth, Thespis was probably in a line of early tragic poets. Some think his innovations were the addition of a prologue and lines (spoken by an actor as a character) to a previously sung narrative work. Almost nothing is known of Thespis. Today, *thespian* refers in general to actors or performers.

Thrust stage See **Stages.**

Tiring-house The backstage space in the Elizabethan public theatre. We know little about this area behind the stage wall used for preparing and maintaining productions. Some reconstructions suggest the space was used for dressing rooms and for storing costumes, furniture, properties, and other equipment.

U

Unity A critical term implying a coherence in which the parts of a play work together to contribute to the whole. *Unity* suggests completeness or a recognizable pattern that ties together beginning, middle, and ending. Aristotle thought a tragedy should have a unified action, meaning a completeness without loose ends or the *deus ex machina* abruptly resolving the play.

Italian critics of the late sixteenth century codified Aristotle's comments on unity of action and themselves established "three unities" of time, place, and action. These unities have often mistakenly been passed down to generations as Aristotle's prescription. The unities so revered by sixteenth-century Italian critics and by seventeenth-century French neoclassical writers were that (1) the action of a play must not cover more than twenty-four hours; (2) it must occur in a single place or room; and (3) it must be entirely tragic or entirely comic with no mixture of plots or characters from either kind of writing. What is interesting is that most Greek tragedies in some way violate these unities.

W

Well-made play (pièce bien faite) A well-made play is a commercially successful pattern of play construction. Its techniques were perfected by the nineteenth-century French playwright Eugène Scribe (1791–1861) and his followers. The well-made play uses eight technical elements for success: (1) a plot based on a secret known to the audience but withheld from certain characters until it is revealed at the climax to unmask a fraudulent character and restore the suffering hero or heroine, with whom the audience sympathizes, to good fortune; (2) a pattern of increasingly intense action and suspense prepared by exposition, contrived entrances and exits, and devices such as unexpected letters; (3) a series of gains and losses in the hero's fortunes, caused by a conflict with a hostile opponent or force; (4) a major crisis in the hero's bad fortune; (5) a revelation scene brought about by the disclosure of a secret that brings a turnabout in the hero's bad fortune and defeats the opponent; (6) a central misunderstanding made obvious to the audience but withheld from the characters; (7) a logical, credible resolution or tying-up of events with appropriate dispensations to good and bad characters; and (8) an overall pattern of action repeated in each act and act climaxes that increase tension over the play's three or four acts.

The features were not new in Scribe's day but represented the technical methods of most great writers of comedy and even serious drama. Scribe and his followers turned the techniques into a formula for commercially entertaining plays as well as serious plays dealing with social and psychological subjects. In plays by Henrik Ibsen, George Bernard Shaw, Oscar Wilde, Arthur Miller, and Neil Simon, we can find well-made play elements underpinning the action.

West End, London The commercial theatre district in central London, equivalent to Broadway, with more than twenty-five theatres located in a small area. Famous West End theatres include the Haymarket, Drury Lane, Aldwych, and Lyceum. The musicals *Cats* and *The Phantom of the Opera* and plays by Tom Stoppard, Michael Frayn, and Alan Ayckbourn have appeared in the West End.

INDEX

I

J

M